Music in Eighteenth-Century Britain

Music in Eighteenth-Century Britain

Edited by

David Wyn Jones

LONDON AND NEW YORK

First published 2000 by Ashgate Publishing

2 Park Square, Milton Park, Abingdon, Oxon OX14 4RN
711 Third Avenue, New York, NY 10017, USA

Routledge is an imprint of the Taylor & Francis Group, an informa business

First issued in paperback 2016

Copyright © 2000 David Wyn Jones

The editor has asserted his right under the Copyright, Designs and Patents Act, 1988, to be identified as the author of this work.

All rights reserved. No part of this book may be reprinted or reproduced or utilised in any form or by any electronic, mechanical, or other means, now known or hereafter invented, including photocopying and recording, or in any information storage or retrieval system, without permission in writing from the publishers.

Notice:
Product or corporate names may be trademarks or registered trademarks, and are used only for identification and explanation without intent to infringe.

British Library Cataloguing-in-Publication Data
Jones, David Wyn
    Music in Eighteenth-Century Britain
    1.Opera – Great Britain – 18th century – History and criticism
    I. Jones, David Wyn
    782.9'033

Library of Congress Cataloguing-in-Publication Data
Jones, David Wyn
    Music in Eighteenth-Century Britain / edited by David Wyn Jones
        p. cm
    Includes index.
    1.Music – Great Britain – 18th century – Congresses.
    I.Jones, David Wyn. II. Cardiff University. Dept. of Music.
    ML285.3.M87 2000
    780'.941'09033–dc21

00–029978

ISBN 13: 978-1-84014-688-2 (hbk)
ISBN 13: 978-1-138-26735-0 (pbk)

Contents

List of plates	vii
List of tables	viii
Library sigla	x
Notes on contributors	xi
Preface	xiv

1   Eighteenth-Century English Music: Past, Present, Future   1
    Peter Holman

Part 1   Institutions and Networks

2   Italian Comic Opera at the King's Theatre in the 1760s:
    the Role of the Buffi   17
    Saskia Willaert

3   Freemasonry and Musical Life in London in the Late
    Eighteenth Century   72
    Simon McVeigh

4   The London Roman Catholic Embassy Chapels and their Music
    in the Eighteenth and Early Nineteenth Centuries   101
    Philip Olleson

Part 2   Genre and Repertoire

5   Italian Violoncellists and some Violoncello Solos Published
    in Eighteenth-Century Britain   121
    Lowell Lindgren

6   Murder most Virtuous: the *Judith* Oratorios of De Fesch,
    Smith and Arne   158
    Eva Zöllner

7   A Reappraisal of Provincial Church Music   172
    Sally Drage

vi CONTENTS

Part 3 Sources and Resources

8 Handel's 1735 (London) Version of *Athalia* 193
   Donald Burrows

9 The Mackworth Collection: a Social and Bibliographical Resource 213
   Sarah McCleave

10 The Papers of C.I. Latrobe: New Light on Musicians, Music
    and the Christian Family in Late Eighteenth-Century England 234
    Rachel Cowgill

Part 4 Individuals and Style

11 Maurice Greene's Harpsichord Music: Sources and Style 261
    H. Diack Johnstone

12 Viotti's 'London' Concertos (Nos. 20–29):
    Progressive or Retrospective? 282
    Robin Stowell

Index 299
    compiled by Jane Holland

List of Plates

3.1 The interior of the Freemasons' Hall   87
(By permission: GB-Lbl.)

4.1 The interior of the Sardinian chapel around 1808   102

5.1 The first known depiction of a violoncello in eighteenth-century
Britain. Designed by Tempest and engraved by John Smith (1702)   123
(By permission: GB-Lbl.)

6.1 William Hogarth: A Chorus of Singers, December 1732   161

6.2 William Hogarth: frontispiece to William Huggins's *Judith*
(London, 1733)   162

7.1 From *11 Anthems on General and Particular Occasions
Interspersed with Symphonies... Being particularly design'd
for the Use of Parochial Choirs* (Nuneaton, 1779)   185

8.1 An opening from the '1735' wordbook for *Athalia*   204
(By permission: Gerald Coke Collection.)

8.2 The recitative 'Chi alla [ha la] pietade' added by J.C. Smith to the
conducting score of *Athalia*   206
(By permission: D-Hs.)

8.3 Conclusion of the aria 'Cor fedele' in the handwriting of J.C. Smith
in the conducting score of *Athalia*   207
(By permission: D-Hs.)

9.1 Title-page of Bemetzrieder's *Music made Easy to every Capacity*
(London, *c.* 1766)   232
(By permission: Cardiff University Library.)

10.1 Reverend Christian Ignatius Latrobe   236
(By permission: National Trust of Australia (Victoria).)

List of Tables

2.1	King's Theatre Opera Companies in the 1760s	30
2.2	Careers of the three *primi buffi*	34
	a Maria Angiola Paganini	36
	b Giovanni Lovattini	46
	c Anna Zamperini	60
2.3	Comic opera productions at the King's Theatre in the 1760s	68
2.4	Arias included in *Bertoldo Bertoldino e Cacasenno* (1749–62)	70
5.1	Italian cellists who performed in eighteenth-century Britain	136
	a Cellists in Britain, 1701–94	137
	b Two unlikely Italian cellists in London, 1702–84	148
5.2	Violoncello solos by twenty-nine composers, nearly all of whom were 'Italian', published in eighteenth-century Britain	149
	a Forty-one solos by Italian composers, published 1725–c. 1795	150
	b Four Italian 'misfits', published 1720–c. 1775	156
	c Three collections by foreign composers other than Italians published c. 1733–c. 1740	157
6.1	Three *Judith* oratorios	164
8.1	Musical sources relating to Handel's 1735 performances of *Athalia*	198
8.2	Overtures to *Athalia*, and use of related movements	200
8.3	Contents of *The Most Celebrated Songs in the Oratorio Call'd Athalia* (Walsh, 1736)	201
8.4	Handel's 1735 version of *Athalia*, based on the scheme from the 'Coke' wordbook	208
8.5	Handel's 1734–35 casts	211
9.1	Chronological development of the Mackworth Collection	215
9.2	Serious operas in the Mackworth Collection	217
9.3	French music in the Mackworth Collection	218
9.4	New publications bought by the Mackworths (ordered by inscribed date)	225
9.5	'Unfashionable' items in the Mackworth Collection (ordered by inscribed date)	226
9.6	Publishers' profile, Mackworth Collection	228

LIST OF TABLES

9.7	Chamber and concerted music in the Mackworth Collection (ordered by published date)	230
10.1	Sacred works by Haydn and Mozart featured in Latrobe's *Selection of Sacred Music*	257
11.1	Greene: The Suites	275
11.2	Greene: Miscellaneous harpsichord pieces	279
11.3	Greene: *Six Overtures* (1745)	281
11.4	Greene: *A Collection of Lessons for the Harpsichord* (1750)	281
12.1	Viotti's 'London' concertos	285

Library Sigla

The following abbreviations for the names of libraries are used in this volume. They are taken from the RISM series (Répertoire International des Sources Musicales).

B-Bc	Belgium: Brussels, Conservatoire Royal de Musique
D-Dlb	Germany: Dresden, Sächsische Landesbibliothek
D-Hs	Germany: Hamburg, Staats- und Universitätsbibliothek
D-Mbs	Germany: Munich, Bayerische Staatsbibliothek
D-WD	Germany: Wiesentheid, Musiksammlung des Grafen von Schönborn-Wiesentheid, private collection
F-Pn	France: Paris, Bibliothèque Nationale
GB-AB	Great Britain, Aberystwyth, National Library of Wales
GB-DRc	Great Britain, Durham, Cathedral
GB-Cfm	Great Britain: Cambridge, Fitzwilliam Museum
GB-Ckc	Great Britain: Cambridge, Rowe Music Library, King's College
GB-Cpl	Great Britain: Cambridge, Pendlebury Library of Music
GB-Cu	Great Britain: Cambridge, University Library
GB-Gu	Great Britain: Glasgow, University Library
GB-Lam	Great Britain: London, Royal Academy of Music
GB-Lbl	Great Britain: London, British Library
GB-Lcm	Great Britain: London, Royal College of Music
GB-Mu	Great Britain: Manchester, John Rylands University Library
GB-Ob	Great Britain: Oxford, Bodleian Library
US-CAh	United States of America: Harvard University, Houghton Library
US-GRB	United States of America: University of North Carolina, Greensboro
US-NYp	United States of America: New York, Public Library at Lincoln Center, Library and Museum of Performing Arts
US-Wc	United States of America, Washington, Library of Congress
US-Ws	United States of America: Washington, Folger Shakespeare Libraries

Notes on Contributors

Donald Burrows is Professor of Music at the Open University, Milton Keynes. He is the author of the 'Master Musicians' volume on Handel and (with Martha Ronish) author of *A Catalogue of Handel's Musical Autographs* (1993). His published editions of Handel's music include *Messiah*, *Belshazzar* and the complete violin sonatas. His is a vice-president of the Georg Friedrich Händelgesellschaft, and Chairman of the Handel Institute.

Rachel Cowgill was a postgraduate student at King's College, London, and wrote her PhD on the English reception of Mozart. Until August 2000 she was Senior Lecturer in Musicology at the University of Huddersfield and has since taken up a lectureship at the University of Leeds. She is one of the deputy directors of *LUCEM* (Leeds University Centre for English Music Studies) and a collaborator on the *Concert Life in 19th-Century London* project.

Sally Drage teaches piano and flute in Cheshire schools and is an experienced singer and director of early music. She is studying for her PhD on performance practice in English provincial church music from *c*.1700 to 1850 and is collaborating with Nicholas Temperley on a volume of psalmody for Musica Britannica.

Jane Holland is a PhD student in the Department of Music, Cardiff University, investigating the relationship between music publishers and the repertoire of the King's Theatre in London in the period 1760–90.

Peter Holman has a busy performing career as Director of The Parley of Instruments, Musical Director of Opera Restor'd and Artistic Director of The Suffolk Villages Festival. He contributes frequently to scholarly journals and conferences and has taught at a number of colleges and universities in Britain and abroad. He is Reader in Historical Musicology at Leeds University. He has written three books: *Four and Twenty Fiddlers, The Violin at the English Court 1540–1690* (1993), *Henry Purcell* (1994) and *Dowland: Lachrimae 1604* (1999).

xii   NOTES ON CONTRIBUTORS

H. Diack Johnstone, University Reader and Tutorial Fellow in Music at St Anne's College, Oxford, is editor of vol. 4 (The Eighteenth Century) of *The Blackwell History of Music in Britain* (1990) and a member of the Editorial Committee of Musica Britannica. He is also the editor of Greene's *Complete Organ Works* (1997).

Lowell Lindgren is Professor of Music and Margaret MacVicar Fellow at the Massachusetts Institute of Technology and specializes in the study of Italian composers of the late Baroque. He has edited cantatas, cello sonatas and trio sonatas, and has written monographs and articles that focus upon Italian music in London, Rome, Vienna and Paris.

Sarah McCleave is Lecturer in Music at The Queen's University, Belfast, where she continues to develop her interests in early opera and theatrical dance. She has published reviews and articles in *The Consort*, *Göttinger Händel Beiträge*, *Handbook for Studies in Eighteenth-Century Music* and the *Mozart Jarhbuch*. From 1996 to 1998, as a Postdoctoral Fellow at Cardiff University, she produced three catalogues of the Mackworth and Aylward Collections.

Simon McVeigh is Professor of Music at Goldsmiths College, University of London. He is the author of *Concert Life in London from Mozart to Haydn* (1993) and of several major articles on musical life in eighteenth- and nineteenth-century London. He is one of the directors of the database project, *Concert Life in 19th-Century London*.

Philip Olleson is Senior Lecturer in Music in the School of Continuing Education, University of Nottingham. He is the editor of *The Letters of Samuel Wesley: Professional and Social Correspondence, 1797–1837* (forthcoming) and the co-editor (with Michael Kassler) of *Samuel Wesley: A Sourcebook* (forthcoming).

Robin Stowell is Professor of Music at Cardiff University. His *Violin Technique and Performance Practice* (1985) was a pioneering work in its field, and he has since published widely. His most recent major publications include a monograph on Beethoven's violin concerto (1998), and a co-authored volume (with Colin Lawson) on historical performance practice (1999), the first of a series of which he is co-editor. He is the editor of and a contributor to *Cambridge Companions* (violin, 1992, and cello, 1999), *Performing Beethoven* (1994) and *The Violin Book* (1999).

NOTES ON CONTRIBUTORS

xiii

Saskia Willaert was a PhD student at King's College, London, and has worked extensively on the management structure and practices of Italian opera companies in London in the eighteenth century. She currently works in the education department of the newly re-opened Museum of Musical Instruments in Brussels.

Eva Zöllner took her PhD in 1998 at the University of Hamburg with a dissertation on English oratorio after Handel. She has lectured at the same university while continuing her research in music and musicians in eighteenth-century Britain. Her publications include articles on Arne, J.C. Smith the younger and Arnold, as well as on German musicians active in London during the eighteenth century.

The Editor

David Wyn Jones is Senior Lecturer in Music at Cardiff University. He has written extensively on music of the Classical period. He is the co-author (with H.C. Robbins Landon) of *Haydn. His Life and Music*, the author *of Beethoven: Pastoral Symphony* (1995) and a biography of Beethoven in the 'Musical Lives' series (1998). Edited volumes by him include *Music in Eighteenth-Century Austria* (1996).

Preface

The essays in this volume have their origin in papers given at a conference on music in eighteenth-century Britain in July 1996, organized by the Department of Music, Cardiff University. Unfortunately, illness prevented Lowell Lindgren from presenting his paper, but it is a pleasure to include it here. Peter Holman, rather than revising his paper, preferred to leave his introductory survey in more-or-less its spoken form.

Although the organizers of the conference, led by Sarah McCleave, were anxious to attract contributions that related to Ireland, Scotland and Wales as well as England, most of the papers and, consequently, the essays in this volume, turned out to be focused on England. In deference to those two essays that are British rather than English in outlook the title of the original conference, 'Music in Eighteenth-Century Britain' has been retained here. Perhaps a future conference and consequent set of essays will be able to explore the issues raised by the bifocal perspective of this volume.

It is a pleasure to record my thanks to Sarah McCleave, who not only organized the conference with a rare eye for detail as well as the overall picture, but also played a critical part in the planning of this book. The Department of Music, Cardiff University underwrote the cost of the music examples and Malcolm Boyd, as ever, was a most willing reader of proofs. Finally, Rachel Lynch of Ashgate deserves the thanks of the contributors and the editor for her commitment to the volume.

DAVID WYN JONES

CHAPTER ONE

Eighteenth-Century English Music:
Past, Present, Future

Peter Holman

There are four German words that everyone concerned with English music has to live with: *das Land ohne Musik* – the land without music. You have all come willingly to this conference, so I presume we can agree that eighteenth-century England was not a land without music, and that the products of its musical culture are worth studying and performing. This has been argued eloquently in print a number of times in recent years, notably in the eighteenth-century volume of the Blackwell History of Music in Britain.[1] But it is worth looking in more detail at how the *Land ohne Musik* judgment came to be made and accepted for so long, and what can be done to change it. Revisionist histories of English music – and of European eighteenth-century music in general – are badly needed and I hope what I have to say will suggest some directions that they might take.

The phrase *das Land ohne Musik* often appears in books on English music, though its origin is a mystery. It was used by Oscar Schmitz for the title of a book published in Munich in 1914, a significant date.[2] Previously Heinrich Heine had expressed similar sentiments, in an article written in French in July 1840 for the *Gazzette d'Augsbourg*.[3]

Ces hommes n'ont d'oreille ni pour la mesure ni pour la musique en général, et leur engoûment contre nature pour le piano et le chant, n'en est que doublement insupportable. Il n'y a véritablement rien d'aussi horrible sur terre que la musique anglaise, si ce n'est la peinture anglaise.

These people [the English] have no ear, either for rhythm or music, and their unnatural passion for piano playing and singing is thus all the more repulsive. Nothing on earth is more terrible than English music, save English painting.

Heine had to admit that the English were fond of music, but managed to turn even that fact into criticism: their passion for piano playing and singing was 'unnatural' and thus 'all the more repulsive'.

Nineteenth-century Germany was the place where musicology was invented: Guido Adler mapped out the main areas of the discipline in an article published in 1885.[4] It is no accident that 'Mediaeval', 'Renaissance', 'Baroque' and

---

[1] *The Eighteenth Century*, H.D. Johnstone and R. Fiske (eds), The Blackwell History of Music in Britain, 4 (Oxford, 1990).
[2] See the correspondence by W. Sheridan, N. Temperley and N. Zaslaw, *Musical Times*, 116 (1975), pp. 439, 625, 877.
[3] Reprinted in *Lutèce. Lettres sur la vie politique, artistique et sociale de la France* (Paris, 1855); modern edn, *Heinrich Heine, Säkularausgabe, Werke, Briefwechsel, Lebenszeugnisse*, vol. 19 (Berlin, 1977), p. 71.
[4] For a useful overview of the subject, see 'Musicology', in *The New Grove Dictionary of Music and Musicians*, ed. S. Sadie (London, 1980), vol. 12, pp. 836–63.

2   MUSIC IN EIGHTEENTH-CENTURY BRITAIN

'Classical', the labels we still use for the main periods of music history, were borrowed by late nineteenth-century German musicologists from art history. In 1888 Heinrich Wölfflin suggested that Jacob Burckhardt's concept of the Baroque in the visual arts could also be applied to literature and music, and in 1919 Curt Sachs applied the concept systematically to music.[5] It is also no accident that our received historical outline of Baroque music traces a central line of development from the Italy of Monteverdi's time to the Germany of J.S. Bach. To some extent, composers are still thought important in so far as they exemplify this historical thread. It helps to explain why, for instance, Albinoni (1671–1751), Vivaldi (1678–1741) and G.B. Sammartini (1700/1–75) receive more attention than a number of equally important Italian contemporaries, for they are the ones thought to have influenced German composers.

Of course, this agenda is part of a larger one that had more to do with nineteenth-century cultural politics than with a proper, balanced evaluation of the total corpus of eighteenth-century music. It privileged what was perceived as the centre – Italy, Germany and Austria – over the supposed periphery – Scandinavia, eastern and central Europe, France, the Iberian peninsula and England. It privileged instrumental music, especially those genres that used Viennese sonata form, over vocal music. And it privileged the work of the professional secular male in concert music over all others, such as church musicians, amateurs and women.

This agenda came to dominate musicological writing in English because many of the founding fathers of American musicology were German, and they were joined in American universities by successive waves of immigration, culminating in the exodus of Jewish musicologists from Nazi Germany before the Second World War. English eighteenth-century music has suffered more than most other areas of musicology from the German-American hegemony of musicological thought, in which Handel, a German, was thought to have dominated English musical life. Even today, most American research into English eighteenth-century music is devoted to Handel. To be fair, it is not difficult to find the same agenda at work in English musicology. The idea that Parry, Stanford and Elgar were part of an English 'Musical Renaissance' presupposes that there had been an earlier period of decline. As recently as 1983 Cambridge University Press entitled a volume *Music in Eighteenth-Century England* even though it consisted of six essays on Handel and his circle, one on Purcell, one on Purcell and Handel, one on Haydn, and only three concerned with all the other composers in eighteenth-century England, or its musical life in general.[6] The irony is that the volume was a memorial to Charles Cudworth, who had done so much to awaken interest in Handel's English contemporaries.

The most persistent observation on musical life in eighteenth-century England is that it was dominated by Handel and other immigrant composers, the

---

[5]   See 'Baroque', in *The New Grove*, vol. 2, pp. 172–8.
[6]   C. Hogwood and R. Luckett (eds), *Music in Eighteenth-Century England: Essays in Memory of Charles Cudworth* (Cambridge, 1983).

implication being that native composers were too feeble, parochial or conservative to offer them much competition. This is such a persuasive idea that it is worth looking at in some detail. It was not a new situation. Immigrants had played an important role in bringing new ideas from the continent ever since the reign of Henry VII. One thinks of the immigrant families that brought new instruments and new types of instrumental music to Henry VIII's court, or Alfonso Ferrabosco I (1543–88) and his crucial role in introducing the madrigal to England, or Angelo Notari (1566–1663), who introduced continuo playing and new types of song in the reign of James I, or Giovanni Battista Draghi (c.1640–1708), whose 1687 ode on St Cecilia's day introduced Purcell (1659–95) and Blow (1649–1708) to new ways of writing for voices and instruments.

It is true that the scale of immigration steadily increased from the reign of Charles II onwards, but this was because England was rapidly becoming one of the leading mercantile powers of the world, with a large middle class willing and able to patronize music. That is why regular commercial concerts began in London earlier than anywhere else, why it became an important music publishing centre in the 1690s, and why it had become the main European centre for harpsichord making by 1750. These developments were not symptoms of weakness or decline, but evidence of a vibrant and complex musical life. Musicians were not attracted to London from all over Europe by the prospect of becoming large fishes in a small, stagnant pond, but because London was the largest and most exciting pond of all, where you did not need to be a big fish to make a fortune.

Indeed, it could be argued that England was the most musical country in Europe in the second half of the eighteenth century, judged by the amount of musical activity of all types. Assuming suffcient wealth and social standing, a music lover in London could choose between a number of rival concert series, the Italian opera, elaborate music in the spoken theatres in plays, masques or pantomimes, and, in the summer, ambitious musical programmes in the various pleasure gardens. Nor was all the musical activity confined to the professional sphere, or to London. We tend to think of the sixteenth and early seventeenth centuries as the golden age of amateur music-making, but there must have been an enormous amount of musical activity in Georgian homes, to judge from the vast amount of vocal and instrumental music of all sorts published mainly or wholly with amateurs in mind. We must not forget, too, that the average Georgian gentleman regularly participated in a form of music-making, however humble, when he sang with his friends in the tavern. The craze for catches and glees reached such a pitch in the late eighteenth century that prizes were instituted for new compositions, and pubs even ran competitions for the best performances.

Perhaps the most impressive feature of English musical life at the time is that it was not confined to the capital, as it tended to be in autocratic and centralized France or Spain. England did not have numerous small courts, each with its own

4   MUSIC IN EIGHTEENTH-CENTURY BRITAIN

musical establishment, as in Germany, or many churches with good choirs and orchestras, as in Italy. However, in the second half of the century most English provincial towns had an amateur musical society that regularly put on orchestral concerts, there were a number of provincial theatre circuits that featured operas and musical plays, and many of the local militias had wind bands that contributed a good deal to the musical life of the towns in which they were stationed. While the provincial cathedral choirs were mostly at a low ebb, there was a vigorous and increasingly complex tradition of music in parish churches, which often involved the performance of elaborate music for choir and instruments by local composers, the subject of Sally Drage's essay in this volume.

A problem with this vigorous musical life was that it was unstructured and decentralized, which meant that there was no central archive to preserve the repertory as in German courts or Italian churches. For this reason, English music tends not to survive unless it was published; there are dozens of composers of the period whose surviving output is more or less confined to their printed collections. Furthermore, the need to keep printed music commercially viable meant that much of the music that did get into print appeared only in an incomplete form. Orchestral songs and cantatas were often printed in compressed score, as were operas, which also suffered from being published without recitatives, dances and choruses; in fact, only a handful of late eighteenth-century English operas survive complete in orchestral form.

My second objection to the 'foreign domination' theory is that there is little sign that immigrants replaced native musicians in lucrative employment, or prevented them from obtaining it. Foreigners were repeatedly encouraged to come to England because they were the purveyors of new musical ideas or new musical technology, but it is striking how often they added a new thread to the tapestry of musical life, enriching the pattern and leaving the existing threads intact. Thus, in the sixteenth century, the Lupo and Bassano families were added to the establishment of Henry VIII's court without displacing existing instrumentalists, and the same is true of the musicians who came to England with the various foreign brides of the Stuarts, or those who were attracted to England's dynamic concert life around 1700. It could be argued that Handel and the other immigrants who staffed the Italian opera company at the Haymarket around 1710 ruined the theatrical ambitions of Englishmen such as John Eccles (c. 1668–1735), John Weldon (1676–1736) and William Corbett (c. 1675–1748), but the English musical theatre soon bounced back, and in the long term Italian opera became just an extra strand enriching the musical life of London.

My most serious objection to the 'foreign domination' theory is that it is based on an anachronistic conception of national and racial identity. Nationalism was developing during the eighteenth century, but it was much less pronounced than in the nineteenth century or in modern times, even though there was a persistent thread of anti-Catholicism in England that must have affected musicians from Catholic countries. But national identity still meant relatively little, particularly to the educated elite that went on the Grand Tour, corresponded with intellectuals with similar interests in other countries, and patronized talented musicians wherever they found them. Charles Burney (1726–1814) typifies this cosmopolitan outlook. He travelled throughout Europe collecting material for his history of music, he corresponded with prominent musicians in a number of countries, and was a strong advocate of modern Italian and German composers such as Galuppi (1706–85), C.P.E. Bach (1714–88) and Haydn (1732–1809), whose progressive styles came closest to his ideal of natural, elegant melody.

There is certainly a logical problem with the received view of English musical history when it asserts that English musical life in the eighteenth century was dominated by immigrants, while at the same time it ignores their contribution to that musical life. Handel, of course, is the exception that proves the rule. It has been common in the past to think of English music only in terms of its native-born composers. But immigrants such as Paisible (d. 1721), Dieupart (d. *c.* 1740), Geminiani (1687–1762), Barsanti (1690–1772), De Fesch (1687–1761), Giuseppe Sammartini (1695–1750), Herschel (1738–1822), Hellendaal (1721–99) and Giordani (*c.* 1733–1806) spent most of their working lives in these islands, and contributed a good deal to musical life. Yet they have suffered from a Catch-22 situation in modern times: English musicologists and performers tend to ignore them because they were foreigners, while they are of little interest in their countries of origin because they left home at an early age, never to return. It is certainly difficult to make sense of some English genres without including the contribution of immigrants. A history of the English concerto grosso (or grand concerto), for instance, needs to take account of Barsanti's op. 3 (1742), De Fesch's op. 10 (1741), Geminiani's op. 2 (1732), op. 3 (1732) and op. 7 (1746), Hellendaal's op. 3 (*c.* 1758), and Sammartini's op. 2 (1728), op. 5 (1747), op. 8 (1752) and op. 11 (*c.* 1756), as well as Handel's op. 3 (1734) and op. 6 (1740). England has always been a nation of immigrants, and it makes no sense to restrict an account of its culture to the work of natives or, more accurately, to the work of the descendants of less recent immigrants.

What is often forgotten is that immigrant composers, anxious to be accepted in England, adapted their own idioms to conform to English taste. Although the basic language of English eighteenth-century music came mostly from abroad, it has a highly distinctive accent, which can often be found as strongly in the work of immigrants as that of native composers. The theatre suites written around 1700 by the Frenchman Jacques or James Paisible and the Moravian Gottfried or Godfrey Finger (*c.* 1660–1730) are as English as those by William Croft (1678–1727) or John Eccles, and the same is true of many of the grand concertos by immigrants just mentioned, to say nothing of John Frederick Lampe's English comic operas or John Christian Bach's Vauxhall songs. Even Handel adopted the English style on occasion. He wrote a Purcellian court ode soon after coming to London, and his Milton oratorio *L'Allegro, il Penseroso ed il Moderato* of 1740

6 MUSIC IN EIGHTEENTH-CENTURY BRITAIN

clearly shows the influence of Thomas Arne's *Comus* written two years earlier, in its vivid nature depiction and in the tuneful ballad style used in some of the arias. Of course, the nature of traditional musical criticism is such that biographers often prefer to see such connections as the influence of the immigrant on the native Englishman, rather than the reverse.

Mention of Handel brings me to the central problem of English eighteenth-century music. We are coming to realize that Handel's domination of English musical life was not so complete as was once thought, at least in his lifetime. He came to London to put on an Italian opera, and Italian opera largely concerned him for the first twenty years of his life in England. In the 1730s he gradually transferred his attention to the new genre of English oratorio, which he effectively invented and which occupied him for the rest of his life. He was supreme in these two genres, and it is striking that, after a few initial attempts, such as Maurice Greene's *Song of Deborah and Barak* (1732) and William Boyce's *David's Lamentation over Saul and Jonathan* (1736), English composers preferred not to challenge him on his own ground. The most notable oratorios by English composers, Arne's *Judith* (1761) and Thomas Linley junior's *The Song of Moses* (1777), were written when he was safely dead. These oratorios have long been unjustly neglected, but they are now beginning to receive their due, as Eva Zöllner's essay in this volume demonstrates.

But Handel's position was not so pre-eminent in other genres. He wrote only a few English songs, hardly anything for the English stage, no English cantatas, and nothing at all for the rapidly developing repertory of catches and glees. All but one of his anthems have orchestral accompaniment, and therefore could not be used in ordinary cathedral or parish church services accompanied just with organ, though they were sometimes performed in adapted versions. Similarly, he wrote no organ voluntaries in the fashionable multi-section idiom of the time, and the only keyboard pieces of his that would have been of use to church organists are the six fugues published around 1735 (HWV605–10), though other pieces were also pressed into service, including solo keyboard versions of overtures and organ concertos. Handel's orchestral music is so frequently performed and recorded today that is easy to forget that it played only a peripheral role in his activities. Although his grand concertos opp. 3 and 6 were very popular at the time, the style of sets by English composers in the middle of the century suggests that they were not so influential as Corelli's op. 6 (1714) or Geminiani's opp. 2 and 3 (1732), which perhaps offered simpler and more formulaic models. Similarly, although Handel's op. 4 (1738) effectively began the English keyboard concerto, his English contemporaries did not imitate them slavishly, and soon began to look abroad for models. Those by William Felton (1715–69) of Hereford are rather Vivaldian, while those by Thomas Chilcot (c. 1707–66) are for harpsichord rather than organ and show the influence of Italian harpsichord composers, including Domenico Scarlatti (1685–1757).

In fact, it could be argued that Handel came to dominate English musical life only long after his death. Certainly, a Handel cult developed even during his lifetime, promoted by a fanatical circle of aristocratic admirers who competed with one another to have his works on their shelves. He was the subject of the first full-length biography of a composer in book form, published by John Mainwaring in 1760;[7] and he was the first composer to be published in a collected edition, edited by Samuel Arnold between 1787 and 1797. But not all of his music stayed in the repertory. The operas were forgotten soon after the composer ceased to put them on, and it is unlikely that the Italian cantatas survived much longer, for the genre was outmoded by the 1750s. I also wonder how long Handel's solo sonatas and the trio sonatas continued to be played. Their genres continued in use, but his opp. 1, 2 and 5 were not republished as frequently in the late eighteenth century as Corelli's opp. 1, 2, 3, 4 and 5. Some of the orchestral music continued to be played by orchestral societies and organizations such as the Concert of Ancient Music, and the keyboard music doubtless remained in use among teachers. But it was the oratorios or, more accurately, a small group of the most popular works or extracts from them that mostly lived on. In part, this was because they spoke powerfully to those touched by the religious revival of the later eighteenth century. William Weber has argued that, by moving religious experience from the church into the theatre or concert hall and from the liturgies of particular denominations to the Bible itself, they created a new arena in which people from different religious backgrounds – Anglican, dissenting, Catholic and Jewish – could meet in harmony.[8]

Handel's oratorios also benefited from the developing choral movement of the time. He had performed them with about twenty singers (soloists, boys and men) and an orchestra of between thirty and forty.[9] However, there were larger-scale performances during his lifetime, particularly at provincial summer music festivals. Some festivals were based on cathedral choirs, though others became a focus for amateurs, and gave amateur singers their first opportunities to perform in concerts. Groups of women from the churches and chapels of northern industrial areas often travelled considerable distances to festivals, and were in great demand. The 1784 Handel Commemoration in Westminster Abbey acted as a further catalyst, since it showed that large-scale performances were viable – Burney, for one, had been sceptical until he heard them[10] – and it inspired imitations around the country, often in quite small places. In many ways, the choral festivals were the precursors of the Victorian choral societies. As the Handel oratorio cult developed it tended to stifle interest in other composers and other types of music, and, for that matter, in those Handel oratorios that had

---

[7]   J. Mainwaring, *Memoirs of the Life of the Late George Frederic Handel* (London, 1760; repr. Buren, 1964, 1975).
[8]   W. Weber, *The Rise of Musical Classics in Eighteenth-Century England: A Study in Canon, Ritual and Ideology* (Oxford, 1992), esp. pp. 103–42.
[9]   D. Burrows, 'Handel's Oratorio Performances', in *The Cambridge Companion to Handel* (Cambridge, 1997), pp. 262–81.
[10]   See, for instance, A. Ribeiro (ed.), *The Letters of Charles Burney, i, 1751–1784* (Oxford, 1991), pp. 423–4, 446.

8 MUSIC IN EIGHTEENTH-CENTURY BRITAIN

only a few choruses. Since oratorio dominated the Victorian musical scene and Handel was the pre-eminent composer of oratorio, it is not surprising that the myth grew up that he had completely dominated English musical life in his own time.

The Handel oratorio cult brings me to what we might call the problem of the past. Eighteenth-century English composers are routinely condemned for being obsessed with the past, and for failing to keep up with new developments from abroad. Of course, it is true that some types of eighteenth-century English music were extremely conservative, but that was nothing new. For centuries English composers had been at least a generation behind their colleagues on the continent. One thinks of the motets of Dunstable and his contemporaries, the pre-Reformation cyclic mass, the Elizabethan madrigal and fantasia, Restoration concerted anthems and odes, and, in the eighteenth century, the concerto grosso or grand concerto. The concerto grosso was dead in Italy by 1720 and in Germany by 1740, but English composers were still writing them while Haydn and Mozart were writing their mature symphonies; the latest one seems to be Charles Wesley's *Concerto Grosso in Seven Parts* (London, *c.* 1782). Of course, there is nothing intrinsically wrong with this, and the English did turn the Corellian concerto into something rich and strange, as they had the cyclic mass, the madrigal and the fantasia. In general, the twentieth century has lost its faith in Progress, but music critics still tend to cling almost subliminally to the Enlightenment idea that novelty is a virtue in itself: that, all things being equal, music written in a progressive style is necessarily better than that written in a conservative style. While that great Enlightenment figure Charles Burney would doubtless have agreed, many English eighteenth-century composers had good reasons for embracing the past.

Up to about 1800 music was a fashionable commodity that rarely outlived its creators by more than a generation. Monteverdi and Schütz were forgotten by the end of the seventeenth century, as were countless of their contemporaries. Palestrina and Corelli continued to be studied as classic exemplars of *stile antico* and *stile moderno* counterpoint, but Britain was the only country where sixteenth- and seventeenth-century music continued to form a living part of the repertory. At the Restoration the newly revived cathedral choirs needed music to sing, and this was initially provided by copying from old collections. But Tudor and Stuart anthems stayed in the repertory even after the need for them had passed, and they were joined by the work of Purcell and his contemporaries. By the middle of the eighteenth century the cathedral repertory had effectively become retrospective, like the repertory of modern cathedrals, or, for that matter, all types of serious music today. The process was greatly assisted by the publication of Boyce's *Cathedral Music* in the 1760s and 1770s and by subsequent publications, such as the volume of Purcell anthems that appeared as part of an abortive collected Purcell edition in the 1790s.[11]

---

[11] W. Boyce, *Cathedral Music, being a Collection in Score of the Most Valuable and Useful Compositions for that Service, by Several English Masters of the Last 200 Years*, i, (London,

EIGHTEENTH-CENTURY ENGLISH MUSIC

Similar things happened in the orchestral repertory. Corelli's op. 6 concertos arrived in England soon after they were published in 1714, and became the foundation of a repertory of English grand concertos. The repertory was initially used by professional orchestras in London – Handel's concertos served as interval music in his operas and oratorios – but it proved to be ideal material for the amateur orchestral societies that were springing up all over England in the middle of the eighteenth century. The difficult *concertino* parts could be taken by hired professionals, leaving the easy *ripieno* parts to amateurs; for this reason grand concertos were usually scored just for strings and flutes, the instruments played by gentlemen. However, some societies kept up with the times in the 1760s and 1770s by adding the more richly scored galant symphonies and overtures, often hiring the players of the socially unacceptable oboes, bassoons, clarinets, horns and trumpets from local militia bands, a practice documented dozens of times in the journals of John Marsh.[12] My local orchestral society in Colchester owned an eclectic collection of concertos and symphonies ranging from Corelli to Dittersdorf (1739–99), and it was reported in 1782 that its concerts consisted of two acts, with five pieces, ancient and modern, in each.[13]

The ancient music movement in eighteenth-century England may have arisen out of the demands of practical music-making in cathedrals and orchestral societies, but it soon acquired a momentum of its own and developed an ideology. William Weber has argued that an interest in old music developed among high Tories opposed to change and concerned for the continuity of England's political and cultural institutions.[14] After 1688 the Whig ascendancy was increasingly concerned with literature rather than music, so Tories such as the musical historian Roger North (*c*. 1651–1734), the collector Thomas Tudway (*c*. 1650–1726) or the religious pamphleteer Arthur Bedford were making quasi-political statements when they interested themselves in old music. By contrast, the Academy of Ancient Music, founded in 1726, seems to have been a sort of cartel of professional musicians opposed to Handel. Its members included many of his rivals, including Bononcini (1670–1747), Galliard (*c*. 1687–1749), Geminiani and Pepusch (1667–1752), and it defined its aims as 'searching after, examining, and hearing performed the Works of the Masters, who flourished before and about the Age of Palestrina: however, not neglecting those who in our own Time have become famous'.[15]

However, the fashion for ancient music in eighteenth-century England needs to be seen in a wider context. The 1730s and 1740s saw the beginnings of an

---

1760), ii (London, 1768), iii (London, 1773); *Anthems and Other Sacred Pieces, Goodison's Edition of Purcell* (London, *c*. 1799).

[12] B. Robins (ed.), *The John Marsh Journals: The Life and Times of a Gentleman Composer (1752–1828)* (Stuyvesant NY, 1998).

[13] Fragments of three sets of printed part-books owned by the author; see P. Holman, 'The Colchester Part-Books', *Early Music*, forthcoming.

[14] Weber, *The Rise of Musical Classics*, esp. pp. 23–74.

[15] C. Hogwood, introduction to J. Hawkins, *An Account of the Institution and Progress of the Academy of Ancient Music* (London, 1770; repr. Cambridge, 1998); see also Weber, *The Rise of Musical Classics*, pp. 56–74.

10   MUSIC IN EIGHTEENTH-CENTURY BRITAIN

interest in the past in the arts in general. There was a fashion in the theatre for old texts, which is why Arne set Milton's *Comus* (1738), why Handel set Dryden's *Alexander's Feast* (1736) and the St Cecilia ode 'From harmony, from heav'nly harmony' (1739), why Boyce set Lord Lansdowne's *Peleus and Thetis* (*c*. 1736) and Dryden's *Secular Masque* (before 1745), and why these were soon followed by the settings of Congreve's *Judgement of Paris* by Giuseppe Sammartini (?1740) and Arne (1742). There was a revival of interest in Shakespeare generated by Macklin and Garrick and their new naturalistic style of acting. The revival of Gothic architecture started at about the same time with Horace Walpole's Strawberry Hill at Twickenham. James Macpherson's supposed versions of Ossian and Thomas Chatterton's fake medieval poems introduced the same spirit to literature in the 1760s. The great histories of music by Burney and Hawkins were part of a developing interest in antiquarian scholarship, and were the counterparts of Edward Gibbon's *History of the Decline and Fall of the Roman Empire* (1776–88), the mid-century editors of Shakespeare, or Thomas Percy's *Reliques of Ancient English Poetry* (1765).

This interest in the antique was part of a wider aesthetic movement in Britain that was really an early manifestation of Romanticism. Romanticism shunned the mundane, rational, urban present in favour of exotic experience, whether it be obtained in some remote past, in the supernatural, in the countryside, or in foreign parts. Hence the development of antiquarian scholarship in all fields, the emerging Gothic horror novel, the new interest in realistic landscape painting, and the increasing popularity of the Grand Tour and of tourism in general. These things happened first in Britain because it was the most advanced society in the world at the time. It had the most developed economy, the most advanced political and social system, and an avant-garde intellectual life. The interest in old music was just one aspect of that intellectual life, though it also fitted well with the traditional conservatism of English musicians.

Thus it is not surprising that English composers in the second half of the eighteenth century began to write in a style that mixed ancient and modern elements: in effect turning the retrospective repertory into a compositional device. I believe that this is an important reason for their neglect, for it offends against late nineteenth-century ideas of unity, originality and consistency in art that still lurk in received critical aesthetic. But such ideas do not seem to have been of much interest to musicians and critics in eighteenth-century England. Indeed, English composers seem to have revelled in the new possibilities that the current interest in old music offered, particularly in large-scale works, where a variety of styles helped them to achieve an agreeable diversity. Thomas Linley Jun. (1756–78) certainly used this device in his major works. In *The Song of Moses*,[16] for instance, he naturally looked to Purcell and Handel for most of the choruses, for the contrapuntal Baroque style was much more exciting and idiomatic for choirs than the simple, homophonic and syllabic idiom developed

---

[16]   GB-Lbl, MS RM 21.h.9; recorded by the Holst Singers and The Parley of Instruments directed by Peter Holman, Hyperion CDA67038 (1998).

EIGHTEENTH-CENTURY ENGLISH MUSIC

on the continent for choral music in the galant style. On the other hand, he looked to Arne and J.C. Bach in most of the arias, not least because the galant solo vocal style involved the use of a much more developed and spectacular type of virtuosity than the outmoded Baroque vocal idiom.

Thomas Arne seems to have been the first composer to realize the potential of what might be called stylistic inconsistency in dramatic works. For instance, in his opera *Artaxerxes* (1762) the airs for the major characters are mostly in an up-to-date galant idiom with spectacular virtuosity and elaborate wind writing, while those for the minor characters tend to be scored for strings and continuo only, and are either Handelian in style or use the simple folk-like style Arne pioneered in the 1730s. Arne also developed inconsistency of another sort in his comic opera *Love in a Village* (1762). This work effectively combines the old ballad opera idiom, which used popular tunes for the airs, and the Italian pasticcio, which brought together arias by a number of composers in one opera. Again, Arne seems to have been trying to aid characterization, and to achieve a greater diversity than was possible within his own style, varied though it was. *Love in a Village* started a vogue for English pastiche operas that lasted well into the nineteenth century. They have been generally ignored or denigrated by modern critics, but Reinhard Strohm and Curtis Price have recently argued that the Italian opera pasticcio should be taken more seriously;[17] the same surely applies to English pastiche operas or, for that matter, pastiche oratorios.

Perhaps stylistic inconsistency is most interesting – and disturbing to conventional critical norms – when it occurs in a single movement. English composers of the 1760s and 1770s began to experiment with combining elements of the ancient and modern styles, and the tendency became more marked at the end of the century, as the sonatas, concertos and symphonies of Samuel Wesley (1766–1827) show. One of the earliest and most interesting examples is the first movement of a violin concerto in F by Thomas Linley Jun., probably written soon after he returned to Bath in 1771 after his studies in Italy. The idiom is basically galant, although the orchestral passages have a series of quiet cadences using the sort of suspensions found in sixteenth- and seventeenth-century music; the strings are doubled by pairs of horns and bassoons.[18] Effects of this sort were to become common in nineteenth-century German music. One thinks of Beethoven's *Die Weihe des Hauses* (*The Consecration of the House*) overture, the slow movement of Schubert's C major string quintet, and many works by Mendelssohn, Schumann and Brahms. But what passes without judgmental comment in German music has often been seen as a problem in English music.

While the influence of the antique in English late eighteenth-century music is certainly striking, not all music was so behind the times. For one reason or

---

[17] R. Strohm, *Essays on Handel and Italian Opera* (Cambridge, 1985), pp. 164–211; C. Price, 'Unity, Originality and the London Pasticcio', in *Bits and Pieces: Music for Theater*, ed. L. Lindgren, *Harvard Library Bulletin*, 2/4 (Winter 1991), pp. 17–30.

[18] GB-Lbl, MS RM 21.h.10; recorded by Elizabeth Wallfisch and The Parley of Instruments directed by Peter Holman, Hyperion CDA66865 (1996).

12   MUSIC IN EIGHTEENTH-CENTURY BRITAIN

another, those genres that have been revived in modern times have mostly been those, such as the anthem, the organ voluntary or the grand concerto, in which tradition was all important. In particular, a false idea of the concerto in eighteenth-century England has emerged because grand concertos happened to have survived in far larger numbers than the more modern solo concertos. This is because they were useful to amateur orchestral societies and were therefore worth publishing, while solo concertos were display vehicles for professionals and therefore remained in manuscript. When, however, the latter do survive they often reveal a surprisingly mature grasp of modern continental idioms. A good example is a violin concerto in G major by Thomas Shaw (*c*. 1755–1830), a rival of Thomas Linley in Bath. He was an almost exact contemporary of Mozart, and probably wrote his violin concerto in the middle of the 1770s when he was about twenty, the same time Mozart was writing his own violin concertos. It is certainly just as up to date as those works and I think it just as good. Yet it and its composer have hardly been noticed in modern times, and it had probably not been played for more than 200 years before it was recorded in 1996.[19]

In the last analysis I wonder whether much fine English music has remained on the library shelf simply because the needs of practical music-making have changed since the eighteenth century. There has been a tendency to revive music that is useful to modern amateurs and students, particularly to those who play wind instruments. Had Thomas Shaw written for the clarinet, the flute or the trumpet, he probably would have been revived long ago. More generally, much of the best eighteenth-century English music was composed in genres such as the occasional ode, English opera and the orchestrally-accompanied song that, for one reason or another, find little place in musical life today. Most people know William Boyce (1711–79) from the *Eight Symphonies in Eight Parts* op. 2 (1760). Although they are undoubtedly charming and cheerful, Boyce would hardly have reckoned them his most significant works. Indeed, they were all written, probably in extreme haste, as the overtures to major vocal works. It is works such as *Solomon* (1742) and *The Secular Masque* (*c*. 1746) that made Boyce's reputation at the time, and deserve our attention today.

But things are changing, and the change has been led by the record companies. An enormous amount of eighteenth-century music now available on CD is still not available in a modern edition, and the reason for this is not just that photocopiers and computer music programs have made the business of producing scores and parts at home much simpler and cheaper. The early recordings of Baroque music concentrated on those areas of the repertory that were of use in modern concert halls, churches or homes. But there is no reason why the repertory should be limited in this way on record, and so in recent years groups all over Europe have begun to record long-forgotten works in hitherto neglected genres. Indeed, the recording industry, pluralistic, decentralized and at

---

[19]   T. Shaw, *A Concerto for the Violin in Nine Parts* (London, *c*. 1785); recorded by Wallfisch and The Parley of Instruments directed by Holman, Hyperion CDA66865 (1996).

times almost anarchic, is effectively chipping away at the monolithic canon of nineteenth-century Teutonic masterpieces. It will eventually destroy it, and I suspect that no-one interested in eighteenth-century English music will mourn its passing.

Part 1
Institutions and Networks

CHAPTER TWO

Italian Comic Opera at the King's Theatre in the 1760s: the Role of the Buffi

Saskia Willaert

Introduction: the Status of the Buffi

The influence of singers in the world of eighteenth-century *opera seria* is well known. Apart from the proverbial capricious behaviour of a blasé *prima donna* or an ambitious castrato disrupting day-to-day programming, examples abound of singers insisting on involvement in the actual construction of an opera. Anna De Amicis, who was to create the role of Giunia in *Lucio Silla*, the new opera planned for the carnival season in 1772 at the Milan opera house, suggested that she might compose her own arias when she heard that the fourteen-year-old Mozart was to write the music.[1] Singers lobbied to have their familiar show pieces inserted in whatever opera they had to perform. In December 1760 the *primo uomo* Filippo Elisi made his London debut and it was said that *Arianna e Teseo*, the opera mounted for the occasion, contained 'several airs of Jomelli, which Elisi introduced in different operas, [and which] were calculated to shew the dexterity and accuracy with which he could form remote intervals'.[2] The social status of top *seria* singers was considerable; they were paid lavishly and moved among the great. Particularly in places such as London, where, according to Burney, 'the audience seems to care little about the Music or the poetry', as long as 'the performer is of the first class, and very miraculous and enchanting', singers of *opera seria* were admired and privileged.[3]

Many *buffi* too enjoyed international popularity and performed at the most famous theatres, but they never reached the social status of their *seria* colleagues. They were generally considered less talented. In 1755 Count Algarotti, learned writer on opera, wrote that because of the 'very limited abilities' of the *buffi*, composers of intermezzi and comic operas were not able to 'indulge their own fancy in a wanton display of all the secrets of their art' (which, in fact, he thought was quite beneficial for the expressiveness of the music).[4] Burney stated that Nicolò Piccinni (1728–1800) in burlettas 'is obliged to produce all his effects with instruments' because in that genre he 'has generally bad voices to

---

[1] See F. Schizzi, *Elogio Storico di Wolfgango Amadeo Mozart*, (Cremona, 1817), translated in C. Eisen, *New Mozart Documents. A Supplement to O.E. Deutsch's Documentary Biography* (Oxford, 1991), pp. 23–4.

[2] C. Burney, *A General History of Music (1776–89)*, ed. F. Mercer (New York, 1957), vol. 2, p. 860.

[3] Ibid., vol. 2, p. 684.

[4] F. Algarotti, *An Essay on the Opera* (London, 1767), p. 46.

18   MUSIC IN EIGHTEENTH-CENTURY BRITAIN

write for – indeed, this kind of drama usually abounds with brawls and squabbles, which it is necessary to enforce with the orchestra'.[5] The burlesque characters the *primi buffi* portrayed were devoid of the grandeur and moral dignity of their serious heroic counterparts. As will be seen, their genre was often viewed as a mere degradation of what was considered the ultimate opera experience: *opera seria*. *Buffi* were much less discussed in reviews and contemporary music histories, they were consistently paid less and enjoyed fewer privileges. Giovanni Lovattini, one of the most popular *buffi* of his time, who sang at the London King's Theatre for many years (1766–72, 1774–75), apparently never earned more than £900 a season, while first singers in *opera seria*, such as Gaetano Guadagni and Giovanni Manzuoli easily received more than £1000.[6] Lovattini's entrance into private *beau monde* circles, outside the opera house, seems to have been restricted: there are no stories of Lovattini or any other *buffo* sharing the table of the great and being showered with gifts, as was the case with top singers of serious opera, such as Giovanni Manzuoli and Ferdinando Tenducci.

Though singers of comic opera did not enjoy the prestige of *seria* singers, a closer view of the mechanisms at work behind a burletta production in London in the 1760s reveals that, contrary to what one would expect, *buffi* often had quite a big impact on what the audience was offered at eminent opera houses such as the King's Theatre.[7] Uncovering this impact in turn helps to explain the working practices of the comic department of the London opera house and to refine our knowledge of the *raison d'être* of comic pasticcios and of English taste for Italian opera in the second half of the eighteenth century.

Italian Comic Opera in London in the 1760s

As for our *opera buffas* or *burlettas*, though we have a multitude of them, yet not one is worth reading. Absurdity, meanness, and a little ribaldry too, are their chief ornaments. Yet our musical composers know at present their trade so well, that they render them pleasing to the numerous vulgar. Every sensible Italian is ashamed of them, and looks with contempt and indignation on those versemongers who write them. But their shame, contempt, and indignation are of no service to their country, as not only the low minded Italians are delighted with them, but even the nations that boast of politeness and taste superior to ours, make it a point to encourage such mongrel compositions.

This is what Joseph Baretti, an Italian residing in London, wrote about *opere buffe* in the 1760s.[8] Burney considered comic opera an inferior 'kind of drama, usually abound[ing] with brawls and squabbles'. Algarotti, on the other hand,

---

[5]   C. Burney, *Musical Tours in Europe*, ed. P.A. Scholes (London, 1959), vol. 1, p. 249.
[6]   See E. Gibson, 'Italian Opera in London 1750–75: Management and Finances', *Early Music*, 17 (1990), 55.
[7]   For the singers engaged at the King's Theatre in the 1760s, see Table 2.1, pp. 30–33.
[8]   J. Baretti, *An Account of the Manners and Customs of Italy; with Observations on the Mistakes of Some Travellers, with Regard to that Country* (London, 1768), vol. 1, p. 180.

could not praise the genre enough, 'wherein the first of all musical requisites, that of expression, takes the lead more than in any other of our compositions'.[9] Obviously Italian comic opera was controversial, capable of evoking indignant, even hostile feelings, as well as delight. For most connoisseurs the true and exalted opera experience was provided by serious opera. References to *opera buffa* being a proletarian genre, merely 'pleasing to the numerous vulgar', peppered much contemporary opera commentary.[10] In places like London, where from the autumn of 1760 onwards both genres were produced at the same theatre during the same season, the juxtaposition led to frequent comparison, mostly to the disadvantage of the comic genre. It is not certain whether Baretti had the English in mind when he referred to those 'nations that boast of taste' and 'encouraged such mongrel compositions'; but if he did, he was wrong.[11] True, when Baretti was writing down the observation, London opera lovers were consumed with enthusiasm for the burletta *La buona figliuola*, while the scheduled *opere serie* were entirely neglected. *La buona figliuola* was to be the most successful and most frequently revived opera in London in the second half of the eighteenth century; but many more burlettas failed, not only through their poor quality but often because of the prejudices of audiences against the genre.

The King's Theatre in the Haymarket was the principal venue for Italian opera in eighteenth-century London. Run as a commercial enterprise, with no subsidies from the court, its system was based on private investments and subscriptions, with an impresario who was responsible for the recruitment of the (almost exclusively Italian) singers and the daily management. The theatre opened its doors every Saturday night and once on a weekday (mostly on a Tuesday night). Expensive and prestigious, it was the place to be for fashionable and aristocratic London.

Italian comic opera had made a stormy entrée in London in the autumn of 1748 when a troupe under the directorship of the eccentric Dr Francesco Crosa arrived at the King's Theatre with a ready-made repertory of the latest hits, including *La commedia in commedia, Don Calascione* and *Orazio,* pasticcios including music by Pietro Auletta (*c.* 1698–1771), Gaetano Latilla (1711–88) and others. Two tumultuous seasons later, however, Crosa was jailed for debt, and the London opera house closed its doors; it re-opened only in the autumn of 1753 with a programme devoted exclusively to serious opera. Slipshod management, intrigues within the *buffo* troupe and the quickly dwindling interest of the public, who missed the stunning diva and the captivating castrato of the *opere serie*, had caused the failure.[12] It was another seven years before

---

[9] Burney, *Musical Tours*, vol. 1, p. 249; Algarotti, *An Essay on the Opera*, p. 46.

[10] Baretti, *An Account of the Manners*, vol. 1, p. 180.

[11] Baretti's *Account of the Manners and Customs of Italy* (1768) was an attack on Samuel Sharp's *Letters from Italy* (London, 1766). Baretti took offence at the 'gross misconceptions' of the English writer about Italy, including the alleged Italian taste for burlettas, ridiculed in Sharp's book.

[12] See R. King and S. Willaert, 'Giovanni Francesco Crosa and the First Italian Comic Operas in London, Brussels and Amsterdam, 1748–1750', *Journal of the Royal Musical Association*, 118 (1993), 246–64.

comic opera was re-introduced at the King's Theatre. By then, *opera seria* too had reached a low point in its popularity with the London audience, due mainly to poor singing and faded pasticcios. When in 1760 the King's Theatre manager Colomba Mattei undertook comic productions, the genre was better received by the audience, though it became an indispensable part of the London opera house programme only from 1773 onwards.

Mattei designed a clever and economical programme and recruitment policy which was to be a blueprint for opera management for the rest of the century: a balanced and varied menu of weekend *opera seria* and weekday burlettas, presented by two separate pairs of principal performers backed by a shared group of second singers. She acquainted the audience with some of the most talented professionals of the *buffo* métier. The Florentine Maria Angiola Paganini, who together with her husband Carlo Paganini, sang at the King's Theatre from 1760 to 1762, had conquered the Italian and Berlin *buffo* theatres during the previous twenty years, acting as an ambassador for Carlo Goldoni's early comic operas (see Table 2.2a, pp. 36–45). In London, people queued up at the theatre entrance to see her perform. The critics were full of praise. Thomas Gray's description offers a picture of her charisma on the stage: 'she is fat, and about forty, yet handsome with all and with a face, that speaks the language of all nations. She is light, alive, ever in motion, and above all graceful: but then her voice, her ear, her taste of singing! good God.'[13] The young Anna De Amicis from Naples was the King's Theatre *prima buffa* during the 1762–63 season. Her appearance on the London stage impressed many. Burney praised her abundantly. 'Her figure and gestures', he wrote, 'were in the highest degree elegant and graceful; her countenance, though not perfectly beautiful, was extremely high-bred and interesting; and her voice and manner of singing, exquisitely polished and sweet. She had not a motion that did not charm the eye, or a tone but what delighted the ear.'[14]

Mattei engaged promising composers and reinstated the position of house composer, whose activities were to go beyond merely arranging and patching up pasticcios: Gioacchino Cocchi (*c.* 1720–after 1788) was the author of the first comic opera composed expressly for the King's Theatre; Johann Christian Bach (1735–82) meticulously selected music for the comic pasticcios. Mattei ensured the presence of a seasoned house poet and pasticheur, Giovanni Gualberto Bottarelli. Three years later, when in the summer of 1763 she closed her books and left the King's Theatre in good grace, without any debts, Mattei had reconciled the London opera audience with the comic genre through hits such as Baldassare Galuppi's *Il filosofo di campagna*, Vicenzo Ciampi's *Bertoldo Bertoldino e Cacasenno* and Giuseppe Scolari's *La cascina*, all settings of librettos by Goldoni.

Towards the end of the decade, the English managers John Gordon, Thomas

---

[13] P. Toynbee and L. Whibley (eds), *The Correspondence of Thomas Gray* (London, 1935), vol. 2, p. 723.
[14] Burney, *General History*, vol. 1, p. 864.

ITALIAN COMIC OPERA AT THE KING'S THEATRE 21

Vincent and Peter Crawford (1766–9), and George Hobart (1769–70) stuck to the same policy of recruitment and programming. In 1766 the universally acclaimed *primo buffo* Giovanni Lovattini entered a long-term relationship with the London opera house and formed successful teams with the gifted *prima buffa* Lavinia Guadagni, sister of the famous castrato Gaetano, and the teenager Anna Zamperini, an excellent singer and actress, whose colourful private lives provided abundant gossip during performance intervals (see Tables 2.2b and 2.2c, pp. 46–67). Two house composers were hired: Pietro Guglielmi (1728–1804) and the young Felice Alessandri (1747–98), husband to Lavinia Guadagni. Carlo Francesco Badini was signed up to collaborate with the poet Bottarelli. Although comic opera remained the little sister of serious opera, scheduled on the less fashionable weekday nights, the managers succeeded in launching some box-office hits which remained popular until the end of the century (Piccinni's *La buona figliuola* and *La schiava*, and Guglielmi's *I viaggiatori ridicoli tornati in Italia*).

Importing Burlettas

The opera managers at the King's Theatre, possibly in agreement with the board of patrons, decided on the genre(s) to be presented and recruited singers accordingly. In the 1760s economic strictures and marketing motives forced the limitation of the expensive production of *opere serie* and prompted the London opera managers to install *opera buffa* troupes. But neither Mattei, who had been a singer of *opere serie* before she turned full-time opera director, nor the English managers Vincent, Gordon, Crawford and Hobart were familiar with the Italian comic repertory, and none of them appears to have been deeply involved in the selection of the individual burlettas to be performed. Only one instance is known in which the management clearly decided on the actual opera programme: it vetoed the planned production of Badini's *I Francesi in Corsica* in the spring of 1770.[15] With its criticism of French imperialism the opera touched too delicate a political nerve to be presented during the precarious peace between France and England in the period after the Seven Years' War and, to Badini's indignation, it was removed from the roster.

The established notion that operas were occasionally imported from Italy in the diplomatic bag (at the instigation of a noble patron) or through British tourists making the obligatory Italian Grand Tour, cannot be substantiated for the London burlettas of the 1760s.[16] Only one comic opera is known to have arrived in England through diplomatic channels. After having seen Goldoni's and Florian Gassmann's *Gli uccellatori* at the Cocomero Theatre in Florence in

---

[15] See the preface to Badini's libretto of *Il disertore* (London, 1770; GB-Lbl).
[16] See for example F. Petty, *Italian Opera in London 1760–1800* (Ann Arbor, 1980), pp. 37–8, discussing British travellers and ambassadors in Italy who could have been possible suppliers of operas for the King's Theatre.

MUSIC IN EIGHTEENTH-CENTURY BRITAIN

April 1761, Horace Mann wrote to Horace Walpole that it was 'the prettiest burletta' he had ever seen, to which Walpole replied three weeks later: 'As we have a rage at present for burlettas [the Paganinis were conquering the London stage during their first season], I wish you would send me the music of your present one, which you say is so charming'.[17] 'I am much obliged to you', he wrote to Mann on the arrival of the copies in January 1762, 'the Uccellatori shall be performed, if they will take it'.[18] Despite Walpole's promotion, the opera was not staged at the King's Theatre until eight years later (18 December 1770), when the singers who had impressed Mann so much in the burletta in Florence in 1761 (Catterina Ristorini and Michele Del Zanca)[19] were engaged at the London opera house. Though an eminent patron and zealous opera lover, Walpole had little influence on the opera repertory.

Surprisingly, the contribution of the London opera house composers to the importation of burlettas was also small. Although Cocchi, Guglielmi and Alessandri all had comic operas in their portfolios when they arrived at the King's Theatre, only Guglielmi had any of his earlier Italian works revived in London: *Il ratto della sposa* and *La sposa fedele* (under the title of *La costanza di Rosinella*), the latter of which may have been co-promoted by Anna Zamperini, who had sung lead roles in Italian revivals of the burletta before (see also Table 2.2c, pp. 60–67). Even separate arias from operas written by King's Theatre composers before they came to London, seem rarely to have been selected for the London opera house productions mounted during their engagement; from the three burlettas Cocchi composed for Venice in the early 1750s to texts by Goldoni (*La mascherata*, *Le donne vendicate* and *Li matti per amore*) only two arias were used for the King's Theatre burlettas presented in the early 1760s when he was the house composer.[20]

Obviously the actual repertory of comic operas performed at the King's Theatre depended largely on the *primi buffi* and the burlettas they had performed before they arrived in the English capital. Once they had arrived at the King's Theatre, they were given almost *carte blanche* concerning the programming of the Tuesday night performances. It was the input of the Paganinis, the De Amicis and Giovanni Lovattini that was pivotal for the rise of comic opera in London.[21] Their repertory in England reveals too close a similarity to that of

---

[17] Mann to Walpole, 25 April 1761; Walpole to Mann, 14 May 1761. W.S. Lewis et al. (eds), *The Yale Edition of Horace Walpole's Correspondence* (New Haven, 1937–83), vol. 21, p. 501 and p. 506.

[18] Ibid., vol. 21, p. 561: to Mann, 4 January 1762.

[19] See C. Sartori, *I libretti italiani a stampa dalle origini al 1800. Catalogo analitico* (Cuneo, 1990–94), no. 24181; libretto *Gli uccellatori* (London, 1770).

[20] 'Donne belle che pigliate' from Cocchi's *La mascherata* was sung in London in *Il mondo della luna* (Act 2, Scene 8) by Carlo Paganini; 'Ma soletto' from Cocchi's *Le donne vendicate* was sung in *Bertoldo Bertoldino e Cacasenno* (2:8) by Giovanni Battista Zonca. See the librettos of *La mascherata* in C. Goldoni, *Opere teatrali. Con rami allusivi* (Venice, 1788–95), vol. 42; *Le donne vendicate* in Ibid., vol. 43; *Il mondo della luna* (London, 1760; preserved in F-Pn); and *Bertoldo Bertoldino e Cacasenno* (London, 1762; GB-Lbl).

[21] Not all principal singers had a big influence on the London repertory. Anna Zamperini may have helped to mount Guglielmi's *La sposa fedele* during her stay in London in

their pre-London career not to have been selected, at least partly, under their guidance. The performance history of such comic pieces as *Bertoldo*, *La favola de' tre gobbi* and, maybe most of all, the pasticcio *La facendiera* convincingly illustrates the impact the Paganinis had on the comic repertory of the opera houses at which they performed (see Table 2.2a, pp. 36–45). While *Bertoldo* and *Li tre gobbi* were also staged by other troupes, *La facendiera* was not; in each of the six known productions of this pasticcio, premièred in Venice in 1746, Maria and Carlo were involved as the principal singers.[22] If the manager of a theatre took care of the recruitment of the necessary singers, the Paganinis would handle the rest: they provided the operas, directed the productions in accordance with the house composer and librettist, and sang the leading roles excellently. Of the eight comic operas performed by the Paganinis at the King's Theatre, at least four belonged to their Italian and Berlin repertory; a fifth one was newly written for London, while another seems to have been supplied by the *seconda buffa*, Teresa Eberardi.[23] It is hardly coincidental that all the burlettas presented by the De Amicis at the King's Theatre in 1762–63 had been performed by them the year before in Dublin, apart from one, *La calamità de' cuori*.[24] The singer who was the most important 'import trader' of Italian burlettas in London in the 1760s was undoubtedly Lovattini. During his first London years every single comic opera staged at the King's Theatre belonged to him (see Table 2.2b, pp. 46–59). Many of the *primi buffi* roles had been written in Italy especially for him. However, the longer he stayed in London, the smaller the number of Italian imports new to the London audience became: his supply of burlettas obviously began to peter out, the shortage being made up by repeat performances (*La buona figliuola*, *La schiava*, etc.) and the composition of new burlettas by Guglielmi, Alessandri, Pugnani (1731–98) and Giordani (*c.* 1733–1806).

As is clear from Table 2.3 (pp. 68–9), imports of Italian productions new to London constituted the main part of the King's Theatre comic repertory in the 1760s, but their number diminished towards the end of the decade. The most notable aspect of the repertory during the decade was the growing proportion of revivals of earlier London productions. From 1760 to 1763 only *Il filosofo di campagna* was shown during more than one season, whereas from 1768–69 onwards at least half of the burlettas performed were revivals of earlier London successes. *La buona figliuola*, *La schiava*, *Il filosofo di campagna* and *I viaggiatori ridicoli* were the most popular. William Weber has written that

---

1766–67, but she was not influential enough to have *Il ratto della sposa* selected, even though the *prima buffa* role had been conceived for her (Venice, 1765); *Il ratto della sposa* was performed in London in 1767–68, with Lavinia Guadagni in the main role. See S. Willaert, 'Italian Comic Opera in London 1760–1770' (PhD diss., University of London, 1999), p. 418 and p. 550.

[22] See Sartori, *I libretti italiani*, nos 9572–7.

[23] Teresa Eberardi had performed in *Le pescatrici* in Cologne, 1758. For the influence of this production on the London performances of the opera, three years later, see Willaert, 'Italian Comic Opera', p. 91.

[24] See the librettos of *La cascina* (Dublin, 1761), *La finta sposa* (Dublin, 1762), *Gl'intrighi per amore* (Dublin, 1762), *Il tutore burlato* [= *Il filosofo di campagna*] (Dublin, 1762) and *Il mercato di Malmantile* (Dublin, 1762), all preserved in GB-Lbl.

24   MUSIC IN EIGHTEENTH-CENTURY BRITAIN

'since opera [in the eighteenth century] was the focus of aristocratic musical taste throughout Europe, the pressure to drop old works for new ones [that is: new to the audience] could not be resisted'.[25] Nevertheless, though they did not constitute a large and permanent standard repertory of operatic classics – something that did not develop until after the middle of the next century – these four burlettas were the first to enjoy success for more than one season and helped to establish a reliable comic stock repertory at the King's Theatre that was to last until the end of the century.[26]

Strikingly, the contribution of *primi buffi* to the dispersal of the comic repertory in the 1760s is obvious in another direction too. Burlettas created especially for the King's Theatre were not much of a hit abroad, but when any of them were revived on the continent, the name of an ex-London singer was invariably to be found in the cast list. The only time Cocchi's burletta, *La famiglia in scompiglio*, was revived outside London was when Maria and Carlo Paganini performed it in Alessandria in 1763; the only occasions when Guglielmi's new London burletta of 1770, *Il disertore*, was presented abroad was when the Zamperini sisters took it to Venice (1771), Lisbon (1772) and Brescia (1777); and the pasticcio *Il tutore e la pupilla*, arranged for the King's Theatre in 1763 by Bach and Bottarelli, had a revival in remote Cadiz when Gaetano Quilici played one of the principal characters. Remarkably, even the composers of the new burlettas, who later embarked on (or continued) a successful career in Italy, did not succeed in promoting their own London creations: Gaetano Pugnani's *Nanetta e Lubino*, Guglielmi's *I viaggiatori ridicoli* and Alessandri's *La moglie fedele* and *Il re alla caccia* seem never to have been performed outside London.

The impact of the *buffi* on the King's Theatre repertory of the 1760s also has implications for modern understanding of taste in eighteenth-century London. Weber points out that the conservatism of the opera audience was accountable for the import of old *opere serie*.[27] The comic repertory imported to London during the 1760s was also subject to a five- to ten-year time lag, most burlettas being written by Goldoni and set to music by Galuppi (1706–85) and Niccolò Piccinni in the 1750s and early 1760s. However, this slightly aged repertory does not necessarily mirror a conservative London taste. The burlettas shown during Mattei's management were on average about eight years old when they arrived in London, not because the audience had a more old-fashioned taste than its Italian counterpart nor because London was at the far end of the opera route, distanced from Italy and the continent.[28] It was because the repertory that the *primi buffi*

---

[25]   W. Weber, *The Rise of Musical Classics in Eighteenth-Century England. A Study in Canon, Ritual, and Ideology* (Oxford, 1992), p. 9.

[26]   For revivals of *La buona figliuola*, *La schiava*, *I viaggiatori ridicoli* and *Il filosofo di campagna* up to the end of the eighteenth century, see Petty, *Italian Opera*, p. 363, p. 364 and p. 374.

[27]   Weber, *The Rise of Musical Classics*, p. 183.

[28]   The history of *Gli uccellatori* proves that copies of a popular Italian burletta could be available in London in fewer than nine months.

brought with them happened to be dated. After the Paganinis had returned to Italy from Berlin in 1756, Maria Paganini sang exclusively in serious operas before she left for London, while her husband revived older productions. The burletta repertory they mastered on their arrival in London in 1760 thus dated mostly from before their journey to Berlin in 1754. Similarly, when the De Amicis arrived in London, they had been travelling for seven years through France, the Netherlands and Ireland since their departure from Italy in 1755. When in the second half of the decade newer music was heard in the London opera house, it was because Lovattini brought in the latest hits from Italy (and Vienna), and when the repertory imported towards the end of the 1760s was again at least three years old, it was because Lovattini, now permanently living in London, had missed the premières of the latest burlettas in Italy.

Obviously English reception of comic operas did not depend entirely on the age of the pieces. True, Londoners loved *Il mondo della luna*, which was ten years old when it reached them, while simultaneously rejecting Tommaso Giordani's new *Il padre e il figlio rivali*. But the same audience instantly grew tired of Vicenzo Ciampi's fourteen-year-old *Bertoldo*, while they could not get enough of Guglielmi's brand new *I viaggiatori ridicoli*. Moreover, for all the alleged trailing behind of the 'conservative' English audience, only a few burlettas (including *Bertoldo* and *Il mondo della luna* in Galuppi's version) saw their last performance in London; many others, such as Domenico Fischietti's *Il signor dottore*, Piccinni's *La schiava* and Galuppi's *Le nozze*, travelled from London to Germany and even returned to Italy.[29] The King's Theatre cannot be stigmatised as a remote outpost of Italian opera culture.

Adapting Burlettas

The fact that *primi buffi* were important suppliers of the repertory would lead one to assume that they would in general also stick to their arias, especially when the songs originally had been conceived for them (as was the case in many of the Paganinis' and Lovattini's repertory pieces). However, a survey of librettos used by the *primi buffi* in London and elsewhere reveals that this was not the case. The notion that principal singers wandered around with the same arias from opera to opera, and that 'substitutions and additions were made generally for the purpose of satisfying the desires of a whimsical singer', cannot be sustained for the *buffi* in London in the 1760s.[30] Comic singers did not rely on suitcase arias. On the contrary, examples abound in which *primi buffi*'s arias from earlier productions were mercilessly replaced in London; occasionally they had to study an entirely new role. At the end of 1748 the Paganinis premièred Goldoni and Ciampi's *Bertoldo Bertoldino e Cacasenno* in Venice. Although

---

[29] See Sartori, *I libretti italiani*, nos 16725, 16680–85, 22002–7, 21184, 21186, 22686–8.

[30] D. Grout, *A Short History of Opera* (New York, 1965), pp. 190–92; see also Petty, *Italian Opera*, p. 41.

26   MUSIC IN EIGHTEENTH-CENTURY BRITAIN

they must have provided the London pasticheurs with the original libretto, only three of the twenty-six original solo arias found their way to the King's Theatre stage (see Table 2.4, pp. 70–71). Maria Paganini retained one from her Venice songs, one from her Berlin revival of 1754 and received no fewer than four new songs. Carlo Paganini changed roles. Scolari's *La cascina*, mounted at the King's Theatre in January 1763 with the two De Amicis in the principal roles, had been presented by the same singers the year before at the Dublin Smock-Alley theatre. Only five of the twenty-three solo arias were kept. Anna De Amicis was given only two of her five Dublin songs; Domenico kept none.

The reasons behind the substitutions are often enigmatic. The fact that some of the arias from, for example, *La cascina*, sung by the De Amicis in Dublin, had already been heard in other London burlettas may have prompted the arrangers to substitute these songs, in anticipation of the audience's need for variety.[31] However, other instances prove that the same pasticheurs did not shy away from a repetition of arias in different burlettas performed before the same audience. One example: 'Oh che tenebre', sung by Carlo Paganini in *Bertoldo* at the King's Theatre in January 1762, was used again a couple of months later in *Il tutore e la pupilla*, now sung by Domenico De Amicis.[32] Substitute arias could even originate from a failed burletta shown during the same season: three arias from the unsuccessful *Lo speziale*, produced in London, May 1769, were apparently transferred to *Le serve rivali*, scheduled some weeks later.[33] And while, for the sake of variety, it would have been acceptable for a burletta previously shown at the London opera house to be updated with new hits, the revivals of *La buona figliuola* in 1768–69, *I viaggiatori ridicoli* and *Il disertore*, both in 1771–72 contained virtually no changes at all, though the company employed new principal singers.[34]

Another reason for adaptation may have been that old imported burlettas, suffering a *coup de vieux*, needed to be brushed up for London use. The fact that *Bertoldo* was fourteen years old when it arrived in the English capital may account for its heavy reworking. The history of *Il filosofo di campagna* also

---

[31] Domenico De Amicis' Dublin aria 'Lenina bellina' had been heard already in the London *Bertoldo Bertoldino e Cacasenno*, his 'Ho per te' in the London *Filosofo di campagna*, and his duet with Anna, 'Occhi belli troppo', in the London *Il tutore e la pupilla*. See the librettos of *La cascina* (Dublin, 1761); *Bertoldo Bertoldino e Cacasenno* (London, 1762); *Il filosofo di campagna* (London, 1761); *Il tutore e la pupilla* (London, 1762); all preserved in GB-Lbl.

Unfortunately, music scores of different versions of any burletta are very rare. This means that in most cases textual concordances have had to be relied upon. Significantly, in those cases where the music has survived, it is clear that the pasticheur retained the music and the text. If an existing burletta was provided with new music, then it was customary to mention the composer in the libretto, either on the preliminary pages or next to the appropriate text, sometimes both. Altogether it seems safe to assume that a textual concordance normally signified a musical concordance too.

[32] See the librettos of *Bertoldo Bertoldino e Cacasenno* (London, 1762); *Il tutore e la pupilla* (London, 1762).

[33] 'T'amo bell'idol mio', 'Ah se in un mar d'affani', and 'É pena troppo barbara' were all newly written (by Felice Alessandri?) for *Lo speziale* and were retrieved in *Le serve rivali*. See the London librettos of both productions from 1769, preserved at GB-Lbl.

[34] See the librettos of *La buona figliuola* (London, 1767 and 1768); *I viaggiatori ridicoli* (London, 1768 and 1772), all preserved in GB-Lbl.

ITALIAN COMIC OPERA AT THE KING'S THEATRE 27

demonstrates how over the years fidelity to the original diminished. However, it did happen that burlettas were sometimes provided with substitute arias that were actually older than the ones they were designed to replace. For example, the London *Il tutore e la pupilla* of 1762 contained an aria ('Ha un gusto') that most probably belonged to Pietro Auletta's *Orazio* of 1737, while the original *Il tutore* (*Gli intrighi per amore*) was premièred in Dublin only the season before (1760).[35] Moreover, rejected older arias were not necessarily disposed of; they occasionally recurred in other London productions.[36]

A typical London adaptation seems to have involved the provision of extra arias for the principal singers, undoubtedly to meet the audience's demand for stars. Maria Paganini and Anna De Amicis, favourites with the London public, nearly always sang more arias per burletta in London than they had done elsewhere, but the addition of arias still does not explain why the original ones or those from an earlier revival needed to be rejected.

Gradually, the picture emerges of an authoritative team of pasticheurs, consisting of the house poet and composer, whether or not assisted by singers, who began work once it was decided which burletta would be produced. They cancelled the arias which were considered unfit for the story or the capacities of the new singers; for example, the misplaced assurance of the *buffo* Giovanni Battista Zingoni, who in two operas previously performed in Dublin had assigned himself a considerable number of arias, was remedied by Bach and Bottarelli when they substantially reduced his contribution.[37] They got rid of songs that they considered unfashionable, did not meet their artistic standards, or that were remembered to have been unsuccessful in productions abroad. Subsequently they looked for more appropriate replacements, mostly provided from a stock of arias built up during the previous seasons, either from earlier London productions or from copies left by the singers.[38] Other songs were newly

---

[35] For the arias in *Orazio*, see F. Walker, '*Orazio*. The History of a Pasticcio', *Musical Quarterly*, 38 (1952), 382–3. Other examples of substitute arias which were older than the original are: 'Bella mia se son', sung in the London *Il mondo della luna* in 1760, and taken from the London revival of *Orazio*, 1748, while the première of *Il mondo* dated from 1750; 'Io sono un libro aperto' in the London production of *Il filosofo* in 1760, originally composed for *Il virtuose ridicole*, which was premièred in 1752, while *Il filosofo* had had its first performance in 1754. See the librettos of *Il mondo della luna* (London, 1760); *Orazio* (London, 1748; GB-Lbl); *Il filosofo di campagna* (London, 1761; GB-Lbl); and *Il virtuose ridicole* (Venice, 1752; F-Pn).

[36] For example, 'Quando si trovano' and 'Non è ver son crudele', both sung by Maria and Carlo Paganini in *Bertoldo* in Berlin, 1754, were used during the Paganinis' first London season in *Il mondo*, not in *Bertoldo*. See the librettos of *Bertoldino alla corte del Re Alboino* (Berlin, 1754; F-Pn); *Il mondo della luna* (London, 1760); and *Bertoldo Bertoldino e Cacasenno* (London, 1762).

[37] His songs in *Il tutore* were reduced from five in Dublin to two in London, in *La finta sposa* from four to two. His limitations as a singer are obvious also from the fact that his roles in Bach's new London *Orione* and *Zanaida* were the smallest parts. See the librettos of *Gli intrighi per amore* (Dublin, 1762); *Il tutore e la pupilla* (London, 1762); *La finta sposa* (Dublin, 1762); *La finta sposa* (London, 1763); *Orione* (London, 1763; GB-Lbl); *Zanaida* (London, 1763; GB-Lbl).

[38] For example, several substitute arias in different burlettas are borrowed from Galuppi's *Il conte Caramella*, never performed in London, but belonging to the repertory of the Paganinis. See the librettos of *Il conte Caramella* (Verona, 1749) in Goldoni, *Opere teatrali*, vol. 40; *Il mondo della luna* (London, 1760); *The Favourite Songs in... La Moglie Fedele* (London: Bremner, 1768).

28 MUSIC IN EIGHTEENTH-CENTURY BRITAIN

written by the house composer, who often furnished the burletta with a new overture or symphony.

One specific type of vocal number, however, was quite consistently retained from the original: the ensemble piece. As the *tutti* and *cori* often incorporated the most essential parts of the action and plot of a burletta and thus largely determined its identity, they proved to be difficult to replace. It may be telling that the only two burlettas which did not retain the ensembles of their models changed their titles in London: *Il tutore e la pupilla* was based on *Gli intrighi per amore*, and *La costanza di Rosinella* was based on *La sposa fedele*.

This process of manipulating an existing score was implied in the remark, reproduced in many London burletta librettos, that the piece had been 'adapted to the taste of the King's Theatre'. The pasticheurs may have been trying to offer entertainments which they thought would work better artistically and commercially under the specific London circumstances than the originals. This is confirmed in a way by the two burlettas that underwent the fewest changes in London, *Il filosofo di campagna* and *La buona figliuola*. They were widely recognized to be musically and dramatically the best, enjoying the most sensational number of revivals everywhere in Europe; hence, the London pasticheurs felt less compelled to 'improve' them.

The picture of house composers and poets collaborating and negotiating over an existing score, consulting the (principal) singers, and manipulating the musical composition, entirely fits in with the well-known concept that an eighteenth-century opera did not possess any of the sacrosanct notions of authorship that a work does now. A burletta was not seen as the expression and intellectual property of a creative individual, as an inviolable piece of art, but as public property, which, nevertheless, was handled with some care and artistic conscience. Arranging an existing score was an opportunity for the 'Compiler of shewing his judgment and taste'.[39] Making a good pasticcio was an artistic activity. 'I hear you are a poet', Casanova said to Bottarelli, when he met him in London in 1763, 'Indeed I am, sir', Bottarelli answered sincerely, 'I have extended the *Didone* and abridged the *Demetrio*'.[40]

It should be noted that very occasionally a cry for an authentic performance was heard. On 24 March 1763 *La serva padrona* was scheduled as an afterpiece to *Il tutore e la pupilla* for the benefit of Anna and Domenico De Amicis; it was presented 'in its own natural beauty, such as it originally came from the hands of the ingenious author Signor Pergolesi, and as it was first done at Naples, in order to give the Nobility and Gentry the most favourable idea of so masterly a piece'.[41] Emphasizing the return to the authentic version of a thirty-year-old piece as a way of advertising an opera and attracting an audience was in fact

---

[39] *The Public Advertiser*, 17 March 1767.

[40] G. Casanova, *History of My Life*, ed. Willard R. Trask (London, 1967–9), vol. 4, p. 389. For the stature and respectability of the pasticcio in the second half of the eighteenth century, see also C. Price, 'Unity, Originality, and the London Pasticcio', in *Bits and Pieces: Music for Theater*, L. Lindgren (ed.), in *Harvard Library Bulletin* 2/4 (Winter, 1991), 21–3.

[41] *The Public Advertiser*, 24 March 1763.

exceptional in the London opera world, dominated as it was by pasticcios and new operas. If a burletta did go from one opera house to another with little alteration, it certainly was not always out of respect for the original piece. When the 1761 revival in Dublin of *Il filosofo* by the De Amicis is compared with their Brussels production of 1759, the congruence immediately catches the eye. It should be noted that Smock-Alley did not house its own composers and poets, so no professional pasticheurs were at hand; all authority to adapt the burletta lay in the hands of the strolling company who decided to change as little as possible. It seems that only well-equipped opera houses, such as the King's Theatre in London, could afford to have their pieces reworked considerably to meet the contextual needs of a production.

30 MUSIC IN EIGHTEENTH-CENTURY BRITAIN

Table 2.1: King's Theatre Opera Companies in the 1760s

Only those theatre seasons are given when comic opera was performed.

Season 1760–61

	Serious		Comic	
primo uomo	Filipo Elisi		Carlo Paganini	*primo buffo*
prima donna	Colomba Mattei		Maria Paganini	*prima donna*
secondo uomo		Pietro Sorbelloni		*uomo serio*
seconda donna		Angiola Calori		*donna seria*
terzo uomo / tenor		Gaetano Quilici		*secondo buffo*
terza donna		Teresa Eberardi		*seconda buffa*
			Christiano Tedeschini	*terzo buffo*

composer / music director	Gioacchino Cocchi
librettist	Giovanni Francesco Bottarelli
leader of the band	Thomas Pinto
manager	Colomba Mattei
treasurer	Joseph Trombetta

Season 1761–62

primo uomo	Filipo Elisi		Carlo Paganini	*primo buffo*
prima donna	Colomba Mattei		Maria Paganini	*prima donna*
secondo uomo		Rosa Curioni		*uomo serio*
seconda donna		Angiola Sartori		*donna seria*
terzo uomo / tenor		Giovanni Battista Zonca		*secondo buffo*
terza donna		Teresa Eberardi		*seconda buffa*
			Pietro Leonardi	*terzo buffo*

composer / music director	Gioacchino Cocchi
librettist	Giovanni Francesco Bottarelli
manager	Colomba Mattei
treasurer	Joseph Trombetta

ITALIAN COMIC OPERA AT THE KING'S THEATRE

Season 1762–63

	Serious		Comic	
primo uomo	Domenico Ciardini		Domenico De Amicis	*primo buffo*
prima donna	Livia Segantini, replaced by Anna De Amicis from Feb. 1763 onwards		Anna De Amicis	*prima donna*
secondo uomo		Giuseppe Giustinelli		*uomo serio*
seconda donna		Giovanna Carmignani and Livia Segantini	Giovanna Carmignani	*donna seria*
terzo uomo / tenor		Gaetano Quilici		*secondo buffo*
terza donna		Marianna Valsecchi		*seconda buffa*
ultima parte		Giovanni Battista Zingoni		*terzo buffo*
ultima parte (from Feb. 1763 onwards)		Clementina Cremonini		*ultima parte*

composer	Johann Christian Bach
librettist	Giovanni Francesco Bottarelli
manager	Colomba Mattei
treasurer	Peter Crawford

Season 1766–67

primo uomo	Tomasso Guarducci		Giovanni Lovattini	*primo buffo*
prima donna	Signora Ponce		Anna Zamperini	*prima buffa*
secondo uomo		Gaspare Savoi		*uomo serio*
seconda donna		Pollo Young		*donna seria*
tenor	Signor Grassi			
bass		Andrea Morigi		*basso caricato*
			Giovanni Zamperini	*secondo buffo*
terza donna		Teresa Piatti		*seconda buffa*
terzo uomo		Leopoldo De Michele		*terzo buffo*
ultima parte	Signora Moser		Margherita Gibetti	*terza donna*

composers	[opera commissions: Matteo Vento, Johann Christian Bach]
librettist	Giovanni Gualberto Bottarelli
leader of the band / first violinist	François-Hippolyte Barthélemon
managers	Thomas Vincent, John Gordon, Peter Crawford
treasurer	Peter Crawford
painters	Vincenzo Conti, Francesco Bigari

MUSIC IN EIGHTEENTH-CENTURY BRITAIN

Season 1767–68

	Serious	Comic	
primo uomo	Tomasso Guarducci	Giovanni Lovattini	*primo buffo*
prima donna	Luisa Campollini	Lavinia Guadagni	*prima buffa*
secondo uomo	Gaspare Savoi		*uomo serio*
seconda donna	Vittoria Querzoli		*donna seria*
tenor	Francesco Moser		
bass	Andrea Morigi		*basso caricato*
terza donna	Teresa Piatti		*secondo buffo*
terza uomo	Leopoldo De Michele		*seconda buffa*
		Angelica Maggiore	*terza donna*

composer / music director	Pietro Guglielmi and Felice Alessandri
librettist	Giovanni Gualberto Bottarelli
translator of librettos	Francesco Bottarelli
leader of the band / first violinist	Gaetano Pugnani
first violoncellist	Signor Manfredi
managers	Thomas Vincent and John Gordon
treasurer	John Gordon
painters	Vincenzo Conti, Francesco Bigari

Season 1768–69

[no serious operas]

Giovanni Lovattini	*primo buffo*
Lavinia Guadagni	*prima buffa*
Domenico Luciani	*uomo serio*
Teresa Giacomazzi	*donna seria*
Giovanni Batt. Bassanese	*secondo buffo*
Anna Gori	*seconda buffa*
Andrea Morigi	*basso caricato*
Leopoldo De Michele	*terzo buffo*
Margerita Gibetti	*terza donna*

composer	Felice Alessandri
librettists	Giovanni Gualberto Bottarelli and Carlo Francesco Badini
leader of the band	Gaetano Pugnani
manager	Thomas Vincent and John Gordon
treasurer	John Gordon
ballet master	Domenico Ricciardi
painter and machinist	Mr Canter

ITALIAN COMIC OPERA AT THE KING'S THEATRE

Season 1769–70

	Serious	Comic	
primo uomo	Gaetano Guadagni	Giovanni Lovattini	*primo buffo*
prima donna	Cecilia Grassi	Lavinia Guadagni and Anna Zamperini	*prima buffa*
secondo uomo	Lorenzo Piatti		*uomo serio*
seconda donna	Teresa Piatti, replaced by Lelia Achiapati from Jan. 1770 onwards	Teresa Piatti, replaced by Antonia Zamperini from Feb. 1770 onwards	*donna seria*
tenor	Benedetto Bianchi		*tenore*
bass	Andrea Morigi		*basso*
		Antonia Zamperini	*seconda buffa*

composer	Pietro Guglielmi
librettists	Giovanni Gualberto Bottarelli and Carlo Francesco Badini
managers	George Hobart, John Gordon (recruitment); backed by a board of noble patrons, presumably incl. George Pitt
treasurer	Peter Crawford
ballet master	Signor Campioni
painters and machinists	Signori Bigari

34   MUSIC IN EIGHTEENTH-CENTURY BRITAIN

Tables 2.2a, 2.2b and 2.2c: Careers of three *primi buffi*

The order of each entry has been standardized in the form year, season and date of the performance; town and theatre in which the performance took place; title, genre and type of the piece performed; role; composer and (continuing on facing page) librettist of the piece as given in the source(s) of the actual performance; the company which gave the performance; additional information and the source(s) for the actual performance. The theatre seasons have been indicated according to the following code: 1 = *carnevale* (carnival); 2 = *inverno* (winter); 3 = *primavera* (spring); 4 = *ascensione* (ascension); 5 = *estate* (summer); 6 = *autunno* (autumn). A letter following the date specifies the date: D = the date of the dedication of the libretto, as given in the source; P = the date of the first presentation of the piece at the particular theatre during season concerned; T = the date of the printing of the libretto, as given in the source. The première of an opera, as given in *The New Grove Dictionary of Opera* (London, 1992) (unless stated otherwise), has been indicated in bold type. The spelling of the titles of the pieces and the names of the company singers have been maintained as in the original source (mainly librettos). The replacement of a singer during the run of the opera has been indicated in the column of the company by a slash (/) followed by the name of the new singer. The spelling of the genres has been standardized. Types of pieces (S = serious opera; C = comic opera) have been added only for operas, not for serenatas, oratorios, concerts, etc. Names of composers and librettist have been given as entered in *The New Grove Dictionary of Opera*. Library sigla and shelf numbers in the source column refer to the libretto used for the entry.

Abbreviations

Bibliographical Sources

AAM	'Chronologia da opera em Portugal', *A Arte Musica,*34–48 (1874)
Brito	Manuel Carlos de Brito, *Opera in Portugal in the Eighteenth Century* (Cambridge, 1989)
IN	*Indice de' Spettacoli Teatrali*, ed. Gio. Battista Cacciò, 17 vols, (Milan, [1772–88])
LS	*The London Stage 1660–1800: a Calendar of Plays, Entertainments and Afterpieces*, Part 4 (1747–76), ed. George Winchester Stone Jun., 3 vols (Carbondale, 1962); Part 5 (1776–1800), ed. Charles Beecker Hogan, 3 vols (Carbondale, 1968); Index, ed. B.R. Schneider (Carbondale, 1979)
Michtner	Otto Michtner, *Das alte Burgtheater als Opernbühne* (Vienna, 1970)

Moreau	Mario Moreau, *Cantores de Opera portugueses* (Lisbon, 1981) vol. 2
NG	*The New Grove Dictionary of Music and Musicians*, ed. Stanley Sadie, 20 vols, London, 1980
OG	*The New Grove Dictionary of Opera*, ed. Stanley Sadie, 4 vols, London, 1992
Piovano	Francesco Piovano, 'Baldassare Galuppi, Note bio-bibliografiche', *Rivista Musicale Italiana*, 13 (1906), 676–726; 14 (1907), 333–65; 15 (1908), 233–74
Piperno	Franco Piperno, 'Buffe e buffi', *Rivista Italiana di Musicologia*, 17 (1982), 240–84
S	Claudio Sartori, *I libretti italiani a stampa dalle origini al 1800. Catalogo analitico*, 7 vols, (Cuneo, 1990–94)
Th.cts	Volumes of theatrical cuttings in the British Library, London
W	Taddeo Wiel, *I teatri musicali veneziani. Catalogo delle opere in musica rappresentate nel secolo XVIII in Venezia* (Venice, 1897)
WW	Robert and Norma Weaver, *A Chronology of Music in the Florentine Theater 1590-1750* (Detroit, 1978)
Zechmeister	Gustav Zechmeister, *Die Wiener Theater nächst der Burg und nächst dem Kärntnerthor von 1747 bis 1776* (Vienna, 1971)

Others

alt.	altered; e.g. Badini, C.F. (alt.): alterations to the original libretto made by Carlo Francesco Badini
C	comic opera
cpsr.	composer
ded. by	dedicated by
dir.	director of the music
Fav. Songs	Favourite Songs
impr.	impresario (also the dedicator)
libr.	libretto
P	première
rec.	recitatives
S	serious opera
sh.	shortened
with alt.	with alteration; e.g. Badini, C.F. (with alt.): Carlo Francesco Badini is the original librettist; alterations have been made in the actual revival

Table 2.2a: Maria Angiola Paganini

	Year / Season		Date	Place	Theatre	Title	Genre	Type	Role	Composer
1	1741	5	/	Pisa	Pubblico	/	/		/	/
2	1742	1	42.01.22 P	Florence	Cocomero	Tito Manlio	dramma	S	Decio and Geminio	Fini, Michele
3	1742	6	42.09.06 P	Florence	Coletti	Marchese sgrana, Il	divertimento giocoso	C	Checchina	Auletta, Pietro
4	1742	6	/	Florence	Coletti	Amore vuol sofferenza	divertimento giocoso	C	Vastarella	Leo, Leonardo
5	1743	1	/	Bologna	Formagliari	Finta cameriera, La	dramma giocoso	C	Betta	Latilla, Gaetano
6	1743	1	/	Bologna	Formagliari	Libertà novica, La	dramma giocoso	C	Flaminia	Capua, Rinaldo di
7	1743	1	43.01.12 D	Bologna	Formagliari	Olimpiade, L'	dramma	S	Argene	pasticcio
8	1743	1	43.02.13 D	Bologna	Formagliari	Cajo Fabricio	dramma	S	Turio	/
9	1743	3	/	Leghorn	S Sebastiano	Finta cameriera, La	divertimento giocoso	C	Giocondo	Latilla, Gaetano
10	1743	6	/	Venice	S Moisè	Orazio	opera bernesca	C	Giacomina	Latilla, G. - G.B. Pergolesi
11	1744	1	/	Venice	S Moisè	Finta cameriera, La	divertimento giocoso	C	Giocondo	Latilla, Gaetano
12	1744	1	/	Venice	S Moisè	Fiammetta, La	opera bernesca	C	Fiammetta	pasticcio
13	/	/	/	/	/	Don Calascione uomo sciocco romano	intermezzi	C	Betta	/
14	1745	6	/	Venice	S Cassiano	Scialacquatore alla fiera, Lo	dramma giocoso	C	Delfina	Orlandini, G. M., *e.a.*
15	1745	6	/	Venice	S Cassiano	**Rigiri delle cantarine, I**	**dramma giocoso**	C	Ersina	**Maggiore, Francesco**

	Librettist	Company	Comments	Source
1	/	/		Piovano1906,724n
2	Noris, Matteo	Giuseppe Ciacchi, Girolama Tearelli, Teresa Imer, Mariana Imer, Nunziata Scardabelli		S,23237; WW,i.291; not in NG, OG
3	Palomba, Antonio	Giuseppe Laschi, Maria Longini, Lucrezia Longini, Gaetano Lanetti, Antonio Lottini, Anna Rigacci		S,14740; WW,i.295-6
4	Federico, Gennaro Antonio	Filippo Laschi, Gaetano Lanetti, Lucrezia Longoni, Maria Longoni, Antonio Lottini, Anna Rigacci		S,01524; WW,i.296
5	/	Eugenia Mellini Fanti, Costanza Rosignoli, Giuseppe Ristorini, Gaspera Becheroni, Francesco Baglioni, Gaetano Maggioni		S,10420
6	/	Giuseppe Ristorini, Francesco Baglioni, Costanza Rosignoli, Luigi Ristorini, \Gaetano Maggioni, Gaspera Becheroni, Annunziata Scartabelli		S,14236
7	/	Pasquale Negri, Margherita Chimenti, Francesco Barlocci, Luigi Ristorini, Annunziata Scattabelli		S,16947
8	Zeno, Apostolo	Francesca Barlocci, Pasquale Negri, Margherita Chimenti, Eugenia Mellini Fanti, Costanza Rosignoli, Girolama Boccabianca		S,04422
9	/	Pietro Compassi, Caterina Chiaveri, Caterina Brogi, Pietro Pertici, Gio. Battista Bianchi, Bartolomeo Cherubini, Anna Gaschi	Pietro Pertici, impr.	S,10421
10	Palomba, Antonio	Pellegrino Gaggiotti, Anna Querzoli, Agata Sani, Grazia Melini, Filippo Laschi		S,17324; W,425
11	Barlocci, Gio. Gualberto	Pellegrino Gaggiotti, Anna Querzoli Laschi, Grazia Melini, Luisa Peruzzi, Filippo Laschi, Catterina Castelli		S,10425; W,443
12	/	Anna Querzoli, Catterina Castelli, Pellegrino Gaggiotti, Grazia Melini, Agata Sani, Filippo Laschi, Giovanni Benvenuti		S,10129; W,426 ('P: 1743,1')
13	/	Carlo Paganini		S,08121
14	Borghesi, Ambrogio	Elisabetta Ronchetti, Rosa Tagliavini, Emanuel Cornaggia, Francesco Amorevoli, Alessandro Cattanei, Carlo Paganini, Margherita Cavalli	'di Firenze'	S,21245; W,447 ('libr.: B. Vitturi'); NG,xiii.824
15	Vitturi, Bartolomeo	Elisabetta Ronchetti, Emanuelle Cornaggio, Rosa Tagliavini, Francesco Amorevoli, Carlo Paganini, Alessandro Cattani, Margherita Cavalli	'di Firenze'	S,19831; W,448; NG,xi.492

Table 2.2a: Maria Angiola Paganini (continued)

	Year / Season		Date	Place	Theatre	Title	Genre	Type	Role	Composer
16	1746	1	/	Venice	S Cassiano	Fata meravigliosa, La	dramma giocoso	C	Carmenta	Scolari, Giuseppe
17	1746	1	/	Venice	S Cassiano	Vedova accorta, La	dramma giocoso	C	Lisetta	Bertoni, F., e.a.
18	1746	4	/	Venice	S Moisè	Facendiera, La	dramma giocoso	C	Checchina	pasticcio
19	1746	4	/	Padua	Obizzi	Facendiera, La	dramma giocoso	C	Checchina	pasticcio
20	1746	6	46.09 P	Prato	Teatro	Finta cameriera, La	divertimento giocoso	C	Giocondo	Latilla, Gaetano
21	1747	1	/	Pisa	Pubblico	Virtuosa moderna, La	intermezzo	C	Elisa	/
22	1747	6	/	Lucca	Teatro	Artaserse	dramma	S	Artaserse	Scarlatti, Giuseppe
23	1748	3	48.05.12 P	Florence	Cocomero	Facendiera, La	dramma	C	Checchina	pasticcio
24	1748	3	48.06.13 P	Florence	Cocomero	Vedova spiritosa, La	dramma giocoso	C	Lisetta	/
25	1748	5	48.07.11 P	Florence	Cocomero	Componimento drammatico (first part)	cantata		Lisinga	/
26	1748	5	48.07.11 P	Florence	Cocomero	Componimento drammatico (second part): La virtuosa moderna	intermezzo	C	Elisa	/
27	1748	6	/	Venice	S Moisè	Semplice spiritosa, La	dramma giocoso	C	Agnesa	'musica a piacere dei cantanti'
28	1748	6	/	Venice	S Moisè	Scuola moderna, La; o sia La maestra di buon gusto	dramma giocoso	C	Drusilla	Ciampi, Vincenzo
29	1749	1	48.12.26 P	Venice	S Moisè	Bertoldo Bertoldino e Cacasenno	dramma comico	C	Menghina	Ciampi, Vincenzo
30	1749	1	/	Venice	S Moisè	Favola de' tre gobbi, La	intermezzo in Anagilda	C	Mad. Vezzosa	Ciampi, Vincenzo

	Librettist	Company	Comments	Source
16	/	Elisabetta Ronchetti, Rosa Tagliavini, Emanuelle Cornaggio, Carlo Paganini, Alessandro Cattani, Francesco Amorevoli, Margherita Cavalli	'di Firenze'	S,09805; W,449; NG,xvii.55
17	Borghesi, Ambrogio	Elisabetta Ronchetti, Emanuele Cornaggia, Rosa Tagliavini, Francesco Amorevoli, Alessandro Cattani, Carlo Paganini, Margherita Cavalli	'di Firenze'	S,24400; W,450
18	/	Nicola Gorri, Luiggia Peruzzi, Carlo Paganini, Alessandro Cattani, Maria Maggini		S,09572; W,470
19	/	Elisabetta Ronchetti, Nicola Gori, Luiggia Peruzzi, Carlo Paganini, Alessandro Cattani, Maria Maggini	Ded. by Maria Angela Paganini 'e compagni'	S,09572
20	/	Margherita Landi, Artemisia Landi, Alessandro Cattani, Carlo Paganini, Carolina Serafin	'di Firenze'	S,10433
21	/	Carlo Paganini	'di Firenze'; ded. by Maria Paganini 'e compagni'	S,25061
22	Metastasio, Pietro	Caterina Fumagalli, Carlo Carlani, Filippo Elisi, Maria Maddalena Parigi, Violante Masi		S,02986; NG,xvi.579
23	/	Margherita Landi, Gaetano Lanetti, Anna Barchetti, Carlo Paganini, Giuseppe Ducci, Antonio Valletti, Giuseppe Compstoff (mute role)		S,09574; WW,i.320
24	Borghesi, Ambrogio	Gaetano Lanetti, Margherita Landi, Anna Barchetti, Carlo Paganini, Giuseppe Ducci, Antonio Valletti, Maria Maddalena Parrini	'di Firenze'	S,24438; WW,i.321
25	/	Margherita Landi, Niccola Berardi	'di Firenze'	S,05999; WW,i.321
26	/	Carlo Paganini		S,05999; WW,i.321
27	Goldoni, C. (with alt.)	Livia Segantini, Rodeginda Travaglia, Anna Bastiglia, Carlo Paganini, Giuseppe Cosino, Catterina Baratti		S,21603; W,494
28	Palomba, A - C. Goldoni	Livia Segantini, Redegonda Travaglia, Carlo Paganini, Anna Bastiglia, Catterina Baratti, Giuseppe Cosmi		S,21392; W,495; NG,iv.509
29	Goldoni, Carlo	Livia Segantini, Anna Bastiglia, Redegonda Travaglia, Cattarina Baratti, sig. Bassani d'anni otto, Carlo Paganini, Francesco Carrattoli, Giuseppe Cosmi		S,04001; W,514; NG,iv.509
30	Goldoni, Carlo	Carlo Paganini, Francesco Carrattoli, Giuseppe Cosimi		S,09831; W,515; NG,iv.509

Table 2.2a: Maria Angiola Paganini (continued)

	Year / Season		Date	Place	Theatre	Title	Genre	Type	Role	Composer
31	1749	3	49.04.13 P	Florence	Cocomero	Catone in Utica	dramma	S	Marzia	Orlandini, G.M. (dir.)
32	1749	3	49.05.21 P	Florence	Cocomero	Arsace	dramma	S	Statire	Orlandini, Giuseppe Maria
33	1749	6	/	Verona	Rena	Facendiera, La	dramma giocoso	C	Checchina	pasticcio
34	1749	6	/	Verona	Rena	Maestra di scola, La	dramma giocoso	C	Drusilla	Ciampi, Vincenzo
35	1750	1	/	Verona	Rena	Bertoldo Bertoldino e Cacasenno	dramma giocoso	C	Menghina	/
36	1750	1	/	Verona	Rena	Favola de' tre gobbi, La	intermezzo	C	Mad. Vezzosa	/
37	1750	3	/	Milan	Regio-Ducale	Arcadia in Brenta, L'	dramma comico	C	Mad. Lindora	/
38	1750	3	/	Milan	Regio-Ducale	Bertoldo Bertoldino e Cacasenno	dramma giocoso	C	Menghina	pasticcio
39	1750	3	/	Milan	Regio-Ducale	Componimento drammatico (first part)	[cantata]		Lisinga	/
40	1750	3	/	Milan	Regio-Ducale	Componimento drammatico (second part:) La favola de' tre gobbi	intermezzo	C	Mad. Vezzosa	/
41	1750	4	50.06 P	Padua	Obizzi	Favola de' tre gobbi, La	intermezzo in Il corsaro	C	Mad. Vezzosa	/
42	1750	4	50.06 P	Padua	Obizzi	Bertoldo Bertoldino e Cacasenno	dramma giocoso	C	Menghina	/
43	1750	/	/	Turin	Carignano	Componimento drammatico (first part)	cantata		Lisinga	/
44	1750	/	/	Turin	Carignano	Componimento drammatico (second part:) Tre gobbi rivali in amore	intermezzo	C	Mad. Vezzosa	/
45	1751	1	50.12.26 P	Florence	Pergola	Tre gobbi rivali, I	intermezzo in Mitridate	C	Mad. Vezzosa	Ciampi, Vincenzo

	Librettist	Company	Comments	Source
31	Metastasio, Pietro	Giuseppe Meisner, Giuseppe Prona, Rosa Tagliarini, Caterina Bartolini, Eleonora Castelli		S,05261; WW,i.325
32	Salvi, Antonio	Giuseppe Porna, Rosa Tagliavini, Giuseppe Meisner, Caterina Bartolini, Maria Eleonora Castelli		S,02876 ('P: 1748,3'); WW,i.325
33	/	Orsola Strambi, Anna Bastiglia, Ottavia Barbarini, Carlo Paganini, Marcantonio Mareschi	'fiorentina'; ded. by the 'compartecipi'	S,09575
34	Goldoni, Carlo	Orsola Strambi, Anna Bastiglia, Carlo Paganini, Ottavia Barbarini, Cattarina Baratti, Marcantonio Mareschi, Antonio Valletti	'fiorentina'; ded. by the 'compartecipi'	S,14642
35	/	Orsola Strambi, Anna Bastiglio, Ottavia Barberini, Caterina Baratti, Carlo Paganini, Marcantonio Mareschi, Antonio Valetti	'fiorentina'; ded. by the 'compartecipi'	S,04004
36	/	Carlo Paganini, M. Antonio Mareschi, Antonio Valletti		S,09832
37	/	Angiola Sartori, Nicola Peretti, Anna Castelli, Carlo Paganini, Giovanni Leonardi, Agostino Bossi		S,02363
38	/	Nicola Peretti, Anna Castelli, Angiola Sartori, Ambrogio Ghezzi, Carlo Paganini, Giovanni Leonardi, Angiolo Tanara		S,04002
39	/	Anna Castelli, Angiola Sartori		S,05994
40	/	Carlo Paganini, Giovanni Leonardi, Ambrogio Ghezzi		S,05994
41	/	Carlo Paganini, Giovanni Leonardi, Marco Antonio Mareschi		S,06699
42	/	Sebastiano Emiliani, Laura Brascagli, Angela Sartori, Marco Antonio Mareschi, Carlo Paganini, Giovanni Leonardi	Ded. by Filippo Dessales	S,04003
43	/	Giuseppe Ucedo, Madalena Pirovana	'di Firenze'	S,05998
44	Goldoni, Carlo	Carlo Paganini, Ambrosini, Pietro Bibiogero	'di Firenze'	S,05998
45	Goldoni, Carlo	Carlo Paganini, Niccola Petri, Antonio Valletti, Giuseppe Compostof	Giuseppe M. Orlandini, impr.	S,23545, 15659; WW,i.330–1

Table 2.2a: Maria Angiola Paganini (continued)

	Year / Season		Date	Place	Theatre	Title	Genre	Type	Role	Composer
46	1751	1	51.01.11 P	Florence	Pergola	Scialacquatore, Lo	intermezzo	C	Mad. Lindora	Orlandini, G. M. or L. Minuti?
47	1751	1	before 51.02.03 P	Florence	Pergola	Vecchio burlato, Il	intermezzo	C	Drusilla	/
48	1751	3	/	Milan	Regio-Ducale	Arcadia in Brenta, L'	dramma comico	C	Mad. Lindora	/
49	1751	3	/	Milan	Regio-Ducale	Mondo della luna, Il	dramma giocoso	C	Lisetta	/
50	1751	6	/	Turin	Carignano	Facendiera, La	dramma giocoso	C	Checchina	/
51	1751	/	51.11.25 P	Turin	Palazzo Duca di Borgogna	Componimento drammatico	/		Giunone	Leoni, Pietro Maria
52	1752	1	51.12 T	Vercelli	T. della città	Facendiera, La	dramma giocoso	C	Checchina	/
53	1752	/	/	Vercelli	T. della città	Mondo della luna, Il	dramma giocoso	C	Lisetta	/
54	1752	5	/	Vercelli	T. della città	Vedova accorta, La	dramma giocoso	C	Lisetta	/
55	1752	6	/	Turin	T. di Torino	Mondo al rovescio, Il; o sia Le donne che comandano	dramma bernesco	C	Cintia	/
56	1754	/	/	Potsdam	Hoftheater	Bertoldino alla corte del re Alboino	intermezzi	C	Menghina	/
57	1757	1	/	Novara	Casa Petazzi	Filosofo di campagna, Il	dramma giocoso	C	Lesbina	Galuppi, Baldassare
58	1758	1	57 T	Milan	Regio-Ducale	Eroe cinese, L'	dramma	S	Ulania	Piazza, Gaetano
59	1758	1	58.01.14 P	Milan	Regio-Ducale	Ipermestra, L'	dramma	S	Elpinice	Galuppi, Baldassare
60	1759	1	58.12.19 D	Lodi	T. di Lodi	Olimpiade, L'	dramma	S	Aristea	Traetta, Tomasso

	Librettist	Company	Comments	Source
46	/	Carlo Paganini, Nicola Petri		S,21243; WW,ii.133
47	/	**Carlo Paganini, Nicola Petri**		**S,24363; WW,ii.134**
48	/	Angiola Cattarina Riboldi, Carlo Ambrogio Gradati, Cattarina Tedeschi, Carlo Paganini, Giovanni Leonardi, Ambrogio Ghezzi		S,02365
49	/	Carlo Paganini, Caterina Riboldi, Gian Ambrogio Grandatis, Caterina Tedeschi, Giovanni Leonardi, Ambrogio Ghezzi		S,15867
50	/	Giuseppa Ucedo, Carlo Paganini, Regina Ronchetti, Madalena Pirovana, Ambrogio Ghezzi, Pietro Bibiogero	'di Firenze'	S,09576
51	/	Gaetano Pompeo Basteris, Teresa Mazzola	'In occasione della nascita del duca di Borgogna'	S,12972; Piperno,243; not in NG, OG
52	/	Carlo Paganini, sig. Allone, Teresa Crespi, Anna Chiari De Hè, sig. Pellerino		S,09577
53	/	Carlo Paganini, Caterina Tedeschi, Giuseppe Quaglia, Ambrogio Ghezzi, Ippolita Mondina, Filippo Sedatti		S,15868
54	/	Carlo Paganini, Ambrogio Ghezzi, Filippo Sidotti, Cattarina Tedeschi, Giuseppe Quaglia, Ippolita Mondini		S,24405
55	Goldoni, Carlo	Carlo Paganini, Giovanni Leonardi, Filippo Sidotti, Cattarina Tedeschi, Giuseppe Quaglia, Ippolita Mondini		S,15842
56	/	Carlo Paganini, Filippo Sidotti		S,03989
57	Goldoni, Carlo	Teresa d'Ucedo, Domenico Jazzi, Carlo Paganini, Pietro Bigiogero, Pietro Leonardi		S,10358
58	Metastasio, Pietro	Giuseppe Tibaldi, Gio. Domenico Giardini, Caterina Gabrieli, Carlo Martinenghino		S,09196; OG,iii.356 ('P: 1757')
59	**Metastasio, Pietro**	**Giuseppe Tibaldi, Caterina Gabrielli, Domenico Ciardini, Carlo Martinenghino, Giuseppe Dondi**		**S,13586; NG,vii.137**
60	/	Pellegrino Ugolini, Rosa Baruffi, Antonio Priorino, Giuseppa Dondi, Giuseppe Viganti	'di Firenze'	S,16974

Table 2.2a: Maria Angiola Paganini (concluded)

	Year / Season		Date	Place	Theatre	Title	Genre	Type	Role	Composer
61	1760	/	60.11.22 P	London	King's	Mondo della luna, Il	dramma giocoso	C	Lisetta	Galuppi, B. / dir.: G. Cocchi
62	1761	/	61.01.06 P	London	King's	Filosofo di campagna, Il	dramma giocoso	C	Lesbina	Galuppi, B. / dir.: G. Cocchi
63	1761	/	61.03.09 P	London	King's	Tre gobbi rivali, I	opera comica	C	Mad. Vezzosa	/
64	1761	/	61.04.28 P	London	King's	Pescatrici, Le	opera comica	C	Lesbina	Bertoni, Ferdinando
65	1761	/	61.11.10 P	London	King's	Mercato di Malmantile, Il	opera comica	C	Lena	Fischietti, Domenico
66	1762	/	62.01.11 P	London	King's	Bertoldo Bertoldino e Cacasenno alla corte del re Alboino	opera comica	C	Menghina	Ciampi, V. / dir.: G. Cocchi
67	1762	/	62.04.03 P	London	King's	Famiglia in scompiglio, La	dramma giocoso	C	Fiammetta	Cocchi, Gioacchino
68	1763	4	63.04 P	Alessandria	Solerio	Famiglia in scompiglio, La	dramma giocoso	C	Fiammetta	Cocchi, Gioacchino
69	1763	6	/	Milan	Ducale	/	/	/	/	/
70	1765	4	65.08 P	Brescia	Erranti	Matrimoni in maschera, I	dramma giocoso	C	Nanna	Rutini, Gio. Marco
71	1767	1	/	Pavia	Omodeo	Didone abbandonata, La	dramma	S	Didone	/
72	1772	6	/	Palermo	S Cecilia	Olimpiade, L'	dramma	S	Aristea	pasticcio
73	1773	1	/	Palermo	S Cecilia	Adriano in Siria	dramma	S	Emirena	pasticcio
74	1773	1	/	Palermo	/	Farnace, Il	dramma serio	S	/	/
75	1773	1	/	Palermo	/	Olimpiade, L'	dramma serio	S	/	/

	Librettist	Company	Comments	Source
61	Goldoni, Carlo	Pietro Sorbelloni, Carlo Paganini, Christiano Tedeschini, Angiola Calori, Gaetano Quilici, Teresa Eberardi		S,15877; LS,iv.826
62	Goldoni, Carlo	Angiola Calori, Pietro Sorbelloni, Carlo Paganini, Christiano Tedeschino, Gaetano Quilici, Teresa Eberardi	'Virtuosa di S.M. il Re di Prussia'	S,10369; GB-Lbl 907.i.9/2; LS,iv.836
63	/	Carlo Paganini, Gaetano Quilici, Christiano Tedeschino		LS,iv.848
64	/	Angiola Calori, Pietro Sorbelloni, Carlo Paganini, Christiano Tedeschino, Gaetano Quilici, Teresa Eberardi	'Virtuosa di S.M. il Re di Prussia'	GB-Lbl 1712.a.57; LS,iv.862
65	/	Carlo Paganini, Rosa Curioni, Angiola Sartori, Giovanni Battista Zonca, Teresa Eberardi, Pietro Leonardi		S,15444; LS,iv.901
66	Goldoni, Carlo	Rosa Curioni, Angiola Sartori, Carlo Paganini, Giovanni Battista Zonca, Pietro Leonardi, Teresa Eberardi	'Virtuosa di S.M. il Re di Prussia'	S,04015; GB-Lbl 11714.b.23; LS,iv.911
67	Bottarelli, Gio. Gualberto	Carlo Paganini, Giovanni Battista Zonca, Angiola Sartori, Rosa Curioni, Teresa Eberardi, Pietro Leonardi	'Virtuosa di S.M. il Re di Prussia'	S,09644; GB-Lbl 907.i.9/5; LS,iv.927
68	/	Carlo Paganini, Nicodemo Calcine, Anna Gallo, Pietro Bigiogero, Anna Penachi, Giacomo Lambertini	'Virtuosa di S.M. il Re di Prussia'	S,09645
69	/	/		Piovano1906,724n
70	/	Bartolomeo Schirolli, Teresa Piatti, Giacomo Cerri, Giuseppa Lombardi, Giuseppe Sechioni, Vincenzo Goresi	'Virtuosa di S.M. il Re di Prussia'; Francesco Putini,	S,15133
71	/	Gio. Domenico Giradini, Giacomo Croce, Teresa Mongis, Carlo Bonomo, Lucia Visconti	'virtuosa di camera di S.M. prussiana'	S,07828
72	/	Nicoló Caldalora, Agnese della Nave, Grazie d'Aniello, Pietro Benedetti, Angela Altieri	'virtuosa di SM de Prussia'	S,17006
73	/	Grazia d'Aniello, Nicolo Caldalora, Agnese della Nave, Pietro Benedetti, Angiola Altieri	'virtuosa di S.M. di Prussia'	S,00433
74	/	Pietro Benedetti, Nicolò Calderola, Grazia d'Aniello, Agnese della Nave, Angiola Altieri		IN1773,37
75	/	Pietro Benedetti, Nicolò Calderola, Grazia d'Aniello, Agnese della Nave, Angiola Altieri		IN1773,37

Table 2.2b: Giovanni Lovattini

	Year / Season		Date	Place	Theatre	Title	Genre	Type	Role	Composer
1	1753	/	/	Ravenna	Pubblico	Uccellatrice, L'	intermezzi	C	Don Narciso	Jommelli, Niccolò
2	1755	1	/	Padua	Obizzi	Mondo alla roversa, Il	dramma giocoso	C	Graziosino	/
3	1755	1	/	Padua	Obizzi	Mondo della luna, Il	dramma	C	Bonafede	/
4	1755	5	55.08.16 D	Bologna	Formagliari	Conte Caramella, Il	dramma giocoso	C	Brunoro	Galuppi, Baldassare
5	1755	6	55.09.14 P	Bologna	Formagliari	Nozze, Le	dramma giocoso	C	Mingone	Galuppi, Baldassare
6	1755	6	55.11 P	Venice	S Samuele	Diavolessa, La	dramma giocoso	C	Falco	Galuppi, Baldassare
7	1756	1	55.12.26 P	Venice	S Samuele	Cascina, La	dramma giocoso	C	Berto	Scolari, Giuseppe
8	1756	1	56.02 P	Venice	S Samuele	Ritornata di Londra, La	dramma giocoso	C	Bar. di Montefresco	Fischietti, Domenico
9	1756	3	/	Milan	Regio-Ducale	Conte Caramella, Il	dramma giocoso	C	Cecco	Galuppi, Baldassare
10	1756	3	56.05.05 T	Milan	Regio-Ducale	Cascina, La	dramma giocoso	C	Berto	Scolari, Giuseppe
11	1756	4	56.08 P	Brescia	Erranti	Donne vendicate, Le	dramma giocoso	C	Flaminio	Cocchi, Gioacchino
12	1756	6	/	Venice	S Samuele	Filosofo di campagna, Il	dramma giocoso	C	Nardo	Galuppi, Baldassare
13	1756	6	/	Milan	Regio-Ducale	Nozze, Le	dramma giocoso	C	Mingone	Galuppi, Baldassare
14	1756	6	/	Venice	S Samuele	Tre matrimoni, I	commedia	C	Freninman	Calandra, Nicola
15	1757	1	56.12.27 P	Venice	S Samuele	Statue, Le	dramma giocoso	C	Mengone	Brusa, Francesco

	Librettist	Company	Comments	Source
1	/	Giuseppe Celesti	'ravennate'	S,24198
2	/	Carlo Bombari, Vittoria Galeotti, Mattio Bovina, Francesca Bovini, Maria Conclin	Giacomo Guaeta, impr.	S,15855
3	/	Vittoria Galeotti, Maria Conclin, Francesca Santarelli Buini, Angiola Candi, Matteo Buini, Carlo Bambari	Giacomo Guaeta, impr.	S,15872
4	Goldoni, Carlo	Rosa Puccini, Maria Monari, Anna Tonelli Bambini, Caterina Tonelli, Michele del Zanca, Giuseppe Cosimi	Bortolo Ganassetti, impr.	S,06373
5	Goldoni, Carlo	Maria Monari, Rosa Puccini, Anna Tonelli Bambini, Michele del Zanca, Caterina Tonelli, Giuseppe Cosimi	Bortolo Ganassetti, impr.	S,16670; NG,vii.137
6	Goldoni, Carlo	Giuseppe Celesti, Antonia Zamperini, Serafina Penni, Giovanni Leonardi, Michele del Zanca, Rosa Puccini		S,07712; W,577; NG,vii.137
7	Goldoni, Carlo	Antonia Zamperini, Giuseppe Celesti, Serafina Penni, Giovanni Leonardi, Rosa Puccini, Michele del Zanca		S,05156; W,588; NG,xvii.55
8	Goldoni, Carlo	Giuseppe Celesti, Antonia Zamperini, Serafina Penni, Giovanni Leonardi, Michele del Zanca, Rosa Puccini		S,19911; W,589; NG,vi.616
9	/	Felice Novelli, Francesca Mocci, Teresa Crespi, Antonia Fassatelli, Giuseppe Cosimi	Ded. by Filippo Dessales	S,06375
10	Goldoni, Carlo	Felice Novelli, Francesca Mucci, Antonia Fasciatelli, Francesca Santarelli, Teresa Crespi, Giuseppe Cosini	Ded. by Filippo Dessales	S,05155
11	Goldoni, Carlo	Giuseppe Cicognani, Serafina Penni, Giovanni Leonardi, Rosa Puccini, Margherita Parisini, Francesca Boini, Michele del Zanca		S,08308
12	Goldoni, Carlo	Bianca Riboldi, Ferdinando Compassi, Anna Tonelli Bambini, Antonio Rossi, Caterina Tonelli, Giuseppe Barbarossa		S,10356; W,591
13	/	Giuseppe Dondi, Rosa Pessina, Agata Ricci, Giuseppe Guadagni, Lavinia Guadagni, Pietro Bigiogero		S,16671
14	Gozzi, Carlo	Bianca Riboldi, Ferdinando Compassi, Anna Bambini, Antonio Rossi, Catterina Tonelli, Giuseppe Barbarossa		S,23554; W,592; NG,iii.612
15	Brusa, Gio. Battista	Bianca Riboldi, Catterina Regis, Anna Tonelli Bambini, Antonio Rossi, Catterina Tonelli, Giuseppe Barbarossa		S,22627; W,598; NG,iii.392

Table 2.2b: Giovanni Lovattini (continued)

	Year / Season		Date	Place	Theatre	Title	Genre	Type	Role	Composer
16	1757	1	/	Venice	S Samuele	Nozze, Le	dramma giocoso	C	Mingone	Galuppi, Baldassare
17	1757	1	/	Venice	S Samuele	Chimico, Il	commedia	C	Volpino	Ciampi, Vincenzo
18	1758	1	/	Rome	Capranica	Duellista fanatico, I	farsetta	C	Don Favonio	Megrino, Giuseppe
19	1758	1	/	Rome	Capranica	Vilanella, La	farsetta	C	Serpillo	/
20	1758	3	58.04.08 D	Bologna	Formagliari	Mercato di Malmantile, Il	dramma giocoso	C	Berto	Fischietti, Domenico
21	1759	1	/	Rome	Tordinona	Amor fra gl'inganni	farsetta	C	Rancio	/
22	1759	1	/	Rome	Tordinona	Arcifanfano re de' matti, L'	farsetta	C	Arcifanfano	Galuppi, Baldassare
23	1759	6	/	Turin	Carignano	Buovo d'Antona	dramma giocoso	C	Buovo d'Antona	Traetta, Tommaso
24	1759	6	/	Turin	Carignano	Filosofo di campagna, Il	dramma giocoso	C	Nardo	Galuppi, Baldassare
25	1759	6	/	Turin	Carignano	Signor dottore, Il	dramma giocoso	C	Bernardino	Fischietti, Domenico
26	1760	1	60.01 P	Rome	Dame	Fiera di Sinigaglia, La	dramma giocoso	C	Orazio	Fischietti, Domenico
27	1760	1	60.02.06 P	Rome	Dame	Buona figliuola, La	dramma giocoso	C	March. della Conchiglia	Piccinni, Niccolò
28	1760	3	/	Bologna	Marsigli Rossi	Buona figliuola, La	dramma giocoso	C	March. della Conchiglia	Piccinni, Niccolò
29	1760	3	/	Bologna	Marsigli Rossi	Signor dottore, Il	dramma giocoso	C	Bernardino	Fischietti, Domenico
30	1760	6	/	Milan	Regio-Ducale	Buona figliuola, La	dramma giocoso	C	March. della Conchiglia	Piccinni, Niccolò

	Librettist	Company	Comments	Source
16	Goldoni, Carlo	Bianca Riboldi, Catterina Regis, Anna Tonelli Bambini, Antonio Rossi, Catterina Tonelli, Giuseppe Barbarossa		S,16674; W,599
17	/	**Bianca Riboldi, Catterina Regis, Anna Tonelli Bambini, Antonio Rossi, Catterina Tonelli, Giuseppe Barbarossa**		**S,05511; W,600; NG,iv.387**
18	/	Giuseppe Orti, Patrizio Rtti, Gio. Batt. Persichino	'da Cesena'; ded. by Gioaccino Puccinelli	S,08601; not in NG, OG
19	/	Giuseppe Orti, Gio. Battista Persichino, Gio. Battista Archari	'da Cesena'; ded. by Gioaccino Puccinelli	S,24884
20	Goldoni, Carlo	Francesca Cioffi, Agata Ferretti, Francesco Carratoli, Anna Bambini, Michele Angelo Potenza, Catterina Ristorini, Isabella Beni	Bortolo Ganassetti, impr.	S,15431
21	/	Tomaso Borghesi, Francesco Carattoli, Francesco Pieri	'di Cesena'	S,01379
22	Goldoni, Carlo	Francesco Carattoli, Tomaso Borghesi, Francesco Pieri	'di Cesena'	S,02400
23	Goldoni, Carlo	Vincenza Baglioni, Giovanna Baglioni, Gaspare Savoj, Clementina Baglioni, Francesco Caratoli, Francesco Baglioni		S,04281
24	Goldoni, Carlo	Giovanna Baglioni, Clementina Baglioni, Francesco Caratoli, Vincenza Baglioni, Gaspare Savoj, Francesco Baglioni		S,10364
25	Goldoni, Carlo	Vincenzia Baglioni, Gaspare Savoj, Giovanna Baglioni, Clementina Baglioni, Francesco Caratoli, Francesco Baglioni		S,21982
26	**Goldoni, Carlo**	**Carlo de Cristoferi, Gaspare Savoj, Giuseppe Giustinelli, Tommaso Borghesi, Francesco Carattoli, Giuseppe Casaccia**		**S,10153; NG,vi.616**
27	**Goldoni, Carlo**	**Gaspare Savoj, Carlo de Cristofori, Tommaso Borghesi, Giuseppe Giustinelli, Francesco Pieri, Francesco Carattoli, Giuseppe Casaccia**		**S,04175; NG,xiv.727**
28	Goldoni, Carlo	Clementina Baglioni, Gaspare Savoj, Giovanna Baglioni, Vincenza Baglioni, Anna Giorgi, Francesco Caratoli, Giacomo Caldinelli		S,04172
29	Goldoni, Carlo	Clementina Baglioni, Gaspare Savoj, Francesco Caratoli, Giovanna Baglioni, Vincenza Baglioni, Giacomo Caldinelli	Bortolo Ganassetti, impr.	S,21983
30	Goldoni, Carlo	Clementina Baglioni, Gaspare Savoj, Filippo Laschi, Francesco Carattoli, Giovanna Baglioni, Vincenza Baglioni, Paola Tradati	Francesco Morone, impr.	S,04174

Table 2.2b: Giovanni Lovattini (continued)

	Year / Season		Date	Place	Theatre	Title	Genre	Type	Role	Composer
31	1760	6	/	Milan	Regio-Ducale	Signor dottore, Il	dramma giocoso	C	Fabrizio	Fischietti, Domenico
32	1761	1	/	Rome	Argentina	Donna di governo, La	dramma giocoso	C	Ridolfo	Galuppi, B., e.a.
33	1761	1	/	Rome	Argentina	Signor dottore, Il	dramma giocoso	C	Bernardino	/
34	1761	3	/	Bologna	Formagliari	Buona figliuola, La	dramma giocoso	C	March. della Conchiglia	Piccinni, Niccolò
35	1761	3	/	Bologna	Formagliari	Tre amanti ridicoli, Li	dramma	C	Onofrio	Galuppi, Baldassare
36	1761	3	61.06.10 D	Bologna	Formagliari	Buona figliuola maritata, La	dramma giocoso	C	March. della Conchiglia	Piccinni, Niccolò
37	1761	6	/	Turin	Carignano	Buona figliuola maritata, La	dramma giocoso	C	March. della Conchiglia	Piccinni, Niccolò
38	1761	6	/	Turin	Carignano	Scaltra spiritosa, La	dramma giocoso	C	Pippo del Gallo	Piccinni, Niccolò
39	1762	1	/	Rome	Capranica	Amante ridicolo deluso, L'	farsetta	C	Baggiano	Piccinni, Niccolò
40	1762	1	/	Rome	Capranica	Buona figliuola zitella, La	farsetta	C	Marchese	Piccinni, Niccolò
41	1762	1	/	Rome	Capranica	Buona figliuola maritata, La	farsetta	C	March. della Conchiglia	Piccinni, Niccolò
42	1762	5	/	Faenza	Remoti	Buona figliuola, La	dramma giocoso	C	March. della Conchiglia	Piccinni, Niccolò
43	1762	5	/	Milan	Regio-Ducale	Filosofo di campagna, Il	dramma giocoso	C	Nardo	Galuppi, Baldassare
44	1762	5	/	Milan	Regio-Ducale	Viaggiatore ridicolo, I	dramma giocoso	C	Cav. Astolfo	Scolari, G. - A. Mazzoni
45	1762	6	/	Milan	Regio-Ducale	Buona figliuola, La	dramma giocoso	C	March. della Conchiglia	Piccinni, Niccolò

	Librettist	Company	Comments	Source
31	Goldoni, Carlo	Clementina Baglioni, Gaspare Savoj, Giovanna Baglioni, Vincenza Baglioni, Filippo Laschi, Francesco Caratoli	Ded. by Francesco Morone	S,21985
32	**Goldoni, Carlo**	**Giuseppe Giustinelli, Gaspare Savoj, Francesco Carattoli, Giovanni Leonardi, Luca Fabri, Caetano Bartolini, Francesco Cecconi**	**A. Lungi and G. Puccinelli, impr.**	**S,08237; NG,vii.504**
33	Goldoni, Carlo	Nicola Benini, Gaspare Savoj, Francesco Carattoli, Luca Fabri, Gaetano Bartolini, Domenico Poggi	Ded. by Giuseppe Balestra	S,21992
34	Goldoni, Carlo	Teresa Zaccarini, Gioachino Caribaldi, Lavinia Guadagni, Margarita Parisini, Isabella Beni, Francesco Carattoli, Giovanni Delpini	Bortolo Ganassetti, impr.	S,04179
35	Galuppi, Antonio	Teresa Zaccarini, Lavinia Guadagni, Margarita Parisini, Isabella Beni, Giovanni Dalpini, Francesco Carattoli, Gioaccino Caribaldi		S,23497
36	**Goldoni, Carlo**	**Teresa Zaccarini, Gioachino Caribaldi, Lavinia Guadagni, Francesco Carattoli, Margarita Parisini, Isabella Beni, Giovanni Delpini**	**Ded. by B. Ganassetti and company**	**S,04241; NG,xiv.727**
37	Goldoni, Carlo	Margarita Caldinelli, Luca Gabri, Gioanna Baglioni, Teresa Zaccherini, Anna Maria Baglioni, Francesco Carattoli, Gioacchino Caribaldi		S,04244
38	Palomba, Antonio	Margarita Caldinelli, Luca Fabri, Gioanna Baglioni, Teresa Zuccherini, Anna Maria Baglioni, Francesco Carattoli, Gioacchino Caribaldi		S,21088
39	/	Luca Fabri, Giovanni Leonardi, Giuseppe Giustinelli	Francesco Simoni, impr.	S,01064
40	Goldoni, Carlo	Luca Fabri, Giuseppe Giustinelli, Giovanni Leonardi	Ded. by Francesco Simoni	S,04186
41	Goldoni, Carlo	Luca Fabri, Giovanni Leonardi, Giuseppe Giustinelli		S,04250
42	Goldoni, Carlo	Chiara Colliva, Gaspare Savoi, Margarita Parisina, Anna Bassani, Giovanna Dacquini, Francesco Caratoli, Gioachino Caribaldi		S,04183
43	/	Clementina Baglioni, Gaspare Savoj, Francesco Caratoli, Giovanna Baglioni, Vincenza Baglioni, Giacomo Caldanelli	Ded. by Giuseppe Galeazzi	S,10370
44	**Goldoni, Carlo**	**Clementina Baglioni, Gaspare Savoj, Vincenza Baglioni, Teresa Piatti, Francesco Caratoli, Giacomo Caldinelli**	**Giuseppe Galeazzi, impr.**	**S,24754; NG,xvii.55**
45	Goldoni, Carlo	Clementina Baglioni, Gaspare Savoj, Francesco Caratoli, Giovanna Baglioni, Vincenzina Baglioni, Maria Teresa Piatti, Giacomino Coldinelli		S,04184

Table 2.2b: Giovanni Lovattini (continued)

	Year / Season		Date	Place	Theatre	Title	Genre	Type	Role	Composer
46	1762	6	/	Milan	Regio-Ducale	Caffè di campagna, Il	dramma giocoso	C	Caligo	Galuppi, Baldassare
47	1763	1	/	Rome	Valle	Cavaliere per amore, Il	intermezzi	C	Florindo	Piccinni, Niccolò
48	1763	1	/	Rome	Valle	Donne vendicate, Le	intermezzi	C	Conte Bellezza	Piccinni, Niccolò
49	1763	4	63.04.29 D	Reggio	Pubblico	Baronessa riconosciuta, La	dramma serio-buffo	SC	March. della Conchiglia	Piccinni, Niccolò
50	1763	4		Reggio	Pubblico	Baronessa riconosciuta e maritata, La	dramma serio-buffo	SC	March. della Conchiglia	Piccinni, Niccolò
51	1763	6	/	Turin	Carignano	Speziale, Lo	dramma giocoso	C	Mengone	Pallavicini, V. - D. Fischietti
52	1763	6	/	Turin	Carignano	Statue, Le	dramma giocoso	C	Mengone	Brusa, Francesco
53	1764	1	/	Rome	Valle	Perucchiere, Il	intermezzi	C	Polidoro	Piccinni, Niccolò
54	1764	1	64.01.01 P	Rome	Valle	Stravaganti, Gli	intermezzi	C	Lelio	Piccinni, Niccolò
55	1764	/		Vienna	Privilegiato	Signor dottore, Il	dramma giocoso	C	Bernardino	Fischietti, Domenico
56	1764	/	/	Vienna	Privilegiato	Mercato di Malmantile, Il	dramma giocoso	C	Rubicone	Fischietti, Domenico
57	1764	/	64.05.19 P	Vienna	Privilegiato	Buona figliuola, La	dramma giocoso	C	March. della Conchiglia	Piccinni, Niccolò
58	1764	/	/	Vienna	/	Buona figliuola maritata, La	dramma giocoso	C	March. della Conchiglia	Piccinni, Niccolò
59	1764	/	64.11.05 P	Vienna	Privilegiato	Nozze, Le	dramma giocoso	C	Mingone	Galuppi, Baldassare
60	1765	2	65.02.11 P	Vienna	Privilegiato	Stravaganti, Gli	commedia	C	D. Alessio	Scarlatti, Giuseppe

	Librettist	Company	Comments	Source
46	Chiari, P. - A. Galuppi?	Clementina Baglioni, Gaspare Savoj, Vincenza Baglioni, Francesco Carattoli, Giacomino Caldinelli	Ded. by Giuseppe Galeazzi	S,04392
47	Petrosellini, Giuseppe	Francesco Battisti, Gaetano Farnassi, Giuseppe Marrochini		S,05340
48	Goldoni, Carlo	Gaetano Farnassi, Francesco Battista, Giuseppe Marrocchini	'da Cesena'; Agostino Palombini, impr.	S,08309; NG,xiv.727
49	Goldoni, Carlo	Angela Guadagni, Giuseppe Pasqualini, Lavinia Guadagni, Francesco Carattoli, Anna Giorgi, Isabella Beni, Lodovico Felloni		S,03821
50	Goldoni, Carlo	Angiola Guadagni, Giuseppe Pasqualini, Lavinia Guadagni, Francesco Carattoli, Anna Giorgi, Isabella Beni, Lodovico Felloni, Vincenzo Morati		S,03822
51	Goldoni, Carlo	Anna Borselli, Luigi Bracci, Francesco Carattoli, Lavinia Guadagni, Anna Giorgi, Antonio Rossi		S,22376
52	Brusa, Gio.Battista	Anna Borselli, Luigi Bracci, Lavinia Guadagni, Francesco Caratoli, Anna Giorgi, Antonio Rossi		S,22631
53	Palombini, Agostino	Francesco Battisti, Venanzio Rauzzini di Camerino, Giuseppe Marrochini	'da Cesena'; ded. by Agostino Palombini	S,18558; NG,xiv.727
54	/	Venanzio Rauzzini, Francesco Battisti, Giuseppe Marrocchini	'da Cesena'; ded. by Agostino Palombini	S,22681; NG,xiv.727
55	/	Anna Maria Cataldi, Catterina Ristorini, Lavinia Guadagni, Francesco Caratoli, Giovanni Ristorini		S,21997; Zechmeister,489
56	Goldoni, Carlo	Angela Masi-Tibaldi, Giacomo Tibaldi, Caterina Ristorini, Francesco Caratoli, Marianna Cataldi, Giuseppe Andreoli		S,15459; Michtner,167; Zechmeister,252
57	Goldoni, Carlo	Anna Maria Cataldi, Lavinia Guadagni, Caterina Ristorini, Francesco Caratoli, Giovanni Ristorini		S,04191; Zechmeister,264,492
58	/	Anna Maria Cataldi, Giovanni Ristorini, Lavinia Guadagni, Catterina Ristorini, Francesco Carattoli, Michele del Zanca		S,04259
59	Goldoni, Carlo	Catterina Ristorini, Lavinia Guadagni, Anna Maria Cataldi, Giovanni Ristorini, Michele del Zanca, Giuseppe Andreoli		S,16682; Zechmeister,495
60	Isaurense, Alcindo	Francesco Caratoli, Angela Masi Tibaldi, Catterina Ristorini, Giovanni Ristorini, Maria Anna Cataldi, Giuseppe Andreoli	'In occasione delle feste per gli sponsali delle loro maesta re e regina de romani'	S,22683; NG,xvi.579

Table 2.2b: Giovanni Lovattini (continued)

	Year / Season		Date	Place	Theatre	Title	Genre	Type	Role	Composer
61	1765	/	65.04.20 P	Vienna	Privilegiato	Schiava, La	azione comica	C	Lelio	Piccinni, Niccolò
62	1765	/	/	Vienna	Privilegiato	Donne vendicate, Le	azione comica	C	Conte Bellezza	Piccinni, Niccolò
63	1765	/	/	Vienna	Privilegiato	Tre amanti ridicoli, Li	dramma giocoso	C	March. Oronte	Galuppi, Baldassare
64	1766	1	/	Venice	S Samuele	Canzon Novissima	cantata nel La donna stravaganta	/		/
65	1766	1	/	Venice	S Samuele	Schiava riconosciuta, La	dramma giocoso	C	Lelio	Scolari, Giuseppe
66	1766	1	/	Venice	S Samuele	Donna stravagante, La	dramma giocoso	C	D. Alessio	Scolari, Giuseppe
67	1766	/	66.10.21 P	London	King's	Stravaganti, Gli; o sia I matrimoni alla moda	comic opera	C	Don Alessio	pasticcio
68	1766	/	66.11.25 P	London	King's	Buona figliuola, La	comic opera	C	Marquis della Conchiglia	Piccinni, Niccolò
69	1767	/	67.01.31 P	London	King's	Buona figliuola maritata, La	comic opera	C	The Marquis	Piccinni, Niccolò
70	1767	/	67.03.12 P	London	King's	Signor dottore, Il	comic opera	C	Bernardino	Fischietti, Domenico
71	1767	/	67.04.09 P	London	King's	Don Trastullo	intermezzo	C	/	Jommelli, Niccolò
72	1767	/	67.11.07 P	London	King's	Schiava, La	comic opera	C	Lelio	Piccinni, N. / dir.: P. Guglielmi
73	1768	/	68.01.26 P	London	King's	Buona figliuola, La	comic opera	C	Marquis della Conchiglia	Piccinni, Niccolò
74	1768	/	68.03.26 P	London	King's	Ratto della sposa, Il	comic opera	C	Gaudenzio	Guglielmi, Pietro
75	1768	/	68.04.21 P	London	King's	Filosofo di campagna, Il	comic opera	C	/	Galuppi, Baldassare

	Librettist	Company	Comments	Source
61	/	Giovanna Baglioni, Francesco Caratoli, Constanza Baglioni	'da Cesena'	S,21179; Zechmeister,498
62	/	Giovanna Baglioni, Francesco Carattoli, Costanza Baglioni	'da Cesena'	S,08312; Zechmeister,495
63	Galuppi, Antonio	Giovanna Baglioni, Anna Maria Cataldi, Costanza Baglioni, Filippo Laschi, Francesco Caratoli, Giuseppe Andreoli		S,23508; Zechmeister,495
64	/	Roschetti, Andrea		S,05003
65	Isaurense, Alcindo	Antonio Pulini, Lucia Moreschi, Teresa Eberardi, Francesca Buini, Antonio Boscoli, Andrea Ronchetti	Venanzio Pengo, impr.	S,21215; W,718
66	Isaurense, Alcindo	Andrea Ronchetti, Teresa Eberardi, Lucia Moreschi, Antonio Boscoli, Antonio Pulini, Francesca Buini, N.N.		S,08271; W,719; NG,xvii.55
67	Bottarelli, G.G. (alt.)	Morigi, sigra. Zamperini, sigra. Piatti, Zamperini, Micheli, sigra. Gibetti		S,22684; GB-Lbl 11775.e.3./3; LS,iv.1190
68	Bottarelli, G.G. (alt.)	Miss Young, Savoi, sigra. Zamparini, Morigi, sigra. Piatti, sigra. Gibetti, Micheli		S,04199; GB-Lbl 11714.b.39/5; LS,iv.1199
69	Goldoni, C. - G.G. Bottarelli	Savoi, Morigi, sigra. Piatti, Mrs Barthelemon, sigra. Zamperini, sigra. Gibetti, Micheli		S,04264; GB-Lbl 11714.aa.13/6; LS,iv.1217
70	Goldoni, C. (with alt.)	Mrs Barthelemon, Savoj, Morigi, sigra. Zamperini, sigra. Piatti, Micheli	Benefit Giovanni Lovattini	S,22001; GB-Lbl 907.i.12/1; LS,iv.1227
71	/	Moriggi, *e.a.*		LS,iv.1234
72	/	Savoj, sigra. Quercioli, Micheli, sigra. Guadagni, Morigi, sigra. Maggiore		S,21181; GB-Lbl 1508/238; LS,iv.1289
73	Bottarelli, G.G. (alt.)	Sigra. Quercioli, Savoi, sigra. Guadagni, Morigi, sigra. Maggiore, sigra. Piatti, Micheli		S,04194; GB-Lbl 11714.aa.22/5; LS,iv.1308
74	Martinelli, G. - G.G. Bottarelli	Sigra. Guadagni, sigra. Maggiore, Savoi, sigra. Piatti, Morigi, Micheli		S,19529; GB-Lbl 11714.aa.21/4; LS,iv.1320
75	/	/	Benefit Giovanni Lovattini	S,10378; LS,iv.1326

Table 2.2b: Giovanni Lovattini (continued)

	Year / Season		Date	Place	Theatre	Title	Genre	Type	Role	Composer
76	1768	/	68.05.24 P	London	King's	Viaggiatori ridicoli, tornati in Italia, I	comic opera	C	Cavalier Gandolfo	Guglielmi, Pietro
77	1768	/	68.11.05 P	London	King's	Amanti ridicoli, Gli	comic opera	C	Ridolfo	Galuppi, B. / dir.: F. Alessandri
78	1768	/	68.12.13 P	London	King's	Donne vendicate, Le	comic opera	C	Count Bellezza	Piccinni, N. / dir.: F. Alessandri
79	1769	/	69.01.28 P	London	King's	Mercato di Malmantile, Il	comic opera	C	Rubicone	Fischietti, D. / dir.: F. Alessandri
80	1769	/	69.03.02 P	London	King's	Re alla caccia, Il	comic opera	C	George	Alessandri, Felice
81	1769	/	69.04.08 P	London	King's	Nanetta e Lubino	comic opera	C	Lubino	Pugnani, Gaetano
82	1769	/	69.05.23	London	King's	Buona figliuola, La	comic opera	C	/	/
83	1769	/	69.06.03 P	London	King's	Serve rivali, Le	comic opera	C	Giannino	Traetta, T. / dir.: F. Alessandri
84	1769	/	69.11.07 P	London	King's	Contadine bizzarre, Le	comic opera	C	Nardone	Piccinni N. / dir.: P. Guglielmi
85	1770	/	70.02.06 P	London	King's	Padre e il figlio rivali, Il	comic opera	C	Asdrubale	Giordani, Tommaso
86	1770	/	70.02.22 P	London	King's	Uccellatrice, L'	intermezzo	C	/	Jommelli, Niccolò
87	1770	/	70.03.31 P	London	King's	Costanza di Rosinella, La [=La sposa fedele]	comic opera	C	Pasqualino	Guglielmi, Pietro
88	1770	/	70.11.06 P	London	King's	Vicende della sorte, Le	comic opera	C	Celidoro	Barthélemon, F.-H. - N. Piccinni - A. Sacchini / dir.: T. Giordani
89	1770	/	70.12.18 P	London	King's	Uccellatori, Gli	comic opera	C	Cecchino	Gassmann, Florian Leopold
90	1771	/	71.02.23 P	London	King's	Pazzie d'Orlando, Le	comic opera	C	Medoro	Guglielmi, Pietro

	Librettist	Company	Comments	Source
76	Goldoni, C. - G.G. Bottarelli	Sigra. Guadagni, Micheli, Morigi, *e.a.*		GB-Lbl 11714.aa.13/7; LS,iv.1333; NG,vii.796
77	Galuppi, A. - G.G. Bottarelli	Sigra. Guadagni, sigra. Gori, Micheli, Morigi, Bassanese, sigra. Gibetti		S,01147; GB-Lbl 907.i.12/2; LS,iv.1365
78	Pizzi, G. - G.G. Bottarelli	Sigra. Giacomazzi, Luciani, sigra. Guadagni, sigra. Gori, Morigi, Bassanese, sigra. Gibetti		S,08314; GB-Lbl 907.i.12/4; LS,iv.1373
79	/	Luciani, sigra. Giacomazzi, Morigi, sigra. Guadagni, sigra. Gori, Bassanese, sigra. Gibetti		S,15467; LS,iv.1382
80	Goldoni, C. (from *The Miller of Mansfield*) - G.G. Bottarelli	Luciani, sigra. Giacomazzi, Bassanese, Morigi, sigra. Guadagni, sigra. Gori, Micheli, sigra. Gibetti		S,19562; GB-Lbl 639.f.27/1; LS,iv.1388
81	Badini, C.F. ('imitated from the French')	Luciani, sigra. Giacomazzi, Morigi, Micheli, sigra. Gibetti, sigra. Guadagni, sigra. Gori, Bassanesi		S,16234; GB-Lbl 907.i.13/1; LS,iv.1396
82	/	/	'Signor Lovatini will perform tonight'	LS,iv.1411
83	Chiari, P. - G.G. Bottarelli	Sigra. Giacomazzi, Luciani, Morigi, sigra. Gori, sigra. Guadagni, Bassanese		S,21864; GB-Lbl 907.i.13/2; LS,iv.1412
84	/	Sigra. Piatti, Piatti, Anna Zamperini, sigra. Guadagni, Morigi, Bianchi, Antonia Zamperini		S,06353; GB-Lbl 907.i.12/6; LS,iv.1435
85	Bottarelli, Gio. Gualberto	Antonia Zamperini, Piatti, sigra. Guadagni, Anna Zamperini, Bianchi, Morigi, sigra. Piatti		S,17689; GB-Lbl 907.i.12/5; LS,iv.1453; NG,vii.394
86	/	[Sigra.] Guadagni	Benefit Giovanni Lovattini	LS,iv.1435
87	/	Anna Zamperini, Morigi, Piatti, Bianchi, Antonia Zamperini, sigra. Piatti		S,06788; GB-Lbl 1342.m.3; LS,iv.1466
88	Goldoni, C. - G. Petrosellini	Giovanni Ristorini, Mrs Barthelemon, Catterina Ristorini, Marianna Demena, Michele del Zanca, Andrea Morigi		S,24855; GB-Lbl 907.i.13/4; LS,iv.1509; NG,ii.195
89	/	Gasparo Savoi, Mrs Barthelemon, sigra. Ristorini, sigra. Demena, Zanca, Andrea Morigi		S,24191; GB-Lbl 907.i.13/3; LS,iv.1518
90	Badini, Carlo Francesco	Zanca, sigra. Ristorini, Savoi, Mrs Barthelemon, Morigi, sigra. Demena		S,18249; GB-Lbl 11714.aa. 21/6; LS,iv.1530; NG,vii.796

Table 2.2b: Giovanni Lovattini (concluded)

	Year / Season		Date	Place	Theatre	Title	Genre	Type	Role	Composer
91	1771	/	71.03.14 P	London	King's	Contadina in corte, La	comic opera	C	Rinaldo	Sacchini, A. / dir.: T. Giordani
92	1771	/	71.04.25 P	London	King's	Schiava, La	comic opera	C	/	Piccinni, N. / dir.: T. Giordani
93	1771	/	71.11.02 P	London	King's	Viaggiatori tornati in Italia, I	comic opera	C	Cavalier Gandolfo	Guglielmi, Pietro
94	1771	/	71.11.23 P	London	King's	Disertore, Il	comic opera	C	Alessio	Guglielmi, Pietro
95	1772	/	72.01.14 P	London	King's	Carnovale di Venezia, Il; o sia La Virtuosa	comic opera	C	Canoro	Guglielmi, Pietro
96	1772	/	72.03.24 P	London	King's	Assemblea, L'	comic opera	C	Giacinto	Guglielmi, Pietro
97	1772	/	72.03.26 P	London	King's	Pazzie d'Orlando, Le	/	C	/	Guglielmi, Pietro
98	1772	/	72.04.06 P	London	Haymarket	Endimione	serenata		Endimione	Bach, Johann Christian
99	1774	1	/	Rome	Dame	Buona figliuola zitella, La	dramma giocoso	C	March. della Conchiglia	Piccinni, Niccolò
100	1774	1	/	Rome	Dame	Finta giardiniera, La	dramma giocoso	C	Contino Belfiore	Anfossi, Pasquale
101	1774	1	/	Rome	Dame	Viaggiatori	dramma giocoso	C	/	Scolari, Giuseppe
102	1774	/	74.12.20 P	London	King's	Buona figliuola, La	/	C	/	/
103	1775	/	75.03.07 P	London	King's	Marchesa giardiniera, La [=La finta giardiniera]	comic opera	C	Conte	Anfossi, P. / dir.: T. Giordani
104	1775	/	75.03.30 P	London	King's	Viaggiatori ridicoli, I	/	C	/	/
105	1775	/	75.05.23 P	London	King's	Donna di spirito, La	comic opera	C	Monsù Carillon	Piccinni, N., e.a.
106	1779	3	/	Cesena	/	Finta giardiniera, La	dramma giocoso	C	Conte Belfiore	Anfossi, Pasquale

	Librettist	Company	Comments	Source
91	/	Mrs Barthelemon, Morigi, sigra. Ristorini, Zanca, sigra. Demena, Ristorini	Benefit sigra. Ristorini	S,06312; GB-Lbl 907.i.14/1; LS,iv.1533
92	Bottarelli, G.G. (alt.)		Benefit Giovanni Lovattini	S,21185; LS,iv.1544
93	Goldoni, C. - G.G. Bottarelli	Sigra. Guglielmi, sigra. Bernardi, sigra. Mengis Boschetti, Morigi, Savoi, Micheli		S,24817; GB-Lbl 639.f.27/3; LS,iv.1581
94	Badini, Carlo Francesco	Andrea Moriggi, Gio. Batt. Ristorini, Lelia Guglielmi, Rosa Bernardi, Gaspare Savoj, Maria Giordani, sigra. Mengis Boschetti		S,07965; GB-Lbl 639.f.27 LS,iv.1587; IN1772,25
95	**Badini, Carlo Francesco**	**Morigi, Savoi, Ristorini, sigra. Guglielmi, sigra. Bernardi, sigra. Mengis Boschetti**		**S,05141; GB-Lbl 907.i.14/4; LS,iv.1600; NG,vii.796**
96	**Goldoni, C. - G.G. Bottarelli**	**Sigra. Giordani, sigra. Guglielmi, Savoj, sigra. Bernardi, Morigi, Leopoldo Micheli**		**S,03218; GB-Lbl 907.i.14/3; LS,iv.1619; NG,vii.796**
97	/	Sigra. Guglielmi		LS,iv.1619
98	**Metastasio, P. - G.G. Bottarelli**	**Sigra. Grassi, sigra. Carara, Savoi**	**Benefit Wendling**	**S,08860; LS,iv.1623; NG,i.843**
99	/	Giuseppe Muschietti, Felice Cerruti, Luigi Marchesi, Alessandro Foschi, Luigi Andreani, Baldassare Marchetti, Giovanni Fabbri Cattaldi		S,04223
100	/	**Baldassare Marchetti, Luigi Marchesi, Giuseppe Muschietti, Felice Cerruti, Alessandro Foschi, Gio. Fabri Cataldi**		**S,10464; IN1774,58; NG,i.422**
101	/	Baldassare Marchetti, Gio. Cataldi, Luigi Marchesi, Alessandro Foschi, Felice Ceruti, Giuseppe Muschietti		IN1774,58
102	/	Fochetti, sigra. Farinella, sigra. Galli, sigra. Sestini, sigra. Spiletta		LS,iv.1857; Th.cts,41
103	/	Sigra. Sestini, Foschetti, sigra. Farinella, sigra. Galli, sigra. Spiletta, Sestini		S,14726; LS,iv.1874
104	/	Fochetti, sigra. Galli, sigra. Faranella, sigra. Spiletta, sigra. Sestini	Benefit Giovanni Lovattini	LS,iv.1881
105	/	Sigra. Sestini, Fochetti, Farinelli, sigra. Galli, sigra. Spiletta, Sestini		S,08241; GB-Lbl 907.i.14/8; LS,iv.1896
106	/	Marianna Santoro, Domenico Madrigali, Elisabetta dal Foco, Giacomo Caldinelli, Andrea Morigi, Geltrude Beltrami		S,10478

Table 2.2c: Anna Zamperini

	Year / Season	Date		Place	Theatre	Title	Genre	Type	Role	Composer
1	1761	3	61.04 P	Venice	Teatro di Murano	Buona figliuola, La	dramma giocoso	C	Sandrina	Perillo, Salvatore
2	1762	1	/	Trieste	Reggio Imperial	**Buona figliuola maritata, La**	**dramma**	S	**Sandrina**	**Scolari, Giuseppe**
3	1762	3	62.04.24 P	Venice	Teatro di Murano	Buona figliuola maritata, La	dramma	C	Sandrina	Scolari, Giuseppe
4	1763	1	/	Bassano	Brochi e Cortellotti	Campagna, La	dramma giocoso	C	Cecca	/
5	1763	1	/	Bassano	Brochi e Cortellotti	Buona figliuola, La	dramma giocoso	C	Sandrina	Perillo, Salvatore
6	1765	6	/	Venice	S Moisè	**Ratto della sposa, Il**	**dramma giocoso**	C	**Aurora**	**Guglielmi, Pietro**
7	1766	1	/	Venice	S Moisè	**Nozze disturbate, Le**	**dramma giocoso**	C	**Ersilla**	**Paisiello, Giovanni**
8	1766	1	/	Venice	S Moisè	**Spirito di contradizione, Lo**	**dramma giocoso**	C	**Cont. Flaminia**	**Guglielmi, Pietro**
9	1766	/	66.10.21 P	London	King's	Stravaganti, Gli; o sia I matrimoni alla moda	comic opera	C	Donna Aurora	pasticcio
10	1766	/	66.11.25 P	London	King's	Buona figliuola, La	comic opera	C	Fanny	Piccinni, Niccolò
11	1767	/	67.01.31 P	London	King's	Buona figliuola maritata, La	comic opera	C	The Marchioness	Piccinni, Niccolò
12	1767	/	67.03.12 P	London	King's	Signor dottore, Il	comic opera	C	Rosetta	Fischietti, Domenico
13	1767	/	67.04.02 P	London	King's	Innamorate del cicisbeo, L'	/	C	Lesbina	/
14	1768	6	/	Turin	Carignano	Amore senza malizia, L'	dramma giocoso	C	Lauretta	Ottani, Bernardo
15	1768	6	/	Turin	Carignano	Serve rivali, Le	dramma giocoso	C	Giacinta	Traetta, Tommaso

	Librettist	Company	Comments	Source
1	Goldoni, Carlo	Elisabetta Cardini, Giuseppe Colonna, Giandomenico Zamperini, Antonia Zamperini, Elisabetta Zamperini, Francesco Ceni, Giuseppe Berera	'fanciulla di anni otto'; ded. by Giandomenico Zamperini 'in versi'	S,04181; W,646; NG,vii.503 ('P: 1760–61')
2	/	**Madalena Pisenti, Giacomo Lambertini, Gio. Domenico Poggi, Anna Gallo, Domenico Lamperini, Giuseppe Berera**	**'Annina Zamperini di anni 9'**	S,04251; NG,xvii.55; OG,ii. 480 ('P: Venice, 24 April 1762')
3	Goldoni, Carlo	Appolonia Orlandi, Giacomo Zambertini, Gio. Domenico Zamperini, Antonia Zamperini, Francesco Ceni	'Annina Zamperini di anni 9'; Giandomenico Zamperini, impr.	S,04248; W,663 ('cpsr.: S. Perillo')
4	/	Giandomenico Zamperini, Antonia Zamperini, Antonio Pesci, Giuseppe Pucini, Marianna Roderghel	'putella d'anni dieci'; ded. by Giandomenico Zamperini	S,04619
5	Goldoni, Carlo	Giandomenico Zamperini, Antonia Zamperini, Marianna Roderghel, Antonio Posci, Giuseppe Pucini	'La putella d'anni dieci'; ded. by Giandomenico Zamperini 'in versi'	S,04188
6	Martinelli, Gaetano	**Francesco Torelli, Rosa Vitalba, Antonio Nasolini, Caterina Bonafini, Giacomo Rizzoli, Bartolomeo Schiroli**		S,19515; W,703; NG,vii.796
7	Martinelli, Gaetano	**Maria Battaglia, Ferdinando Compassi, Francesco Torelli, Rosa Vitalba, Catterina Bonafini, Giacomo Rizzoli, Bartolomeo Schirolli**	*Parti uguali* with **Maria Battaglia**	S,16762; W,714; NG,xiv.100
8	Martinelli, Gaetano	**Maria Battaglia, Francesco Torelli, Rosa Vitalba, Catterina Bonafini, Giacomo Rizzoli, Bartolomeo Schilori, Paolo Sibilla**	*Parti uguali* with **Maria Battaglia**	S,22390; W,715; NG,vii.796
9	Bottarelli, G.G. (alt.)	Morigi, sigra. Piatti, Lovattini, Zamperini, Micheli, sigra. Gibetti		S,22684; GB-Lbl 11775.e.3/3; LS,iv.1190
10	Bottarelli, G.G. (alt.)	Miss Young, Savoi, Lovattini, Morigi, sigra. Piatti, sigra. Gibetti, Micheli		S,04199; GB-Lbl 11714.b.39/5; LS,iv.1199
11	Goldoni, C. - G.G. Bottarelli	Savoi, Lovattini, Morigi, sigra. Piattai, Mrs Barthelemon, sigra. Gibetti, Micheli		S,04264; GB-Lbl 11714. aa.13/6; LS,iv.1217
12	Goldoni, C. (with alt.)	Mrs Barthelemon, Savoj, Morigi, Lovattini, sigra. Piatti, Micheli	Benefit Giovanni Lovattini	S,22001; GB-Lbl 907.i.12/1; LS,iv.1227
13	/	Antonia Zamperini, Giandomenico Zamperini, Maria Zamperini	Benefit Anna Zamperini	LS,iv.1233
14	Chiari, Pietro	Antonia Zamperini, Brigida Lolli Anelli, Francesco Bussani, Antonio Napolioni, Alessandro Giovannola		S,01732
15	/	Brigida Lolli Anelli, Antonia Zamperini, Francesco Bussani, Alessandro Giovannola, Antonio Napolioni		S,21861

Table 2.2c: Anna Zamperini (continued)

	Year / Season	Date		Place	Theatre	Title	Genre	Type	Role	Composer
16	1768	6	/	Turin	Carignano	Sposa fedele, La	dramma giocoso	C	Rosinella	Guglielmi, Pietro
17	1769	/	69.11.07 P	London	King's	Contadine bizzarre, Le	comic opera	C	Auretta	Piccinni, N. / dir.: P. Guglielmi
18	1770	/	70.02.06 P	London	King's	Padre e il figlio rivali, Il	comic opera	C	Nannina	Giordani, Tommaso
19	1770	/	70.03.13 P	London	King's	Buona figliuola, La	/	C	Buona figliuola	/
20	1770	/	70.03.31 P	London	King's	Costanza di Rosinella, La [=La sposa fedele]	comic opera	C	Rosinella	Guglielmi, Pietro
21	1770	6	/	Turin	Carignano	Astuta cameriera, L'	dramma giocoso	C	Lisetta	Astarita, Gennaro
22	1770	6	/	Turin	Carignano	Lavandara, La [=Il marchese villano]	dramma giocoso	C	Vespina	Galuppi, Baldassare
23	1771	6	/	Venice	S Moisè	Disertore, Il	dramma giocoso	C	Rosetta	Guglielmi, Pietro
24	1771	6	/	Venice	S Moisè	Anello incantato, L'	dramma giocoso	C	Felicita	Bertoni, Ferdinando
25	1772	1	/	Venice	S Moisè	Isola di Alcina, L'	dramma giocoso	C	Alcina	Gazzaniga, Giuseppe
26	1772	1	/	Venice	S Moisè	Contessa di Bimbinpoli, La	dramma giocoso	C	Contessa di Bimbinpoli	Astarita, Gennaro
27	1772	5	/	Lisbon	Rua dos Condes	Anello incantato, L'	dramma giocoso	C	Felicita	Bertoni, Ferdinando
28	1772	5	/	Lisbon	Rua dos Condes	Disertore, Il	dramma giocoso	C	Rosetta	Guglielmi, Pietro
29	1772	6	/	Lisbon	Rua dos Condes	Isola di Alcina, L'	dramma giocoso	C	Alcina	Gazzaniga, Giuseppe
30	1773	1	/	Lisbon	Rua dos Condes	Antigono	dramma	S	Berenice	Majo, Gian Francesco de

	Librettist	Company	Comments	Source
16	Chiari, Pietro	Brigida Lolli Anelli, Antonia Zamperini, Francesco Bussani, Vincenzo Goresi, Alessandro Giovannola, Antonio Napolioni		S,22443
17	/	Sigra. Piatti, Piatti, sigra. Guadagni, Lovattini, Morigi, Bianchi, Antonia Zamperini	*Parti buffe uguali* With Lavinia Guadagni	S,06353; GB-Lbl 907.i.12/6; LS,iv.1435
18	Bottarelli, Gio. Gualberto	Antonia Zamperini, Piatti, Lovattini, sigra. Guadagni, Bianchi, Morigi, sigra. Piatti	*Parti buffe uguali* with Lavinia Guadagni	S,17689; GB-Lbl 907.i.12/ 5; LS,iv.1453; NG,vii.394
19	/		'La Buona Figliuola = Zamperini'	LS,iv.1461
20	/	Lovattini, Morigi, Piatti, Bianchi, Antonia Zamperini, sigra. Piatti		S,06788; GB-Lbl 1342.m.3; LS,iv.1466
21	/	Benedetto Bianchi, Francesco Mongeri, Teresa Montanari, Maddalena Ricci, Vincenzo Focchetti, Luigi Pagnanelli		S,03338; OG,i.231
22	Chiari, Pietro	Teresa Montanari, Maddalena Ricci, Benedetto Bianchi, Francesco Mongeri, Vincenzo Focchetti, Luigi Pagnanelli		S,14150; OG,ii.340
23	Badini, Carlo Francesco	Filippo Laschi, Antonia Zamperini, Elisabetta Sartori, Paolo Bonaveri, Vincenzo Fochetti, Antonio Beccari	Ferdinando Cerri, impr.	S,07965; W,769
24	Bertati, Giovanni	Antonia Zamperini, Elisabeth Sartori, Filippo Laschi, Paolo Bonaveri, Giovanni Morelli, Antonio Beccari	Ferdinando Cerri, impr.	S,01954; W,770; NG,ii.647
25	Bertati, Giovanni	Antonia Zamperini, Filippo Laschi, Elisabetta Sartori, Paolo Bonaveri, Antonio Beccari, Giovanni Sforzini, Giovanni Morelli		S,13794; W,779; IN1772,56; NG,vii.206
26	Bertati, Giovanni	Filippo Laschi, Antonia Zamperini, Paolo Bonaveri, Giovanni Morelli, Antonio Beccari, Elisabetta Sartori, Giovanni Sforzini		S,06457; W,780; IN1772,56; NG,i.661
27	Bertati, Giovanni	Antonia Zamperini, Teresa Turchi, Giuseppe Trebbi, Nicodemo Calcina, Antonio Marchesi, Massino Giuliani		S,01956; Brito,146
28	Badini, C.F. (with alt.)	Giuseppe Trebbi, Antonia Zamperini, Antonio Marchesi, Vincenzo Goresi, Anna Sestini, Massimo Giuliani, Antonio Pesci		S,07966; AAM,xli.3; Brito,146
29	Bertati, Giovanni	Antonia Zamperini, Anna Sestini, Giuseppe Trebbi, Nicodemo Calcina, Antonio Marchesi, Vincenzo Goresi, Massimo Giuliani		S,13791; Brito,146
30	Metastasio, Pietro	Antonio Tedeschi, Sebastiano Folicaldi, Antonia Zamperini, Massino Giuliani		S,02164 ('P: 1772,6'); IN1773,21; Brito,146

Table 2.2c: Anna Zamperini (continued)

	Year / Season	Date	Place	Theatre	Title	Genre	Type	Role	Composer
31	1773	1 /	Lisbon	Rua dos Condes	Contessa di Bimbimpoli, La	dramma giocoso	C	/	Astarita, Gennaro
32	1773	2 /	Lisbon	Rua dos Condes	Cidde, Il	dramma	S	Climene	Sacchini, Antonio
33	1773	2 /	Lisbon	Rua dos Condes	Betulia liberata, La	dramma sacro	S	Giuditta	/
34	1773	3 /	Lisbon	Rua dos Condes	Molinarella, La	dramma giocoso	C	Metilde	Piccinni, Niccolò
35	1773	5 /	Lisbon	Rua dos Condes	Finte gemelle, Le	dramma giocoso	C	Isabella	Piccinni, Niccolò
36	1773	5 /	Lisbon	Rua dos Condes	Giardiniera brillante, La	intermezzo	C	Lenina	Sarti, Giuseppe
37	1773	5 /	Lisbon	Rua dos Condes	Orfane svizzere, Le	dramma giocoso	C	Rosina	Boroni, Antonio
38	1773	6 /	Lisbon	Rua dos Condes	Sposa fedele, La	dramma giocoso	C	Rosinella	Guglielmi, Pietro
39	1774	3 /	Lisbon	Rua dos Condes	Impresa d'opera, L'	dramma giocoso	C	Mad. Tortorella	Guglielmi, Pietro
40	1774	3 /	Lisbon	Rua dos Condes	Isola d'amore, L'	intermezzo	C	Belinda	Sacchini, Antonio
41	1774	5 /	Lisbon	Rua dos Condes	Amore senza malizia, L'	dramma giocoso	C	Lauretta	Ottani, Bernardo
42	1774	6 /	Lisbon	Rua dos Condes	Calandrano, Il	dramma giocoso	C	Zerbinetta	Gazzaniga, Giuseppe
43	1775	1 /	Lisbon	Rua dos Condes	Geloso, Il	dramma giocoso	C	Mad. Doralice	Silva, Alberto Giuseppe Gomes da
44	1776	4	76.05.11 P	Venice	S Benedetto	Antigona	dramma	S	Antigona	Mortellari, Michele
45	1776	5 /	Venice	S Benedetto	Aristo e Temira	pastorale		Temira	Bertoni, Ferdinando

	Librettist	Company	Comments	Source
31	Bertati, Giovanni	Gius. Trebbi, Nicodemo Calcina, Ant. Marchesi, Vinc. Goresi, Gio. Stogler Sestini, Antonia Zamperini, Anna Sestini, Vittoria Turchi, Antonio Tedeschi, Massimo Giuliani		IN1773,21; Brito,147
32	Pizzi, Giovacchino	Giuseppe Trebeschi, Sebastiano Folicaldi, Antonia Zamperini, Massimo Giuliani, Anna Sestini		S,05579; AAM,xli.4; Brito,148 ('P: Jan. 1774?')
33	Metastasio, Pietro	Sebastiano Folicaldi, Antonia Zamperini, Giuseppe Trebbi, Antonio Tedeschi, Massimo Giuliani		S,04067; Brito,148
34	/	Sebastiano Folicaldi, Giuseppe Trebbi, Nicodemo Calcina, Antonia Zamperini, Anna Sestini, Massimo Giuliani		S,15826; Brito,148
35	Petrosellini, Giuseppe	Giuseppe Trebbi, Marcantonio Marchesi, Antonia Zamperini, Vincenzo Goresi, Maria Giovacchina, Massimo Giuliani		S,10579; Brito,148
36	/	Sebastiano Folicaldi, Antonio Marchesi, Antonia Zamperini		S,11773; Brito,148
37	Chiari, Pietro	Antonia Zamperini, Giuseppe Trebbi, Innocenzo Schettini, Maria Giovacchina, Vincenzo Goresi		S,17392; Brito,148
38	Chiari, Pietro	Sebastiano Folicaldi, Giuseppe Trebbi, Vincenzo Goresi, Antonia Zamperini, Cecilia Zamperini, N.N.		S,22470; Brito,148
39	/	Giuseppe Trebbi, Antonia Zamperini, Innocenzo Schettini, Maria Giovachina, N.N., Vincenzo Goresi	*parte buffe uguali* with Giovanna Stocler	S,12880; IN1774,25; Brito,149–50
40	Metastasio, Pietro	Giuseppe Trebbi, Innocenzo Schettini, Antonia Zamperini	*parte buffe uguali* with Giovanna Stocler	S,13835; IN1774,25; Brito,150
41	Chiari, Pietro	Sebastiano Folicaldi, Giuseppe Trebbi, Antonia Zamperini, Maria Giovacchina, Vincenzo Goresi	*parte buffe uguali* with Giovanna Stocler	S,01746; IN1774,25; Brito,150
42	Bertati, Giovanni	Giuseppe Trebbi, Innocenzo Schettini, Maria Giovacchina, Vincenzo Goresi	*parte buffe uguali* with Giovanna Stocler	Moreau72; IN1774,25; Brito,150
43	Tonioli, Girolamo	Giuseppe Trebbi, N.N., Cecilia Zamperini, Vincenzo Goresi, Maria Gioacchina, N.N.		S,11435; Brito,151; not in NG, OG
44	Roccaforte, Gaetano	Giacomo David, Cristofolo Arnaboldi, Maria Antonia Zamperini, Giuseppe Coppola, Paolina David		S,02093; W,836; OG,ii.474
45	Salvioli, Count de	Angiolo Monani Manzoletto, Maria Antonia Zamperini, Giovanni Sforzini		S,02651; not in W

Table 2.2c: Anna Zamperini (concluded)

	Year / Season		Date	Place	Theatre	Title	Genre	Type	Role	Composer
46	1776	5	/	Venice	S Benedetto	Orfeo ed Euridice	dramma	S	Euridice	Bertoni, Ferdinando
47	1776	6	76.09.06 P	Florence	Pergola	Due contesse, Le	dramma giocoso	C	Contessina	Paisiello, Giovanni
48	1776	6	76.10.16 P	Florence	Pergola	Marchese villano, Il; o sia La lavandara astuta	dramma giocoso	C	Vespina	Caruso, L., *e.a.*
49	1777	1	/	Venice	S Moisè	Dama immaginaria, La	azione teatrale	C	Eurilla	Astarita, Gennaro
50	1777	4	/	Venice	S Moisè	Armida	dramma	S	Armida	Astarita, Gennaro
51	1777	4	/	Brescia	Erranti	Dama immaginaria, La	dramma giocoso	C	Eurilla	Astarita, Gennaro
52	1777	4	/	Brescia	Erranti	Disertore, Il	dramma giocoso	C	Rosetta	Guglielmi, Pietro

	Librettist	Company	Comments	Source
46	Calzabigi, Ranieri de	Cav. Gaetano Guadagni, Giuseppe Copola		S,17444; not in W
47	Petrosellini, Giuseppe	Giovacchino Garibaldi, Gio. Battista Gherardi, Antonia Zamperini, Eusebio Pellicioni		S,08453; WW,ii.360–1
48	Chiari, P., *e.a.*	Giovacchino Caribaldi, Giovanni Gherardi, Antonia Zamperini, Filippo Laschi, Eusebio Pelliccioni		S,14762; WW,ii.363–4
49	**Bagliacca, Pietro Antonio**	**Antonia Zamperini, Andrea Toti, Gio. Battista Brocchi**	**Alberto Bottari, impr.**	**S,07071; W,855; OG, i.231 ('P: Brescia, 1777')**
50	**Migliavacca, Giann'Ambrogio**	**Domenico Cremonini, Domenico Bedini, Gio.Battista Seni, Antonia Zamperini, Lorenzo Piatti**	**Ded. by Giuseppe Borghi**	**S,02697; W,857; NG,i.661**
51	Bagliacca, Pietro Antonio	Antonia Zamperini, Antonio Nazolini, Santo Pirazzini, Angela Passia, Domenico Cremonini	Francesco Gallerani, impr.	S,07069
52	/	Antonia Zamperini, Antonio Nazolini, Verginio Bondichi, Santo Pirazzini, Domenica Bortolini, Domenico Cremonini	Francesco Gallerani, impr.	S,07967

Table 2.3: Comic opera productions at the King's Theatre in the 1760s

Season	Total	New imports	Newly written for the King's Theatre	Repeat productions
1760–61	3	1. *Il mondo della luna.* P: Venice, San Moisè, 29 Jan. 1750. C. Goldoni - B. Galuppi 2. *Il filosofo di campagna.* P: Venice, San Samuele, 26 Oct. 1754. C. Goldoni - B. Galuppi 3. *Le pescatrici.* P: Venice, San Samuele, 26 Dec. 1751. C. Goldoni - F. Bertoni	/	/
1761–62	5	1. *Il mercato di Malmantile.* P.: Venice, San Samuele, 26 Dec. 1757. Goldoni - D. Fischietti 2. *Bertoldo Bertoldino e Cacasenno.* P: Venice, San Samuele, 26 Dec. 1748. C. Goldoni - V. Ciampi 3. *Le nozze di Dorina.* P: Bologna, Formagliari, 14 Sep. 1755. C. Goldoni - B. Galuppi	1. *La famiglia in scompiglio.* P: London, King's Theatre, 3 Apr. 1762. G.G. Bottarelli - G. Cocchi	1. *Il filosofo di campagn*
1762–63	4	1. *Il tutore e la pupilla.* P: Dublin, Smock-Alley, 29 Jan. 1762 (*Gl'intrighi per amore*). Pasticcio 2. *La cascina.* P: Venice, San Samuele, 26 Dec. 1755. C. Goldoni - G. Scolari 3. *La calamità de' cuori.* P: Venice, San Samuele, 26 Dec. 1752. C. Goldoni - B. Galuppi 4. *La finta sposa.* P: Bologna, Formagliari, 11 Jan. 1755. C. Goldoni - G. Latilla	/	/
1766–67	4	1. *Gli stravaganti.* P: Vienna, Burgtheater, 11 Feb. 1765. A. Isaurense - G. Scarlatti	/	/

		2. *La buona figliuola.*
		    P: Rome, Dame, 6 Feb. 1760.
		    C. Goldoni - N. Piccinni
		3. *La buona figliuola maritata.*
		    P: Bologna, Formagliari, 10 June 1761.
		    C. Goldoni - N. Piccinni
		4. *Il signor dottore.*
		    P: Venice, San Moisè, autumn 1758.
		    C. Goldoni - D. Fischietti		

1767–68	7	1. *La schiava.*
		    P: Rome, Valle, 1 Jan. 1764 (Gli stravaganti).
		    C. Goldoni - N. Piccinni
		2. *Il ratto della sposa.*
		    P: Venice, San Moisè, autumn 1765.
		    G. Martinelli - P. Guglielmi
			1. *La moglie fedele.*
			    P: London, King's Theatre, 27 Feb. 1768.
			    G.G. Bottarelli - F. Alessandri
			2. *I viaggiatori ridicoli.*
			    P: London, King's Theatre, 24 May 1768.
			    G.G. Bottarelli - P. Guglielmi
				1. *La buona figliuola maritata*
				2. *La buona figliuola*
				3. *Il filosofo di campagna*

1768–69	12	1. *Gli amanti ridicoli.*
		    P: Venice, San Moisè, 18 Jan. 1761 (I tre amanti ridicoli).
		    A. Galuppi - B. Galuppi
		2. *Le donne vendicate.*
		    P: Rome, Valle, carnival 1763.
		    C. Goldoni - N. Piccinni
		3. *Il re alla caccia.*
		    P: Venice, San Samuele, autumn 1763.
		    C. Goldoni - B. Galuppi
		4. *Lo speziale.*
		    P: Venice, San Samuele, 26 Dec. 1754.
		    C. Goldoni – V. Pallavicini and D. Fischietti
		5. *Le serve rivali.*
		    P: Venice, San Moisè, autumn 1766.
		    P. Chiari - T. Traetta
			1. *Nanetta e Lubino.*
			    P: London, King's Theatre, 8 Apr. 1769.
			    C.F. Badini - G. Pugnani
				1. *I viaggiatori ridicoli*
				2. *La buona figliuola*
				3. *La schiava*
				4. *Il mercato di Malmantile*
				5. *Il filosofo di campagna*
				6. *La moglie fedele*

1769–70	9	1. *Le contadine bizzarre.*
		    P: Venice, San Samuele, autumn 1763.
		    G. Petrosellini - N. Piccinni
		2. *La costanza di Rosinella.*
		    P: Venice, San Moisè, carnival 1767 (La sposa fedele).
		    P. Chiara - P. Guglielmi
			1. *Il padre e il figlio rivali.*
			    P: London, King's Theatre, 6 Feb. 1769.
			    G.G. Bottarelli - T. Giordani
			2. *Il disertore.*
			    P: London, King's Theatre, 19 May 1770.
			    C.F. Badini - P. Guglielmi
				1. *I viaggiatori ridicoli*
				2. *Il filosofo di campagna*
				3. *La schiava*
				4. *La buona figliuola*
				5. *Il signor dottore*

Sources: C. Sartori, *I libretti italiani a stampa dalle origini al 1800. Catalogo analitico*, 7 vols, Cuneo, 1990–94; *The New Grove Dictionary of Opera*, ed. Stanley Sadie, 4 vols, London, 1992; *The New Grove Dictionary of Music and Musicians*, ed. Stanley Sadie, 20 vols, London, 1980

Table 2.4: Arias included in *Bertoldo Bertoldino e Cacasenno* (1749–62)

Content of London version, 1762		Venice, 1749 (P)	Milan, 1750	Padua, 1750	Berlin, 1754	London, 1755		London, 1762
1	*Quando s'incontrano* Bdo.[1]	I,4*	I,8	I,8		I,5	I,6 (sh.)²	
2	*Ma soletto* Bdo.						II,8	From Goldoni's *Le donne vendicate* [P: Venice, 1751, G. Cocchi]
3	*Per donna non voglio* Bdo.						III,3	
4	*Menghina bellina m'ha detto* Bno.[3]						I,4b*	From Goldoni's *La cascina*, Venice, 1756, G. Scolari (P); also in *Le nozze di Dorina*, Rome, 1760, B. Galuppi
5	*Maledetti quanti siete* Bno.	II,3	II,3*	II,3*		II,1b	I,8a*	
6	*Un segreto o donne* Bno.				I,1d*		II,4*	
7	*Oh che tenebre* Bno.						II,7a*	
8	*A riveder io torno* Bno.	III,8	III,4*	III,5a*	III,2*(sh.)	III,4b	III,4*(sh.)	
9	*Ahi ahi non farò* Cac.[4]	I,7b	I,3b	I,3b	I,1b	I,2b	I,3b	
10	*Voglio andar* Cac.		II,7	II,7		II,3a	II,5 (sh.)	
11	*Che bel contento* Cac.	III,10	III,7	III,7	III,3b (tutti)	III,5 (tutti)	III,6c (tutti)	
12	*Questo del sesso* Dan.[5]						I,2	
13	*E' di donna bel* Dan.						II,6	From Goldoni's *I bagni d'Abano* (1st part) [P: Venice, 1753, B. Galuppi and D. Fischietti]
14	*Se nessuno ora* Dan.						III,2	From Goldoni's *Il mercato di Malmantile*, Venice, 1758, D. Fischietti (P); incl. in *Fav. Songs in... Bertoldo*, London, [1762]
15	*Ciascun mi dice* Men.[6]				I,1c**	I,2c	I,4a**	Incl. in *Fav. Songs in.. Bertoldo*, London, [1762]: "Ciampi"
16	*Ho una testa* Men.						I,5*	From Goldoni's *La buona figliuola maritata* [P: Bologna, 1761, N. Piccinni]
17	*Largo largo* Men.	II,2**			II,1a**	II,1a	II,1a**	
18	*Io non mi curo* Men.						II,1b**	
19	*Sior Bertoldo mio garbato* Men.						II,7b**	Incl. in *Fav. Songs in. Bertoldo*, London, [1762]: "Ciampi"
20	*Son allegra* Men.						III,6b**	Incl. in *Fav. Songs in... Bertoldo*, London, [1762]: "Ciampi"

#	Title	Role							Notes
21	*Pupilli amate*	Re[7]						I,7	
22	*A trionfar mi chiama*	Re						II,3	Also in Metastasio's *La Didone abbandonata*, Rome, 1726, Leonardo Vinci
23	*Amor lusinghiero*	Re						III,5	
24	*Al caro porto*	Reg.[8]						I,1b	
25	*Non sei federele*	Reg.						II,2	
26	*Se il loco*	Reg.						III,1	
27	*Più bella è la Campagna*	Cac.-Bno.		III,5	III,5b	III,3a		III,6a	
28	*Oh caro amabile*	Re-Reg.						II,9	
29	*Ferma ferma non conviene*	Bdo.-Bno.-Men.	I,15	I,12	I,12	I,2	I,6b	I,8b	
30	*Dolce amor*	tutti			I,1a			I,1a	
31	*Qua si fatica*	tutti	I,7a	I,3a	I,3a	I,1a	I,2a	I,3a	
32	*Vuo' conoscere*	tutti	II,18	II,15	II,15		II,7	II,10	
33	*Dolce diletto*	tutti	III,11	III,8	III,8		III,6	III,7	

Notes: * aria sung by Carlo Paganini **aria sung by Maria Paganini
[1] Bdo. = Bertoldo [2] sh. = shortened [3] Bno.= Bertoldino [4] Cac. = Cacasenno
[5] Dan. = Dandina [6] Men.= Menghina [7] Re = Alboino Re [8] Reg. = Ipsicrateo Regina

CHAPTER THREE

Freemasonry and Musical Life in London in the Late Eighteenth Century

Simon McVeigh

Introduction

The early Hanoverian period witnessed a proliferation of clubs and societies in London: voluntary associations of men devoted variously to intellectual pursuits – literary, antiquarian, philosophical, scientific – and to convivial socializing.[1] This was closely allied to the rise of the coffee-house and tavern culture, a milieu encouraging debate among the leisured and business classes of the mixed urban society in London, and indeed such clubs frequently held their meetings at such venues. Prominent musical organisations such as the Castle Society or the Academy of Ancient Music, both formalized in the 1720s and both meeting at City taverns, should certainly be viewed in much the same light.

So too in some respects should the development of speculative freemasonry, formalized in Britain in 1717 by the uniting of four lodges into a Grand Lodge. Though derived from a craft guild background (operative freemasonry), the movement had already largely been transformed into a gentlemen's organization not dissimilar to other societies in Britain, and often sharing certain enlightenment ideals with them.[2] Masonic rhetoric emphasized that the path towards wisdom and virtue was through fraternalism, expressed in two directions in which music played a major part: externally in a mutual benevolence (including charity towards needy brethren and support for their theatre or concert benefits), and internally in private sociability. The lodge, in the succinct summary of one contemporary masonic lecturer, was 'a place of safe retirement where we may securely enjoy generous freedom, innocent mirth, social friendship, and useful instruction'.[3]

---

[1] M.A. Clawson, *Constructing Brotherhood: Class, Gender, and Fraternalism* (Princeton, 1989), pp. 54–5; R.W. Weisberger, *Speculative Freemasonry and the Enlightenment* (Boulder, 1993), pp.37–8. I am indebted to John Hamill and John Ashby of the Library and Museum of the United Grand Lodge of England, and also to Rachel Cowgill, Claire Nelson and Ernest Warburton, for their assistance in the preparation of this article.

[2] Standard histories of freemasonry in England include [A.S. Frere], *Grand Lodge 1717–1967* (Oxford, 1967) and J. Hamill, *The Craft: a History of English Freemasonry* (London, 1986). For more searching and provocative analyses of the social role of freemasonry see M.C. Jacob, *The Radical Enlightenment: Pantheists, Freemasons and Republicans* (London, 1981) and *Living the Enlightenment: Freemasonry and Politics in Eighteenth-Century Europe* (New York, 1991). The latter has been a particularly valuable source for this study. The principal study of musicians and freemasonry is R. Cotte, *La musique maçonnique et ses musiciens*, rev. edn (Paris, 1987); see also W. Barrett, 'Masonic Musicians', *Ars Quatuor Coronatorum*, 4 (1891), 90–96.

[3] Lecture of 1776 quoted in Jacob, *Living the Enlightenment*, p. 59.

A striking early example of the importance of music in masonic recreation is provided by the Philo-Musicae et Architecturae Societas, a musical society attached to the Queen's Head Lodge. Founded on 18 February 1725, its most prominent musical light was Francesco Geminiani (1687–1762), who had been initiated at the lodge on 1 February.[4] Appointing him 'perpetual Dictator' of the musical performances, the society immediately subscribed to Geminiani's latest publication (a set of concerti grossi arranged from Corelli's op. 5), and the advancement of his career as well as general guidance on musical taste seems to have been one objective. On 10 June Geminiani was asked to find four musicians to assist the performances, and among those he selected was his colleague from Lucca, Francesco Barsanti (1690–1772). But essentially this was a musical society of lodge members, minor merchants as well as professional musicians, meeting to play instrumental music for their enjoyment and improvement, and there is no evidence of any particular masonic agenda. Music was already being perceived as an activity combining intellectual rewards with practical enjoyment, in a spirit of fraternity that could encompass a wide range of society as well as of technical prowess.

Yet freemasonry represented more than just another club or philosophical society, as both Margaret Jacob and Mary Ann Clawson have argued.[5] In the first place, the increasingly centralized organization of freemasonry, and the uniformity of its rituals and symbols, engendered a rare universality across the nation, and, in the form of masonic songs, a universality of musical culture that few organizations, perhaps not even the Church, could match.[6] Furthermore its system of ethical conduct played a major role in the development of modern civil society: teaching how to organize and participate, and developing loyalty and personal responsibility as part of a collective endeavour. More specifically, it encouraged decorum and civilized behaviour, fostering the well-mannered gentleman in the interests of public order. This aspect is well documented in connection with masonic audiences at the theatres, whose behaviour contrasted markedly with normal playhouse rowdiness.[7] It is tempting to suggest that audiences at concerts in the Freemasons' Hall (here by contrast with upper-class insouciance) may have been inspired towards more attentive listening, not only by the presence of freemasons but also by the surroundings and ritual associations. Revealing in this connection are the laws of the Castle Society, not a masonic institution but one much exercised with the regulation of behaviour:

---

[4] Records in GB-Lbl Add. MS 23202; see also E. Careri, *Francesco Geminiani (1687–1762)* (Oxford, 1993), pp. 15–18. Geminiani's elevation to 'Fellow Craft & Master' on 12 May is the earliest known mention of the third degree of Master Mason.
[5] Jacob, *Living the Enlightenment*, pp. 29–32; Clawson, *Constructing Brotherhood*, p. 55.
[6] Further on masonic song, see H. Poole, 'Masonic Song and Verse of the Eighteenth Century', *Ars Quatuor Coronatorum*, 40 (1927), 7–29; A. Sharp, 'Masonic Songs and Song Books of the Late Eighteenth Century', *Ars Quatuor Coronatorum*, 65 (1952), 84–95. (The volume numbering system follows that used in standard indexes, whereby the transactions of the Quatuor Coronati Lodge are cited by year of presentation: publication was generally in the following year.)
[7] H. W. Pedicord, 'White Gloves at Five: Fraternal Patronage of London Theatres in the Eighteenth Century', *Philological Quarterly*, 45 (1966), 277–8.

74 MUSIC IN EIGHTEENTH-CENTURY BRITAIN

laws forbidding walking around or conversation during the performance, as well as inappropriate interruptions or comment.[8] It seems likely that other self-consciously serious-minded institutions such as London's two ancient music societies adopted similar strictures, foreshadowing nineteenth-century attitudes towards concert behaviour and listening in silence.

Still more significantly, the self-created image of freemasonry as a secret and esoteric brotherhood, its mystical initiation rites and myths, and its elaborate rituals enacted in a quasi-religious temple suggest that it should not be regarded as a purely secular programme, but rather as allied to the 'new religiosity of the mind' characteristic of the eighteenth century.[9] Nor, in any case, was British freemasonry anything other than theistic in the broadest sense, its all-embracing concept of 'Grand Architect of the Universe' satisfying not only deists and pantheists but also the orthodox and devout. Representing in the arts such mystical concepts with due solemnity, without falling back on standard religious topoi, was not an easy assignment. In architecture, the favoured neo-Augustan style – filtering the classical orders through the Renaissance mirror of Palladio – reflected order, stability and symmetry, in accordance with a Newtonian view of a harmonious and ordered universe. This was a conscious appeal to a higher past: already in 1735 *The Free Mason's Pocket Companion* confidently observed 'the Arts of the fam'd Augustan Age revive amongst us', a sentiment less elegantly picked up in masonic song: 'We drove the rude Vandals and Goths off the stage, / Reviving the art of Augustus' fam'd age'.[10] This suggests a parallel with the eighteenth-century appreciation for ancient (i.e. Renaissance) music, which, at least in the form of madrigals, was certainly a feature of masonic meetings. More strikingly, contemporary masonic composers drew on images of the Renaissance in their own ceremonial music and glees. Benjamin Cooke, a leading figure in the later history of the Academy of Ancient Music, went further, writing madrigals and a deliberately backward-looking setting of Collins's *Ode on the Passions*; this even includes a part for the ancient double pipe ('tibiae pares') and concludes with a noble exhortation in neoclassical C major: 'O bid our vain endeavours cease, Revive the just designs of Greece, Return in all thy simple state!' No doubt the ode was performed at the Academy at Freemasons' Hall, and it was certainly performed at a benefit there for the orphaned James Bartleman in 1785.

The masonic appeal to moderation and stability is directly reflected in eighteenth-century debate about the effects of music. Its ability to transport the listener with religious enthusiasm on the one hand or with sensual ecstasy on the other (both suggesting emotional abandon) raised passionate voices in Hanoverian England, mainly in the context of sacred music and Italian opera, though they are equally relevant to discussions about freemasonry. The former

---

[8] S. McVeigh, *Concert Life in London from Mozart to Haydn* (Cambridge, 1993), pp. 3–4.

[9] M.C. Jacob, 'Private Beliefs in Public Temples: the New Religiosity of the Eighteenth Century', *Social Research*, 59 (1992), 59–84.

[10] Jacob, *Living the Enlightenment*, p. 57; 'The Deputy Grand Master's Song'.

was seen as violating the discipline of freemasonry as well as its essential fraternalism; while the latter suggested the profligacy and corruption that flowed from excessive luxury and self-indulgence. Yet, just as freemasonry did not abjure worldly advancement (indeed wealth was seen as a reflection of human endeavour and a reward for personal industry), so music was accepted as a valuable luxury, provided it remained within bounds. Moderation in the masonic approach towards music, even a certain vein of puritanism, mirrored the attitude of City musical societies towards what they perceived as the sensual frivolity of West End concerts and Italian opera. Thus music in English masonic ritual, as on the continent, symbolized harmony and moderation in its restricted devotional tone, inevitably drawing on religious musical images, yet at the same time suggesting a universal antiquity through chordal writing (often symbolically in three parts) and predominantly diatonic harmony.

In addition to its quasi-religious contribution to ritual, music played a further vital role in freemasonry. The English glee, a latter-day form of madrigal often with strongly contrasting sections, embodied the ideals of freemasonry to perfection: uniting disparate contrapuntal lines, usually three, into a single harmony, and disparate sections into a single whole. It was also the genre intended for widespread amateur participation, certainly among the educated classes (recalling London's innumerable glee clubs from the Noblemen and Gentlemen's Catch Club to local tavern societies). Masonic meetings always concluded in conviviality, where wine flowed freely and sociable songs and glees were sung; and communal participation, even if only in the choruses to masonic songs, was clearly a central feature. Music provided a common ground for 'innocent mirth' and good company, smoothing over social distinctions of breeding and education that would have been revealed by conversation.

Furthermore, music and drinking ritualized and thereby validated the pleasurable side of lodge meetings, attributing to enjoyment a metaphor for higher causes. Lines such as the following from 'The Grand Warden's Song' were more than routine drinking-song platitudes: 'Let faithful Masons' healths go round, / In swelling cups all cares be drown'd, / And hearts united 'mongst the Craft be found / ... My brethren, thus all cares resign, / Let your hearts glow with thoughts divine, / And veneration show to Solomon's shrine.' This link between loftier ideals and their immediate pleasurable enaction was emphasized by aspects of musical style: for there was much in common between glees and the odes heard at the formal meeting shortly before. A popular ode to freemasonry was William Hayes's 'Comus away', essentially a glee celebrating, in turn, science, commerce, arts and industry, then loyalty to the king, liberty and honour, followed by sacred truth and justice, and ending with a chorus 'Hail! Hail! Masonry! thou faithful, kind instructer of the human mind.' This vocal presence was a characteristic feature of English masonry: though instrumental music was heard (for example for processions, funeral marches and other ceremonial aspects), there was no distinctive association with particular instruments or tonal sonorities as at Viennese lodges.

The social agenda of freemasonry – stressing fraternity, equality and the value of liberty – was openly egalitarian, and even in Britain there remained an underside of radicalism, expressed in allegiance to a variety of anti-establishment causes. One such was Jacobitism, and it is possible that the cellist and publisher James Oswald (1711–69) was not only associated with the Jacobite movement in the 1740s but that he advanced the cause through his masonic connections in Scotland. There is no evidence, however, that his much discussed Society of the Temple of Apollo was a formal masonic organization, though its title is certainly suggestive, nor, as yet, that he was involved in masonic activities in London.[11]

In general, however, British freemasonry, far from fomenting revolutionary aspirations as on the continent, became increasingly aligned with establishment values: loyalty to King and government, to the Hanoverian succession, and to the Protestant church.[12] Partly this loyalism was engendered by its ideals of harmony and moderation, which demanded a stable and cohesive social order. An innate tension, therefore, persisted between an idealistic, utopian vision of a perfectible society (the masonic meeting as a private model for public action), and a confirmation of social stability and the status quo. There was indeed a paradox at the heart of the masonic ideal that blunted the force of any more radical agenda: 'Fraternal binding also obscured the social division and inequities of rank and degree endemic to the lives of the men who embraced "equality" and "liberty"... As tradesmen and gentlemen, doctors and merchants, broke bread together and practised fraternity, they obfuscated the real divisions of wealth, education, and social place that existed between them.'[13] Dissident ideas were made harmless by their representation in song: 'Let Monarchs run mad after riches and power, / Fat Gown-men be dull, and Philosophers sour, / While the claret goes round, and the company sings, / We're wiser than Sages, and greater than Kings.'[14] Usually, egalitarianism was sublimated in masonic lore, in a way that paradoxically appears to celebrate subservience towards rank and hierarchy: 'Tho' sometimes in Concert sublimely we sing, / Whilst each Brother Mason joins hand with a King / [Chorus] And Princes disdain not companions to be, / with a Man that is own'd for a Mason & free.'[15]

Many aristocrats were indeed members of London lodges; and as British freemasonry became, according to John Money, a 'quasi-chivalric national

---

[11] See F. Kidson, 'James Oswald, Dr Burney, and "The Temple of Apollo"', *Musical Antiquary*, 2 (1910–11), 34–41; R. Lonsdale, *Dr. Charles Burney* (Oxford, 1965), pp. 28–34; J. Purser, *Scotland's Music* (Edinburgh, 1992), pp. 186–7. *Pace* Lonsdale, the society did give concerts at least from 1755 to 1761: advertisements give the venue as Queen Square, and Oswald's music shop as the source of tickets (see *Public Advertiser*, 8 October 1755, 23 August 1759, 27 October 1760, 2 January and 19 October 1761).

[12] J. Money, 'Freemasonry and the Fabric of Loyalism in Hanoverian England', in E. Hellmuth (ed.), *The Transformation of Political Culture: England and Germany in the Late Eighteenth Century* (Oxford, 1990), pp. 235–74.

[13] Jacob, *Living the Enlightenment*, p. 45.

[14] Cited in ibid., p. 63.

[15] 'Begin, O ye Muses!' in Thomas Hale, *Social Harmony* (Liverpool, 1763).

affinity group' the royal family took a leading role in the upper echelons of its organization.[16] Following the initiation of Frederick, Prince of Wales, in 1737, almost the entire royal family became freemasons (though not, significantly, George III); and in 1782 the King's brother, the Duke of Cumberland, became Grand Master, to be succeeded on his death in 1790 by the Prince of Wales. Though both were active and highly visible supporters of cosmopolitan modern music, the loyalist trend within freemasonry in the later decades of the century favoured more traditional British musical icons. Loyalism and a popular patriotism were alike reflected in the use of 'Rule, Britannia' as a masonic song and Handel's coronation anthems as ceremonial music. Furthermore, what is known of the music preferred in lodges suggests that solid English vocal music and baroque concertos were favoured, the same repertoire preferred in the bourgeois music societies of the City (and in contrast with the modern German symphonies and Italian arias of fashionable West End concert series).

In principle it was a central tenet of freemasonry that it crossed barriers of class, religion and political allegiance: 'We have no idle prating, of either Whig or Tory, but each agrees to live at ease, & sing or tell a story', as 'The Steward's Song' admonishes. In truth, there remained a certain exclusiveness, of course: most glaringly in the exclusion of women (unlike on the continent); and members were expected to be literate, of good character and affluent enough to be able to pay their dues. Indeed, it was to counter a growing perception of exclusivity that the breakaway 'Antients' (in fact a new branch) were formed in 1751, primarily directed at shopkeepers and artisans. Nevertheless freemasonry certainly did bring together a wide range of London society – merchants, bankers and substantial tradesmen, professionals, men of letters and the arts, as well as nobility and gentry – in a way scarcely conceivable elsewhere. The explicitly positive assessment of productive labour, of achievement through merit and 'sober striving', through virtue and learning, validated the emerging bourgeoisie and, by implication, the social mobility that resulted; according to John Money, 'Hanoverian Freemasonry expressed and ritualised middle-class cultural formation and self-replication at several crucial points.'[17]

In these circumstances it is scarcely surprising that musicians should have taken to freemasonry with enthusiasm, their professional status uncertain, rather uneasily embracing the educated organist with a cathedral or university background, the virtuoso with pretensions to acceptance in high society, the manufacturing and commercial world of instrument making and music selling, the artisan who scraped a living in the playhouse pit. Certainly for those lower down the scale freemasonry represented an opportunity for association with the merchants and professionals who made up much of the membership. Though attendance at a lodge meeting meant giving up an evening of work, many

---

[16] J. Money, 'The Masonic Moment; or, Ritual, Replica, and Credit: John Wilkes, the Macaroni Parson, and the Making of the Middle-Class Mind', *Journal of British Studies*, 32 (1993), 386.

[17] Ibid., 370.

78 MUSIC IN EIGHTEENTH-CENTURY BRITAIN

musicians played an active part in prominent (if not the most exclusive) lodges, clearly reflecting the importance of social status on the one hand and of fraternization with potential clients or contacts on the other.

A vital issue for musicians was the religious tolerance professed by freemasonry, which welcomed not only dissenting Protestants, but also Catholics and Jews. Lord Petre, Grand Master from 1772 to 1776, was himself a Catholic, as were some indigenous musical masons such as the Webbes. This tolerance was a cause of some unrest in the decades around 1780 (the year of the anti-Catholic Gordon riots), when it was perceived that some Britons were being excluded from membership, while foreigners, many of them Catholic, were freely admitted.[18] Certainly this category would have included most Italian musicians and converts such as J.C. Bach, for whom freemasonry must have provided a welcome sense of inclusion in British society.

Musicians and Freemasonry

It is tempting to look for masonic alliances throughout the structure of musical life in London. Freemasonry provided an obvious form of association for advancement, through professional connections between performers, impresarios and music sellers, and through meeting with patrons. Many musicians from all walks of musical life were freemasons, as were numerous music sellers such as Robert Bremner, Robert Birchall and John Bland. Some caution is surely necessary, however, for most important musicians from Geminiani to Samuel Wesley (1766–1837) were connected with freemasonry at some point in their lives. One can only speculate as to the opportunity that membership of a specific lodge provided for career advancement; and musical constituencies and patronage seem often to have been confirmed rather than been established by masonic connections. However, study of the musical membership of London lodges and of their masonic activities reveals not only the confirmation of musical constituencies but also surprising associations across the normal boundaries of musical life in London; and there are also links among lodge membership with patrons.

Geminiani's masonic connections and musical activities have already been described. Notable freemasons of the earlier eighteenth century included Maurice Greene (1696–1755), and possibly William Boyce (1711–79), but not, so far as can be determined, Handel (even though the chaplain at Cannons in the late 1710s was John Desaguliers, the most influential figure in English freemasonry of the period). Ruth Smith has pointed out that two of Handel's oratorio heroes, Solomon and Cyrus, are potent figures in masonic culture; while acknowledging the possibility of a masonic interpretation, she nevertheless hazards a guess that

---

[18] Ibid., 376–7.

FREEMASONRY AND MUSIC IN LONDON

'freemasonry did not influence the librettist or public understanding of their works'.[19]

As the eighteenth century progressed, lodges developed particular characters and associations, and several were known for their literary or artistic connections.[20] Four lodges stand out for their musical membership and affiliations (see Appendix 3.1, pp. 92–4). The Somerset House Lodge developed a strong musical tradition, based on the English musical fraternity.[21] Early members include Abraham Fisher, initiated at Old Horn Lodge before 1768 and no doubt to be identified with John Abraham Fisher, the Covent Garden leader and composer; he was shortly to be joined by his patron, Lord Tyrawley. Three musicians were admitted in 1777: Samuel Arnold, Redmond Simpson, and one Wood, probably to be identified with the alto singer. The following year the lodge moved to the Freemasons' Tavern, where it specifically encouraged music by appointing musicians as honorary members, or 'serving brethren', to lead the singing after lodge business; these were masons but not full members, paying no initiation fees or dues (all those initiated in 1783 were, however, raised to the third degree of Master Mason during the following year). Other prominent musicians, though not so identified, included the distinguished organists Thomas Sanders Dupuis and Benjamin Cooke, both also raised to Master Mason in 1784. Thus most leading English glee composers and singers attended the Somerset House Lodge – many of the same musicians who assisted at the Noblemen and Gentlemen's Catch Club, the Glee Club, and private glee parties; and also the principal performers at Harrison and Knyvett's prestigious Vocal Concerts, founded in 1792. The music seller John Bland was also a member, in 1785 presenting the lodge with two of his latest publications, music by fellow members Samuel Arnold and John Danby – no doubt the *Anacreontic Songs* and first book of *Catches, Canons and Glees*, respectively. In 1805 the Somerset House Lodge committee itemized its library of songs and glees, which then included Warren's well-known collections, the Ladies' Collection published by Bland, and others by Webbe, Dupuis, Spofforth and so on. The library at some point also acquired part-books for Handel overtures, and concertos by Felton (1715–69), Chilcot (1707?–66), Castrucci (1679–1752), Geminiani and others; whether these were actually played or were simply a donation remains unclear.[22]

The Lodge of Antiquity, one of the four original lodges, was split by schism in 1778, when William Preston (a controversial Scottish printer and the leading masonic teacher of the day) was expelled; the immediate cause was a relatively minor disagreement, but underlying it was an issue over egalitarianism and

---

[19] R. Smith, *Handel's Oratorios and Eighteenth-Century Thought* (Cambridge, 1995), p. 12.

[20] Weisberger, *Speculative Freemasonry*, p. 38; Pedicord, 'White Gloves', 281.

[21] The standard history is A.W. Oxford, *No. 4: An Introduction to the History of the Royal Somerset House and Inverness Lodge* (London, 1928).

[22] Oxford, *No. 4: An Introduction*, Appendix B.

80   MUSIC IN EIGHTEENTH-CENTURY BRITAIN

democracy.[23] The lodge was split into two branches, both of which subsequently attracted significant musicians. Preston's branch is the more interesting in the musical context. His system of masonic teaching was organized around what was known as the Chapter of Harodim, and music clearly played a significant part in the meetings, one of which is described below; the musicians, apparently invited or employed since none of them was a member, are otherwise unknown. But in 1778 Samuel Wesley was initiated here, during a turbulent period of his life (he had incurred the consternation of his family through his Catholic inclinations, a serious accident was causing intense mental distress and his father died the same year). Wesley became a figure of some importance in the lodge, rising to Junior Deacon in 1789, and acting on occasion as secretary. In 1789 he was joined by a prominent Catholic musician, Samuel Webbe (1740–1816), the singer and glee composer, who had already been initiated at the Somerset House Lodge. Also a member of Preston's Lodge of Antiquity was Benjamin Henry Latrobe, superintendent of the Moravian brethren in England; his son Christian Ignatius Latrobe, composer of Moravian and Anglican church music, was later a pioneering publisher of Catholic sacred music from the continent.

In 1790 the rift was healed and the two branches of the Lodge reunited. At the same time Preston founded the Harodim Lodge No. 558, 'in order to bring the Chapter of Harodim into regular communication with Grand Lodge'. Webbe was a founder member and he was a leading representative of the Harodim Lodge at a meeting on 6 December 1792 when a final union with the Lodge of Antiquity was resolved. Webbe's closeness to Preston was reflected in his receiving a mourning ring in Preston's will. There may be an element of subversiveness in all of this: both Webbe and his son, also a member of the Harodim Lodge, played a prominent role in the politically radical London Corresponding Society during the 1790s. It was certainly characteristic of Samuel Wesley to be attracted to an alternative culture, though he later became an orthodox member of the masonic establishment as Grand Organist from 1812 to 1818.[24]

Other lodges attracted a different musical clientele. The Lodge of the Nine Muses, formally constituted on 25 March 1777, was strongly inclined towards the arts, and the membership showed some bias towards Italians: alongside many *conti* and artists were the violinist Luigi Borghi (*c.* 1745–*c.* 1806) and Felice Giardini (1716–96). Other early members, however, were the leaders of the German musical community: J.C. Bach (1735–82), C.F. Abel (1723–87) and Wilhelm Cramer (1746–99), the last-mentioned already initiated elsewhere, as will be seen. All three joined in 1778, shortly after the initiation of Bach's patron Augustus Greenland. It is striking that Giardini had only recently become

---

[23]   The standard history is W.H. Rylands and C.W. Firebrace, *Records of the Lodge Original, No. 1. Now the Lodge of Antiquity, No. 2* (London, 1911–26).

[24]   On the Webbes' political activism see A.V. Beedell, *The Decline of the English Musician, 1788–1888* (Oxford, 1992), p. 61; and Samuel Wesley's letter of 17 February [1813], GB-Lbl Add. MS 11729, f. 51 (I am indebted to Philip Olleson for bringing this to my attention). Further on Wesley see also P. Fox, 'A Biographical Note on Samuel Wesley (1766–1837), the First Grand Organist', *Ars Quatuor Coronatorum*, 92 (1979), 64–81.

FREEMASONRY AND MUSIC IN LONDON 81

reconciled to the 'Teutonic interest', and had probably begun to play at the Bach-Abel concerts in 1776.[25] Also in the Nine Muses were the painter G.B. Cipriani and the engraver Francesco Bartolozzi, a partnership already connected with both Italian and German camps, responsible for title-pages for Bach's publications and benefit tickets for Giardini. They were also responsible for an ornamental frontispiece for the 1784 edition of the masonic Constitutions (see p. 87). Unlike the Somerset House Lodge, the Nine Muses met in the heart of the West End, at the Thatched House Tavern in St James's Street, the same venue used by other prestigious lodges such as the Prince of Wales.

A fourth lodge, the Pilgrim Lodge or Pilger Loge, was founded by Johann Leonhardi (a German lawyer, civil servant and polymath) and constituted on 24 August 1779.[26] As the only German-speaking lodge in London, it attracted Germans and Austrians visiting or resident in London, including diplomats, City merchants and members of the royal household. The lodge maintained strong links with continental courts, and it is likely that this provided an entrée for those from the arts. A number of German-speaking musicians, including Anton Kammell (1730–by 1787) and J.P. Salomon (1745–1815), were among its earliest members; another, initiated in 1792, was the flautist Christoph Papendiek, a court employee well known as Salomon's friend and supporter. The example of Salomon, however, should alert commentators to the dangers of making unsubstantiated assertions about masonic connections. He was already a mason before his arrival in England, but this did not directly result in his involvement with concerts at Freemasons' Hall. More significant for his career may be the fact that he belonged to a different lodge from most of the principal concert performers, and subsequently followed his own path. Likewise there is no evidence that Haydn maintained masonic contacts in London, nor can it be confirmed that he visited the Pilger Loge, as has sometimes been suggested.[27]

It is, however, striking that one musician who did achieve great influence in the music profession was also a power within freemasonry. Redmond Simpson, the Irish son-in-law of Matthew Dubourg, was a successful oboist of some reputation during the 1760s, playing at Covent Garden Theatre, Vauxhall Gardens and in the Queen's chamber orchestra. But the arrival in 1768 of J.C. Fischer (1733–1800) changed the course of his career: recognizing Fischer's

---

[25] The standard history is *An Account of the Lodge of the Nine Muses No. 235 from its Foundation in 1777 to the Present Time* (London, 1940). See also E. Warburton, 'Johann Christian Bach und die Freimaurer-Loge zu den Neun Musen in London', *Bach-Jahrbuch*, 78 (1992), 113–17; S. McVeigh, *The Violinist in London's Concert Life, 1750–1784: Felice Giardini and his Contemporaries* (New York, 1989), p. 182.

[26] The standard history is N. O'Leary, *The History of Two Hundred Years of Pilgrim Lodge No. 238* (London, 1979); members are listed in *Festgabe für die erste Säcular-Feier der ger. u. voll. St. Joh.-Loge "Der Pilger" No. 238* (London, 1879). See also C. Nelson, 'The Masonic Connections of Haydn's Impresario Johann Peter Salomon', *Ars Quatuor Coronatorum*, 110 (1997), 177–91.

[27] Recent studies of Haydn's masonic connections are J. Webb, 'Joseph Haydn – Freemason and Musician', *Ars Quatuor Coronatorum*, 94 (1981), 61–82; J. Hurwitz, 'Haydn and the Freemasons', *Haydn Yearbook*, 16 (1985), 5–98; and D.P. Schroeder, *Haydn and the Enlightenment: the Late Symphonies and their Audience* (Oxford, 1990), pp. 33–43.

82   MUSIC IN EIGHTEENTH-CENTURY BRITAIN

superior powers Simpson turned towards the exercise of power well beyond his musical abilities. Acting in modern parlance as a 'fixer', he began to engage orchestral personnel for more famous impresarios. Some were resentful of his carefully nurtured power; Charles Dibdin (1745–1814) bitterly reflected the opinions of the slighted, saying that Simpson specialized in exerting 'injury to the cause of *real genius*'.[28] Simpson's power-base seems to have been built on his masonic connections. In April 1777 he joined the Somerset House Lodge, the same year he became heavily involved in the musical activities at Freemasons' Hall. In January he was invited by the committee to manage their anniversary concert (described below, p. 85); and he was soon responsible for bringing more famous musicians into the Freemasons' Hall orbit, in order to boost the musical performances there. The committee suggested Fischer himself and J.C. Bach, or other 'capital performers', offering to initiate them by dispensation at a committee meeting free of expense; they apparently declined, for on 24 May it was Wilhelm Cramer and John Crosdill who were admitted into the first two degrees and raised to Master Mason.

The following January, Simpson was appointed an honorary member of the committee. He had clearly established himself as a figure of some stature, designated 'Esq' in the records, and he was soon to become a prominent figure in the (Royal) Society of Musicians, acting alongside Arnold as a principal assistant director to the 1784 Handel Commemoration. On his death Simpson was worth an astonishing £10,000, according to a newspaper obituary; certainly he was sufficiently well-off to donate £25 to masonic charities in 1784, and to donate four well-known portraits (Handel, Corelli, Geminiani and Purcell) to the Royal Society of Musicians.[29]

Music and Freemasonry

Turning to music within the masonic ritual itself, little is known about regular practice in eighteenth-century London, though it is clear that instrumental 'solemn music' and anthems or odes in honour of masonry played an important part. The most detailed surviving account describes a meeting of Preston's Lodge of Antiquity on 5 March 1777, a Chapter Night held at the Mitre Tavern. Eighteen members and nine visitors were present, as well as five additional musicians: Bros. Buckland, Bowman, John Mallet, Robert Cotton and Foy. The order of ceremony is worth quoting in full, as it reveals the importance of music, both instrumental and vocal, in alternation with teaching in the Prestonian manner.

---

[28]   C. Dibdin, *The Musical Tour* (Sheffield, 1788), p. 169.
[29]   *The World*, 25 June 1787; *Proceedings of the Grand Lodge of England 1770 to 1813*; B. Matthews, *A History of the Royal Society of Musicians 1738–1988* (London, 1988), pp. 56–60.

FREEMASONRY AND MUSIC IN LONDON

Lodge opened in the Third Degree in an adjacent Room, Procession entered the Lodge Room, and the usual ceremonies being observed, the Three Rulers were seated. A piece of music was then performed, and the 12 Assistants entered in procession and after repairing to their stations the Chapter was opened in solemn form. Brother Barker then rehearsed the Second Section. A piece of music was then performed by the instruments. Brother Preston then rehearsed the third Section. An Ode on Masonry was then sung by three voices. Brother Hill rehearsed the 4th Section, after which a piece of solemn music was performed. Bror. Brearley rehearsed the 5th Section, and the funeral procession was formed during which a solemn dirge was played and this ceremony concluded with a Grand Chorus. Bror. Berkley rehearsed the 6th Section, after which an anthem was sung. Bror. Preston then rehearsed the 7th Section, after which a song in honour of masonry, accompanied by the instruments was sung. The Chapter was then closed with the usual solemnity, and the Rulers and twelve Assistants made the procession round the Lodge, and then withdrew to an adjacent Room, where the Master's Lodge was closed in due form.[30]

Much more completely documented, and of considerable interest, is the ceremony for the dedication of the first Freemasons' Hall in 1776.[31] The need for a centre of freemasonry in London, combining a spiritual home for the Grand Lodge with a large meeting hall, was first discussed in 1768; a site was eventually identified in Great Queen Street near Drury Lane Theatre, behind a house that was to become the Freemasons' Tavern. The foundation stone was laid on 1 May 1775 (with an anthem 'To Heaven's high Architect' set to the music of 'Rule, Britannia') and the building was completed a year later. Austere in its classical restraint, the hall measured some 100 feet long, 43 feet wide, and 60 feet high, with a narrow gallery along each side supported by fluted pilasters. The ceiling was decorated with a representation of the sun surrounded by the signs of the zodiac (Plate 3.1, p. 87). Such a grand building was significant not only for its physical presence, as a potent reminder of the significance of masonry (to which end a moderate ostentatiousness was entirely appropriate), but it was also a symbolic reference to the Divine Architect of the Creation, analogous to the building of Solomon's Temple.

The ceremony of dedication, held on 23 May 1776, was therefore naturally invested with due solemnity and celebration, music playing its part in both aspects in a manner analogous to a coronation, and, John Money has observed, foreshadowing the symbolism and something of the scale of the Handel Commemoration at Westminster Abbey eight years later.[32] The minute books of

---

[30] Rylands and Firebrace, *Records of the Lodge Original*, i. 287. See also J. Morehen, 'Masonic Instrumental Music of the Eighteenth Century: a Survey', *Music Review*, 42 (1981), 215–24.

[31] This section is largely drawn from the records preserved in the Library of the United Grand Lodge, especially the minutes of the Freemasons' Hall Committee (reproduced by kind permission of the Board of General Purposes of the United Grand Lodge of England), *Proceedings of the Grand Lodge of England 1770 to 1813*, handbills and tickets. It also draws on newspaper advertisements and reviews, listed in S. McVeigh, *Calendar of London Concerts 1750–1800*, database, Goldsmiths College, University of London. See also J. Stubbs and T.O. Haunch, *Freemasons' Hall: the Home and Heritage of the Craft* (London, 1983) and *Survey of London*, 5/ii, p. 62.

[32] Money, 'The Masonic Moment', 369.

84   MUSIC IN EIGHTEENTH-CENTURY BRITAIN

the Hall committee reveal a great deal about the organization of the Dedication music, which was entrusted to John Abraham Fisher (1744–1806). He himself contributed a new anthem and a large-scale ode with full orchestral accompaniment. After various changes of plan, the final programme included four other items: the anthem from the foundation stone ceremony, a march,[33] Handel's coronation anthem 'Zadok the Priest' and an older ode entitled 'Wake the lute' (see Appendix 3.3, pp. 96–100).[34] The minutes (unusually) list all the performers: three soloists (Joseph Vernon, Frederick Reinhold and Thomas Norris); a chorus of thirty-three including boys from St Paul's; and an orchestra of thirty, directed by Samuel Arnold at the organ. Many of the performers were appropriately attired masons, including Arnold himself; non-masons had to leave with the ladies during the central Dedication ceremony. The total bill for the music came to £105 7s, including £50 to Fisher, who provided an organ and music books gratis. With further expenses of some £30, the whole made only a slight loss, amounting to £1 9s 7d.

The score of the new anthem and ode, largely in Fisher's autograph, is preserved in the Library of the United Grand Lodge, together with almost all the part books used in the ceremony (which reveal, incidentally, that strings and chorus performed two to a part) (see Appendix 3.2, p. 95). The text of the anthem ('Behold how good and joyful a thing') was taken from Psalm 133, an appropriate song in praise of brotherly unity; this was selected by William Dodd, the ambitious and increasingly self-serving clergyman, now Grand Chaplain, who was soon to be embroiled in scandal (on 27 June 1777 he was hanged at Tyburn for forgery).[35] The text of the ode was contributed by an unnamed member of the Alfred Lodge at Oxford University; the opening Strophe relays the mystery of the Creation (the work of the Grand Architect of the Universe obviously mirrored by the fine new building); an Antistrophe invites music to offer its 'tender votive strains'; and an Epode provides a paean to Virtue, Love and the Wisdom that eschews earthly vanities.

Most of Fisher's music is written in an attractive early classical style, close to that of J.C. Bach: its harmonic blandness is somewhat compensated by a colouristic use of winds (one aria has two obbligato bassoons). Yet Fisher made some attempt to capture a more elevated tone, almost inevitably by references outside his natural idiom, especially images recalling church music or oratorio. The central Grave of the overture introduces a triple-time hymnic texture in devotional manner, and some of the vocal music also recalls this sentimental standby of the contemporary anthem. Other choruses obviously emulate Handel in their D-major splendour, punctuated by some rather short-winded attempts at

---

[33] Included in Thompson's *Pocket Collection of Favourite Marches* (Morehen, 'Instrumental Music', 222).

[34] The order of ceremony for the 1776 Dedication is preserved in the published *Proceedings of the Grand Lodge of England 1770 to 1813;* it can also be found in *The Book of Constitutions,* 4th edn (London, 1776) and in *The Institutes of Freemasonry, to Which are Added a Choice Collection of Epilogues, Songs etc.* (Liverpool, 1788).

[35] Money, 'The Masonic Moment', 358–95.

fugal interludes. Two choruses begin with violin figurations building up to the first choral entry in the manner of 'Zadok the Priest', a familiar image of the religious sublime, evoking awesome majesty, but also serving as an appropriate metaphor for enlightenment. The final chorus draws on another Handelian device, the orchestral postlude with separate chords dying away, as in 'Glory to God' (*Messiah*), introducing a note of reflection and perhaps humility before the continuation of the ceremony.

The subsequent history of the anthem and ode proved controversial. The committee believed that the composer's fee was an outright payment covering rights both to future performance and to publication. Eventually Fisher conceded the first point but held out for publication rights, claiming to have received an offer of £70 from an unnamed third party; he then optimistically suggested sharing publication costs and profits if the Freemasons' Society would raise 200 subscriptions of half a guinea. Negotiations became increasingly acrimonious; eventually the committee granted Fisher an extra £30 for the full rights, which the members decided to pay out of their own pockets rather than reveal the matter to the Grand Lodge. In some dudgeon they returned a donation of £20, to show contempt for his conduct ('not only unjustifiable but very ungenteel'); and petitioned the Grand Lodge to have him struck off the list of freemasons. Certainly Fisher did not attend the committee further, and Simpson took his place in the organization of concerts.

The music was never published, but it was heard again at an anniversary concert and ball the following year commemorating the dedication of the hall (Fisher's name was pointedly omitted from the advertising).[36] Many of the by-now familiar names recurred among the principals: Simpson as manager and Arnold as director, the soloists Vernon, Norris, Wood and Reinhold, as well as Cramer, Crosdill and Fischer from the Bach-Abel concerts, a crossover of cultures highly unusual in concert life in London at the time. Attendance at this concert was confined to masons and their lady guests, but this restriction was lifted the following year, presumably as a fund-raising and propagandist gesture; and by 1779 the programme had drifted away from Fisher's Dedication music towards an unashamedly modern plan of symphonies, concertos and arias. Despite this, the profit amounted to only £8 4s 6d, and as a consequence it was decided to discontinue the venture.

The hall was also used for masonic charitable causes, reflecting not only the strongly philanthropic vein within freemasonry, but also the traditional alliance of charity with music. One series of annual concerts made substantial profits for a masonic charity. The Royal Cumberland Freemasons' School was founded in 1788 for the daughters of deceased and indigent masons (fifteen initially), with the Duchess of Cumberland as patroness.[37] The prime mover in its establishment

---

[36] The only performance in modern times was at Andrew Pearmain's Prestonian Lecture, 'Music and Masonry', in 1988.

[37] R.M. Handfield-Jones, *The History of the Royal Masonic Institution for Girls 1788–1974* (London, 1974); *A Brief Account of the Freemasons' Charity, for Female Children* (copy in Guildhall Library, London, GMus 146).

86   MUSIC IN EIGHTEENTH-CENTURY BRITAIN

was Chevalier Bartholomew Ruspini, dentist to the nobility, and a founder member of the Nine Muses and other lodges. The committee included the violinist Barthélemon (1741–1808) and music sellers Henry Holland and Francis Broderip, as well as the banker for the Professional Concert, Thomas Hammersley. Naturally musical masons were involved in the fund-raising concerts: the first in 1788 brought together two teams, the former partnership of Arnold and Cramer, and, from the Academy of Ancient Music, now resident at the hall, Cooke and Barthélemon. The programme was no longer masonic, although the following year Barthélemon did promise a concerto with a 'masonic rondeau'.

A plan was then mooted for a larger schoolhouse across the river in St George's Fields, which eventually opened in 1795; numbers rose to sixty-two, and though music was not central to the girls' education, they were paraded in their identical dresses to sing during concert intervals. Patronized by the Prince of Wales, fund-raising concerts from 1794 onwards were organized on a grand scale, though apparently without rehearsal, as confirmed by the well-known anecdote of Haydn refusing to direct a symphony under these conditions.[38] In addition to providing valuable publicity, the concerts played a significant financial role, raising as much as £270 in 1798. The organizers during the 1790s included once again Arnold and Cramer, together with Dupuis and later George Smart, whose son played a piano concerto at the 1799 concert. The latter, by now Sir George Smart (1776–1867), went on to be Grand Organist (succeeding Samuel Wesley in 1818), as well as the most important concert administrator in London. Further concerts in aid of the school were held more sporadically in the early nineteenth century under his direction.

By no means all concerts at the hall were masonic in origin, as it was readily available for hire for subscription and benefit concerts. The standard charge was modest at ten guineas a night, with perhaps an extra two guineas for setting up the orchestra or for the hire of the organ (and sometimes security was asked against damage). Reductions were often agreed in cases of particular hardship or in recognition of masonic service, with Simpson responsible for negotiations until his death in 1785. It was essentially a commercial operation, and the minutes record concern when the high level of revenue and prestige attracted in the early years tailed off to near extinction in the late 1790s. Benefit promoters were therefore not necessarily masons, though many names on the list are familiar from their masonic connections; it is worth remembering that most of London's musical world must have attended concerts at the heart of freemasonry at some time.

---

[38]   H.C. Robbins Landon, *Haydn: Chronicle and Works. Haydn in England 1791–1795* (London, 1976), p. 299.

FREEMASONRY AND MUSIC IN LONDON 87

Plate 3.1 The interior of the Freemasons' Hall

88   MUSIC IN EIGHTEENTH-CENTURY BRITAIN

The hall was never one of the more fashionable venues in London; the effect of the masonic connection is impossible to gauge, but its location half-way between the West End and the City was certainly not in its favour for the beau monde. From the promoter's point of view, on the other hand, it was considerably larger than Hanover Square (which measured 79 feet by 32 feet) and it could readily accommodate choral music in an imposing setting. Among the most notable events here were Philidor's three performances in 1779 of his *Carmen saeculare*, a large-scale setting of Horace's hymn in honour of Apollo and Diana. Although this impressive secular ode is not overtly masonic, it was an ideal venue; and indeed there was no obvious place in London's concert structure for such a work, which united the English affection for Horace's verse with the French choral tradition. Subscription concerts hardly ever used a chorus, and certainly not for a serious work on this scale; while it might have found a place in the Lenten oratorio series (which could after all accommodate the mythical *Acis and Galatea*), biblical stories were the norm for new works here. Furthermore, Philidor's music often evokes an antique and devotional style, with its solemn wind writing; Roger Cotte has suggested that there may be deliberate masonic overtones here.[39] The following season Carl Stamitz (1745–1801) preferred Freemasons' Hall for his benefit, presumably as a suitable venue for his *Canticum sacrum* (a setting of Latin psalms 'with grand Chorusses') and a grand chorus to celebrate Admiral Rodney's recent naval successes. His subsequent behaviour was, however, anything but fraternal; he left the country without paying for the hall, so the committee impounded an organ hired from Benjamin and Flight, who had to haggle for over a year and then pay seven guineas for its release.

A number of attempts were made to use the hall for more durable subscription series. In the autumn of 1776 a proposal for a ten-week 'select musical meeting' was received from Sir Charles Whitworth; at the same time the committee approved a scheme for a Freemasons Concert at the hall, an eight-concert series for 250 subscribers (with two lady guests), not restricted to masons. Neither came to fruition. Scarcely more successful was a series in 1783 in opposition to the Earl of Abingdon's concerts at the Hanover Square Rooms.[40] Leonhardi, founder of the Pilgrim Lodge, was responsible for proposing the idea on behalf of 'the Most eminent Musical Performers' headed by one Baron Kaas. Initial advertisements promised Cramer, Fischer and other Hanover Square luminaries, but then Abingdon banned his performers from taking part, despite the pleas of the Duke of Manchester on behalf of the Freemasons' Society. An alternative orchestra was brought in, led by Leonhardi's fellow mason Salomon (not, it should be noted, the first choice), but the series failed, with only one concert taking place, on 10 March. The hall was also the venue later in the decade for various series of readings and music, a temporarily popular middle-brow format

---

[39]   Cotte, *La musique maçonnique*, pp. 90–95.
[40]   S. McVeigh, 'The Professional Concert and Rival Subscription Series in London, 1783–1793', *Royal Musical Association Research Chronicle*, 22 (1989), 27.

alternating recitations from Shakespeare and Milton with songs, glees and instrumental items.

But a much more important institution had already become associated with the hall: the Academy of Ancient Music. In origin a coterie of enthusiasts for a specialist repertoire, the society had steadily grown in size and ambition, and by the 1780s it resembled a semi-public subscription series with a professional orchestra and a strong City representation (including ladies). It thus emulated the more fashionable subscription series in the West End but at the same time distinguished itself through a broad-ranging repertoire stretching back to the Renaissance. In January 1784 the concerts were transferred from the nearby Crown and Anchor Tavern to the Freemasons' Hall. This was not only a larger and grander milieu, an assertion of social and cultural status by the wealthier bourgeoisie and a venue no doubt familiar to the many freemasons among them, but it also allowed a more impressive and commodious platform; and in 1786 the hall commissioned an organ from Samuel Green for 200 guineas. The result was an amphitheatre arrangement for the chorus and orchestra, described in detail in Doane's *Musical Directory for the Year 1794*: a main platform some five feet high, with chorus and soloists ranged around the conductor at the harpsichord, and three further platforms rising in semicircular fashion towards the organ crowning the ensemble (it was joined by long keys to the harpsichord).[41] This was where Haydn made his triumphant first public entrance in 1791, due entirely to the fact that Salomon was by now leader of the Academy, and through no masonic connection.[42] Unfortunately the hall minutes add little to our knowledge of the latter years of the Academy, mainly comprising practical details concerning the furnishings and the organ. The Academy paid twenty guineas a season for the hire of the organ, which it agreed to keep in good repair. In 1793, however, the Academy successfully petitioned for a reduction in its annual hire fee, pleading ever-rising expenses; but it soon became apparent that it had overreached itself, and after the 1795 season it returned to earlier principles as a private society at the Crown and Anchor Tavern.

Though its secrets and rituals were carefully guarded – this was one of the targets of periodic anti-masonic movements – there was also a public face to freemasonry. Numerous masonic songs, glees and odes were available in print;[43] and occasionally masonic tunes were used in piano rondos and the like (in the next century, masonic polkas and quadrilles). In addition strong masonic connections within the theatrical world were revealed in two rather distinct directions. The first was attendance at the English playhouses by parties of lodge members, particularly on feast days when the Grand Master might be invited as a

---

[41]   McVeigh, *Concert Life*, pp. 209–11.
[42]   Landon, *Haydn in England*, pp. 36–7.
[43]   For example, *The Free Masons Songs* (published by Robert Bremner in 1761) and Thomas Hale, *Social Harmony* (1763).

90 MUSIC IN EIGHTEENTH-CENTURY BRITAIN

guest after a celebratory dinner.[44] Such occasions were noted in the press, even in advertisements, and special masonic prologues and epilogues were given; evidence that masonic audiences were known for their orderly and civilized behaviour has been mentioned above. Theatrical benefits could also invoke charity on behalf of distressed masons, their widows or orphans; and on any of these occasions masonic songs were often to be heard, especially in the entr'acte between main piece and afterpiece. As has been seen, concert benefits were sometimes also used in this way, though rarely is the masonic connection made so apparent. Marybone Gardens in the 1760s provides a striking exception. In 1763 'Brother Lowe', the celebrated tenor, invited freemasons to join in the chorus of the 'Fellow Craft's Song', sung on this occasion to the tune of 'Rule, Britannia'. The following year a certain Squibb introduced a new 'Ode in Honour of Freemasonry', again inviting audience participation and changing the date of the concert to suit freemasons; and Lowe repeated this ode in 1766 and 1768, no doubt to reinforce the charitable message of his heavy losses as proprietor of Marybone.[45]

Secondly, some theatrical productions took an explicitly masonic theme.[46] The earliest of these was *The Generous Freemason*, a ballad opera with music by Galliard (*c.* 1687–1749) and others, first produced during Bartholomew Fair on 20 August 1730, and subsequently a popular favourite at the fairs and (briefly) at the small Haymarket Theatre. Much more public in its acclaim was the unlikely sounding *Harlequin Freemason*, a highly successful pantomime whose popularity perhaps reflected the public profile of the hall dedication ceremony.[47] The first performance took place at Covent Garden on 27 December 1780, and a number of lengthy descriptions survive, as does some of the music by Charles Dibdin. The production reflected the current trend in pantomime towards elaborate spectacle and pageantry, usually exploiting national characteristics as an opportunity for extravagant *mis-en-scène* and costumes. In the opening scene, three masons are found working on a figure of 'that great building, MAN' (a common masonic image). Harlequin emerges from the figure and receives a magic trowel from Hiram that enables the usual pantomime burlesque. The story is even thinner than usual – little more than an excuse for a variety of colourful national escapades – but the finale returns to the masonic theme: an imposing procession of the principal Grand Masters from the Creation onwards, 'in the habits of their respective ages and countries', accompanied by representations of

---

[44] Pedicord, 'White Gloves at Five', 276–85.

[45] *Public Advertiser*: 28 June 1763, 26 July 1764, 26 September 1766, 28 September 1768.

[46] H.W. Pedicord, 'Masonic Theatre Pieces in London 1730–1780', *Theatre Survey*, 25 (1984), 154–7.

[47] Ibid., 160–65; W.A. Taylor, 'English Pantomime in London in the Period 1779 to 1786' (PhD diss., University of Wales College of Cardiff, 1997), vol. 1, pp. 81–5, vol. 2, pp. 343–9. The text of the vocal pieces, together with an explanation of the procession, was published in 1780; Dibdin included the overture and five vocal numbers in *The Lyrist* (1781). Pedicord also mentions a Dublin masonic oratorio, *Solomon's Temple*, with music by Richard Broadway, with the suggestion that it might have been performed at London lodges.

buildings associated with them. The music by Dibdin, not known to be a mason himself but ever the opportunist, included a ceremonial overture, and several masonic songs, glees and choruses (for example, 'Behold the model of our art', 'The sun's a freemason, he works all day' and 'Fill a capacious bowl'). None of this was presented in a spirit of mockery or satire, even if it did provide the opportunity for an irreverent comic song, borrowed from *The Quaker*, in which the master builder Solomon discourses on the first law of wisdom: before you start a major project, make sure you get paid in advance.

There were those who thought the incongruity of *Harlequin Freemason* even more ridiculous than usual for a pantomime ('former part to my taste unpleasing – Harlequin in dumb show; why he is said to be a freemason, I cannot divine'[48]). Yet there is no sign that the Grand Lodge made any objection to freemasonry being paraded in this way; indeed its success may have provided a welcome relief after a period of some internal dissent over questions of social exclusivity and religious toleration (the Gordon riots were only six months past). The final scene presciently foreshadows the reconciliation of the Modern and Antient branches, which eventually took place in 1813. Certainly the general public does not appear to have found anything controversial or objectionable about freemasonry being portrayed with unashamed propaganda on the public stage. The popularity of *Harlequin Freemason* was a sure sign that freemasonry had become accepted as a central feature of London life: furthermore it was taken for granted that music played a central role in this projection.

---

[48] Quoted in Pedicord, 'Masonic Theatre Pieces', 163.

92 MUSIC IN EIGHTEENTH-CENTURY BRITAIN

Appendix 3.1: Musical Members of Selected Lodges

Note: *I* = initiated; *J* = joined/admitted (i.e. already initiated at another lodge)

Somerset House Lodge (now Royal Somerset House and Inverness Lodge No. 4)

Old Horn Lodge united with and took the name Somerset House Lodge, 10 January 1774.

Fisher, Abm. [John Abraham]	member before 1768
Arnold, Dr. [Samuel]	*J* 14/4/1777
Redmond Simpson, Esq.	*J* 14/4/1777
Wood (musician)[1]	*J* 14/4/1777
Smith, J[ohn] Stafford (musician)	*I* 16/1/1779
Dyne, [John] (musician)	*I* 16/1/1779
Webbe, Samuel (musician)	*I* 16/1/1779 [see also Lodge of Antiquity below]
Danby, John (musician)	*I* 16/1/1779
Ayrton, Edmund (musician)	*I* 16/1/1779
Knyvett, [Charles] (musician)	*I* 16/1/1779
Dupuis, T[homas] S[anders], Esq.	*I* 22/12/1783 [index gives 20/12/1783 for this and succeeding five entries]
Osmond, Thomas (musician) [or Osmand]	*I* 22/12/1783 (honorary member)
Dighton, Robert (musician) [or Deighton]	*I* 22/12/1783 (honorary member)
Hobler, John Paul, jun. (musician)	*I* 22/12/1783 (honorary member)
Hindle, John (musician)	*I* 22/12/1783 (honorary member)
Luther, John C. (musician)	*J* 22/12/1783 (honorary member, from St Andrews Lodge)
Harrison, Samuel (musician)	*I* 26/1/1784 (initiated into first, passed to second degree, already was hon. member)
Cooke, Benjamin, Mus.D.	*I* 25/10/1784 (initiated and passed)
Sale, [John]	*I* 13/3/1786 (initiated and passed)
Gore, Israel	*I* 24/4/1786 (initiated and passed)

The following were admitted during 1786–89 *or* as honorary musical members *or* did not take up membership:

Aylward, Theodore	1786
Ban[n]ister, Charles	1792

---

[1] Those designated 'musician' may all have been honorary members (cf. a minute of 7/1/91 recommending termination of the membership of the following musical honorary members, due to non-attendance: Dighton, Hindle, Osmond, Harrison and Knyvett).

FREEMASONRY AND MUSIC IN LONDON

Bartleman, James	1790
Bellamy, Thomas, jun.	1792
Bland, John	1785
Dignum, Charles	1789
Guichard, John	1788
Lacey [Lacy], Willoughby	1786
Leate [= Leete?], Robert	1795
Nield, Jonathan	1795
Page, John	1790
Parsons, William	1787
Rheinhold [Frederick C. Reinhold]	1783
Sale, John Bernard [Barnard]	1798
Sedgwick, [Thomas]	1800
Spofforth, Reginald	1795
Vi[ga]noni, [Giuseppe]	1800
Webbe, Samuel, jun.	1790 [see also Lodge of Antiquity below]

Source: A.W. Oxford, *No. 4: An Introduction to the History of the Royal Somerset House and Inverness Lodge* (London, 1928)

Lodge of Antiquity (originally No. 1, now No. 2)

One of the four lodges originally forming Grand Lodge, 24 June 1717.
Between 1778 and 1790 there were two branches, headed by Noorthouck (N) and Preston (P); Harodim Lodge was founded by Preston in 1790 and merged with the Lodge of Antiquity in 1792 (see p. 80)

Birchall, Robert	*J* 1781 (N, from Lodge of Brotherly Love)
Cramer, John	*J* 1789 (N)
Wesley, Samuel	*I* 1788 (P; expelled 1791; Somerset House Lodge 1808; Grand Organist 1812–18)
Webbe, Samuel	*J* 1789 (P; also Harodim Lodge) [see also Somerset House Lodge above]
Field, John	*J* 1792 (from Harodim Lodge)
Webbe, [Samuel] jun.	*J* 1792 (from Harodim Lodge) [see also Somerset House Lodge above]

Source: W.H. Rylands and C.W. Firebrace, *Records of the Lodge Original, No. 1. Now the Lodge of Antiquity, No. 2* (London, 1911–26)

94 MUSIC IN EIGHTEENTH-CENTURY BRITAIN

Lodge of the Nine Muses (founded 14 January 1777; constituted 25 March 1777, now No. 235)

Borghi, Esq. [? Luigi Borghi]	*J* 14/1/1777
Cramer, Wilhelm	*J* 13/2/1778 (*I* by Freemasons' Hall Committee, 24/5/77 [not 24/4], with John Crosdill)
Abel, Chas. Fred.	*J* 13/2/1778
Giardini, Felici [Felice]	*J* 12/3/1778
Bach, John Chris.	*I* 15/6/1778
Kellie, Earl [Thomas Alexander Erskine]	*J* 21/2/1780
Viganoni, G[iuseppe]	*I* 1/7/1796

Other members include Ruspini (*J* 14/1/1777), Cipriani (*J* 23/1/1777), Bartolozzi (*I* 13/2/1777), Carlini (*J* 13/2/1778), William Taylor (*I* 15/6/1778) and Zoffany (*J* 21/2/1780).

Principal source: *An Account of the Lodge of the Nine Muses No. 235* (London, 1940)

Pilgrim Lodge (Pilger Loge) (founded 5 August 1779, constituted 24 August 1779, now No. 238)

Kammel, Anton	*I* 17/11/1779
Grosse, Samuel	*J* 6/4/1782
Salomon, [Johann] Peter	*I* 24/4/1782
Kirchhoff, Joh. Andreas	*J* 24/11/1784
Papendiek, Christoph	*I* 29/2/1792

Source: *Festgabe für die erste Säcular-Feier der ger. u. voll. St. Joh.-Loge "Der Pilger" No. 238* (London, 1879)

FREEMASONRY AND MUSIC IN LONDON

Appendix 3.2: Music for the 1776 Dedication Ceremony (Library of the United Grand Lodge, M/5)

Music:
- i   Anthem in C, 'To Heaven's high Architect all praise' [to music of Arne, 'Rule, Britannia']
- ii   March in D
- iii   Fisher, Anthem in A, 'Behold, how good and joyful' [Ps. 133]
- iv   Fisher, Ode compos'd for the Opening of the Free Masons Hall, 'What solemn sounds on holy Sinai rung'
- v   Handel, Coronation Anthem, 'Zadok the Priest'
- vi   Ode on Masonry, 'Wake the lute and quiv'ring strings'

Full score
105 folios [modern numbering 1–74, 74A–104], 236mm x 290mm; some folios signed by the composer.
- i   choral refrain, bass line only, in pencil
- ii   bass line only
- iii   full score, autograph, except final chorus in the hand of the principal copyist
- iv   full score, autograph, except: overture, movements 2 and 3, bass line only (principal copyist); final chorus (principal copyist)

Parts
Mostly in the hand of the principal copyist, with some pencil corrections and performance markings.
2 treble chorus (i iii iv), treble chorus (iv); 4 alto chorus (i iii iv), alto chorus (i iii iv vi), alto chorus (v); 3 tenor chorus (i iii iv); bass chorus (i iii iv); ob/fl1, ob/fl2, bns (i iii iv); hn1, hn2, tpt1, tpt2, timp (i iv); 3 vln1 (i ii iii iv); 2 vln2 (i ii iii iv), vln2 (i iii iv); vla (i iii iv); vcl (i ii iii iv).

Note: At the end of the Freemasons' Hall Committee Minute book, Vol. 2, there is a list of parts lent to St John's Lodge, Newcastle: 1 organ, bound [score?], 4 vln1, 4 vln2, 2 vla, 2 vcl, ob1, ob2, bns, hn1, hn2, tpt1, tpt2, drums, 3 [solo] vocal parts (Norris, Vernon, Reinhold), 14 chorus parts and 3 miscellaneous vocal parts.

96 MUSIC IN EIGHTEENTH-CENTURY BRITAIN

Appendix 3.3: Performances at Freemasons' Hall 1775–1800

MASONIC PERFORMANCES

1/5/1775 Foundation Stone Ceremony

Anthem ['To Heaven's high Architect']

23/5/1776 Dedication Ceremony

Music for procession
  Introduction
Anthem ['To Heaven's high Architect'], music 'Rule, Britannia', as at
        Foundation Stone Ceremony
  Exordium by Grand Secretary, return of implements
Old ode ['Wake the lute'?] [probably replacing Solemn piece of music: 8th
        Corelli]
  During Dedication ceremony:
Solemn music by the organ, three times
  After Dedication ceremony:
New anthem: Fisher ['Behold, how good and joyful'] Ps. 133
  Oration by Grand Chaplain
Coronation Anthem ['Zadok the Priest']
  Donations proclaimed [Omitted: favourite piece of music]
New ode: Fisher, 'What solemn sounds on holy Sinai rung'
  [Omitted: Another piece of music, and a song in honour of the ladies]
Music for procession

Performers [spellings verbatim]
Instrumental: Arnold [organ/conductor], Baumgarton [leader?], Mazzinghi,
Nofere, Borghi, Agus, Lowe, Smith, Jones, Dunvault, Leiffler, Linton, Blanc,
Scovel, Scouler, Bulkeley, Feidler, Sharpe, Simpson, Jones, Nelson, Smart,
Lang, Valentine, Jones, Shaw, Willims, Cordicelli, Gray, Ashley, Sarjant (total
31)
Vocal: [Soloists] Vernon, Reinhold, Norris. [Chorus] Du Bellamy, Old Field,
Chard, Freind, Reynoldson, Machon, J Pemberton, Johnson, Luther, Billington,
Wilson, Randall, Baker, Clarke, Donin, Popplewell, Fox, Ayrton, Burton sen.,
Forbes, Burton jun., Simpkinson, Real, Webb, Denbigh, Reiley, Wamsley,
Harrison Mr, 5 boys from St Paul's (total 36)

FREEMASONRY AND MUSIC IN LONDON

20/3/77 Anniversary concert and ball

1. [Fisher], Dedication Ode, 'What solemn sounds', Vernon, Reinhold, Norris; vcl solo, Crosdill; Anthem, 'To Heaven's high Architect', <Wood> Norris [music, 'Rule, Britannia']; [Handel], Hallelujah Chorus.
2. Vln conc, Linley jun.; Ode, 'Wake the lute', Vernon, <Norris> Wood, Reinhold [full text]; ob conc, Fischer; [Handel], Coronation Anthem, 'Zadok the Priest'.
Public Advertiser, 20/3: cond. Arnold, lead Linley jun., no Vernon.
Minutes, 19/2: managed by Simpson; 11/4: thanks to Arnold, Simpson, Fischer, Vernon, Reinhold, Norris, Wood, and others, who performed gratis.

20/2/78 Anniversary concert and ball

1. [Fisher], Dedication Ode, 'What solemn sounds', Vernon, Champness, Wood [full text, by member of the Alfred Lodge, Oxford University]; vcl solo, Crosdill; ob conc, Fischer; [Handel], Hallelujah Chorus.
2. Bach, new ov, 2orch; vdag solo, Abel; Haydn, str qt; vln conc, Cramer; [Handel], Coronation Anthem, 'Zadok the Priest'.
Minutes, 3/1, 24/1: managed by Simpson; open to non-masons for first time.
Public Advertiser, 20/2: complete programme, with Reinhold instead of Champness.

13/5/79 Anniversary concert and ball

1. Stamitz ov; vln-vla duet, Cramer, Stamitz; song, Tenducci; vcl solo, Crosdill; song, Sgra Prudom.
2. Arnold ov; song, Tenducci; vln conc, Cramer; song Sgra Prudom; ob conc, Fischer.
Minutes, Proceedings, and *Public Advertiser*, 6/5, 12/5: managed by Simpson, dir. Arnold, Lamotte replaced Cramer; profit £8 4s 6d.

ROYAL CUMBERLAND FREEMASONS' SCHOOL BENEFITS

3/6/88   Cond. Cooke, Arnold; dir. Barthélemon, Cramer
25/5/89 Dir. Cooke, Barthélemon (vln conc with masonic rondeau)
24/3/94 Managed by Arnold, Dupuis (directors) and Cramer (leader); profit £136 2s 9d.
30/3/95 Managed by Arnold, Dupuis (directors), Cramer (leader); profit £204 14s 11d.
5/2/96   Managed by Arnold, Dupuis (directors), Cramer (leader); profit £197
1797   Managed by Arnold, Cramer, Smart; profit £217 14s 5d.
8/3/98   Managed by Arnold (dir./org.), Cramer (leader), Smart; profit £270 17s 11d.
12/4/99 Managed by Arnold (dir./cond.), Cramer (leader), Smart; profit £154 17s.

CONCERT SERIES

Hall hire fees are given in parentheses; gn = guinea (£1 1s)

1776   Proposal for twelve-concert series of oratorios and sacred music during Lent: refused.

1776–7 Proposal for concert series by Sir Charles Whitworth: eight concerts (50gn) or ten (60gn): agreed, but no further mention.

1776–7 Proposal for concert series by Rowland Berkeley, with Henry Dagge (members of the Hall Committee): eight concerts Dec to Mar (Freemasons Concert, not limited to masons): agreed, but no further mention.

1779   26/2, 5/3, 12/3: three performances of Philidor's *Carmen saeculare* (10gn each).

1780   22/3 etc: three nights of Arnold's Liberal Academy of Eloquence (10gn each).

1783   Nine-concert series proposed by Bro. Leonhardi on behalf of 'eminent Musical Professors'; initially advertised performers included Harrison, Cramer, Duport and Fischer. First and only concert on 10/3 with different performers led by Salomon (see McVeigh, *RMA Research Chronicle*, 22 (1989), 27). Minutes 14/3: the concerts directed by Baron Kaas had not succeeded through the influence of a nobleman [the Earl of Abingdon] in preventing some of the principal musicians and singers from performing there, despite the intervention of the Duke of Manchester.

1784–95 Academy of Ancient Music: to 1789 dir. Cooke, lead Barthélemon; 1789-90 cond. Arnold, lead Salomon; 1790-91 cond. Arnold, lead Salomon; 1793   cond. Arnold, lead Cramer; 1794 cond. Arnold, lead Salomon; 1795 [cond.] Arnold, lead Hindmarsh (1784 £31 10s; 1789 £105; 1793 £105; 1794 £94 10s; 1795 £84).

1786   8/3 to 5/4: five nights of Trew and Percy's Readings and Singing (£8 15s. each).

1786   16/5 to 4/9: at least seven nights of Lacy's Readings and Music, music directed by Billington (£8 15s. each).

1786–7 23/11 to 19/1: six nights of the same; ?26/1 to 28/2: three further; 17/3 one further, but music directed by Mahon.

1788   26/2 to ?15/4: three nights of Trew, Danby and Ashley's Readings and Music (10gn each: but because of losses, only charged for two nights).

1795   20/2 to 27/3: ten nights of Holman, Fawcett, Incledon and Pope's Readings and Vocal Music (8gn each).

1795   Proposed eight-concert series by Barthélemon to employ French emigrants (50gn); probably never took place.

SINGLE BENEFIT CONCERTS

14/5/77	Middlesex Hospital: Fisher, new oratorio, *Providence* (10gn)
21/5/77	Borghi (10gn)
12/3/78	Giardini (10gn)
27/3/78	Cramer (12gn)
3/4/78	Fischer (12 gn: Crosdill and Cervetto cancelled 10gn bookings)
9/4/78	Miss Harrop (17gn)
28/5/78	Middlesex Hospital: Fisher, *Providence* (12gn)
18/3/79	Miss Harrop (17gn)
10/12/79	Family in great distress – Ganthony (10gn or £10)
15/2/80	City of London Lying-In Hospital: Fisher, *Providence* (10gn)
24/2/80	Webbe (10gn)
26/5/80	Stamitz (15gn)
15/2/81	City of London Lying-In Hospital: Fisher, *Providence* (10gn)
4/5/81	Webbe (10gn)
31/5/81	Hinner (14gn)
1782	? Middlesex Hospital (10gn)
21/2/83	Webbe (10gn)
11/4/83	Harrison (10gn)
28/4/83	Mrs Weichsell (10gn)
1/5/83	Evans (10gn)
20/2/84	Webbe (5gn, because of his attention to the Society)
4/3/84	Thomson, librarian, Academy of Ancient Music
27/1/85	Bartleman, patronage of Academy of Ancient Music (gratis, as orphan)
7/2/85	Kirchhoff
10/3/85	Webbe [5gn]
6/5/85	Mr and Mrs Barthélemon (5gn, as he performs at Academy of Ancient Music)
27/5/85	Crotch (7gn, as Mrs Crotch a widow)
2/6/85	Widow – Mrs Maguire (10gn)
13/2/86	Humane Society: Callcott new ode (gratis, in recognition of their 'rescuing from the jaws of Death many of our fellow Creatures')
23/2/86	Webbe [5gn]
27/3/86	Mr and Mrs Barthélemon (8gn)
6/4/86	Lockhart (10gn)
20/12/86	Young lady – Miss Maguire (10gn)
16/2/87	Webbe [5gn]
20/4/87	Lockhart (12gn)
24/4/87	Trew: Readings and Music (10gn)
7/6/87	[Rees]: Readings and Music (10gn)
22/3/88	[Des Mullins]: English Readings and Concert (10gn)
10/4/88	Webbe [5gn]
25/4/88	Lockhart [12gn]

100 MUSIC IN EIGHTEENTH-CENTURY BRITAIN

26/4/88   Ossulston Dispensary
14/5/88   Courtenay
25/3/89   Miss Leary
16/4/89   Webbe
1/5/89   Lockhart
15/5/89   General Lying-In Hospital
23/2/90   Miss Bertles
2/3/90   Salomon
11/3/90   Webbe
23/3/90   Cizo, patronage of Academy of Ancient Music
29/3/90   Huttley
28/4/90   Miss Leary
10/3/91   Webbe
22/3/92   Miss Leary
2/5/93   Arnold, patronage of Academy of Ancient Music
25/4/97   Gentleman under pecuniary embarrassments: Readings, Recitations
          and Music

Sources: Minutes of the Freemasons' Hall Committee; *Proceedings of the Grand Lodge of England 1770–1813*; handbills and tickets in the Library of the United Grand Lodge; *A Brief Account of the Freemasons' Charity, for Female Children* [London, 1814] (Guildhall Library, GMus 146); newspaper advertisements and reviews (McVeigh, *Calendar of London Concerts 1750–1800*, database, Goldsmiths College, University of London)

CHAPTER FOUR

The London Roman Catholic Embassy Chapels and their Music in the Eighteenth and Early Nineteenth Centuries

Philip Olleson

Throughout the seventeenth century and for most of the eighteenth, the London embassy chapels of Roman Catholic powers played a crucial role in the history of Roman Catholicism in England. Conducting or attending Roman Catholic worship was illegal, part of the penal legislation enacted in the sixteenth and seventeenth centuries that also discriminated against Roman Catholics in terms of their access to education, membership of the professions and property rights. The embassies of foreign powers, however, were technically on foreign soil and thus outside the jurisdiction of English law. Consequently, their chapels became places in which Roman Catholic rites could be celebrated openly and without fear of prosecution, and over the years they became the main centres for Roman Catholicism in London.[1] Three of the largest chapels also developed elaborate musical traditions and were central to the history of Roman Catholic church music in England in the eighteenth century.[2] With the passing of the Catholic Relief Acts of 1778 and 1791 most of the penal laws were repealed, the few remaining prohibitions being finally swept away by the Catholic Emancipation Act of 1829.[3] With Roman Catholic worship no longer illegal, the *raison d'être* of the embassy chapels disappeared, and they became anachronistic relics of a former age.

This essay is a broad survey of the embassy chapels and their music from the early eighteenth century until 1829, the date of closure of the Portuguese chapel. By this time the Bavarian and Sardinian chapels had already closed as embassy chapels and had re-opened as public places of worship. Despite this change of status, their musical and other traditions remained largely intact, and they were still generally known by their former names. For this reason, it is appropriate here to include some discussion of their later history.

---

[1] For histories of Roman Catholicism in England, see E. Norman, *Roman Catholicism in England: From the Elizabethan Settlement to the Second Vatican Council* (Oxford, 1986); J. Bossy, *The English Catholic Community 1570–1850* (London, 1975).

[2] The fullest survey of the music remains R. Darby, 'The Music of the Roman Catholic Embassy Chapels in London, 1765 to 1825' (Mus M diss., University of Manchester, 1984).

[3] B. Ward, *The Dawn of the Catholic Revival in England, 1781–1803* (London, 1909); B. Ward, *The Eve of Catholic Emancipation: Being the History of the English Catholics during the first Thirty years of the Nineteenth Century* (London, 1912).

Plate 4.1 The interior of the Sardinian chapel around 1808

THE LONDON ROMAN CATHOLIC EMBASSY CHAPELS 103

Locations and buildings

Throughout the seventeenth and eighteenth centuries a number of embassies of Roman Catholic powers in London offered public access to their chapels.[4] Of the eight or nine chapels in operation at one time or another during the period, the Portuguese, Bavarian and Sardinian embassy chapels stand out as the most important in terms of their stability and continuity, the extent of their provision, and the strength of their liturgical and musical traditions, and these are the main focus of this survey.

From 1724 to 1747 the Portuguese Embassy was at 23 and 24 Golden Square, the chapel occupying part of the rear of the same site with a frontage to Warwick Street.[5] In 1747 the embassy moved to 74 South Audley Street, close to its junction with South Street.[6] Access to the stables, coach-house and other outbuildings owned by the embassy was through a yard to the rear and the side of the main building giving on to South Street, and it was here that a chapel was either constructed or adapted from an already existing building. A plan of 1808 indicates that it measured only around 45 ft square; it is apparent from the inventories of the chapel (see below) that it was a two-storied galleried building, possibly modelled on the nearby Grosvenor Chapel, South Audley Street, built only a few years earlier in 1730.[7] The main access to the chapel was from South Street, with alternative access through a passage from the embassy itself. This arrangement was doubtless in the interests of security: at times of anti-Catholic unrest, when embassy chapels were among the first targets of the mob, the South Street entrance could have been shut off to allow access only through the embassy. The chapel closed when the embassy left South Audley Street in 1829, and was demolished a few years later. A volume containing inventories of the contents of the chapel and details of its customs and establishment is still at the embassy; its contents are discussed below. Apart from one incomplete manuscript choir book dating from late in the history of the chapel,[8] none of its musical archive appears to have survived.

Following the move of the Portuguese to South Audley Street in 1747, their former premises in Golden Square were taken over by the Bavarian embassy. The Warwick Street chapel was attacked in the Gordon riots in June 1780 and the

---

[4]   For the embassy chapels and their locations, see T.G. Holt S.J., 'The Embassy Chapels in Eighteenth-century London', *London Recusant*, 2 (1972), 19–37; B. Ward, *Catholic London a Century Ago* (London, 1905); J.H. Harting, *Catholic London Missions from the Reformation to the Year 1850* (London, 1903).

[5]   *Survey of London, Vol. 31: The Parish of St James Westminster. Part Two: North of Piccadilly* (London, 1963), pp. 158–9 and 168–72.

[6]   *Survey of London, Vol. 40: The Grosvenor Estate in Mayfair. Part Two: The Buildings* (London, 1980), pp. 309–10, p. 340, and Fig.7 4.

[7]   For the Grosvenor Chapel, see N. Pevsner, *The Buildings of England: London I: The Cities of London and Westminster*, 3rd edn. rev. B. Cherry, (Harmondsworth, 1973), pp. 488–9.

[8]   Novello-Cowden Clarke Collection, Brotherton Library, University of Leeds, entitled 'Masses in 2, 3 and 4 parts composed by V. Novello. Choir copy No. 3'. The inclusion of material that also appears in Novello's *A Collection of Sacred Music* (1811) suggests that it was probably compiled before this date.

104   MUSIC IN EIGHTEENTH-CENTURY BRITAIN

interior destroyed, and with it probably most, if not all of its library of music. In 1788, on the departure of the Bavarian embassy from Golden Square, the site was purchased for the erection of a new Roman Catholic chapel: this was Our Lady of the Assumption and St Gregory, Warwick Street, which opened in March 1790. Although no longer formally an embassy chapel, it retained some of its links with the Electors of Bavaria, was partly supported by them, and was generally known as the Bavarian Chapel. It still survives, one of a small number of Roman Catholic churches built in the earliest days of emancipation, and the only one to have a direct connection with the embassy chapels.[9] The church houses the only substantial collection of manuscript music from the period, although only two of its over twenty volumes contain music written before 1791.[10]

The Sardinian chapel at Duke Street (now Sardinia Street), Lincoln's Inn Fields, had the longest continuous history – there had been a chapel on this site since the reign of James II – and survived the longest of all the eighteenth-century chapels.[11] After a serious fire in 1759 which destroyed the previous building, a new chapel by Jean Baptist Jacque was built. Like the Bavarian chapel, it was attacked in the Gordon riots and the interior destroyed; it re-opened after repairs in February 1781. It ceased to be an embassy chapel in 1798 when the embassy moved from Lincoln's Inn Fields, and re-opened the following year supported by public subscription and contributions from the King of Sardinia, who became its patron and protector. Like the Bavarian chapel, it retained its former name, and was known as the Royal Sardinian Chapel until as late as 1853. It was demolished in 1909 to make way for the building of Kingsway and was replaced by the present-day church of St Anselm and St Cecilia, Kingsway. It is the only embassy chapel for which there is any visual documentation: an acquatint by Augustus Charles Pugin and Thomas Rowlandson of the interior around 1808 is included in Rudolf Ackermann's *Microcosm of London* (Plate 4.1),[12] and a number of photographs are included in later histories.[13] No musical archives of the chapel survive.

Worship at the embassy chapels

The style of worship in the embassy chapels during the eighteenth century has been described by Edward Norman as 'baroque and triumphalist, bringing the atmosphere of the European counter-reformation to English worship'.[14] Much of

---

[9]   *Survey of London 31*, pp. 168–70, Plates 12c and 13, Fig. 21; Pevsner, pp. 497–8.
[10]   For a description and catalogue of this archive, see Darby, 'The Music of the Roman Catholic Embassy Chapels in London', p. 33 and Appendix 1.
[11]   J.H. Harting, *A History of the Sardinian Chapel, Lincoln's Inn Fields*, (London, 1905).
[12]   [W. H. Pyne and W. Combe], *The Microcosm of London, or, London in Miniature*, (London, 1808–10) vol. 1, facing p. 114.
[13]   See Harting, *A History of the Sardinian Embassy Chapel*, facing pp. 4, 14, 18 and 97; Ward, *Catholic London a Century Ago*, facing p. 88.
[14]   Norman, *Roman Catholicism in England*, p. 50.

THE LONDON ROMAN CATHOLIC EMBASSY CHAPELS   105

its flavour is conveyed by the contents of a volume relating to the Portuguese chapel still in the possession of the Portuguese Embassy in London.[15] Begun in October 1739, it contains inventories in French of the contents of the chapel in 1739 and 1757, a list of chaplains and lay staff in 1739 (periodically updated thereafter) and an account of usages and customs.

With their detailed listing of the furniture and fittings of the chapel and their descriptions of vestments, linen and other accoutrements of worship, the inventories convey a wealth of information on how worship was conducted in the Portuguese chapel and, by implication, in the other largest embassy chapels.[16] In the same way, the list of clergy conveys the size of the chapel establishment: there were no fewer than eight chaplains, supported by a number of external priests, a sacristan, an organist, an organ-blower and a porter. This large establishment was needed for the extensive programme of services provided, as set out in detail in the account of usages and customs. There were eight masses per day: six Low Masses, beginning at 6.00 a.m. in summer and 7.00 a.m. in winter, followed by High Mass at 11.00 a.m. and a final Low Mass at noon or 12.30 p.m. High Mass and Vespers were sung every Sunday and on specified feasts. There was Compline after Vespers on Wednesdays in Lent, and the Holy Week Office was observed in its entirety. There were also special services for the birthdays of the Portuguese royal family and the feast days of some saints with specifically Portuguese connections; one was Elizabeth of Portugal (1271–1336), who was probably the patron saint of the chapel. Although there were no doubt minor changes in organization over the years, the entry for the chapel in Coghlan's *Laity's Directory* for 1793 shows that the extent of its programme remained substantially the same over fifty years later.

The music of the chapels: plainsong and polyphony

There is little contemporary information about the role of music in the embassy chapels in the first half of the eighteenth century. The inclusion of an organ in the 1739 Portuguese chapel inventory and of an organist and organ-blower in its list of staff at the same time indicates that music was a regular part of worship there, as it no doubt was at the other main chapels.[17] The only books listed in this inventory, however, are 'un psalterium pour le choeur', two missals, and

---

[15]   The registers of births and marriages of the chapel are also held by the embassy. For the volume of inventories, see J. C.M. Weale (ed.), *Registers of the Catholic Chapels Royal and of the Portuguese Embassy Chapel 1662–1829. Vol. 1: Marriages* Catholic Record Society Publications Vol. 38 (London, 1941), xxv–xxvii. See also P. Olleson, 'The Portuguese Embassy Chapel and its Registers', *Catholic Ancestor*, 5 (1995), 144–51. I am grateful to Professor Dr Graça Almeida Rodrigues for confirming the present location of these volumes.

[16]   For details of gifts of vestments sent to the Sardinian chapel in 1764 and 1782 see Harting, *A History of the Sardinian Chapel*, pp. 23–7.

[17]   At the time of the 1739 inventory the organist was Jacques Gass, who was paid a stipend of £1 10s. (£1.50) per month. He was succeeded in August 1743 by Jean Baptiste Coopere (*sic*), who after his death in January 1747 was in turn succeeded by Louis Dors. No further names of organists are recorded, and nothing else is known of these three.

106   MUSIC IN EIGHTEENTH-CENTURY BRITAIN

one antiphonal, supplemented at some unspecified later stage by another missal and antiphonal. A page of entries made around 1748 records the addition at that time of 'two books of plainchant, one for the morning, one for the afternoon' ('Deux livres de Plain Chant, un pour le Matin, l'autre pour l'après midy') (i.e. for Mass and Vespers). Six scarlet soutanes and twelve surplices for 'the choir children' ('les Enfants de Choeur') are also listed, but it is not clear whether these would have been for choristers or altar boys. There is no evidence concerning the place of music at this time at the Bavarian or Sardinian embassy chapels.

In the absence of any manuscript material from the period, it is impossible to tell what part in the services any choir might have had, or what they might have sung. It is apparent, however, from the publication in 1748 of two plainchant treatises in London that plainchant was sung congregationally in the chapels at this time, and the role of the choir may not have extended much, if at all, beyond supporting the singing of the congregation.[18] The continuing strength of the plainchant tradition is shown by the publication in 1782 by J.P. Coghlan of *An Essay on the Church Plain Chant*, the same publisher's *Plain Chant for the Chief Masses* (1788) and his subsequent plans, ultimately abortive, for an ambitious compilation of plainchant for choir use, to be entitled *Gregorian Note, in Red and Black of the Largest Size, for the Choir*.[19]

The *Essay on the Church Plain Chant* is in three parts. Part 1 is an elementary instruction manual for reading Gregorian notation, described in one of Coghlan's catalogues as containing 'the best and most easy Rules for a Person, unacquainted with divine Harmony, to obtain a perfect Knowledge of it';[20] Part 2 consists of 'Several Anthems, Litanies, Proses and Hymns as they are sung in the Public Chapels [i.e. the embassy chapels] at London'; Part 3 is 'A Supplement of Several Anthems, Litanies, Proses and Hymns which have been omitted in the Second Part yet are sung in the Public Chapels at London.' The provision of bass parts to many of the items in Parts 2 and 3 demonstrates that the prevailing method of performance of plainchant was with organ accompaniment. The publication of an *Essay on the Church Plain Chant* was an attempt to raise what its publisher and authors saw as the current low standard of performance of congregational plainchant.[21] As its introduction stated:

---

[18] *The Art of Singing: or, A short and easy Method, for Obtaining a perfect Knowledge of the Gregorian Note*, published by Thomas Meighan Senior, and *The true Method to learn the Church Plain-Song*, published by J. Marmaduke. For plainchant traditions, see B. Zon, 'Plainchant in the Eighteenth-Century English Catholic Church', *Recusant History*, 21 (1993), 361–80; B. Zon, *The English Plainchant Revival* (Oxford, 1999), pp. 72–103.
[19] Zon, *The English Plainchant Revival*, pp. 89–103.
[20] Catalogue dated 15 November 1780, quoted in Zon, 'Plainchant in the Eighteenth-Century English Catholic Church', pp. 364–5.
[21] Authorship of the anonymous *Essay* has often been ascribed to Samuel Webbe I. Bennett Zon has pointed out, however, that more than one hand was involved in the compilation and that Webbe cannot have been the main compiler, although he may have had a subsidiary role. He argues strongly that the main author was the influential plainsong scribe John F. Wade (1711–86). See Zon, 'Plainchant in the Eighteenth-Century English Catholic Church', pp. 366–7; Zon, *The English Plainchant Revival*, pp. 94–6.

THE LONDON ROMAN CATHOLIC EMBASSY CHAPELS   107

While we admit the sanctity of the institution, can we forbear regretting the great neglect in the cultivation of [plainchant]? We observe, that those whom nature has blest with a moderate share of vocal powers, can contribute in general to raise social mirth by a song, yet when every heart and every voice should join in hymning the Deity, alas they are dumb. If we consider the great effect that is produced in divine service by a few untutored voices; how much greater must the effect be, if every individual in a congregation, capable of singing, should join in a well regulated choir, and all united by the powerful harmony of a well-touched organ.[22]

In fact, by the time of publication of Coghlan's *Essay* the practice of singing parts of the services to polyphonic settings had been established for some years, and it was widely believed that this was the cause of, or at least had contributed to, the declining standards of congregational plainchant performance. There appears to be no contemporary statement of this view, but it was expressed in an articulate historical survey of Roman Catholic church music in England which formed part of an anonymous review of Vincent Novello's *The Evening Service* in the *Quarterly Musical Magazine and Review* (henceforth *QMMR*) for 1823:

> The Gregorian chant... has been gradually disappearing during the last forty or fifty years, and is now almost wholly discontinued in England. This may perhaps be attributable, in some degree, to the difficulty found by the generality of organists in accompanying the Gregorian Masses, &c. with appropriate harmonies; for as no copies were published but those containing the mere *melody*, and that too printed in the old square and lozenge-shaped character, the organist was left entirely to his own skill, to adapt whatever bases his fancy suggested, and to supply correct and grammatical harmonies to the singular modulations and transitions with which this wild style of music abounds. This could be no easy task, especially to those organists whose knowledge of harmony was confined, and who therefore would naturally give encouragement to the introduction of other music, in which the bases and chords were supplied ready to their hands.
>
> Another cause has probably arisen from the employment of *regular singers* in choirs, instead of the clergy as formerly; the latter were content to sing the old chants in *unison*, but the former would naturally wish to display their abilities in *part-singing*, as well as in solos, duets, &c. thus requiring a wider scope than the ancient Gregorian allows. But a still more effective cause has perhaps been the gradual *change of taste* in the musical part of the congregations (induced originally by this employment of professional performers), and the consequent necessity on the part of the proprietors and conductors of the various Catholic Chapels, to bring forward such compositions as would be most attractive and satisfactory to those who attended the service.[23]

The author of the *QMMR* account identifies 'the first attempt to introduce a deviation from the Gregorian style' as the publication in 1766 of *Sacred Hymns, Anthems, and Versicles* by Charles Barbandt, organist of the Bavarian chapel,[24]

---

[22] *An Essay on the Church Plain Chant*, Introduction, [i]–ii.

[23] Anon., review of Vincent Novello's *The Evening Service*, *Quarterly Musical Magazine and Review*, 5 (1823), 198-206.

[24] *Sacred Hymns, Anthems, and Versicles, for Morning and Evening Service, on all Sundays and Festivals throughout the year; taken out of the public Liturgy of the Church, and set to Music in a manner no less solemn than easy, and proper to promote the Divine Worship and excite*

108　　　　　　　MUSIC IN EIGHTEENTH-CENTURY BRITAIN

describing the contents of the volume as being in 'a light, trivial, French style' and adding that their performance was 'principally, if not entirely, confined to the chapel for which they were written'.[25]

Barbandt's collection is in two parts. The first, for 'Morning Service' (the Mass), includes simple and straightforward settings in three or four parts of Proper texts for all the major feasts of the Church year, together with 'Domine salvum fac' (the prayer for the monarch), 'Tantum ergo', and the 'Dies Irae' from the Requiem Mass; the second includes fifty-five hymns for use at Vespers and Compline. As the first collection of Roman Catholic church music to be published in England since Byrd's *Gradualia* of 1605–7, Barbandt's *Sacred Hymns* was undoubtedly a landmark, and the very fact of its publication indicates the spirit of toleration prevailing in England at the time. The *QMMR* reviewer's statement that it marked the 'first attempt to introduce a deviation from the Gregorian style' may, however, be erroneous: it seems probable that similar collections would have been in use at the time at the other chapels – collections that were never published and were subsequently lost or destroyed.

In fact, it is clear that settings of the Ordinary of the mass were in regular use in the embassy chapels at least by the late 1760s, and probably earlier. The evidence is from entries made during the period February 1767 to September 1790 in the diary notebooks of the Roman Catholic woollen-draper and enthusiastic amateur musician William Mawhood (1724–97).[26] Although Mawhood's main place of worship was the Sardinian chapel, where he sang in the choir and sometimes played the organ, he was also involved in the music of the Bavarian and Portuguese chapels, moving easily from chapel to chapel in a way which may have been typical of other Roman Catholic musicians at the time. His diary entries relating to church music consist typically of no more than a note of where he attended mass and whose setting was performed. Despite their brevity, they are an invaluable source of information about the repertory of the embassy chapels, enabling us to be more precise about composition dates of music that did not appear in print until much later. The masses mentioned by Mawhood during the late 1760s and 1770s include at least two by Samuel

---

the Devotion of the Faithful (London, 1766). The title is also given in French and Latin. For a discussion of the collection, see Darby, 'The Music of the Roman Catholic Embassy Chapels in London', pp. 10–17. For Barbandt (1716–76 or later), who was organist of the Bavarian chapel from 1764, see E. Zöllner, 'English Oratorio after Handel', in M. Burden and I. Cholij (eds), *A Handbook for Studies in Eighteenth-Century English Music V* (Oxford, 1996), 21–39.

[25]　Review of *The Evening Service*, *QMMR*, 5 (1823), 205.

[26]　E. E. Reynolds (ed.), *The Mawhood Diary: Selections from the Diary Note-Books of William Mawhood, Woollen-Draper of London, for the Years 1764–1790*, Catholic Record Society Publications Vol. 50 (London, 1956). The complete diaries take up forty-nine small notebooks with a total of over 4,000 pages and probably 500,000 words, covering the period from 14 July 1764 to 18 October 1790. Mawhood started the diaries as business memoranda, but gradually began to introduce items of a more personal nature, and Reynolds's selection includes everything of Roman Catholic interest. Entries concerning music heard by Mawhood at the chapels occur during the period February 1767–September 1790. See also E.E. Reynolds, 'The Mawhoods of Smithfield and Finchley', *Biographical Studies*, 1 (1951), 59–77; E.E. Reynolds, 'Some Catholic Musicians of the Eighteenth Century', *Biographical Studies*, 1 (1951), 149–56.

Webbe I (1740–1816), two by Thomas Augustine Arne (1710–78),[27] at this time the organist of the Sardinian chapel, one by Stephen Paxton (1735–87) and one by Francesco Pasquale Ricci (1732–1817). All were to appear in the published collections by Webbe and others from the 1780s and early 1790s: two masses by Webbe were included in his *A Collection of Sacred Music as Used in the Chapel of the King of Sardinia* (c. 1785) and a further six appeared in his *A Collection of Masses, with an accompaniment for the organ, particularly design'd for the use of small choirs* (1792), which also contained the masses by Paxton and Ricci which Mawhood recorded having heard in 1770 and 1777 respectively. The two Arne masses recorded by Mawhood are both now lost in their original forms, although a two-part arrangement of a mass in G was discovered in 1981.[28]

As the Mawhood diaries clearly show, the Webbe publications of the 1780s and early 1790s are compendiums of the repertory of the embassy chapels from the late 1760s on.[29] According to the *QMMR* reviewer, writing over thirty years later, 'from their simplicity of style and facility of expression, [they] were admirably adapted to the powers of a small choir, and soon became in almost universal request.'[30] In fact, the music of the Webbe publications to a large extent formed the basis of Roman Catholic repertory in the period immediately following emancipation, and – as is apparent from many later editions – many pieces remained in use well into the middle of the nineteenth century and beyond. Ex.4.1 is typical of much of the writing in many of these volumes: plain and straightforward, largely note-against-note, with the organ doubling the vocal parts. More elaborate writing, and independent organ parts, are reserved for solo passages (Ex.4.2).

Webbe's *A Collection of Masses* and its companion-volume *A Collection of Motetts or Antiphons* (also published in 1792) provided music for most liturgical

---

[27] Mawhood first recorded performing an Arne mass in 1767. Entries for 1 and 3 January 1773 refer to performances of 'Dr Arne's Old Service' and 'Dr Arne's New Service', suggesting a composition date for the latter of late 1772. For a discussion of settings by Arne of the 'Libera me' from the Requiem Mass and of 'O salutaris hostia', see Darby, 'The Music of the Roman Catholic Embassy Chapels', pp. 17–30 and Appendix 1.

[28] See J.P. Rowntree, 'Lulworth Chapel and a missing Arne Mass', *Musical Times*, 128 (1987), 347–9. A mass by Arne was also announced in Webbe's *A Collection of Modern Church Music consisting of masses &c composed by... Webbe, Paxton, Ricci, and Dr. Arne* (1791). The only two extant copies of this publication are incomplete, however, containing only the first twenty-four pages. It is probable that these were all that were published, as the plates were re-used in Webbe's *A Collection of Masses* the following year. Further contemporary information on Arne's masses is given by the author of the unsigned 'Music of the English Catholic Chapels', *Catholic Gentleman's Magazine*, 1 (1818), 573–4: '[Arne] composed for the choir of the Sardinian ambassador two masses, – one in four, the other in three parts; – the latter did not please, the former was exquisite. It is, what all church music should be, solemn and impressive; the harmony correct and simple; the melody slow and graceful. Unfortunately, the thinness of the Catholic choirs in those times, made them drop the contra-tenor and tenor parts, and sing only the canto and base. This entirely spoilt the beauty of the composition.' The author was almost certainly Charles Butler; parts of the article are repeated word for word in his *Historical Memoirs of the English, Irish and Scottish Catholics* (London, 1819–21), vol. 2, pp. 355–6.

[29] For an extended discussion of these publications, see Darby, 'The Music of the Roman Catholic Embassy Chapels in London', pp. 35–56.

[30] Review of *The Evening Service*, *QMMR*, 5 (1823), p. 206.

Ex. 4.1 Samuel Webbe I: Mass in F (*A Collection of Masses* (1792)): opening of Kyrie

occasions, drawn from repertory that was probably in use in all three major chapels. Although the title of the earlier *A Collection of Sacred Music as Used in the Chapel of the King of Sardinia* links its contents to one chapel, it cannot be assumed that the works it contains were exclusively performed there, and it is no doubt significant that several well-used copies of this collection are to be found in the archives of the Bavarian Chapel.[31]

Samuel Webbe and Samuel Wesley

Although information about the organization of the music of the chapels in the 1770s and 1780s is far from abundant, there can be no doubt about the central

---

[31]   Darby, 'The Music of the Roman Catholic Embassy Chapels in London', p. 32.

Ex. 4.2 Samuel Webbe I: Mass in F (*A Collection of Masses* (1792)): from the Gloria

importance of Samuel Webbe I. He had been Barbandt's assistant at the Bavarian chapel, and appears to have become an important figure in Catholic church music from the mid-1760s, if not earlier. According to most accounts, he became organist of the Portuguese chapel in 1776, probably holding the post until the appointment of Vincent Novello (1781–1861) in 1797 or 1798. At the same time he was organist of the Sardinian chapel, having succeeded George Paxton following the latter's death in October 1775.[32] As is known from Mawhood, he was also involved with the music of the Bavarian chapel, and may in fact have had overall control of the musical organization of all three major chapels. His music dominates the publications of the 1780s and the 1790s and is well represented in the early publications of Vincent Novello. At the Sardinian chapel, he gave free instruction in church music every Friday evening, and was thus highly influential in training the next generation of Catholic church

---

[32] *Mawhood Diary*, 26 October 1775.

112 MUSIC IN EIGHTEENTH-CENTURY BRITAIN

musicians.[33] Amongst his known pupils were Vincent Novello and (almost certainly) Samuel Wesley.

Almost nothing is known about the circumstances in which the young Samuel Wesley (1766–1837) began to be involved with the embassy chapels from around September 1778 or even earlier.[34] Almost the only evidence comes from his first compositions for the Roman rite, which are dated from November 1780 onwards. Although these point unequivocally to his active involvement with one or other of the embassy chapels it is impossible to say which. Wesley's connection with the embassy chapels would certainly have brought him into contact at an early stage with Webbe, who would have welcomed him into his choir at either the Sardinian or the Portuguese chapel, or both. Here, week by week, Wesley would have become familiar with the repertory of the chapels and laid the foundations of a lifelong interest in Gregorian chant. Under these circumstances, it would have been natural for him to attend Webbe's Friday evening instruction sessions at the Sardinian embassy chapel and, in time, and with Webbe's encouragement, to begin to compose for the chapels. We may further conjecture a more personal dimension to the relationship and a friendship with Webbe's son Samuel II (1770–1843), who later became a professional musician and an associate of Wesley.

Wesley's Latin church music of the early 1780s, mostly consisting of short motets or antiphons, provides further insights into the embassy chapel choirs of the time.[35] None of this music has been published, but two items have appeared on a recent recording: one is an extended setting of the Magnificat for SSA and organ from 1783; the other is a later arrangement for five voices of a setting of around 1781 of 'Ave regina coelorum' in which the original scoring for SA and organ can readily be imagined. Both pieces show the easy fluency and tunefulness also to be heard in Wesley's orchestral music of the period and an inventiveness which far outstrips the rather pedestrian nature of much of the contents of the Webbe publications.[36]

In later life Wesley was at pains to claim that his first involvement with Roman Catholicism arose out of a fascination with its music rather than its doctrines. Whatever the truth of this, it was no doubt on these grounds that he was able to assuage (if not entirely to lay to rest) the anxieties that his involvement must have caused his family. But in May 1784 he converted, marking the event by writing a large-scale setting of the mass which he subsequently despatched to Pope Pius V in Rome. In its size and scope – it is

---

[33] J.P. Coghlan, *The Laity's Directory* (London, 1793).

[34] This date derives from a passage in a letter from Wesley's father to his mother of 5–7 September 1778 (John Rylands University Library of Manchester, Methodist Archives and Research Centre, DDCW 7/36): 'Sam will have many more escapes. Great will be his trials; but the Lord will deliver him out of all.... Sam wants more pains to be taken with him. If I should not live to help him, it will lie all upon you. Make him a living Christian, and he will never wish to be a dead Papist.'

[35] For Wesley's Latin church music, see J. Marsh, 'The Latin Church Music of Samuel Wesley' (PhD diss., University of York, 1975).

[36] *Samuel Wesley: Sacred Choral Music*, Choir of Gonville and Caius College, Cambridge, directed by Geoffrey Webber (ASV CD GAU 157, 1996).

THE LONDON ROMAN CATHOLIC EMBASSY CHAPELS 113

scored for soloists, chorus and orchestra and plays for around ninety minutes – the *Missa de Spiritu Sancto* is quite unlike any of his previous Latin church music. It bears no relationship to the repertory of the embassy chapels, could not have been performed in any London chapel of the day, and is probably best regarded as a presentation work in which Wesley was able to display both the strength of his religious commitment and his compositional prowess.[37] After 1786, Wesley's involvement with the music of the chapels declined, for reasons probably connected with an increasing disenchantment with Roman Catholicism from around this time. From now on, his connection with the chapels would be intermittent, and as a musician with a fascination with the rituals and music of Roman Catholicism coupled with a strong distaste for its doctrines. A group of further compositions from around 1798–1800 indicates a renewed interest in Roman Catholic church music that coincided with a more general return to composition after years of relative inactivity, and may have been connected with the beginning of his friendship with Vincent Novello, recently appointed as organist of the Portuguese chapel.[38] A yet later group is connected with Wesley's involvement with the Portuguese chapel as assistant to Novello during the period *c.* 1811–24.

The final period

The period between the passing of the second Catholic Relief Act in 1791 until the closure of the Portuguese embassy chapel in 1829 was a brilliant sunset. As already mentioned, by 1798 the Portuguese chapel was the only one to retain its original status, the Bavarian and Sardinian chapels each having closed as an embassy chapel and re-opened as a public place of worship. In fact, the change of status did not greatly affect the operation of the chapels, their musical traditions, or the way they were perceived by most people, and it is convenient to consider their history alongside that of the Portuguese chapel in its final years.

For much of the 1790s and the whole of the first decade of the nineteenth century there is little fresh information about any aspect of the activities of the chapels, and no further publications of music; it can be assumed that the publication of the Webbe collections of 1791 and 1792 had for the moment satisfied any increased demand for new repertory that had followed the second Relief Act. As detailed above, Wesley appears to have renewed his interest in Roman Catholic church music around 1798 and his compositions from this time may well have been written for the Portuguese chapel. Wherever they were performed, such pieces as his settings for double choir of 'Deus majestatis

---

[37] Samuel Wesley, *Missa de Spiritu Sancto*, ed. F. Routh (London, 1997). See also P. Olleson, 'Spirit Voices', *Musical Times*, 138 (September 1977), 4–10, revised and expanded as 'Samuel Wesley and the *Missa de Spiritu Sancto*', *Recusant History*, 24 (1999), 309–19.
[38] For Novello's life and career, see M.C. Clarke, *The Life and Labours of Vincent Novello* (London, 1864); R. Hughes, ed., *A Mozart Pilgrimage: Being the Travel Diaries of Vincent and Mary Novello in the Year 1829* (London, 1955); M. Hurd, *Vincent Novello – and Company* (London, 1981).

intonuit' (1799) and 'Dixit Dominus' (1800)[39] point to the existence at this time of at least one choir capable of singing complex polyphony in up to eight parts, and look forward to 'In exitu Israel' (1810), Wesley's most celebrated work to a Latin text.

The best evidence of the repertory of the Portuguese chapel in the first decade of the nineteenth century, however, is provided by Vincent Novello's first publication, the two-volume *A Collection of Sacred Music as performed at the Royal Portuguese Chapel in London* (1811). As its title implied, this was – like the earlier Webbe volumes – largely a compendium of existing repertory. Also like the earlier Webbe volumes, it was published by subscription, and the large number of subscribers (301, subscribing for 472 copies) and the lavishness of production indicates the strength of demand for such a work. As Novello explained in his introduction:

> Most of the following Pieces were written at different intervals for the sole use of the Portuguese Chapel and without any view to future Publication; but from their having been found not ill adapted to the Powers of a small Choir and more particularly in consequence of the very great scarcity of similar productions, so many applications were made from Persons who were desirous of possessing Copies, that I at last resolved to alter my original intention.

In addition to his own compositions, which he implied were those in the current repertoire of the Portuguese chapel, Novello included a number of adaptations from the music of other composers, beginning a trend that he would continue in later publications:

> In order to afford Variety (by contrast with the simplicity of my own little compositions) & at the same time to give real value to the Collection, I have selected and inserted some of the most approved pieces from the masterly productions of Mozart, Haydn, Durante. Several of these, however, in their original state were so very long that it would have been impossible to have performed them, without extending the duration of the service to an unusual and inconvenient length. As the only alternative therefore was abridgement, or total omission, I preferred the former, and ventured to curtail and alter some of the movements, so as to reduce them within the customary limits.

In fact, *A Collection of Sacred Music* contained an eclectic mixture of the old and the new: by Novello, both Webbes, Wesley, the continental composers listed in Novello's introduction, and others including J.S. Bach, whose chorale 'Liebster Jesu, wir sind hier' is adapted to form a Tantum ergo. One particular feature of Volume 2 was a 'Selected Mass': a compilation of music by a variety of composers, including Novello himself, Durante, Haydn, Mozart and Pergolesi. Also included in this volume was a new arrangement by Novello of 'Adeste Fideles', for long associated with the Portuguese chapel and generally known as 'the Portuguese hymn'.

The publication of Novello's *A Collection of Sacred Music* was a major landmark: the first collection of music specifically associated with the Portuguese chapel, and also Novello's first venture into music publishing.

---

[39]   Included on ASV CD GAU 157.

THE LONDON ROMAN CATHOLIC EMBASSY CHAPELS   115

Following its evident success, Novello rapidly expanded his publishing ventures with subsequent volumes of Roman Catholic service music which included *Twelve Easy Masses* (3 vols, 1816), *A Collection of Motetts for the Offertory* [1822?], *The Evening Service* (1822), masses by Mozart and Haydn, church music by Purcell and selections from music in the Fitzwilliam Museum, Cambridge.[40]

Further information on the Portuguese chapel and its operation in the early nineteenth century is found in the large group of over 170 letters that Wesley wrote to Novello between May 1811 and the end of 1825 and which makes up a large part of his professional and social correspondence. It seems likely that the beginning of the correspondence – of which only Wesley's half has survived – coincided with or closely followed Wesley's appointment as Novello's assistant at the Portuguese chapel and was in some way connected with it; it extended up to and beyond Novello's resignation from the chapel in April 1824. The letters are exceptionally wide-ranging in their subject matter and cover a good deal more than Portuguese chapel affairs, but contain much informal discussion of chapel business: the music to be performed (which included on occasion masses by Haydn and Mozart), reports on the outcomes of services undertaken by Wesley in Novello's absence, and Wesley's comments, not invariably respectful, on the chaplains and other staff of the chapel. Extracts from two letters will convey some of the character of the correspondence as a whole. On 9 July 1814, Wesley reported on High Mass on the previous day, when he had been deputizing for Novello.

> I mounted Guard, selon ma Promesse for you yesterday.– We could not get up any thing very magnificent, because your Honour's Worship & Glory had omitted to leave the Key of your Bum-Fiddle Box.– We therefore determined upon Webbe's grand Chromatic Mass in G Major, which was accordingly carried to Execution.– Little Prina, however, in his Zeal for the good of the Church, would resolve (in Spite of my Veto) to run to your House for the Key, which he did, & brought it, but we had done with the Gloria first, (I think) & your Brother judiciously observed that it were better to do what was easy with a *small* Choir (as was the Fact) than risk the spoiling excellent Music requiring a large one.–[41]

The ironic reference to Webbe's 'grand Chromatic Mass in G' is presumably to the notably diatonic work in Webbe's 1785 volume. On another similar occasion in January 1816, Wesley reported:

> We cooked the Hash yesterday as well as we could without you, & I think the Mass went very well: we had Ricci's Kyrie, Gloria, Sanctus & Agnus, & the selected Credo, & Roman Domine... . The Feast was "of the Name of Jesus," & Turle & Prina sang "O Jesu Pastor bone," that fine treacly Lollypop of old Webbe, but it had quite a ravishing Effect, upon the *Ladies* especially.[42]

---

[40]   Hurd, *Vincent Novello – and Company*, pp. 23–8.
[41]   Wesley to Novello, 9 July 1814 (GB-Lbl Add. MS 11729, f. 66). For Wesley's letters to Novello, see P. Olleson (ed.), *The Letters of Samuel Wesley: Professional and Social Correspondence, 1797–1837* (Oxford, forthcoming).
[42]   Wesley to Novello, [15 January 1816] (GB-Lbl Add. MS 11729, f. 127).

116 MUSIC IN EIGHTEENTH-CENTURY BRITAIN

Among many other points of interest, the Wesley letters contain evidence of the further decline of plainchant, despite the best efforts of Wesley and Novello to promote it. The depth of commitment to plainchant of Wesley, Novello, and a group of fellow-enthusiasts who included the eminent Roman Catholic lawyer Charles Butler (1750–1832) and the wealthy architect and antiquarian Joseph Gwilt (1784–1863) can be seen in the discussion, in the letters of 1811–12, of plans for the publication of a volume of plainchant harmonisations, to include 'all the Introits, Tracts, Offertories, Post Communions, Antiphons & Hymns'.[43] This ambitious scheme was to have been underwritten by Gwilt, but the scheme eventually came to nothing, partly at least because of the difficulties caused by discrepancies between the various books of chant in use in London at the time.[44] A little later, in the context of a discussion of his poor prospects of gaining a good fee for the sale of the copyright of one of his own plainsong harmonizations, Wesley commented: 'As the Gregorian is beginning to be proscribed *by the Clergy themselves*, it is plainly an unfavourable Epoch to reckon upon its Encouragement, even when presented with florid Advantages.'[45] The precise background to this remark is not clear, but Wesley's reference later in the same letter to 'the sudden & silly Revolution taking Place in your Choir' seems to point to a move within the Portuguese chapel towards the jettisoning of plainchant in favour of polyphonic settings, especially when taken in conjunction with his postscript, parodying the Magnificat antiphon for the fifth Sunday after Epiphany:

> Scrape together all the Gregorian Masses & Anthems, & bundle them all up for a good Bonfire on the 5th of November, but make a correct Copy on vellum Paper of all Webbe's & David Perez's Church Music, together with all other Pieces for divine Service by Portugueze authors, who have uniformly & happily defied the hacknied Rules of Counterpoint adopted by Handel, Haydn, Mozart & such old fashioned tight-laced Pedants.

Voices like those of Wesley and Novello were no doubt in the minority, however, and the overwhelming tendency was towards the further reduction of the amount of plainchant in the service, even when presented with 'florid advantages'. By 1820, Charles Butler, while commenting approvingly on performances at Roman Catholic chapels of masses by Haydn, Mozart and others, felt the need to put on record his 'decided wish that the ancient Gregorian song was restored to its pristine honours'.

> Sacred music in the modern Italian style is more pleasing; but it is little calculated to promote devotion, the only legitimate object of music composed for the church.– *There*, let that music, and that music only be performed, which is, at once, simple, and solemn, and which all can feel, and in which most can join. Let it be strictly confined to pure melody; let the congregation be taught to sing it in exact unison, and with subdued voices; let the accompaniment be full and chaste, never overwhelm the voice; and, if it can be managed, in chaunting the psalms, let the trebles and tenors sing alternately... . And let it be

---

[43] Wesley to Novello, 11 November [1811] (GB-Lbl Add. MS 11729, f. 10).
[44] Wesley to Novello, 27 June [1812] (GB-Lbl Add. MS 11729, f. 94).
[45] Wesley to Novello, 5 December [1812] (GB-Lbl Add. MS 11729, f. 41).

THE LONDON ROMAN CATHOLIC EMBASSY CHAPELS

accompanied by a Novello:– A service, thus performed, will excite the finest feelings of piety, promote rational devotion, and, in time, equally satisfy the scientific and the unlearned.[46]

Three years later, the anonymous reviewer of Novello's *Evening Service* was recording that the only portions of plainchant retained in the mass were 'the parts sung by the priest at the altar, and the responsiones': 'These Mr Novello has endeavoured to preserve as long as possible, by arranging them for six voices, and giving them the rich and harmonious effect required by the admirers of the modern school, and he has published them in a seventh book of motets.' At Vespers, however, 'the *chants* for the psalms, and the Gregorian hymns, have stood their ground hitherto against all attempts to supersede them. How long this may be the case, it is not easy to calculate, but Mr Novello has done all in his power to preserve them for the admirers of these old melodies, by forming them into a complete collection.'[47]

In fact by the second decade of the century, if not before, the elaborate music of the three main Catholic chapels had turned them into fashionable places of resort. Novello's eldest daughter Mary recorded in her biography of her father how 'it became a fashion to hear the service at the Portuguese chapel; and South Street, on a Sunday, was thronged with carriages waiting outside, while their owners crowded to suffocation the small, taper-lighted space within.'[48] Later, in her autobiography, she commented how her father's organ playing 'attained such renown that it attracted numerous persons, even among the nobility, whose carriages waited for them outside while they lingered to the end of the service, and after; for it was playfully said that his "voluntaries" – intended to "play out" the congregation – on the contrary, kept them in, listening to the last note.'[49]

Meanwhile, the Bavarian chapel became known as 'the shilling opera' from its practice of featuring some of the leading Italian opera singers at its services and charging for admission to its galleries. One notable occasion there must have been in 1818, when the soloists in a performance of a mass by Manuel Garcia (1775–1832) included Garcia himself and Giuseppe Naldi (1770–1820). These two were the stars of the opera house, to be seen in the evenings on the stage of Covent Garden as the Almaviva and Figaro in the first London performances of Rossini's *Il barbiere di Siviglia*.

With the closure of the Portuguese chapel in late 1829 a long tradition came to an end. The embassy chapels had originally developed to provide ways in which London Catholics could worship without falling foul of the penal laws, and the three major chapels had over time developed substantial music traditions. Following the Relief Acts of 1778 and 1791 the Bavarian and Sardinian chapels in turn became public places of worship, leaving the

---

[46] Butler, *Historical Memoirs of the English, Irish and Scottish Catholics*, vol. 2, p. 359.
[47] Review of *The Evening Service*, *QMMR*, 5 (1823), 206.
[48] Clarke, *The Life and Labours of Vincent Novello*, p. 4.
[49] M.C. Clarke, *My Long Life: an Autobiographic Sketch* (London, 1896), p. 11.

Portuguese chapel as the only remaining embassy chapel in the strict sense after 1798. In view of the radically altered situation following emancipation, it is perhaps surprising that the Portuguese chapel remained in operation for as long as it did. Any explanation for its continued existence must be speculative, but part of the answer may lie in the prestige of the musical tradition that had been built up by Webbe and then continued by Novello; another may be in the personal role played by William Victor Fryer (1768–1844), the principal chaplain, a close personal friend of Novello, the dedicatee of his *A Collection of Sacred Music*, and godfather to several of his children.[50] Whatever was the case, it is peculiarly appropriate that the final work to be heard at the chapel before its closure was Mozart's Requiem, and we can see its performance in November 1829 as being as much a requiem for the passing of an era as for Mozart's sister, whose death the performance commemorated.

---

[50]   Clarke, *My Long Life*, pp. 10–11.

Part 2
Genre and Repertoire

CHAPTER FIVE

Italian Violoncellists and some Violoncello Solos Published in Eighteenth-Century Britain

Lowell Lindgren

In 1824, the anonymous author of 'On the Rise and Progress of the Violoncello' began with a stirring affirmation: 'The violoncello has been rising since the beginning of the last century into estimation, and may now be said to enjoy an almost equal reputation with the violin as a concerto instrument, and as an accompaniment its merits as well as its character are far higher.' The author then devoted a page to stringing, a page to general technical advice and eighteen pages to career summaries of more than eighty 'professors' who 'stood pre-eminently high in their performance' during the years 1725–1824.[1] He mentioned British engagements for only ten of these 'professors', but he reserved his highest praise for a contemporary Briton, Robert Lindley (b. Rotherham 1776, d. London 1855).

> As a violoncellist, Lindley perhaps can overcome greater difficulties than any performer that ever lived – and as an accompanist, in point of knowledge and execution, he is second to none. His tone is rich, powerful, and sweet, and his upper notes are most beautiful. His concertos are peculiar, and are suited to every species of audience. He introduces, amid most extraordinary difficulties, with a quaint yet elegant humour, popular old airs, and plays them in a style of characteristic simplicity. He is enjoying all the honours and emoluments such high attainments invariably procure. There is no concert of any note, and no festival at which Lindley is not a prominent attraction.[2]

In 1794, Lindley 'succeeded Sperati as principal violoncello at the opera'.[3] Sperati is the last of the twenty-nine Italians listed in Table 5.1a (pp. 137–48). During the eighteenth century they had been the most prominent cellists in Britain, and were presumably praised by contemporaries – as Lindley was – for technical agility, tone quality and distinctive compositions. Unfortunately, Charles Burney is the only contemporary who critically evaluated and compared

---

[1] *The Quarterly Musical Magazine and Review*, 6 (1824), 351–63 and 475–82. In his text, he rarely cites his source. He mentions Burney several times, but his main source was clearly E.L. Gerber, *Historisch–biographisches Lexicon der Tonkünstler* (Leipzig: J.G.I. Breitkopf, 1790–92). Gerber first worked professionally as a cellist, and he wrote three concertos for the instrument, according to van der Straeten, *History of the Violoncello*, pp. 189–90. When a complete citation for a source is given in Table 5.1 (pp. 136–49), an abbreviated version is given in these notes.

[2] 'On the Rise and Progress of the Violoncello', p. 480. The author had already placed Lindley above all others on p. 353, and a frank discussion of his twenty-two-year-old son ends the article on p. 482: 'W[illiam] Lindley is, most unfortunately, extremely nervous, arising from a weak state of health, and he therefore plays in public under great disadvantages. It is to be hoped that he will recover his health and with it his nerve. What he can do in private is most extraordinary.'

[3] Ibid., p. 479.

122 MUSIC IN EIGHTEENTH-CENTURY BRITAIN

a few of them in print. His pithy comments, found in *A General History of Music* (1789), are cited in Table 5.1a, even though they may sometimes tell less about a cellist's abilities than about Burney's inclination to favour a new fashion and deride whatever preceded it.

The first and most notable predecessor for Table 5.1 is found in Pohl's *Mozart und Haydn in London* (1867; vol. 2, p. 371). His table is no more than a chronological list of the surnames of cellists in London between 1750 and 1792 together with the year of their public debut. It is a far from perfect list, yet it provides an excellent starting point, for it reflects Pohl's careful search through newspapers and periodicals at the British Museum in 1863–6.[4] Another notable predecessor is van der Straeten's *History of the Violoncello* (1914), in which each cellist is placed in the chapter concerning his country of origin, even when he mainly worked elsewhere. On his title-page, van der Straeten claimed that his volume was 'the result of thirty years' research', and he seems to have collected (somewhat uncritically) and then summarized all that was known to him concerning the instrument and its practitioners. In the twenty-six-page chapter concerning England, for example, he provides information about one bass violinist and eleven cellists, then discusses two princes of Wales who were cellists: Frederic Lewis (1707–51)[5] and George Frederic August (1762–1830), who became George IV in 1820.[6] He continues by summarizing the careers of three more cellists and the contents of the first nine tutors he had found, published in 1745/46–*c*.1800. He ends by discussing or at least mentioning thirty more cellists, the first of whom is Robert Lindley. Since James Cervetto is the only performer discussed in both van der Straeten and Table 5.1 below, his information about forty-six other Englishmen appropriately complements the data given here.

---

[4] Pohl told of his search through 'the rich collection of English journals in the British Museum' ('der reichen Sammlung englischer Zeitschriften im British-Museum') in his introduction, then listed those he saw in his bibliography (*Haydn und Mozart in London*, vol. 1, p. v and vol. 2, p. viii).

[5] In 1733, Philippe Mercier painted three versions of 'A Music Party', in which Prince Frederick plays a cello solo with intense concentration. Two demure sisters play the continuo part on the harpsichord and mandolin, while a third sister looks at the viewer, not at the open book on her lap. The version in the National Gallery has been reproduced in many places, for example in van der Straeten, plate 34. All three versions are briefly discussed in M. De-la-Noy, *The King who Never Was: The Story of Frederick, Prince of Wales* (London & Chester Springs, PA, 1996), pp. 107–8 (see also ill. 6), and in *Handel: A Celebration of his Life and Times, 1685–1759*, ed. J. Simon (London, 1985), no. 112 (and colour plate facing p. 152). According to the entry for 3 August 1732 in Egmont, *Diary*, vol. 1, p. 290, the twenty-five-year-old prince was, as 'an amusement', 'learning the bass–viol[in!], for he could not always be in company ... He said he hoped soon to play well enough to be admitted of my concert'. Egmont must have heard him play before 5 November 1733, when he 'complimented ... him on his great progress in playing on the bass viol[in!]' (ibid., vol. 1, p. 412).

[6] His study with and fondness for the 'fire and brilliancy' of John Crosdill (b. London 1755, d. Escrick, Yorks., 1825), his appreciation for the 'sweetness and mildness' of James Cervetto (Table 5.1a, no. 24) and his delight in singing made him 'not only a musician amongst princes, but a prince amongst musicians', according to Robert Huish, *Memoirs of George the Fourth* (London, 1831), vol. 1, pp. 45–6.

Plate 5.1 The first known depiction of a violoncello in eighteenth-century Britain. Designed by Tempest and engraved by John Smith (1702)

124 MUSIC IN EIGHTEENTH-CENTURY BRITAIN

Tables 5.1 and 5.2 constitute the chief outcome of this foray into what at first seemed a clearly defined topic, represented by the title of this article. The following introduction to the tables will deal with three problematic words in the title: 'Italian', 'violoncello' and 'solo'. The other main words are unproblematic: 'published' means that the manuscript sources copied or extant in Britain are not discussed in this article;[7] 'eighteenth century' refers to 1701–1800; and 'Britain' includes England, Ireland, Scotland and Wales. All but Wales are represented in this article.

'Italian'

An 'Italian' in Table 5.1 is anyone known to have been born in Italy, to have had a father born there, or suspected to have had Italian ancestry. Table 5.1a includes sixteen cellists whose birthplace is known. Thirteen were born in Italy, but at least two of them – Haym (no. 1) and Chelleri (no. 11; cf. Keller) – must have had a father or grandfather who was born in Germany. Three were born to Italian fathers who lived outside Italy: Dall'Abaco (no. 17), whose father, Evaristo Felice, lived in Munich; Alexis Magito Jun. (no. 23), whose father worked in The Hague; and James Cervetto (no. 24), whose father was employed as a cellist in London (no. 13).

The other thirteen cellists on Table 5.1a were presumably Italian. The surnames for eleven of them end with a vowel. The other two were not known by their surnames (Goodsens and Chaboud), but rather as 'Signor Francisco' (no. 2) and 'Signor Pietro' (no. 3). Since the latter was trained in Bologna, perhaps he was born in northern Italy. Charles Scola (no. 21) was possibly a son of the Neapolitan musician named Adamo Scola, and may well have been born after his father had settled in London. Siprutini (no. 22) was, according to Leopold Mozart, a Dutch Jew who had travelled to Italy and Spain before coming to London. Because of his surname, it is surmised that his ancestry was Italian. Nothing seems to be known about the pre- or post-British days of a number of these performers, e.g., Pardini, Bocchi, Caruso and Sperati (nos. 6, 9, 20 and 29). It can only be assumed that none of them was a Briton, as Francis Fleming did *c.* 1750: 'that if any person of merit in the musical world should unfortunately have his name end with a consonant, he seldom succeeds; on the contrary, a name that flows with an *ini*, an *ani*, or a *gobioni*, hardly ever fails of making a fortune'. As a result, he 'italianised' his name, at least for one benefit concert in Salisbury, where the printed bills and the advertisement in newspapers listed him as 'Signior Turko Francisco Fleminiani, &c. &c.'. 'His scheme ... succeeded to a miracle; the room was greatly crowded; the people all round Sarum came to the performance; others, who were dying the week before, were brought in litters to hear this famous Italiano'.[8]

---

[7] An article by the author concerning manuscript sources is in preparation.

[8] Fleming, *The Life and Extraordinary Adventures* (see Table 5.1a, no. 18), vol. 2, pp. 91–2, 98–9.

VIOLONCELLISTS AND VIOLONCELLO SOLOS

Britain must have provided a safe haven and financial lure for Italian cellists during the eighteenth century, because most of those listed in Table 5.1a stayed for an extended period. Only five remained for as little as one to three years (nos. 5, 11, 15, 17 and 25), and the first of them was primarily a bass singer, who was hired at the opera house for only one season; he was only incidentally a bass viol(in)ist. The twenty-four others seem to have stayed for a minimum of eight years each. Note that the span of years given for each performer on the table represents the first and last known years of his stay in London. Some cellists may have come earlier than the first year, and many may have stayed later than the second. Ten of them stayed in Britain until death (nos. 1–2, 7–8, 13–14, 16, 21, 24 and 28), while ten others died on the continent. Some of the remaining nine may have died in Britain (nos. 3, 6, 9, 19–20, 22–23, 27 and 29).

'Violoncello'

In 1572, Andrea Amati made the earliest extant cello at Cremona.[9] In 1657, an English musical amateur in Lucca wrote to his brother in London about the predominance of the cello in Italy: 'The instrumental music is much better than I expected. The organ and violin they are masters of, but the bass viol they have not at all in use; and to supply its place they have the bass violin with four strings, and use it as we do the bass viol'.[10] In England, Germany and France the bass violin made relatively slow headway, because refined musicians continued to prize the six-string viol for its soloistic and other capabilities until the middle of the eighteenth century. According to Burney five Italian cellists who began to perform in London around 1739 (Table 5.1a, nos. 13–17) 'brought the violoncello into favour, and made us nice judges of that instrument'.[11] As a result, viol playing must have quickly fallen out of favour. The last great eighteenth-century gamba player in England was Carl Friedrich Abel (b. Cöthen 1723, d. London 1787). In 1789, Burney (b. Shrewsbury 1726, d. London 1814) praised his magnificent achievements, but commented trenchantly upon the instrument, which Burney unequivocally loathed.

> All lovers of Music lamented that he had not in youth attached himself to an instrument more worthy of his genius, taste, and learning, than the viol da gamba, that remnant of the old chest of viols, which, during the last century, was a necessary appendage to a nobleman or gentleman's family throughout Europe, previous to the admission of violins, tenors [= violas], and bases [= cellos and double basses] in a private house or public concert... The tone of the

---

[9] J. Dilworth, 'The Cello: Origins and Evolution', in *The Cambridge Companion to the Cello*, ed. R. Stowell (Cambridge, 1999), p. 7.

[10] Letter of 1 October 1657, written by Thomas Hill and printed in *Familiar Letters which passed between Abraham Hill, Esq., ... and Several Eminent and Ingenious Persons of the Last Century*, ed. anon. (London: W. Johnston, 1767), p. 17. For further evidence, see E. Cowling, *The Cello*, new edn (New York, 1985), pp. 56–7.

[11] *A General History of Music*, vol. 2, p. 1005. Burney was first at London in 1744–51, and he returned there in 1760. Thus the first cellists on Table 5.1a that he heard, or perhaps performed with, would have been nos. 13, 14 and 16.

126   MUSIC IN EIGHTEENTH-CENTURY BRITAIN

instrument will do nothing for itself, and it seems ·with Music as with agriculture, the more barren and ungrateful the soil, the more art is necessary in its cultivation. And the tones of the viol da gamba are radically so crude and nasal, that nothing but the greatest skill and refinement can make them bearable. A human voice of the same quality would be intolerable.[12]

Perhaps a Briton accustomed to bass parts played suavely by viols would have written just as caustically about the strident sound of a cello when the first Italian cellist arrived in England in 1701. This pioneer, as shown on Table 5.1a (p. 137), was a Roman named Haym. In 1694 he was conjecturally the 'Nicola' – just as Amadei (no. 7 on Table 5.1a) was the 'Pippo' – on a list of twenty-four professional 'violoncelli' in the papal city.[13] In 1697, the printed register of teachers at the Seminario Romano identified Haym's instrument as the 'violone', while that of 1699 identified it as the 'violoncello'.[14] A year after his arrival in London, a letter written by the violinist Gasparo Visconti expressed hope that 'il caro Signor Aimi, il nostro caro violoncello', would play at a concert given during the opening of Parliament in 1702.[15]

When it was new, the cello was identified by a bewildering variety of names.[16] By the early eighteenth century, only three alternatives were still common: bass violin in Britain, basse de violon in France, and violone in Italy.[17] In Haym's first two publications, trio sonatas issued by Estienne Roger at Amsterdam in 1703–4, the bass part-books are therefore marked 'violone o leuto'. In his op. 2, the solo parts for the first nine sonatas are labelled 'violino primo' and 'violino secondo', while in the next two works they are marked 'violino solo' and 'violoncello';[18] it seems as if the term 'violoncello' was reserved for a solo part, while 'violone' referred to a continuo part. It seems

---

[12]   Ibid., vol. 2, pp. 1019–20. Early eighteenth-century comments about the difficulty of playing the instrument, made in 1710 by Roger North and in 1715–16 by Dudley Ryder, are cited in J.A. Sadie, 'Handel: In Pursuit of the Viol', *Chelys: The Journal of the Viola da Gamba Society*, 14 (1985), 12.
[13]   Oscar Mischiati, 'Una statistica della musica a Roma nel 1694', *Note d'archivio per la storia musicale*, new ser., 1 (1983), 222.
[14]   Lindgren, 'The Accomplishments of ... Haym', 251.
[15]   Ibid., p. 255. Visconti's letter was addressed to the violinist Nicola Cosimi, who had travelled with Haym to London. The decorative title-page for Cosimi's *Sonate da camera* of 1702 is shown in Plate 5.1, because it is the first known depiction of a cello in eighteenth-century Britain and because it illustrates the transformation of an Italian original by British artists. It was designed by [Pierce?] Tempest and engraved by John Smith. Only two copies are known to survive: one precedes the musical score in B–Bc (T15.093), while the other is a separate folio in GB-Lbl, Department of Prints and Drawings (John Smith, III, folio 33). Tempesti's model was the frontispiece to Corelli's *Sonate a violino e violone o cimbalo*, op. 5 (Rome, 1700). It is noteworthy that in Corelli's frontispiece, designed by Antonio Meloni and engraved by Girolamo Frezza, the angelic cellist is not playing, has no musical score in front of him, is not looking at the viewer, and is placed at the lower right–hand corner. By comparison, the Tempesti/Smith cellist is a focal point of the design.
[16]   See P. Allsop, 'Ensemble Music: In the Chamber and the Orchestra', *The Cambridge Companion to the Cello*, pp. 160–62.
[17]   J. Gunn, *The Theory and Practice of Fingering the Violoncello* (London: Author, *c.* 1793), p. 21. This passage is cited in Cowling, *The Cello*, pp. 57–8.
[18]   Lindgren, 'The Accomplishments of ... Haym', 335–8.

VIOLONCELLISTS AND VIOLONCELLO SOLOS

highly unlikely that Haym's violone part was intended for an instrument other than the violoncello.[19]

When Haym died in 1729, the term 'violoncello' must have still been new enough in Britain to require clarification, for his obituary describes him as 'deservedly famous for divinely touching the *Violoncello*, or *Four-string Base*'.[20] During his career in London, he was at least twice cited as a player of the six-string viol. According to a contract of January 1706, which he signed for the theatrical production of his adaptation of *Camilla*, he promised to play the 'Bass Violl' during its performances (see Table 5.1a, no. 1). When he was hired to serve the Earl of Carnarvon, letters of 1715–18 refer to him as 'Mr Hyems y[t] plays upon the Base Viol' or, more succinctly, a 'Bass', while the lists of servants refer to him as a performer on the cello and violone.[21] While he might have played the viol, or might have played one of the many hybrid instruments fabricated in seventeenth-century Italy,[22] it seems far more likely that the above-cited contract and letter writers were not yet acquainted or familiar with the term violoncello.

The same problem is apparent in ten orchestral lists from between *c.* 1707 and *c.* 1713: the three or four players are five times listed as 'violoncelli', are three times grouped with other 'bases', and are twice named 'bass viols'.[23] The problem still appears in Egmont's diary entries of 1732–3, when he refers to Prince Frederick's learning and playing upon the bass viol, which is surely a mistake for the bass violin or violoncello.[24] Between 1700 and 1740, the bass viol tradition remained alive to varying degrees in northern Europe. In England, some music and a few tutors were published.[25] A notable example is Giovanni [i.e., Johannes] Schenk, *Select Lessons for the Bass-Viol, of Two Parts* (Walsh and Hare, 1703, RISM S 1455; rpt. Walsh, *c.* 1730).[26] This collection had first been published as *La nymphe di Rheno, per due viole di gamba solo*, op. 8

---

[19]   In some cases, 'violone' may well indicate an instrument that has a double bass range. This is the principal point made in A. Planyavsky, *The Baroque Double Bass Violone*, trans. J. Barket (Lanham, MD, and London, 1998). But Corelli's 'violone' was almost certainly a violoncello; see D. Watkin, 'Corelli's Op. 5 Sonatas: *Violino e violone o cimbalo?*', *Early Music*, 24 (1996), 645–63. Watkin provides much intriguing evidence for his main point, namely, that a cello playing the bass part alone should play chords.

[20]   *The Weekly Medley*, 9 August 1729.

[21]   Beeks, 'Handel and Music for the Earl of Carnarvon', pp. 3, 8 and 12.

[22]   They are described in Dilworth, 'The Cello', pp. 12–13.

[23]   *Vice Chamberlain Coke's Papers*; the five are on pp. 31, 127, 151, 158 and 159; the three on pp. 33, 69 and 77; and the two on pp. 119 and 192. 'Bases' is sometimes a comprehensive term, including several instruments; on pp. 151 and 158, where 'violoncelli' are named, 'bassi' refers to double bassists and bassoonists.

[24]   See note 5, above.

[25]   Eleven viol tutors, dated 1603–1722, are listed in A. Simpson, 'A Short-Title List of Printed English Instrumental Tutors up to 1800, held in British Libraries', *RMA Research Chronicle*, 6 (1966), 27–33. The first tutor for the 'bass violin' on Simpson's list (pp. 36–7) was issued in 1754 and reissued in 1756–9. Sadie, 'Handel: In Pursuit of the Viol', 12, asserts that 'new methods and music suitable for the viol were published in a trickle' after 1712; in support of this point, she cites M. Tilmouth, 'A Calendar of References to Music in Newspapers Published in London and the Provinces (1660–1719)', *RMA Research Chronicle*, 1 (1961; rpt. 1968), 40, 55–6, 65, 81 and 99.

[26]   Smith, *A Bibliography* (see Table 5.2a, no. 3, p. 150), no. 136, and Smith and Humphries (S&H on Table 5.2), no. 1333.

128   MUSIC IN EIGHTEENTH-CENTURY BRITAIN

(Amsterdam: Estienne Roger, *c.* 1700; RISM S 1451). In 1737, it was still listed in Le Cène's *Catalogue des livres de musique, imprimés à Amsterdam*, in which the sole category of works for bass instruments is headed 'Pièces pour la viole de gambe'. It includes eighteen works, all by non-Italians, for one or more viols, and, appended near the end, only four works for 'basse de violon' or 'violoncelli'. The only Italians represented are Carlo Passionei (*c.* 1716–22; RISM P 1004–5) and Giorgio Antoniotti (*c.* 1735), whose print consists primarily of works designed (or at least designated) for 'due violoncelli overo due viole di gamba' (see Table 5.1a, no. 18). Britons had, it seems, embraced the 'rise and progress of the violoncello' (to quote the author referred to in the opening paragraph) about three decades earlier than their continental neighbours.

Bass viol and bass violin are remarkably similar terms, and it seems likely that some of the published references to the 'bass viol' during the first quarter of the eighteenth century were slips of the pen. References to solos on viols as well as cellos are therefore included in Table 5.1a. Since viols had apparently disappeared from the Italian musical scene by 1660, it is striking that the two players who were advertised only as gamba players were the Italians Zanoni and Chelleri (nos. 5 and 11), each of whom played only once in public. In the earliest known reference to 'Mr Francisco', he is named as a bass-violist (see no. 2). 'Francisco' is, however, placed among the 'violoncellos' in five operatic documents. The advertisements for concert appearances of 'Signior Francisco' do not name his instrument, but after 1711 'Francisco Goodsens' was a 'bass violin' in the Chapel Royal.[27] 'Signor Pietro' (no. 3) apparently played several instruments very well. He was a bassoonist in the opera orchestra from 1707 until at least 1712, a soloist on the bass viol and German flute at concerts of 1707–19, then a cellist rather than a bassoonist in the last known plan of 1720 for the new Royal Academy of Music.[28]

The first British newspaper to print the name of the novel instrument was apparently *The Daily Courant* of 22 December 1718. It advertised a concert in which 'the Violoncello, Signior Pipo', would accompany 'the small Eccho Flute played by Paisible'; he presumably also accompanied the other flautist and the two violinists named in the notice.[29] In *The Edinburgh Courant* of 13 May 1707, the instrument had earlier been referred to by its alternative English name:

---

    [27] He is listed as a 'Bass Violin in the Chapel' in the index to *Records of English Court Music*, vol. 9, p. 141. In the documents, his instrument is apparently named only on the list of performers for 31 July 1713, where it is identified as a 'violn' (*Records*, vol. 2, p. 115). On this document, his name is preceded by those of the two organists and the one lutanist; so he is clearly placed among the continuo players. He is in the same place on the list for 25 May 1714 (*Records*, vol. 2, p. 117). Thus his 'violn' must have been a bass violin. Sadie, 'Handel: In Pursuit of the Viol', p. 12, relates that 'his Chapel Royal part–books dating from the second decade of the century reveal by their range and character of line that a cello rather than a viol was increasingly preferred'.

    [28] It is not entirely clear why 'Sig' Pietro' was moved from one location to another in this plan. According to Milhous and Hume, 'New Light on Handel and the Royal Academy of Music in 1720', p. 161, 'Pietro was moved from bassoon to violoncello and not replaced at bassoon'.

    [29] Tilmouth, 'A Calendar', p. 104.

VIOLONCELLISTS AND VIOLONCELLO SOLOS

'Ralph Agutter of London, lately come to Edinburgh, ... makes the Violin, Bass Violin, Tenor Violin, the Viol de Gambo [*sic*], the Lute Quiver, the Trumpet Marine, the Harp'.[30] With regard to whether the instrument was a cello or a viol, the most puzzling concert advertisement is probably that of 29 April 1719, which included 'a solo on the Bass Viol and German flute played by Pietro and Signor Pipo'.[31] Since Pietro Chaboud played both of the named instruments, perhaps there were instead 'solo[s] on the Bass Viol and German flute played by Pietro and [accompanied by] Signor Pipo [Amadei]. If the notice indeed refers to a single solo, Pietro must have played the flute while Pippo accompanied him on the bass viol[in?]. Three years later, Amadei was credited with composing and performing a concerto for the bass viol, as will be noted below.

'Solos'

The genre designations on the forty-one title-pages listed in Table 5.2a (pp. 150–55) include twenty-six 'solos', six 'sonatas', five 'duets', and one each for 'sonatinas', 'sonatas or trios', 'lessons or divertimentos' and 'divertiments'. Within nearly every volume of 'solos', the heading for each piece is 'sonata'; thus there is no generic distinction between these two terms. Most of the title-pages specify a single performer for the figured bass part; thirteen name a harpsichord, twelve another cello, eight a 'bass', no. 1 'the Harpsicord or bass Violin', and no. 23 'a Bass or Harpsichord'. The non-specific 'basso continuo' or 'thoroughbass' is given five times (for nos. 3, 8, 14, 30 and 31), and no designation is given for the lower part of no. 7. Two of the collections on Table 5.2a are written for three rather than two performers: no. 5, by Cervetto Sen., is for 'three violoncellos or two violins and a bass', while no. 17, by Galeotti, is for 'two violoncellos with a thorough bass for the harpsichord'. These two collections thus contain trio (rather than solo) sonatas, as indicated by Cervetto's title, *Six sonatas or trios*. The alternative instrumentation specified in his title was undoubtedly placed there in order to boost sales. Treble alternatives for the cello are similarly indicated in the titles of nos. 6, 19, 40 and 41, while a 'fagotto' alternative is named for no. 3 only.

    The overwhelming prevalence of two-part pieces is undoubtedly explained by their eminent suitability for teaching purposes. In lessons, the student could play one part while the teacher played the other. Many of the collections seem to be designed for near-beginners or amateurs. Four prints appealed to such practitioners in their titles: Lanzetti, *Six solos after an easy & elegant taste* (no. 15); Cirri, *Six easy solos* (no. 23); Cervetto Jun., *Twelve divertiments in an easy stile* (no. 29); and Cirri, *Six solos ... in an easy pleasing taste proper for young practitioners* (no. 33). The keys are likewise 'easy' and fashionably 'galant'. Each collection primarily or exclusively utilizes major keys

---

[30]   Ibid., printed on the insert labelled 'Author's note on the second printing'.
[31]   Ibid., p. 106.

130   MUSIC IN EIGHTEENTH-CENTURY BRITAIN

with few sharps or flats. In order of popularity, they are C, D, G, F, A and B flat. The key of A minor is found slightly less frequently than B flat major. Other minor keys were less than half as frequent as A; in descending order of frequency, they are D, G, C and E minor.

The types of difficulty found in a solo changed as the favoured texture moved away from two motivically interrelated parts, which are often found in prints of 1725–50, to two sharply contrasting parts. The latter texture, which consists of a graceful melodic line plus a repeated-note accompaniment, is close to ubiquitous in works from 1750 to 1800.[32] Only six collections preserved the contrapuntal texture, the balance between major and minor (in which two or three of the six works are in minor keys),[33] and the four-movement structure (slow – fast – slow – fast) of the Baroque church sonata. They were all issued in the 1730s and 1740s: Marcello (1732), Galliard (1733; see Table 5.2c), Merci (c. 1735), Porpora/Costanza (1745; see Table 5.2b), Geminiani (1747) and Bononcini &c. (1748). In the vast majority of the collections, each piece has three movements; at least two of them are in binary form, and the last is typically a minuet. The clear focus is on the lyrical character of the top part, which is illustrated in most prints included in Table 5.2a, for example, Lanzetti (1737), Cervetto Sen. (1748, 1750 and 1761), Pasqualino de Marzis (1748 and 1751), Galeotti (1763 and 1766), and Siprutini (two of 1764). Lyricism is likewise the focus of the one- and two-movement duets composed by Cocchi (1764) and Giordani (1780) respectively.

The above comments indicate that the cello solos printed in eighteenth-century Britain were aimed at the musical amateur, so that tuneful melodies and a lack of textural complexities were considered cardinal virtues. Nevertheless, some composers manifested their compositional skills by writing in learned textures. The trios by Cervetto Sen. (c. 1741) and Galeotti (1763) provide excellent examples, and many prints have at least one sonata that is distinctively difficult. Difficulties abound in the first collection of solos by Pasqualino de Marzis (1748); but many of the compositional features of these works may not be his own, because he seems to have appropriated at least one-and-a-half of the six works from other composers (see Table 5.2a, no. 9, p. 152). Caporale's six solos provide a far greater problem in terms of attribution, because five of them

---

[32]   This change from Baroque to pre-Classic texture has been discussed many times. See, for example, W.S. Newman, *The Sonata in the Baroque Era*, 3rd edition (New York, 1972), and Newman, *The Sonata in the Classic Era*, 2nd edition (New York, 1972). Some of the prints listed on Table 5.2 are among the many mentioned in Newman's books and in Cowling, *The Cello*, pp. 82–127. The stylistic differences between the Italian Baroque and pre–Classic cello sonatas in one private collection are discussed in L. Lindgren, 'Count Rudolf Franz Erwein von Schönborn (1677–1754) and the Italian Sonatas for Violoncello in His Collection at Wiesentheid', *Relazioni musicali tra Italia e Germania nell'età barocca*, Atti del VI Convegno internazionale sulla musica italiana nei secoli XVII–XVIII, Loveno di Menaggio (Como), 11–13 luglio 1995, ed. A. Colzani, N. Dubowy, A. Luppi and M. Padoan (Como, 1997), pp. 270–90.

[33]   The only print with a preponderance of minor keys is the earliest on Table 5.2, that is, Table 5.2b, no. 1 (1720). Since its solo part was written for the violin rather than the cello, it is not discussed in this article. It should nevertheless be noted that its twelve solos include eight in the minor key, which extend from four flats to three sharps (F, C, D, D, A, B, B, F sharp), and four in the major, extending from four flats to four sharps (A flat, B flat, A, E).

VIOLONCELLISTS AND VIOLONCELLO SOLOS

are identical to violin sonatas by Niccolò Pasquali. The cello and violin versions were both published in 1746 (see Table 5.2a, no. 7, p. 151).[34] Pasquali and his brother had first performed in London a year earlier (see Table 5.1a, no. 19). By the time Caporale's solos were published, Caporale and the Pasquali brothers had apparently left London for Dublin (see Table 5.1a, no. 16). Galliard implies this in his dedication of *XII solos for the violoncello, VI of Sig' Caporale & VI compos'd by M' Galliard*, to the Prince of Wales: 'The Work which I now humbly offer to your *Royal Highness's* acceptance will suffer by the loss of *Sig' Caporale*, who was engaged with me in the design, and whose Excellent performance wou'd have made it the more Entertaining.' If Pasquali did compose these works, he presumably played them at London in 1745, and they could not have been published under Caporale's name in 1746. But if anyone unscrupulous had obtained a copy of Caporale's works in 1745, he might have easily sold them to a Parisian publisher as new creations by Pasquali. This problem remains unresolved.

Newspaper advertisements for most (but far from all) of the concerts given in eighteenth-century London are cited in summary form in *The London Stage, 1660–1800*. Most (but not all) of these entries supply information on the date of performance, the genre and the player.[35] The first advertised genre for the cello was – rather surprisingly – a concerto. It was played on 14 March 1722, at the concert given in the Drury Lane Theatre for the benefit of the violinist Stefano Carbonelli. In addition to songs, the programme included two solos and nine concertos, one of which was a 'Concerto on Bass Viol[in?] composed and performed by Pippo'.[36] Since Amadei had been a professional cellist from *c.* 1685, 'Bass Viol' is presumably an error. If, as seems likely, he played a solo in 1722,[37] then no cello concerto was heard until 11 February 1736, when Caporale's benefit concert included 'two solos and two concertos on Violoncello by Carporali [*sic*]'.[38] Haym conjecturally played cello solos shortly after his arrival at London in 1701,[39] but the first advertised 'solo' was played at Hickford's on 10 May 1732, when a concert organized by Mr and Mrs De Fesch included 'a Solo, composed, and perform'd by Mr St. Helene, on the Bass Viol,

---

[34] A privilege for Pasquali's print was obtained on 17 May 1746; see A. Devriès, *Édition et commerce de la musique gravée a Paris dans la première moitié du XVIIIe siècle: Les Boivin, Les LeClerc* (Geneva, 1976), p. 235.

[35] Throughout this article, I have relied upon entries in *The London Stage*. They provide a brief summation of the notice in a single newspaper and do not divulge either the differences between various papers or the changes made in successive advertisements for an event. Judith Milhous and Robert Hume are currently re-editing *The London Stage*, part 2 (1700–29), and they have generously given a pre-publication copy of the first section (1700–11) to major libraries, such as The Harvard University Theatre Collection and GB-Ob. Their addenda and corrigenda are bountiful, and exceedingly useful to scholars.

[36] *London Stage*, part 2, p. 668.

[37] No concerto written by him is known. His only extant sonata has been published in Lindgren, 'Count Rudolf Franz Erwein von Schönborn', pp. 295–8.

[38] *London Stage*, part 3, p. 551.

[39] Two cello sonatas that he wrote at Rome in the 1690s are extant in manuscript; they will be published in my forthcoming edition of his instrumental music for A-R Editions.

132   MUSIC IN EIGHTEENTH-CENTURY BRITAIN

another on the Violoncello, the first Time of his performing in Publick'.[40] Since a Frenchman may well have mastered both the bass viol and cello, the content of this notice is plausible.

Advertisements from the eighteenth century utilize the words 'solo' and 'concerto' to the near exclusion of other generic terms. Thus the word sonata appears only for three performances given by Jean-Pierre Duport in 1770.[41] 'Solos' were played at about forty-five events recorded in *The London Stage*. The seventeen 'soloists' included eight of the twenty-nine Italian cellists listed in Table 5.1a: Pasqualino de Marzis (1733), Lanzetti (1733–54), Caporale (1733–41), Pasquali Jun. (1745), Caruso (1756), Siprutini (1762), Cirri (1764–74) and Cervetto Jun. (1777). Another three who played 'solos' were French: St. Helene (1732), Duport (1770–72) and Jean-Baptiste Janson (1772). The remaining six were British: John Biggs (1736), Mr Jones (1748), Benjamin Hallet (1751–2), Stephen or William Paxton (1761–5), John Crosdill (1770–75) and Robert Mason (1791).

Cello 'concertos' must have been significantly more attractive than 'solos', since they were heard at about seventy-five events listed in *The London Stage*. The seventeen cellists included seven Italians: Amadei (1722), Caporale (1736–44), Cervetto Sen. (1742–63), Pasqualino (1753–59), Cervetto Jun. (1769–79), Siprutini (1762–65) and Cirri (1764–72). The other ten who played concertos were the Frenchmen Duport (1770–72) and Janson (1772), the German Johann Baptist Mara (1787–8), and the Englishmen John Gordon (1744–62), Jones (1750–52), an unidentified Paxton (1764–75), Crosdill (1773–84), Mason (1786–92), Robert Lindley (1792–4) and Charles Ashley (1793–1800).[42]

Many sources other than *The London Stage* need to be consulted in order to complete the picture of cellists and their repertoire in eighteenth-century Britain; others that have been utilized for Table 5.1 are cited in its bibliography.[43] If references to the solos and concertos mentioned in such sources are added to those found in *The London Stage*, the names of the two Italians – Bocchi and Magito – who are known to have played only outside London could be added to the above list of 'soloists'. But the primary alterations would affect the last three decades of the century. The most notable among them would be a marked increase in the number of British cellists and in the number of solo and concerto performances given by them, especially by Crosdill, Lindley and Cervetto Jun. Twenty-seven of the twenty-nine Italian cellists listed in Table 5.1a had arrived by 1764, and many British and a few French played the leading role after

---

[40]   Ibid., part 3, p. 217.

[41]   Ibid., part 4, pp. 1463, 1465 and 1474.

[42]   For specific dates and descriptions of these events, see the entry for each cellist in the index volume for *The London Stage*.

[43]   Four of them are· Boydell, *A Dublin Musical Calendar*; James, 'Concert Life in Eighteenth–Century Bath'; McVeigh, 'The Professional Concert and Rival Subscription Series in London, 1783–93'; and Robbins Landon, *Haydn: Chronicle and Works. Haydn in London, 1791–1795*. A fifth source is J. Burchell, *Polite or Commercial Concerts? Concert Management and Orchestral Repertoire in Edinburgh, Bath, Oxford, Manchester and Newcastle, 1730–1799* (New York and London, 1996).

c. 1770. The primary significance of Italian cellists is that they were the pioneers who – as Burney stated – introduced the British to the cello and to the music they had written for it.

The 'concerto' deserves special attention, because it was the genre most frequently named in the advertisements for solo appearances by cellists in 1736–1800, and it remained the leading genre thereafter. This is made clear by the author of the 1824 article that was cited at the beginning of this survey. He rejoiced in the 'reputation' of the violoncello 'as a concerto instrument', praised its insuperable 'merits as well as its character' in a supporting role, and defined the 'peculiar' character of Lindley's concertos. As a supporting instrument, it had always flourished. While newspaper advertisements of 1718–28 mention cellists who accompanied violinists or flautists, those of 1790–1800 mention those who accompanied singers, presumably with a solo or an obbligato part.[44]

The first known publication of solo cello music by a British composer is in this popular genre: John Garth's *Six Concertos, for the violoncello, with four violins, one alto viola, and basso ripieno*, dedicated to his Royal Highness, the Duke of York (London: John Johnson, J. Walsh and T. Smith, 1760).[45] Like his father (Frederick Louis, Prince of Wales), the dedicatee, Edward August (1739–67), played the cello;[46] and he employed the Italian cellist Zappa between *c.* 1764 and 1767 (see Table 5.1a, no. 27, p. 147).[47] Even though there are seven part-books (two were printed for each of the violin parts), the texture is that of a quartet, because the viola plays during the ritornellos, but is silent (or perhaps doubles the bass line) while the soloist is playing.[48]

No Italian composer published works entitled concertos in Britain until Gianbattisa Cirri did so in his op. 14 of *c.* 1775 (Table 5.2b, no. 4, p. 156). His title correctly describes their texture: *Six concertos in four parts, for the violoncello obligato with two violins and a bass*. In solo passages, the obbligato cello plays passage work that, as in Garth's works, is relatively simple (the solo passages in Haydn's cello concertos are, in comparison, fiendishly difficult). About a decade earlier, a collection of trio sonatas by Francesco Uttini (Table 5.2b, no. 3, p. 156) had included one 'sonata' with the quartet texture

---

[44] See, for example, the entries for Amadei in 1718–19 (*London Stage*, part 2, pp. 495 and 536), Pardini in 1724–8 (part 2, pp. 770, 912 and 967), Mason in 1790–93 (part 5, pp. 1229, 1236, 1329, etc.) and Ashley in 1791–1800 (part 5, pp. 1333, 1435, 1521, etc.). The first entry concerning Pardini implies that he served as accompanist for the named soloists; he might have played a solo in addition to accompanying soloists at all three of his benefit concerts.

[45] Smith and Humphries, *A Bibliography ... Walsh*, no. 686, and RISM G 432. This or another edition of the collection was engraved by William Clark and published in Edinburgh by Robert Bremner, then reissued *c.* 1780 in London by Welcker (RISM G 433).

[46] See *Music in Britain: The Eighteenth Century*, ed. H. Diack Johnstone and R. Fiske (Oxford, 1990), p. 317, for an occasion in 1761 when Sir William Herschel played the violin and the duke played the cello. Charles Avison and John Garth were also present, so one or both of them might have played the thorough bass on the harpsichord.

[47] Frederick's third son, William Henry (1743–1805), Duke of Gloucester, apparently followed in the footsteps of an elder brother and his father, since the cellist Cirri was his teacher from *c.* 1665 to *c.* 1775 (see Table 5.2a, nos. 23 and 32).

[48] I have seen only no. 2 in B flat major and no. 5 in D minor, as edited by Gerald Finzi for Hinrichsen Edition (1954 and s.d.).

134   MUSIC IN EIGHTEENTH-CENTURY BRITAIN

found in Cirri's concertos. The scoring discussed above requires only four or five players: one soloist accompanied by two violins, a continuo player and sometimes (as in Garth's case) a filler part in the viola. This is the characteristic texture of Italian cello concertos of the eighteenth century. It is well illustrated by the sinfonias for cello collected by Count Schönborn at Wiesentheid; since only one part-book is extant for any instrumental part in these pieces, they were presumably played as chamber rather than orchestral music.[49] A similar scoring might have been employed for J.C. Bach's 'New Concerto for two *Violins*, and a *Violoncello*', which was played during the performance of *Alexander's Feast* at the King's Theatre on 31 March 1775.[50]

The first Italian works published in Britain that may have utilized this concerto texture were by Porpora and Costanza (Table 5.2b, no.2). The title-page of the print implies that they might be scored like the concertos discussed above: *Six sonatas for two violoncellos and two violins with a thorough bass for the harpsichord.* According to RISM P 5123, both of the violin parts survive at D-Mbs. I have seen neither this copy nor the one at GB-Lam, but have seen the copies at GB-Lbl, where the three part-books marked 'violino' are identical, and US-Wc, which has only one 'violino' part book. The remaining part book in both libraries is labeled 'violoncello obligato col suo basso'. In 1980, Klaus Stahmer edited Sonata V from the copy in GB-Lbl, and in his preface he noted that the three extant parts provide a 'harmonic texture not ... lacking completeness' and that the second violin part was probably never published, so that 'the whole remained a torso'. Since Walsh does not attribute individual pieces to either composer, Stahmer shrewdly lists both of them as composers of the piece he edited. Perhaps at least one of the four extant copies of the print does have a second violin part. If not, then a manuscript copy of it may materialize. Sonatas III and IV (but not Sonata V) in this print do survive in a manuscript at US-NYp JOG 72–29.v.29, ff. 1–12 and 17–22. The former is entitled 'Sonata di Violoncello Solo con V.V. e Basso Del Sig[r] Nicolò Porpora', and its score for solo cello and bass is supplemented by parts for violin 1, violin 2 and bass. The latter is entitled 'Sinfonia di Violongello con V.V. e Basso Del Sig[r] Nicolò Porpora'; it has the two-part score, but no parts.

During the eighteenth century, at least twenty-nine Italian cellists performed in Britain, and at least forty-one prints containing Italian cello solos and three prints containing Italian cello concertos were published. Only the first publication, dated 1725, included pieces for the old viola da gamba as well as the new violoncello. The novel instrument was a fashionable commodity in eighteenth-century Britain. This point is illustrated by Frederick, Prince of Wales, who began to play it in 1732, by his second and third sons, the dukes of York and Gloucester, who began to play it in the 1760s, and by his grandson,

---

[49]   Lindgren, 'Count Rudolf Franz Erwein von Schönborn', p. 271.
[50]   *London Stage*, part 4, p. 1881. This piece might be the only one by Bach in J.C. Bach, C.F. Abel and Anton Kammel, *Six Sonatas for two violins and a violoncello, with a thorough bass for the harpsichord* (London: Welcker, 1777), no. 1. Its thematic incipits are given in C.S. Terry, *J. C. Bach*, 2nd ed. (London, 1967), p. 311.

VIOLONCELLISTS AND VIOLONCELLO SOLOS

George August Frederick, Prince of Wales (later George IV), who began to play it in the 1780s. It is known that the sons of Frederick Louis studied with the Italians Zappa and Cirri, and it seems likely that teaching was the primary means of support for many if not most of the Italian cellists living in England. Their publications must have provided the basic material for their teaching. Galliard and De Fesch, two non-Italian foreigners who had settled in London, capitalized on the new fashion by each publishing two collections of cello sonatas in 1733–40.[51] By 1739, the new fashion had also spread to Paris, and Lanzetti's '1 œuvre' and De Fesch's '2 œuvre' were among the first four collections of cello sonatas published by Le Clerc. By 1768, close to thirty prints of cello sonatas were advertised by Le Clerc.[52] A few relationships between London and Paris prints are mentioned in Table 5.2, and a closer examination will undoubtedly reveal many others. The following tables should likewise be viewed as a working draft, and I keenly look forward to reading any emendations and additions. To adapt Alexander Pope: 'To err is human, to supplement divine'.

•

---

[51] See Table 5.2b, nos. 1–3, and Table 5.2a, no. 7. After Galliard (b. Celle c. 1687, d. London 1749) and De Fesch (b. Alkmaar 1687, d. London c. 1757), the next non–Italians whose works were published in London were three generations younger: Jean-Baptiste Sébastien Bréval (b. Paris 1753, d. Colligis, Aisne 1823) and Jean-Balthasar Tricklir (b. Dijon 1750, d. Dresden 1813).

[52] Devriès, Édition et commerce, p. 116, or Devriès and F. Lesure, Dictionnaire des éditeurs de musique français, vol. 1: Des origines à environ 1820, Catalogues (Geneva, 1979), nos. 122 and 133. See also E. Selfridge-Field, 'Vivaldi's Cello Sonatas', Vivaldi vero e falso: Problemi di attribuzione, ed. A. Fanna and M. Talbot (Florence, 1992), pp. 128–32.

136   MUSIC IN EIGHTEENTH–CENTURY BRITAIN

Table 5.1: Italian cellists who performed in eighteenth–century Britain

For each performer, the entry is preceded by the time span that he is known to have spent in Britain. Whenever possible, the entry focuses on his performance activity in Britain. It does not summarize his compositional activity. If any works by him are found in Table 5.2 (pp. 149–57), they are listed at the end of the entry.

In smaller type, sources are listed for the information given in the entry. The following sources are referred to more than once.

[Baretti, Giuseppe,] *The Voice of Discord, or the Battle of the Fiddles / La voix de la discorde, ou la bataille des violons* (London: W. Owen and T. Snelling, 1753)

Beeks, Graydon, 'Handel and Music for the Earl of Carnarvon', *Bach, Handel, Scarlatti: Tercentenary Essays*, ed. P. Williams (Cambridge, 1985), pp. 1–20

A Biographical Dictionary of Actors, Actresses, Musicians, Dancers, Managers and Other Stage Personnel in London, 1660–1800, ed. P.H. Highfill, Jun., K.A. Burnim and E.A. Langhans, 16 vols (Carbondale, 1973–93)

Boydell, Brian, *A Dublin Musical Calendar, 1700–1760* (Dublin, 1988)

Burney, Charles, *A General History of Music from the Earliest Age to the Present Period*, ed. F. Mercer, 2 vols (rpt. New York, 1957)

Deutsch, Otto Erich, *Mozart: A Documentary Biography*, trans. E. Blom, P. Branscombe and J. Noble (London, 1965)

Egmont, Viscount Percival, afterwards Earl of, *Diary: 1730–47*, 3 vols (London, 1920–23)

Farmer, Henry George, *A History of Music in Scotland* (London, 1947)

Hawkins, John, *A General History of the Science and Practice of Music*, 2nd edn, 2 vols (rpt. New York, 1963)

James, Kenneth, 'Concert Life in Eighteenth-Century Bath' (University of London, PhD diss., 1987)

Kaul, Oskar, *Geschichte der Würzburger Hofmusik im 18. Jahrhundert* (Würzburg, 1924)

Lindgren, Lowell, 'Musicians and Librettists in the Correspondence of Gio. Giacomo Zamboni (Oxford, Bodleian Library, MSS Rawlinson Letters 116–38)', *RMA Research Chronicle*, 24 (1991)

The London Stage, 1660–1800, ed. W. Van Lennep, E.L. Avery, A.H. Scouten, G.W. Stone, Jun., and C.B. Hogan, 5 parts in 11 vols., plus an index vol. compiled by B.R. Schneider, Jun. (Carbondale, 1960–79)

McVeigh, Simon, 'The Professional Concert and Rival Subscription Series in London, 1783–93', *RMA Research Chronicle*, 22 (1989), 1–135

Milhous, Judith, Gabriella Dideriksen, and Robert D. Hume, *Italian Opera in Late Eighteenth Century London*, vol. II: *The Pantheon Opera and its Aftermath* (Oxford, forthcoming)

VIOLONCELLISTS AND VIOLONCELLO SOLOS

Milhous, Judith, and Robert D. Hume, 'New Light on Handel and the Royal Academy of Music in 1720', *Theatre Journal*, 35 (1983), 149–67

Mozart, *Briefe und Aufzeichnungen, Gesamtausgabe*, ed. Stiftung Mozarteum Salzburg, prepared by W.A. Bauer and O.E. Deutsch, vol.1: 1755–76 and vol.2: 1777–9 (Kassel, 1962)

The New Grove Dictionary of Music and Musicians, ed. Stanley Sadie, 20 vols (London, 1980)

The New Grove Dictionary of Opera, ed. Stanley Sadie, 4 vols (London, 1992)

Pohl, Karl Ferdinand, *Mozart und Haydn in London* (Vienna, 1867)

Price, Curtis, Judith Milhous and Robert D. Hume, *Italian Opera in Late Eighteenth–Century London*, vol. I: *The King's Theatre, Haymarket, 1778–91* (Oxford, 1995)

[Raguenet, François,] *A Comparison between the French and Italian Musick and Operas, translated from the French; with Some Remarks*, trans. and ed. anon. (London: William Lewis, 1709; rpt. Farnborough, 1968)

Records of English Court Music, ed. A. Ashbee. 9 vols (Snodland, Kent; Aldershot; and Brookfield, VT, 1986–96)

Robbins Landon, H.C., *Haydn: Chronicle and Works. Haydn in England, 1791–1795* (London, 1976)

Straeten, Edmund S.J. van der, *History of the Violoncello, the Viol da Gamba, their Precursors and Collateral Instruments* (London, 1914)

Vice Chamberlain Coke's Theatrical Papers, 1706–15, ed. from the manuscripts in the Harvard Theatre Collection and elsewhere by J. Milhous and R.D. Hume (Carbondale, 1982)

Table 5.1a: Cellists in Britain, 1701–94

1701–29 1. **Haym**, Nicola Francesco (b. Rome 1678, d. London 1729), performed at Rome until October 1700, when he and the violinist Nicola Cosimi surreptitiously left for London in order to serve Wriothesley Russell, Marquess of Tavistock and soon-to-be Duke of Bedford. Cosimi returned to Italy in 1705, but Haym remained in London. He flourished by arranging scores and librettos for theatrical productions. For the first of them, Giovanni Bononcini's *Camilla*, he contracted 'to play his part on ye Bass Violl at all times when ye said Opera shall be performed between the date hereof [14 January 1705/6] and the End of May next'. If he remained in town, for further compensation he would 'performe on ye Bass Viol... not exceeding three days in a week during the said Month of June next'. From 1720 on, he was one of the two leading cellists in the new Royal Academy of Music. According to his obituary, he was famed for 'divinely touching' the violoncello and for recondite scholarly endeavours in the *belles-lettres*.

L. Lindgren, 'Nicola Cosimi in London, 1701–1705', *Studi musicali*, 11 (1982), 229–34; *Vice Chamberlain Coke's Theatrical Papers*, nos. 17–96 passim; Raguenet, p. 53n; Milhous and Hume, pp. 158–60; Giovanni Bononcini, *Camilla: Royal*

138   MUSIC IN EIGHTEENTH–CENTURY BRITAIN

College of Music, MS 779, introduced by Lindgren, Music for London Entertainment, 1660–1800, ser. E, vol. 1 (London, 1990), Appendix, pp. 3–4; Lindgren, 'The Accomplishments of the Learned and Ingenious Nicola Francesco Haym (1678–1729)', *Studi musicali*, 16 (1987), 247–380.

1703–41   2. **Goodsens**, Francisco (d. London 1741), was presumably one of the three musicians – 'Mr *Dean* upon the *Violin*, Mr *Francisco* upon the *Bass–Viol*' and Mr *Smith* upon the *Hautboy*' – who were termed 'as Celebrated as any now living' in *Heraclitus Ridens* for 26 October 1703, then derided as 'Eminent Crowdero's' in *The Observator* of 30 October 1703. Earlier that year a 'Signior Francisco' had performed twice in public: on 5 March with 'the Famous Seniora Anna, lately come from Rome', and on 18 May with 'Mr Dean'. 'Francisco' was one of three violoncellists who played for operas at the Queen's Theatre in 1707–13. On 14 June 1710, 'Signior Francisco' organized a concert for his own benefit (see no. 3 below for a comment on one piece). On 27 October 1711, Francis(co) Goodsens was admitted to the Chapel Royal as musician in ordinary, to serve as a bass violinist. Perhaps he was also the 'Mr. Francisco' who set words by Charles De la Faye for a masonic piece performed on 24 April 1731. Since he is 'Signior Francisco' in three advertisements and 'Francisco' in most other references, it seems likely that he was either born in Italy or had Italian ancestry.

Vice Chamberlain Coke's Theatrical Papers, nos. 17–117 *passim*; *London Stage*, part 2, pp. 33 and 36, and part 3, p. 132; *Biographical Dictionary*, vol. 6, pp. 266–7; Hawkins, vol. 2, p. 784; *Records of English Court Music*, vol. 2, pp. 108, 115–17, 131–2, 149, 152, 159 and 175–7, and vol. 5, pp. 242 and 244.

Francisco Lodi the lutanist was also known as 'Signor Francisco'. He was employed by James II before 1688, and the Duke of Bedford paid him for playing at one of his residences (perhaps at Woburn) in May 1702. Lodi might have settled in Ireland, because he died there in 1703.

Records of English Court Music, vol. 2, p. 21, and vol. 5, p. 87; G.S. Thomson, *The Russells in Bloomsbury, 1669–1771* (London, 1940), p. 130; O. Edwards, 'Espionage, a Collection of Violins, and *Le bizzarie universali*: A Fresh Look at William Corbett', *Musical Quarterly*, 73 (1989), p. 331, n. 47.

1707–25   3. **Chaboud**, Pietro (fl. Italy *c.* 1690, d. London *c.* 1725), described himself 'musico sonatore di fagotto e serpente' and 'humilissimo servitore delle Signorie loro Ill.me' in his undated petition (*c.* 1690?) to serve the 'Signorie' of San Petronio in Bologna. 'Signor Pietro' was in London by 1707, when he served James Butler, second Duke of Ormonde, and was one of three bassoonists in the opera orchestra. At public concerts in 1707–19, he played the German flute and bass viol. At a concert on 14 June 1710, the traveller Uffenbach found 'a most charming [flute] concerto' to be the 'most notable of all', and the 'man who played the viol di gamba with such uncommon excellence is an Italian called Signor Pietro, and he is under the patronage of the Duke of Ormond'. Pietro might have served the Duke of Chandos in 1718, and did serve from 1720 as a cellist in the orchestra of the new Royal Academy of Music.

O. Gambassi, *La cappella musicale di S. Petronio: maestri, organisti, cantori e strumentisti dal 1436 al 1920* (Florence, 1987), p. 471; *Vice Chamberlain Coke's Theatrical Papers*, nos. 17–117 *passim*; *London Stage*, part 2; *Biographical Dictionary*, vol. 3, p. 134, and vol. 11, p. 308; Zacharias Conrad von Uffenbach, *London in 1710*, trans. and ed. W.H. Quarrell and M. Mare (London, 1934), pp. 66–7; Beeks, p. 8; Milhous and Hume, pp. 158–61.

1710–17   **4. Schiavonetti** (Zanetti), Giovanni (d. 1730), was married to the singer Elisabetta Pilotti, who sang at the London opera house for six seasons: 1710–13 (under Queen Anne) and 1714–17 (under George I). In 1707, when the couple was serving at the Hanover court, Schiavonetti is listed (as 'Pilotti') among the cellists in a tentative plan for the London opera orchestra. His name reappears (as 'Zanetti' or 'Pilotti') in plans for the season of 1710, in plans for the Duchess of Shrewsbury's concerts (of 1712–13?), and as one of those owed money for services rendered to the opera house in February 1713. In the London librettos for *Rinaldo* (1711) and *Ambleto* (1712), Elisabetta Pilotti is listed as a servant of Princess Sophia, Electress of Hanover (1620–1714). In librettos for *Ernelinda* (1715), *Amadigi* (1715), *Lucio Vero* (1715 and 1716) and *Clearte* (1716), she is listed as 'Servant to her Royal Highness the Princess of Wales'. Schiavonetti was perhaps a member of the orchestra in 1714–17, when he is listed as the receiver of sums paid by George I for the benefit performances given by his wife. Princess Caroline must have been fond of the pair, because – if we can believe their claim – she still subsidized them in 1725, with a grant of 1000 *scudi* a year. In 1722–24 they were employed (with a 'junger Schiavonetto', who played the oboe and was perhaps their son) at Bishop Schönborn's court in Würzburg, while in 1726 they were at the ducal court in Stuttgart.

Vice Chamberlain Coke's Theatrical Papers, p. 199 and nos. 17, 89, 95–6 and 117; *Biographical Dictionary*, vol. 11, pp. 311–12; Lindgren, no. 172; Kaul, p. 21 (where 'Pilotti' is misspelled 'Bellotti'); D. Burrows and R.D. Hume, 'George I, the Haymarket Opera Company and Handel's *Water Music*', *Early Music*, 19 (1991), 324–7; R. Krauss, *Das Stuttgarter Hoftheater von den ältesten Zeiten bis zum Gegenwart* (Stuttgart, 1908), p. 20. Schiavonetti's year of death is given in W. Dean's entry in *The New Grove Dictionary of Opera*, vol. 3, p. 1013.

1714–15   **5. Zanoni**, Angelo (b. Venice; fl. 1710–32), was a bass employed at Italian opera houses in 1710–13, 1716–27 and 1732. On 9 May 1715, near the end of his single season in London, he organized a benefit concert. The singers were Elisabetta Pilotti, Diana Vico and himself. In addition, there were 'several Solos on the Bass–Viol[in?] to be perform'd by him'.

C. Sartori, *I libretti italiani a stampa dalle origini al 1800*, Indici, vol. 2 (Cuneo, 1994), p. 683; *London Stage*, part 2, p. 355; *Biographical Dictionary*, vol. 16, p. 372.

1714–55   **6. Pardini**, Charles (fl. 1714–55), organized benefit concerts in 1714–28, served the Duke of Chandos in 1718–20, and from 1720 on played violoncello for performances given by the new Royal Academy of Music. Francesco Geminiani selected him as the continuo cellist for the performances given at a masonic lodge in 1725–26. He was active in the Royal Society of

140 MUSIC IN EIGHTEENTH-CENTURY BRITAIN

Musicians from its foundation in 1739 until 1755. He was conceivably from Lucca, where Father Pier Vincenzo Pardini served in 1707–52 as a musician in the royal chapel.

London Stage, part 2; *Biographical Dictionary*, vol. 11, p. 196; Beeks, pp. 8 and 17; Milhous and Hume, pp. 158–61; W.H. Rylands (ed.), *The Book of the Fundamental Constitutions and Orders of the Philo Musicæ and Architecturæ Societas, London, 1725–27*, Quatuor Coronatorum Antigrapha, 9 (London, 1900), 78, 80, 95, 97, 130 and 182; L. Nerici, *Storia della musica in Lucca*, Memorie e documenti per servire alla storia di Lucca, vol. 12 (Lucca, 1880), p. 210. In two of the three documents cited by Milhous and Hume, the surname is spelled Perdini.

1715–25   7. **Amadei**, Filippo, called Pippo (b. Rome *c*. 1665, d. London *c*. 1725), was the exemplary cellist in Rome, who was 'deservedly to be admired', according to the Raguenet edition of 1710. He performed for Roman cardinals and various churches in the city from 1685 until January 1715, when he and the Castrucci brothers (both of whom were violinists) went to London with the Earl of Burlington. In London, he performed at public concerts in 1718–22. In 1720 he became the principal cellist for the new Royal Academy of Music.

Raguenet, p. 51n; *London Stage*, part 2; *Biographical Dictionary*, vol. 1, pp. 68–9; Lindgren, no. 35a; Lindgren, 'Parisian Patronage of Performers from the Royal Academy of Musick (1719–28)', *Music and Letters*, 58 (1977), 8; Milhous and Hume, pp. 158–60.

1716–29   8. **Ariosti**, Attilio (b. Bologna 1666, d. London 1729), entered the monastic order of the Servites in 1688, served the Duke of Mantua in 1696, then – at the behest of the duke – went to serve the Electress Sophie Charlotte in the Protestant court at Berlin in 1698. The Servite Order demanded his return, but he did not leave Berlin until 1703, when he went to Vienna; he was appointed an imperial diplomat in 1708. After the death of Joseph I in 1711, he entered the diplomatic service of the Duke of Anjou, the future Louis XV. After he went to London in 1716, he stayed there, except for a diplomatic mission to Paris in 1720–22. When listing his accomplishments, the Duke of Mantua wrote in 1698 that Ariosti 'played various instruments masterfully' ('suona maestralmente varij istromenti'), while Leibniz in 1703 likewise wrote that 'he is accomplished on several instruments' ('il s'entend en plusieurs instruments de musique'). The trustworthy Hawkins is the only writer known to have termed him a cellist: 'Attilio was a celebrated performer on the violoncello; but he was most distinguished for his performance on ... the Viol d'Amore'.

L. Lindgren, 'Ariosti's London Years, 1716–29,' *Music and Letters*, 62 (1981), 331–51; A. Ebert, *Attilio Ariosti in Berlin (1697–1703)* (Leipzig, 1905), pp. 67 and 91; Hawkins, vol. 2, p. 866.

1720–29   9. **Bocchi**, Lorenzo (fl. Edinburgh 1720, d. Edinburgh 1729), went to Edinburgh in July 1720 with Mr Gordon, who had lately been 'travelling in Italy'. His companion must have been the Scottish tenor Alexander Gordon, who had just sung for the first season (2 April to 25 June 1720) of the Royal Academy of Music in London. Bocchi, whom an Edinburgh newspaper heralded as 'the second master of the violoncello in Europe', probably remained in Scotland until 1724, when he gave concerts in Dublin. He was back in Edinburgh by 1729. (See also Table 5.2a, no. 1.)

Farmer, pp. 284, 292–3, 301 and 309; Boydell, pp. 40–41 and 272; Nicholas Carolan, Introduction to *A Collection of the Most Celebrated Irish Tunes proper for the Violin, German Flute or Hautboy. PleaRar keh na Rough set w.*[th] *Different Divisions, Bass & Corus, as performed at the Subscription Consort by Senior Loranzo Bocchi* (Dublin: Iohn & William Neal, [1724]; facsimile by The Folk Music Society of Ireland, 1986), pp. xxiii–xxv.

1720–32   10. **Bononcini**, Giovanni (b. Modena 1670, d. Vienna 1747), was trained in Bologna, worked in Rome and Naples in 1692–7, went to Vienna to serve Leopold I and Joseph I, then returned to Rome in 1714 to serve the Viennese ambassador, who died in 1719. According to the Raguenet edition of 1710, he was 'indisputably the first' among cellists. In London he might have played in the orchestra of the Royal Academy of Music during the five seasons that he composed for it (1720–24 and 1727). He is known to have played at private concerts, most notably those at the home of Henrietta, Duchess of Marlborough (d. 1733), the patroness who subsidized him munificently in 1724–31. After leaving London, he went to Paris, Madrid and Lisbon before returning to Vienna in 1736. (See also Table 5.2a, no. 11.)

Raguenet, p. 51n; *Biographical Dictionary*, vol. 2, pp. 207–10; L. Lindgren in *New Grove Dictionary of Opera*, vol. 1, pp. 541–4.

1725–7   11. **Chelleri**, Fortunato (b. Parma 1690, d. Kassel 1757), was of German heritage (Chelleri is probably an Italian form of Keller). He served as Kapellmeister to Prince-Bishop Johann Philipp Franz von Schönborn in 1722–4. After the death of Schönborn on 17 August 1724, he requested release from service, which was granted on 20 November 1724. Thus he may well have been the 'Signor Chelleri' who, at the tenor Gaetano Rocchetti's benefit on 12 April 1725, played a 'solo on the bass viol[in?] ... , being the first time of his appearing on the English stage'. In August 1725, when Riva, the Modenese ambassador to Britain, was with George I in Hanover, he spoke with Schiavonetti and Pilotti, who had served with Chelleri in Würzburg. They claimed to have placed Chelleri (who was with them in Hanover) in the service of Landgrave Karl of Hesse–Kassel, and said that he had written two operas expressly for England, which he had sold to the Royal Academy of Music. Perhaps his endeavour to gain employment at the Academy was the main reason for his trips to England in 1725 and 1726–7. Lost manuscripts containing thirteen cello sonatas by him are in the sale catalogue of Nicolas Selhof. His only extant solo work for the instrument is apparently a 'concerto con violoncello obligato', dated 1742, which he presumably wrote for Count

142   MUSIC IN EIGHTEENTH-CENTURY BRITAIN

Schönborn, an avid cellist, whose brother (Johann Philipp) had been Chelleri's employer in 1722–4.

London Stage, part 2, p. 818; *Biographical Dictionary*, vol. 3, p. 188; Lindgren, no. 172; Kaul, pp. 18–21; N. Selhof, *Catalogue d'une très belle bibliothèque de livres,... d'une partie très considerable de livres de musique,... ainsi qu'une collection de toutes sortes d'instruments,... lesquels seront vendus publiquement aux plus offrants, Mercredie le 30 Mai 1759 & jours suivants* (The Hague: la Veuve d'Adrien Moetjens, 1759), nos. 2157–8; F. Zobeley, *Die Musikalien der Grafen von Schönborn-Wiesentheid*, Part I: *Das Repertoire des Grafen Rudolf Franz Erwein von Schönborn (1677–1754)*, vol. 2: *Handschriften*, ed. F. Dangel-Hofmann (Tutzing, 1982), no. 531.

1725–33   12. **Rolli**, Giovanni (b. Rome *c.* 1690?, d. Todi 1745), was the blind brother of the poet and librettist Paolo Antonio Rolli (b. Rome 1687, d. Todi 1765). In London he gave cello lessons and played at private concerts. He was presumably still there in 1733, when he published *Six Italian cantatas & six lessons upon the harpsichord* (RISM R 2082). He was in Todi by October 1734.

Lindgren, nos. 161, 172a–b, 186a, 313 and 347b.

1728–83   13. **Cervetto** Sen., Giacobbe Basevi, called Cervetto (b. Venice *c.* 1682, d. London 1783), reportedly came to London in 1728 in order to sell musical instruments. He apparently began to play the cello for theatre orchestras in the 1730s. He certainly played in the Drury Lane orchestra in 1742–4, and was apparently still playing – at least for summer concerts in Vauxhall Gardens – at the age of 98. Burney lists him and the next four Italians – Pasqualino, Lanzetti, Caporale and Dall'Abaco – as those who 'brought the violoncello into favour, and made us nice judges of that instrument'. Burney furthermore judged the technical command and musical knowledge of Pasqualino and Cervetto Sen., to be infinitely better than that of Caporale, yet by comparison they had a 'raw, crude, and uninteresting' tone. In 1753, Baretti published a spoof concerning Francesco Vanneschi's attempt to form an opera company: 'He has engaged a Band of Players upon the Violin and other Instruments with very little Money... Lieutenant [John] Gordon will dispute the Ground against the Nose of Cervetto and the Legs of Pasqualino [in the French version printed on the facing page: 'contre le rinoceroté Cervetto et le gambu Pasqualino']; and although I am acquainted with his Courage and Valour, yet I fear he will be overpower'd by Numbers, and this Field of Battle will be his last'. (Cervetto was commonly called 'Nosey' by Londoners, because of his physical appearance not his behaviour.) After 1768, the 'Sig. Cervetto' featured at events was most likely his son (see no. 24 below). (See also Table 5.2a, nos. 5, 10, 12 and 16.)

Baretti, pp. 18–19 and 50–51; Burney, vol. 2, pp. 1005 and 1012; Pohl, vol. 2, p. 371; Straeten, pp. 151–4; *London Stage*, part 3; *Biographical Dictionary*, vol. 3, pp. 130–32; Lindgren, nos. 389–91; James, p. 532.

VIOLONCELLISTS AND VIOLONCELLO SOLOS

1732–66 14. Pasqualino di Marzis (d. London 1766) is presumably 'Sig. Pasquale', the cellist who performed 'in public for the first time' on 24 April 1732, then organized a benefit for himself – 'the famous Italian Violoncello' – on 5 May 1732. 'Pasquelini' played at Egmont's concert on 9 February 1733. Baretti and Burney implied that he was technically very fluent (see the evaluations cited in the preceding entry). He spent *c.* 1736–*c.* 1746 in Ireland, where he played for Mercer's Hospital benefits in Dublin, and for four years resided with and taught the children of George Berkeley, Bishop of Cloyne. He performed again in London from 1748 until at least 18 June 1762. He is among the subscribers to Antoniotto's *L'arte armonica* (1760), as noted in no. 18 below. (See also Table 5.2a, nos. 9, 11 and 13.)

Egmont, vol. 1, p. 325; Baretti, pp. 50–51; Burney, vol. 2, p. 1005; Pohl, vol. 2, p. 371; *London Stage*, parts 3–4; *Biographical Dictionary*, vol. 11, p. 232; Boydell, p. 287; A.C. Fraser, *Life and Letters of George Berkeley*, The Works of George Berkeley, vol. iv (Oxford, 1872), pp. 309–10.

1733 & 1754 15. Lanzetti, Salvatore (b. Naples *c.* 1710, d. Turin *c.* 1780), was termed 'virtuoso of the violoncello and servant to H. M. the King of Sardinia' in an advertisement for his benefit concert on 7 May 1733. The 'Lonzetti' who played a solo at the performance of Handel's *Acis and Galatea* on 13 February 1754 is possibly the same person. (See also Table 5.2a, nos. 4, 6 and 15.)

Burney, vol. 2, p. 1005; Pohl, vol. 2, p. 371; Straeten, pp. 166–7; *London Stage*, part 3, p. 297, and part 4, p. 409; *Biographical Dictionary*, vol. 9, p. 152.

1733–58 16. Caporale, Andrea (fl. London 1733, d. Dublin 1758), was the principal cellist in the opera orchestra at the King's Theatre in 1733–4 (according to the advertisement for his benefit concert on 22 March 1734). He thus participated in Handel's productions, not in those of the rival Opera of the Nobility. Egmont's private concert of 15 February 1734 included, 'on the violoncello, Signor Caporali'. Caporale was presumably not 'Signor Caprara, the great bass fiddle', who played for Egmont's concert of 8 March 1734. He played in numerous concerts, such as the series of twenty Friday performances at Hickford's during the first half of 1740. He and the violinist Michael Christian Festing often played together. According to Burney, he was 'no deep musician, nor gifted with a very powerful hand', yet 'was always heard with great partiality, from the almost single merit, of a full, sweet, and vocal tone'. His last known performance in London was on 14 February 1745. Perhaps he moved to Dublin, for he is known to have performed there in December 1753, September 1754, May 1755, February 1757 and February 1758. (See also Table 5.2a, nos. 7 and 11.)

Egmont, vol. 2, pp. 30 and 50; Burney, vol. 2, pp. 1003 and 1005; Straeten, pp. 160–61; *London Stage*, part 3; *Biographical Dictionary*, vol. 3, pp. 49–50; Boydell, pp. 188, 200, 206, 223, 235 and 273.

144   MUSIC IN EIGHTEENTH–CENTURY BRITAIN

1736   17. **Dall'Abaco**, Giuseppe Clemente Ferdinando (b. Brussels 1710, d. Arbizzano di Valpolicella, near Verona, 1805), was the son of the composer Evaristo Felice (b. Verona 1675, d. Munich 1742). He served the Elector of Cologne at Bonn from 1729, and became the director of chamber music in 1738. His only known public appearance in London was at a benefit concert on 15 April 1736. He moved to Italy in 1753, and was created a baron in 1766. 'Barone' precedes his name in many copies of his works.

Burney, vol. 2, p. 1005; Straeten, pp. 164–5; *London Stage*, part 3, p. 573; *Biographical Dictionary*, vol. 4, p. 126.

1742–60s   18. **Antoniotto**, Giorgio (b. ?Milan *c*. 1692, d. Milan 1776), was living in Holland when his only musical publication appeared: *XII sonate, le prime cinque a violoncello solo e basso, e le altre sette a due violoncelli overo due viole di gamba*, op. 1 (Amsterdam: Le Cène, *c*. 1735; RISM A 1275). He was in England by 1742, when he accompanied a raucous violinist named Kneller at Bath. He also played at Bristol in 1745 and again at Bath in 1749. While in England, he may have played only in the provinces. Two cellists, '*Signor* Pasqualino' (no. 14 above) and '*Mr*. Alexis Magito' (no. 23 below), are among the subscribers to his *L'arte armonica*, or *A Treatise on the Composition of Musick*, trans. anon. (London: John Johnson, 1760).

S. Hansell in *New Grove Dictionary of Music*, vol. 1, p. 493; F. Fleming, *The Life and Extraordinary Adventures, the Perils and Critical Escapes of Timothy Ginnadrake [i.e., Francis Fleming], that Child of Chequer'd Fortune* (Bath: R. Cruttwell, for the Author, 1771), vol. 2, pp. 89–90 and 102–4; James, p. 445.

1745–57   19. **Pasquali** Jun. (b. after 1718), performed with his elder brother, the violinist Niccolò (b. *c*. 1718, d. Edinburgh 1757), at a concert in London on 1 April 1745. The brothers played at Bristol in September 1747, then apparently went to Dublin, where a masque by Nicolò was produced in February 1749 with 'Machinery & Scenes... contrived and executed by Pasquali Junior, brother to Signor Pasquali'. At Edinburgh in October 1752, a concert featured, for 'the first time in this Kingdom', the 'Violin Signor Pasquale and Signor Pasquale, junior, on the Violoncello'. In Baretti's spoof of 1753, he is presumably 'Pasquali le cadet', who is clearly opposed to the vengeful actions recommended by other musicians: 'What then shall we do? (exclaimed the youngest Pasquali) shall we suffer in silence? Alas, my Friends! (added he with a sigh) This I fancy would be the wisest Resolution!' He possibly remained in Edinburgh until his brother died in 1757. He is conceivably the Francis Pasquali who worked as a publisher and double bass player at London in 1760–94.

Baretti, pp. 38–9; Pohl, vol. 2, p. 371; *London Stage*, part 3, p. 1163; *Biographical Dictionary*, vol. 11, pp. 230–32; James, pp. 861–2; Boydell, p. 123; Nicolò Pasquali, *Thorough–Bass Made Easy*, introduced by J. Churchill (London: Robt Bremner, *c*. 1760; facs. London, 1974), p. ii.

VIOLONCELLISTS AND VIOLONCELLO SOLOS 145

1748–56   20. Caruso, Signor (?–?), accompanied an aria sung at the opera house on 26 April 1748 'on the saltero, which was never performed in any concert before'. In 1750, 'Carusi' played the same instrument (a cither viol with five double strings) at a concert in Edinburgh. The only other known reference to his presence in Britain is on 12 August 1756, when he played a cello solo at the Drury Lane Theatre. Perhaps he was employed as a cellist at one of the theatres.

London Stage, part 4, pp. 49 and 549; *Biographical Dictionary*, vol. 3, p. 93; Farmer, p. 281.

1750s–1817   21. Scola, Charles (d. London 1817), was possibly a son of Adamo Scola (fl. London 1728, d. London 1748), a 'virtuoso of Naples' who played harpsichord, taught music, copied musical manuscripts, edited music and perhaps engraved prints. Charles played violoncello in the opera orchestra and in professional concerts for at least five decades (1750s–90s). It was presumably Charles (rather than another Scola) who played the viola at some choral events.

Pohl, vol. 2, p. 371; O. Edwards in *New Grove Dictionary of Music*, vol. 17, pp. 54–5; *The London Stage*, parts 4–5; *Biographical Dictionary*, vol. 13, pp. 234–5; Mozart, p. 193; McVeigh, pp. 32, 50, 57 and 65; Price, Milhous and Hume, pp. 286 and 321; Milhous, Dideriksen and Hume, appendices 1 and 2.

1758–69   22. Siprutini, Emanuel (b. Holland?), was 'a great virtuoso on the cello; he is the son of a Dutch Jew; after travelling through Italy and Spain he found the Jewish faith and its ceremonies and commandments laughable' ['ein grosser Virtuos auf dem Violoncello; er ist eines Holländischen Juden Sohn; er fand den Jüdischen Glauben und ihre Ceremonien und Gebote, nachdem er Italien und Spanien durchgereiset, lächerlich'] (Leopold Mozart, letter of 13 September 1764). In London, he is known to have performed publicly in 1758–65, and he led an orchestra at Bath in December 1761. By July 1767 he and the violinist Giardini were selling music and instruments at a warehouse in the Haymarket. By April 1769 he and a different partner were operating at a similar warehouse in the Strand. (See also Table 5.2a, nos. 19–20, 28 and 30–31.)

Pohl, vol. 2, p. 371; Mozart, vol. 1, pp. 164–5 and 193; *London Stage*, part 4; *Biographical Dictionary*, vol. 14, p. 102; James, p. 1004; S. McVeigh, *The Violinist in London's Concert Life, 1750–84* (New York and London, 1989), pp. 125 and 166.

1760–67   23. Magito, Alexis Jun. (b. The Hague 1689), was born about a decade after his Italian father had moved to The Hague. At Rotterdam *c.* 1738–40, he engraved a set of trio sonatas by Duni that was dedicated to Carl Bentinck and a set of concertos by Wassenaer that was dedicated to Count William Bentinck. He must have arrived in England before 1760, since he is 'Mr. Alexis Magito' on the list of subscribers to Antoniotto's *L'arte armonica* (London, 1760; see no. 18 above). He is 'Mr. Alexis' in advertisements for concerts at Cambridge in 1767. A handwritten note identifies 'Alexis' as the cellist in a well-known caricature of a concert in Cambridge. He is presumably

146   MUSIC IN EIGHTEENTH–CENTURY BRITAIN

the engraver of his only published opus, which was printed for him and sold in Cambridge. (See also Table 5.2a, no. 22.)

R. Rasch and K. Vlaardingerbroek (eds), *Unico Wilhelm van Wassenaer, 1692–1766, Componist en staatsman* (Walburg Pers, 1993), pp. 16–18, 47, 80 and 289–90; C. Hogwood and R. Luckett (eds.), *Music in Eighteenth-Century England: Essays in Memory of Charles Cudworth* (Cambridge, 1983), dust cover, frontispiece, and pp. xv–xviii: Hogwood, 'A Note on the Frontispiece: *A Concert in Cambridge*'.

1760s–1837   24. **Cervetto** Jun., James (b. London 1747 [or 49?], d. London 1837), was the natural son of Cervetto Sen. They played together at various events during the 1760s. Burney declared that, as a child, James already 'had a better tone, and played what he was able to execute, in a manner much more *chantant* than his father. And, arrived at manhood, his tone and expression were equal to those of the best tenor voices.' In 1771, James was accepted into the Queen's private band, and for the rest of the century he was often a soloist at concerts and a principal cellist in various orchestras. In 1782, an attempt to oust him from the opera band in favour of Crosdill was not successful. In 1789 he 'lost his favourite violoncello' in the fire at the opera house. (See also Table 5.2a, nos. 26, 29, 35, 37 and 40–41.)

Burney, vol. 2, p. 1012; Pohl, vol. 2, p. 371; Straeten, pp. 314–16; *London Stage*, parts 4–5; *Biographical Dictionary*, vol. 2, 132–4, and vol. 10, p. 78; McVeigh, pp. 27–34, 36, 40–44, 49–54, 57–60, 65–9 and 74–84; S. Sadie, 'Music in the Home II', *Music in Britain: The Eighteenth Century*, ed. H. Diack Johnstone and R. Fiske (Oxford, 1990), pp. 318 and 325; Robbins Landon, p. 283; F.C. Petty, *Italian Opera in London, 1760–1800* (Ann Arbor, 1980), pp. 158–9, 186, 195, 224–5 and 238; Price, Milhous and Hume, pp. 285–6, 321 and 633; James, p. 532; S. McVeigh, *Concert Life in London from Mozart to Haydn* (Cambridge, 1993), pp. 45, 80, 85, 122 and 200.

1764   25. **Graziani**, Carlo (b. Asti *c.* 1730, d. Potsdam 1787), is known to have played publicly only once in London, on 22 May 1764. He and his wife, a singer, performed at Frankfurt in September 1770. He then moved to Berlin as cello teacher to the future Frederick William II.

Pohl, vol. 2, p. 371; Straeten, p. 168; Mozart, vol. 1, p. 192; Deutsch, pp. 33–4; Graziani, *Sonatas for Violoncello and Basso*, ed. M.E. Parker (Madison, 1997), p. vii.

1764–80   26. **Cirri**, Gio. Battista (b. Forlì 1724, d. Forlì 1808), began his London performances at the June 1764 concert given for the benefit of 'Miss Mozart of Eleven, and Master Mozart of Seven Years of Age, Prodigies of Nature'. He was also featured at their July 1765 concert and at many other events, especially oratorio performances, through March 1774. Some of his publications were obviously designed for teaching purposes (e.g., opp. 7 and 11). In *c.* 1765–*c.* 1775 he served as music master to the Duke of Gloucester, brother of George III and son of the late Frederick Louis, Prince of Wales. He returned to Forlì in 1780. (See also Table 5.2a, nos. 32–4, and Table 5.2b, no. 4.)

VIOLONCELLISTS AND VIOLONCELLO SOLOS

Pohl, vol. 2, p. 371; Straeten, p. 167; Deutsch, pp. 35–6 and 45; Mozart, vol. 1, p. 193; *London Stage,* part 4; *Biographical Dictionary,* vol. 3, p. 289; *Enciclopedia della musica,* ed. C. Sartori (Milan, 1963), vol. 1, p. 486.

1764–71   27. **Zappa**, Francesco (b. Milan?), dedicated his *Six trios à deux violons avec la basse* (London: Welcker, 1765; RISM Z 88) to the Duke of York. His patron, Edward August (1739–67), was brother to George III and the Duke of Gloucester (see no. 26 above). The dedication is signed 'Londres ce 1 Juin 1765, François Zappa'. It relates that the duke, when travelling in Italy, had honoured Zappa 'by taking some music lessons from me which provided me with the occasion to admire the delicate and refined taste that you have for this lustrous science, and at the same time to imprint in my heart feelings of the deepest gratitude' ['de prendre de moi quelque leçon de Musique m'a donnè lieu d'admirer le goût delicat et rafinè qu'elle a pour cette Illustre Science, et en même tems a gravé dans mon coeur les sentimens de la plus vive reconnoissance']. The duke left his London home on 1 September 1763 and returned there exactly one year later. He was in Italy from 28 November 1763 until 17 August 1764, and thus had ample time to improve his cello playing by taking lessons from Zappa, who subsequently served the duke in London. He reportedly termed himself the duke's music master on the title-page of his *Sei trio,* op. 2 (London: Welcker, 1766; RISM Z 83). 'Mr. Zappa Violoncellist' is one of the musicians that Leopold Mozart met during his stay in London (late April 1764–July 1765). Between October 1764 and November 1766, Zappa occasionally performed with the violinist Francesco Pasquale Ricci in Dutch cities, but he possibly resided in London until 1770, when Welcker published his *Six trios,* op. 4. He was in Germany by autumn 1771, and performed at The Hague in 1788–90. On 12 February 1778, Leopold Mozart wrote angrily to Wolfgang, who was at Mannheim, advising him not to carry out a plan, which was 'only for dim-wits, half-composers and scribblers, people like *Schwindl, Zappa, Ricci etc*' ['nur eine sache für kleine Lichter, für Halb-Componisten, für Schmierer, für einen *Schwindl, Zappa, Ricci etc.*'].

Mozart, vol. 1, p. 195, and vol. 2, p. 277; *The Tour of his Royal Highness Edward, Duke of York, from England to Lisbon... Genoa,... Turin, Milan, Parma, Florence,... Rome, Bologna,... Venice* (London: J. Dixwell, 1764); R. Eitner, *Biographisch-bibliographisches Quellen-Lexikon,* 2nd edn in 11 vols (Graz, 1959), vol. 10, p. 330; G. Salvetti in *New Grove Dictionary of Music,* vol. 20, p. 644; M. de Smet, *La musique a la cour de Guillaume V, Prince d'Orange* (Utrecht, 1973), pp. 41, 59, 109–20, 132, 146 and 150–56; R. Rasch, 'The Italian Presence in Musical Life of the Dutch Republic', in P. Chiarelli (ed.), *The Diaspora of Italian Music and Musicians in the XVIIIth Century* (Turnhout, Belgium, forthcoming). Zappa's *Sonata a tre* in D major for 'violoncello obligato', 'violin' and 'violoncello basso' has been published in Early Cello Series 23, ed. N. Pyron and C. Barritt (Grancino Editions, 1983); no source is cited, but it may well be a manuscript in D–Dlb (listed by Eitner).

1782–92   28. **Tonioli**, Girolamo (d. London 1792), was a cellist at the opera house during at least 1782–5, then the staff librettist who arranged texts for the Pantheon seasons of 1790–92. Perhaps he was related to the violist Antonio

148   MUSIC IN EIGHTEENTH–CENTURY BRITAIN

Tonioli, who played in the Pantheon orchestra in 1790–92, as well as to Vincenzo Tonioli, who published *Sei duetti a due violini* (London: Walker, *c.* 1800); RISM T 958.

Biographical Dictionary, vol. 15, p. 26; Price, Milhous and Hume, pp. 35n, 286, 297, 318, 321 and 637; C. Price, 'Italian Opera and Arson in Late Eighteenth–Century London', *Journal of the American Musicological Society*, 42 (1989), 87–90; Milhous, Didericksen and Hume, ch. 8 and appendices 1 and 2.

1787–94   29. **Sperati**, John (?–?), reportedly first performed at London in 1787. He served as the principal cellist at operatic performances from 1791 to 1794, when Robert Lindley succeeded him. He also played for various concert and oratorio performances.

Pohl, vol. 2, pp. 23, 146–8, 249 and 371; *Biographical Dictionary*, vol. 14, pp. 218–19; McVeigh, pp. 85, 88, 89 and 130; Robbins Landon, vol. 3, pp. 89–90 and 183–4; Milhous, Didericksen and Hume, appendices 1 and 2.

Table 5.1b: Two unlikely Italian cellists in London, 1702–84

1702–11   1. **Saggione**, Giuseppe Fedeli, called Saggione (fl. Venice 1680, d. Paris 1733), was an instrumentalist (primarily a trombonist?) at San Marco in Venice from 1680 onwards. His first concert in London was apparently on 26 December 1702, when he was termed 'Mr Joseph Saggione, a Venetian'. Songs he had set in Italian and French were sung by Signora Joanna Maria Lindelheim on 23 January 1703, when he was called 'Signior Sajoni lately arriv'd from Italy'. When she sang them again on 1 February 1703, her accompanists were named: 'Signior Gasperini [i.e., Gasparo Visconti, violinist] and Signior Saioni'. He likewise accompanied Maria Margarita Gallia (whom he married) on 1 June 1703, 20 April and 16 November 1704, and 4 April 1707; and he accompanied 'Signiora Lovicina' on 29 January 1706. From 1707 until at least 1711, he played 'double base' in the opera orchestra. He presumably settled in Paris before publishing his *Sonate a violino e basso*, op. 1 (Paris: Foucault, 1715); RISM F 157. His only other instrumental publication is *Six sonates a deux violonceles* [sic], *violes, ou bassons, qui peuvent se jouer sur deux violons en les transposant à la quinte. Il y a une musette, et une chaconne, et un menuet à la fin* (Paris: L'Autheur, Le Sr Boivin, Le S^r Le Clerc, 1733); RISM F 158. It seems plausible that he would have played the violoncello (instead of another bass instrument) when he was the only continuo player supporting a solo singer at a private or public concert.

London Stage, part 2; *Biographical Dictionary*, vol. 13, pp. 169–70; *Vice Chamberlain Coke's Papers*, pp. 31–245 *passim*; E. Selfridge-Field in *New Grove Dictionary of Music*, vol. 6, p. 447.

1784   2. **Chiabrano**, (Gaspare Giuseppe) Gaetano (b. Turin 1725, d. Turin after 1800), served the royal chapel in Turin during his entire career. He has occasionally been identified with the 'Capperan' who played for various events at Paris in 1755 and the 'Chabran' who played for concerts at London in 1784. But advertisements of 1784 (mentioned by McVeigh) list 'Chabran' as a violinist, not a cellist. It was therefore Gaetano's brother Francesco who worked as a performer in London. The publication of two violoncello sonatas by Chabran at London in *c.* 1785 was therefore not related to any visit by Gaetano. (See also Table 5.2a, nos. 25 and 38.)

Straeten, pp. 171–2; Bouquet–Boyer, 'Note biografiche sulla famiglia Chiabrano', in Gaetano Chiabrano, *44 sonate da camera per due violoncelli obbligati, per violoncello e basso, per violoncello solo o fagotto e basso,* Libro I: Sonate 1–15, ed. A. Pais, Monumenti musicali italiani, vol. 12 (Milan: Suvini Zerboni, 1988), vi–xviii; *Biographical Dictionary,* vol. 3, 134–6; McVeigh, p. 32.

Table 5.2: Violoncello solos by twenty-nine composers, nearly all of whom were 'Italian', published in eighteenth-century Britain

For each item, paragraph 1 lists the date, composer (surname in bold-face type), title, opus number, dedicatee and number of subscribers. In titles, only the first word and proper nouns are capitalized, and the following abbreviations are used: vc = violoncello, vcs = violoncellos, bc = basso continuo and tbh = thorough bass for the harpsichord. The date is italicized when known from a title-page, dedicatory page or advertisement in a newspaper. Dates in roman type have been derived from the following sources: W.C. Smith and C. Humphries [hereafter S&H], *A Bibliography of the Musical Works published by the firm of John Walsh during the years 1721–1766* (London, 1968); *The British Union-Catalogue of Early Music printed before the year 1801,* ed. E.B. Schnapper, 2 vols (London, 1957); *The Catalogue of Printed Music in the British Library to 1980,* ed. L. Baillie and R. Balchin, 62 vols (London, 1981–87). I have not examined copies of the following prints: Table 5.2a, nos. 28–32 and 37–41.

Paragraph 2 names the publisher (in London, unless otherwise indicated), then refers to the letter and number of each item (except Table 5.2a, no. 11) in RISM A I: *Einzeldrucke vor 1800,* ed. K. Schlager and O.E. Albrecht, 9 vols (Kassel, 1971-81), which has been supplemented through to letter R in *Addenda et Corrigenda,* ed. I. and J. Kindermann, vols. 11–13 (1986–98). For four items (Table 5.2a, nos. 7, 11 and 25, and Table 5.2b, no. 2), references are then given to page numbers in RISM B I: *Recueils imprimés, XVIIIe siècle,* ed. F. Lesure (Munich-Duisburg, 1964). For thirteen items (Table 5.2a, nos. 2, 4–7, 9–11 and 17; Table 5.2b, nos. 1–2; and Table 5.2c, nos. 1 and 3), references are then given to item numbers in S&H. Any comment concerning reissues, composer(s) or contents is then added.

Paragraph 3 lists some recent facsimile and other editions.

150   MUSIC IN EIGHTEENTH–CENTURY BRITAIN

Table 5.2a: Forty-one solos by Italian composers, published 1725–*c.* 1795

1725 Jul 27   1. **Bocchi**, Lorenzo, *A musicall entertainment for a chamber. Sonatas for violin* [4], *flute* [4], *vc* [2], *and six string bass* [viola da gamba, 2] *with a tbh or bass violin. Lastly a Scotch cantata, with the instrumentall parts after the Italian manner*, op. 1; dedicated to James, Duke of Hamilton and Brandon; ninety-three 'subscribers' (most of them Scottish) for 120 copies and thirty-three 'additional subscribers' (nearly all of them Irish) are listed.

     Dublin: Iohn & William Neal; RISM B 3233; cf. RISM B 3232. The date of the print is given by Nicholas Carolan in his facsimile edition *of A Collection of the Most Celebrated Irish Tunes* (see Table 5.1a, no. 9), pp. xxi and xxiv. The text of the cantata is by Allan Ramsay; see D. Johnson, *Music and Society in Lowland Scotland in the Eighteenth Century* (London, 1972), p. 191.

     Facsimile by King's Music, Redcroft, Huntingdon, Cambs [*c.* 1990].

1732 Oct 28   2. **Marcello**, Benedetto, *Six solos for a vc with a tbh*, op. 2.
John Walsh; RISM M 449; S&H 984.
Facsimile in Performers' Facsimiles, no. 155, New York [*c.* 1996].

c. 1735   3. **Merci**, 'Luidgi, di natione Inglesa', *VI sonate a fagoto o vc col bc*, op. 3.

     Printed for the author & sold by Sam[ll] Weaver & John Johnson; RISM M 2313. 'Luis Mercy' was the name he gave on his first two collections of flute solos. The first, RISM M 2311, is dated 2 December 1718 in W.C. Smith, *A Bibliography of the Musical Works Published by John Walsh during the years 1695–1720* (London, 1948), no. 553. It was dedicated to his employer, the Earl of Carnarvon, in whose documents his surname is spelled Merci (Beeks, p. 8). His op. 2 is listed in RISM M 2312. The precise Italianate version cited above is also found on another print marked op. 3: *VI sonate a fluto traverso, violoncello o cembalo* (London: Author, [*c.* 1735?]; RISM M 2314. Merci is listed here (rather than on Table 5.2c) because his ancestry is possibly French-Italian.

     Edited by George Longazo (St Cloud, MN: Medici Music Press, 1982).

1737   4. **Lanzetti**, Salvatore, *VI solos for two vcs with a tbh*.

     Benj[n] Cooke; RISM L 641. Solos I–IV and VI were derived from sonatas 1–5 in Lanzetti, *XII sonate a vc solo e bc*, op. 1, dedicated to Frederick, Prince of Wales (Amsterdam: Gerhardo Federico Witvogel, [1736]); RISM L 638. Reissued with Cooke's plates c.1745 by John Johnson; RISM L 642. Reissued by I. Walsh on *28 Nov 1747* in a new order (III, IV, II, V, VI, I) and with a new title: *Six solos for two vcs or a German flute and a bass*, op. 2; dedicated to Frederick, Prince of Wales; RISM L 643 (add US-GRB Scholz Collection); S&H 924 provides the year of Cooke's print. Walsh re-utilized the title and dedication found on his Lanzetti print of *c.* 1745 (see no. 6 below).

VIOLONCELLISTS AND VIOLONCELLO SOLOS

Edition – based on the Walsh print – by N. Pyron, C. Barritt and P. Foster in Early Cello Series (hereafter ECS) 11a–11b (Grancino Editions, 1982). Facsimile of the Walsh print in Grancino Editions 8211-F [c. 1982]. Facsimile of the Amsterdam edition of *XII sonate*, Op. 1, in *The Eighteenth-Century Continuo Sonata* (New York, 1991), ed. J. Adas, vol. VII: *Mid Eighteenth-Century Cello Sonatas*, pp. 81–149.

c. 1741   5. **Cervetto** Sen., Giacob Basevi called Cervetto, *Six sonatas or trios for three vcs or two violins and a bass*; dedicated to Leonora Salvadori; fifty-eight subscribers for sixty-nine copies are listed.

Author; RISM C 1721. Reissued by Walsh on *1 Apr 1741* without the list of subscribers; RISM C 1722; S&H 349.

Edited by N. Pyron, C. Barritt and W. Stewart in ECS 5a–5c (Grancino Editions, 1982–6). Facsimiles of the three partbooks ('violino primo o vc', 'violino secondo o vc', 'basso o cembalo') in Grancino Editions 8205-F [c. 1982].

c. 1745   6. **Lanzetti**, *Six solos for two vcs or a German flute and a bass*; dedicated to Frederick, Prince of Wales.

I. Walsh; RISM L 644 (add US-GRB Scholz Collection); S&H 923.

1746   7. **Caporale**, Andrea, & Johann Ernst **Galliard**, *XII solos for the vc, VI of Sig' Caporale; & VI compos'd by M' Galliard*; dedicated to the Prince of Wales.

John Johnson; RISM C 916, C 917 and G 248; RISM, p. 361; S&H 316 (Walsh also sold this print). Galliard's solos had already been issued separately, on *1740 Dec 11*, and were reissued separately, on *28 Nov 1747* (S&H 661 and 662). Since Galliard is a German composer, his other collection of sonatas is listed on Table 5.2c. Caporale's solos I–III and V–VI are identical to nos. I–V in [Niccolò] **Pasquali**, *Sonate a due violonzelli, o per violino e basso o cembalo*, engraved by Tessarin (Paris: Madame Boivin, M^r le Clerc, Melle Castagnerie, [c. 1745?]); RISM P 992. Pasquali's solo part is written in the treble clef.

Edition of Galliard's six by N. Pyron in ECS 9a–9b (Grancino Editions, 1982); the facsimile of them in Grancino Editions 8209-F [c. 1982] is defective, because the source utilized (GB-Lbl e.277/2) has Caporale's pp. 20–22 in place of Galliard's pp. 20–22. Edition of Caporale's six by N. Pyron and C. Barritt in ECS 10a–10b (Grancino Editions, 1982); facsimile of them in Grancino Editions 8210-F [c. 1982].

1747   8. **Geminiani**, Francesco, *VI sonate di vc e bc*, p. 5, 'in which he has endeavoured to make them useful not only for those who desire to improve themselves on the solo instrument, but also for those who accompany on the harpischord' ['nelle quali egli à procurato di renderle non solo utile a quelli che bramano perfettionarsi sopra il detto stromento ma ancora per quelli che accompagnano di cembalo'].

152   MUSIC IN EIGHTEENTH–CENTURY BRITAIN

'Philips sculp.'; RISM G 1509 (add US-GRB Scholz Collection). The musical plates are identical to those in Geminiani, *Sonates pour le vc et bc... dans lesquelles il a fait une ètude particuliere pour l'utilitè de ceux qui accompagnent*, op. 5; dedicated to Monseigneur le Prince d'Ardore (The Hague: Author, 1746); RISM G 1508.

Facsimile of the 1747 edition by King's Music, Redcroft, Huntingdon, Cambs [*c.* 1991]. Facsimiles of the 1746 edition by Studio per edizioni scelte, Florence, 1988, and by Performers' Facsimiles, no. 74, New York [*c.* 1989].

1748 Jan 16   9. **Pasqualino de Marzis**, *Six solos for two vcs.*
I. Walsh; RISM P 995; S&H 1171. Sonata I is attributed to Ant. **Caputi** in D-WD MS 516, and movements 1–2 of Sonata VI to G.B. **Costanzi** in D-WD MS 550.

Edited by N. Pyron, C. Barritt and W. Stewart in ECS 21a–21b (Grancino Editions, 1983–8).

1748   10. **Cervetto Sen.**, *Twelve solos for a vc with a tbh*; dedicated to Karl Theodor, Elector Palatine; 135 subscribers are listed.

Author; RISM C 1726. For letters of Nov–Dec 1747 that concern this forthcoming publication, see Lindgren, 'Musicians and Librettists' (see Table 1), nos. 389–91. Reissued *c.* 1750 by Walsh without the list of subscribers, but with 'Op. 2' added; RISM C 1727; S&H 348.

Edition of solos V, VI, IX and XII by W. Conable (Kassel: Bärenreiter, 1987).

1748   11. [Giovanni] **Bononcini, Pasqualini** [de Marzis], [Giuseppe] **St Martini**, [Andrea] **Caporale**, [Wenceslaus Joseph] **Spourni** and [Giovanni] **Porta**, *Six solos for two vcs, composed by Sig^r Bononcini and other eminent authors.*

J. Simpson; RISM, p. 361 (add US-GRB Scholz Collection); S&H 215 (Walsh began selling it in 1764). The solo by St Martini that Pasqualino played at Hickford's on 20 April 1733 might have been the one published in this collection. Spourni's solo is no. 5 in his *Six sonates pour deux violoncelles*, op. 4, engraved by Mlle Michelon (Paris: Le Clerc le cadet, Le Clerc, M^{mme} Boivin, s.d.); RISM S 4177. It is not known whether Spourni was of Italian descent.

Edited by N. Pyron and W. Stewart in ECS 36a–36b (Grancino Editions, 1986).

c. 1750   12. **Cervetto** Sen., *Six solos for a vc with a tbh*, op. 3.
John Johnson; RISM C 1736 (wrongly placed among the works of Cervetto, Jun.).

1751   13. **Pasqualino de Marzis**, *Six solos for two vcs*, op. 2.
J. Johnson; RISM P 996.

1758 14. **Lapis**, Santo, 'Maestro di Capella Italiano', *X solos for the vc with a tbh*, op. 15.
R. Liesem for the author, 'Wm Smith Sculp.'; RISM L 665; cf. RISM L 666.

c. 1760 15. **Lanzetti**, *Six solos after an easy & elegant taste for the vc with a tbh.*
For Claudius Heron at Mr Burchell's Toy Shop; RISM L 647. This is a reprint of his *Sei sonate di vc e basso*, op. 6 (Paris: Auteur, s.d.); RISM L 646. Facsimile in *The Eighteenth-Century Continuo Sonata* (New York: Garland, 1991), ed. J. Adas, vol. VII: *Mid Eighteenth-Century Cello Sonatas*, pp. 245–75.

1761 16. **Cervetto Sen.**, *Six lessons or divertimentos for two vcs*, op. 4.
John Johnson; RISM C 1730.

1763 May 12 17. **Galeotti**, Stefano, *Six sonatas for two vcs with a tbh.*
I. Walsh; RISM G 137; S&H 650.

1764 May 14 18. **Cocchi**, Gioacchino, *Six duets for two vcs*, op. 3.
Walsh; RISM C 3249; S&H 388.

c. 1764 19. **Siprutini**, Emanuel, *Six solos for a vc or a violin with a tbh*, op. 1.
For the author, by T. Bennett; RISM S 3512 (add US-CAh and US-GRB Scholz Collection). Reissued *c.* 1764 by Thompson and Sons; RISM S 3513.

1764 20. **Siprutini**, *Six solos for a vc with a tbh*, op. 3, dedicated to Evelyn Pierepont, Duke of Kingston.
Printed for the author and sold by Charles and Samuel Thompson; RISM S 3516.

c. 1765 21. **Guerini**, Francesco, *Six solos for a vc with a tbh*, op. 9.
J. Johnson; RISM G 4863.

c. 1765 22. **Magito**, Alexis, *Six sonate for the vc e basso*, op. 1.
Printed for the author and sold by John Wynne at his music shop in Cambridge; RISM M 133.
Edited by N. Pyron and C. Barritt in ECS 19a–19b (Grancino Editions, 1983–6). Facsimile in Grancino Editions 8219-F [*c.* 1983].

c. 1765 23. **Cirri**, Gianbattista, 'Teacher to his Royal Highness the Duke of Gloucester', *Six easy solos for a vc accompanied by a bass or harpsichord, and three duets for a violin or German flute and vc obligato*, op. 7.
Welcker, for the author; RISM C 2520.

154   MUSIC IN EIGHTEENTH-CENTURY BRITAIN

Facsimile by A. Forni, Sezione IV N. 131, Sala Bolognese, May 1977. Edited by L. Malusi and A. Zanotelli, *Sei sonate facili*, op. 7 (Padua: G. Zanibon, 1981).

1766   24. **Galeotti**, *Six solos for a vc with a tbh*, op. 3.
W. Randall and I. Abell; RISM G 140. Nos. 1–4 were derived from nos. 2–3 and 5–6 in Galeotti, *Sei sonate per vc solo e basso*, op. 1 (Paris: Le Clerc, [1765?]); RISM G 138.

1767   25. **Chiabrano**, Gaetano, and Francesco de **Piantanida**, *Six solos for a vc with a tbh*.
R. Bremner; RISM P 2030; RISM, p. 361 (add US-GRB Scholz Collection and US-NYp). Nos. 1–3 and 5 are assigned to 'Chiabrano', nos. 4 and 6 to 'Piantanido' [*sic*].

1768   26. **Cervetto Jun.**, James, *Six solos for the vc with a tbh*, op. 1, dedicated to the Earl of Pembroke.
Author, 'Pasquali sculp.'; RISM C 1731. Reissued *c.* 1775 by Bremner; RISM C 1732.

c. 1770   27. **Galeotti**, *Six sonatas for a vc and bass*.
Welcker; RISM G 139 (add US-GRB Scholz Collection).

c. 1770   28. **Siprutini**, *Six solos for a vc with a tbh*, op. 5.
[?Author], RISM S 3517. Reissued *c.* 1775 by Welcker; RISM S 3518.

1771   29. **Cervetto Jun.**, *Twelve divertiments in an easy stile for two vcs*, op. 2.
Author; RISM C 1733.

1775   30. **Siprutini**, *Six solos for a vc with a tb*, op. 6.
R. Wornum; RISM S 3519.

c. 1775   31. **Siprutini**, *Six solos for a vc with a tb*, op. 7.
Author, engraved by J. B. Scherer; RISM S 3520.

c. 1775   32. **Cirri**, 'Teacher to his Royal Highness the Duke of Gloucester', *Eight duets for 2 vcs*, op. 8, dedicated to the Prince of Brunswick-Lüneburg.
John Johnson, for the author; RISM C 2521. Reissued *c.* 1775 by Welcker; RISM C 2522 (add US-GRB Scholz Collection).
Facsimile by A. Forni, Sezione IV N. 148, Sala Bolognese, February 1972.

c. 1775   33. **Cirri**, *Six solos for a vc and a bass, in an easy pleasing taste proper for young practitioners*, op. 11.
A. Hummel; RISM C 2523. Reissued *c.*1775 by Welcker; RISM C 2524.

VIOLONCELLISTS AND VIOLONCELLO SOLOS

Nos. 1–3 edited by H. Müller, *Drei Sonaten für vc und bc* (Wilhelmshaven: Heinrichshofen, 1970).

c. 1775   34. **Cirri,** *Six solos for the vc and a bass,* op. 15, dedicated to William Ward; the frontispiece is an engraved portrait of 'Ioanes Baptista Cirri Foroliviensis'.

Welcker; RISM C 2528 (add US-GRB Scholz Collection).

1777   35. **Cervetto** Jun., *Six solos for the vc and a bass,* op. 3, dedicated to Sir Edward Walpole.

Printed for the author and sold by J. Duckworth; RISM C 1735. Reissued c.1790 by William Forster; RISM C 1737.

Facsimile in *The Eighteenth-Century Continuo Sonata* (New York: Garland, 1991), ed. J. Adas, vol. VIII: *Late Eighteenth-Century Cello Sonatas,* pp. 161––97.

c. 1780   36. **Giordani,** Tommaso, *Six duettos for two vcs,* op. 18, dedicated to Lord Poleraine.

Longman and Broderip; RISM G 2316 (add US-GRB Scholz Collection).

Edited by Kh. Schultz-Hauser (Mainz: B. Schött's Söhne, 1963) from *Six duos à deux violoncelles,* op. 4 [*sic*] (Berlin: J.J. Hummel, s.d.); RISM G 2318. Hummel's engraver copied the Longman and Broderip print.

1781   37. **Cervetto** Jun., *Twelve sonatinas for a vc and a bass,* dedicated to Thomas Dundas, op. 4.

Author; RISM C 1738 (add US-GRB Scholz Collection). Reissued *c.* 1790 by William Forster; RISM C 1739.

c. 1785   38. **Chabran** [i.e., Gaetano Chiabrano?], *Two solos for the vc and bass ... played with the greatest applause by Messrs* [sic] *Crosdill.*

J. Bland; RISM C 1771.

1785   39. **Galeotti,** *Two solos for a vc and bass... performed ... by... Messrs. Crosdill, Cervetto, &c.,* op. 1.

William Forster; RISM G 141. According to *The Catalogue of Printed Music in the British Library,* these two solos were derived from nos. 1 and 4 in Galeotti, *Sei sonate per vc solo e basso,* op. 1 (Paris: Le Clerc, [1767?]); RISM G 138.

c. 1795   40. **Cervetto** Jun., *Six duetts for two vcs or a violin and vc,* op. 5.

Robert Birchall; RISM C 1740.

c. 1795   41. **Cervetto** Jun., *Three duetts for two vcs or a violin and vc,* op. 6.

Robert Birchall; RISM C 1741.

156   MUSIC IN EIGHTEENTH–CENTURY BRITAIN

Table 5.2b: Four Italian 'misfits', published 1720–c. 1775

1720 Feb 1 1. **Valentini**, Giuseppe, *XII solos for the violin or vc with a tbh*, op. 8.

I. Walsh & I. Hare; RISM V 119; Smith, *A Bibliography of... John Walsh during the years 1695–1720* (see Table 5.2a, no. 3, p. 150), no. 577. Reissued *c.* 1730 by I. Walsh; S&H 1497. Each piece in the Walsh print is headed 'Allettamento', which confirms that his source was one of the two earlier editions. Both were entitled *Allettamenti per camera a violino e violoncello o cembalo*, op. 8 (Rome: Mascardi, 1714; RISM V 117; and Amsterdam: Estienne Roger & Michel Charles Le Cène, [*c.* 1715]; RISM V 118). The solo part is in the treble clef in all three editions. In the *Allettamenti*, the solo is for violin, the accompaniment for cello or harpsichord. Did Walsh & Hare intentionally alter or unintentionally mistranslate the earlier title? No matter which is true, this collection is more apt for Table 5.2b than for Table 5.2a. Eighteen movements were plagiarized in Henry Eccles, *Premier livre de sonates à violon seul et la basse*, gravez par Roussel (Paris: Foucaut, Grégoire, auteur, 1720; RISM E 203), nos. 1, 4, 8 and 9; see W. Barclay Squire, 'Henry Eccles's Borrowings', *Musical Times*, 64 (1923), 790.

Edition (based on the Walsh & Hare print) by N. Pyron, F. Guèneux, C. Barritt and W. Stewart in ECS 20a–20d (Grancino Editions, 1983–6).

1745 Jan 24 2. **Porpora**, Nicolò, and Gio. Batta. **Costanza** [Costanzi], *Six sonatas for two vcs and two violins with a tbh*.

I. Walsh; RISM P 5123; RISM, p. 364; S&H 1226 and 1223 (an advertisement of 9 Apr 1745). No sonata is attributed to either composer.

No. 5 edited by K.H. Stahmer (Wilhelmshaven: Heinrichshofen, 1980); his edition lacks the second violin part, which may never have been printed.

1768 Oct 18 3. **Uttini**, Francesco, *Six sonatas for two violins and a bass; the third and sixth with additional obligato parts, one sonata [the third] for the violoncello, and the other [the sixth] for the harpsichord*, dedicated by Fougt to the Society for the Encouragement of Arts, Manufactures and Commerce of Great-Britain.

Henry Fougt; RISM U 133. The third work is a quartet. Its obbligato cello part resembles that in Cirri's op. 14 (see no. 4 below).

c. 1775 4. **Cirri**, *Six concertos in four parts for the vc obligato with two violins and a bass*, op. 14.

Welcker; RISM C 2507. Reissued *c.* 1780 by Longman & Broderip; RISM C 2506. All passages, whether marked *tutti* or *solo*, are scored for all four parts; in solos, the obbligato cello is sometimes the fastest-moving part.

Edition (based on the Welcker print) by N. Pyron in ECS 35a–35f (Grancino Editions, 1987).

VIOLONCELLISTS AND VIOLONCELLO SOLOS

Table 5.2c: Three collections by foreign composers other than Italians, published *c.* 1733–*c.* 1740

1733 May 1   1. **Galliard**, Johann Ernst, *Six sonatas for the bassoon or vc with a tbh.*
John Walsh; RISM G 246 (add US-GRB Scholz Collection); cf. RISM G 247; S&H 664. Reissued c.1740 by Walsh; S&H 665.
Facsimile by Éditions Minkoff, Geneva, 1995.

c. 1733   2. **Fesch**, Willem De, *XII Sonatas, six for a violin, with a tb ... and six for two vcs*, op. 8; dedicated to Lord Teynham; seventy-six subscribers for seventy-seven copies are listed.
Ben. Cooke; RISM F 629 (add US-GRB Scholz Collection). Sonatas VII–XII in this print are identical with *VI sonatas for a vc with a tbh*, op. 8 (John Johnson, *c.* 1733); RISM F 630.
Facsimile of the Johnson print in Performers' Facsimiles, no. 55, New York [*c.* 1988]. Edited by W. Schultz, *Sechs Sonaten für Violoncello und bezifferten Bass* (Leipzig: Peters, 1961).

c. 1740   3. **Fesch**, *VI Sonatas for a vc solo, with a tbh*, op. 13; dedicated to Peregrine, Duke of Ancaster and Kesteren.
s.l., s.n; RISM F 639. Reissued by Walsh on *2 Nov 1757*; RISM F 640; S&H 544–5.
Edited by W. Kolneder (Heidelberg: Willy Müller, 1982).

CHAPTER SIX

Murder Most Virtuous:
The *Judith* Oratorios of De Fesch,
Smith and Arne

Eva Zöllner

One of the most intriguing heroines of the Apocrypha, Judith of Bethulia, who liberates her people by murdering the enemy general Holofernes, is probably best known through the many paintings that she inspired throughout the ages: portrayals by Tintoretto, Caravaggio, Cranach, Botticelli, Titian, Rembrandt and others show the heroine either in the act of committing the murderous deed or, in relaxed and triumphant attitude, presenting the head of Holofernes to the viewer. Apart from the visual arts, however, the Judith legend was also a source of inspiration to poets and dramatists from Hans Sachs and Friedrich Hebbel to Johann Nestroy and Jean Giraudoux, as well as to composers of operas such as Serov (1863) and Honegger (1926) and oratorios, most notably settings of Pietro Metastasio's famous *Betulia liberata* of 1734.[1]

The eighteenth century saw the creation of no fewer than three English oratorios on the subject, all composed by contemporaries of Handel: the first English *Judith* oratorio was written by Willem De Fesch (1687–1761) in 1733 and was followed by two mid-century versions, by John Christopher Smith Jun. (1712–95), composed in the period ?1755–8, and Thomas Augustine Arne (1710–78), composed in 1761.

As an oratorio character, Judith undoubtedly has many advantages that must have made her very attractive to the three composers in question: pious and virtuous on the one hand, courageous, alluringly beautiful and daring on the other, she makes an ideal heroine, particularly since the high point of her story, the killing of Holofernes, while offering high drama, is, thanks to Judith's noble motives, 'the Bible's most approved of murder'.[2] Apart from the heroine herself, the legend also offers ample room for dramatic scenes, such as choruses for the opposing Bethulians and Assyrians, and there is also the additional attraction of Judith's opponent, the cunning Holofernes. Small wonder, therefore, that De Fesch, Smith and Arne deemed the legend appropriate for an oratorio.

The main elements of the story as described in Chapters 7–15 of the Book of Judith are as follows. The city of Bethulia is besieged by Assyrian troops under the command of their general Holofernes. With the water supply cut off, the city

---

[1] The most recent and far-reaching study of the Apocryphal heroine and her impact on Western culture is M. Stocker, *Judith: Sexual Warrior* (New Haven, London, 1998). For Judith and her portrayal in English and German literature see E. Purdie, *The Story of Judith in German Literature* (Paris, 1927).

[2] H. Diack Johnstone and R. Fiske (eds), *The Blackwell History of Music in Britain*, vol. 4: *The Eighteenth Century* (Oxford, 1990), p. 217.

THE *JUDITH* ORATORIOS   159

is doomed to surrender within a matter of days. In this desperate situation it falls on the beautiful and virtuous Judith, the widow of Manasseh, to save her city. With only one servant to accompany her, she sets out for the Assyrian camp and, pretending to have lost faith in the Bethulian cause, she is allowed to enter it. Struck by her beauty, Holofernes is instantly taken in and is all too easily convinced that Judith has come merely to surrender herself to him. He invites her to a banquet, in the course of which he becomes drunk and eventually falls asleep. With nobody else about, Judith takes advantage of the situation, beheads Holofernes and, under cover of darkness, leaves the camp together with her servant. The next morning, Holofernes's decapitated corpse is found, and the Assyrian troops disperse in terror and confusion. Safely arrived in Bethulia, Judith is celebrated and the story ends with general rejoicing

Willem De Fesch's *Judith* is one of the earliest English oratorios, preceded only by Handel's *Esther* and Maurice Greene's short *Song of Deborah and Barak* of 1732. The first performance of De Fesch's *Judith* took place at Lincoln's Inn Fields on 16 February 1733, and a second – a benefit performance for De Fesch – is known to have been given at the Crown and Anchor tavern on 29 February 1740. A former chapel master of Antwerp Cathedral, De Fesch had settled in London in the early 1730s, where he was listed as 'a respectable professor on the violin', often appearing as a concert violinist. Unfortunately, a short aria for Judith, 'Gayly smiling',[3] is the only complete musical item of his oratorio that has survived. Any manuscript scores or part-books that may have existed are lost. The libretto, however, can truthfully be described as one of the most intriguing, dramatic and colourful of its time. It was written by William Huggins (1696–1761), who later pursued a career as a translator, publishing an English version of Ariosto's *Orlando Furioso* in 1757; his translation of Dante's *Divina Commedia*, however, never reached fruition. It is not known whether Huggins had recourse to earlier dramatizations of extracts from the legend and it is perfectly possible that he worked directly from the Scriptures.[4] The decision to write the work at all was presumably inspired by the performances of Handel's *Esther* in London in 1732. According to Charles Burney, Huggins had taken an eager and indeed active interest in the performances which took place at the Crown and Anchor tavern on 23 February, 1 March and 3 March 1732: 'Soon after this [the private performances of *Esther* at the house of Bernard Gates] it was twice performed by the same children, at the Crown and Anchor, by the desire of William Huggins, esq. a member of that Society[5] [...] who furnished the dresses.'[6]

---

[3] One copy of which is in GB-Lbl, H.1601. c. (13), dated *c*. 1750. The aria has been printed in the *New Oxford History of Music*, vol. 6 *Concert Music 1630–1750* (London, 1986), pp. 35–6.

[4] In her list of Judith plays Purdie lists a *Siege of Bethulia* 'performed at Bartholomew's Fair, on Lee and Harper's stage' in 1732, but it is not certain whether there was any connection between this and Huggins's dramatization of the legend. Purdie, *The Story of Judith*, p. 16.

[5] It is not exactly clear to which of the two societies involved in the *Esther* performances Burney refers: the first two performances were organized by the Philharmonic

160   MUSIC IN EIGHTEENTH-CENTURY BRITAIN

It seems probable that these performances, which were given at Huggins's instigation, inspired him to try his hand at a similar project himself. In fact, there are some parallels to be found in the respective librettos: both *Esther* and *Judith* oratorios centre around a strong-minded and brave heroine, who puts her own life at risk in trying to save her people; Judith has to confront Holofernes, whereas Esther pleads the cause of her people before King Ahasuerus, her husband, even though by doing so she puts her own life at risk, since she dares to appear unsummoned before him. A few other parallels could be drawn – Haman in his rage for the blood of the Israelites closely resembles Holofernes, with the two characters even sharing similar lines of verse – but it would be futile to try to search for any closer relationship between the two pieces. Nevertheless, given Huggins's close involvement in the *Esther* performances, his one and only oratorio libretto that he finished shortly after can safely be assumed to have been inspired by this experience.

William Huggins was a close friend of William Hogarth, the eminent painter and engraver. Hogarth apparently took some interest in De Fesch's and Huggins's project, as is evident from two of his engravings. The well-known 'Chorus of Singers', which dates from December 1732, shows a rehearsal of *Judith*; the singers are in the process of rehearsing the first chorus in Act I, Scene I of the oratorio, 'The world shall bow to the Assyrian throne' (Plate 6.1). For the published edition of the libretto, which was issued in 1733,[7] Hogarth provided Huggins with a design for an engraving to be used as a frontispiece (Plate 6.2). It shows Judith in front of Holofernes's tent, shortly before the murder. While Holofernes, oblivious to what is to befall him, sleeps undisturbed, Judith casts her eyes heavenwards, holding the sword rather inexpertly in her left hand by the cutting edge. The inscription 'per vulnera servor morte tua vivens' ['saved by your wounds, alive when you are dead'] is taken from Book X of Virgil's *Aeneid*.

About twenty-five years went by before the Judith legend was again taken up by an English oratorio composer: John Christopher Smith Jun., who, together with John Stanley (1712–86), had taken over Handel's oratorio series at Covent Garden, set a new Judith libretto written by his friend Robert Price of Foxley. No dates of any public or private performances of this work are known. In his article on Smith in *The New Grove Dictionary*,[8] Roger Fiske listed

---

Society, the third by the Academy of Ancient Music. Huggins may have been a member of either; see also W. Dean, *Handel's Dramatic Oratorios and Masques* (London, 1959), p. 204.

[6] C. Burney, *An Account of the Musical Performances* (London, 1785), pp. 22 and 100–101.

[7] This was not the wordbook used in connection with any actual performances (of which no copy seems to have survived). It was issued well in advance of the première and the title-page does not refer to any specific performance, nor does the list of characters give any information about the singers. Some copies of the libretto were published without the frontispiece. Copies that include Hogarth's engraving are in GB-Lbl, 162.h.9. and the Huntington Library. For more detailed descriptions of the two engravings see R. Paulson (ed.), *Hogarth's Graphic Works* (New Haven, London, 1965), vol. 1, pp. 149–51 and 264–5.

[8] R. Fiske, 'J.C. Smith' in S. Sadie (ed.), *New Grove Dictionary of Music and Musicians* (London, 1980), vol. 17, p. 415.

Plate 6.1 William Hogarth: A Chorus of Singers, December 1732

Plate 6.2 William Hogarth: frontispiece to William Huggins's *Judith* (London, 1733)

THE *JUDITH* ORATORIOS 163

Judith as having been composed in 1758. While this is not an unlikely date, Fiske's source for this information is not known. Evidence gained from the manuscript score of Smith's *Judith,* held in the Hamburg Staats- und Universitätsbibliothek (D-Hs MA/669), may help to clarify the situation: the score was obviously used for performances on more than one occasion; there are numerous cuts, some of the arias were shortened, other numbers omitted or later, alternative versions added in Smith's own hand. Barbara Small[9] identified the watermarks of the main body of the manuscript as Hans-Dieter Clausen's Cr I and II,[10] which appear to have been in use between 1755 and 1758, which makes it likely that the oratorio was written within this period, at any rate shortly before Thomas Arne's famous *Judith* of 1761. Even though information regarding the performance dates of almost all of Smith's oratorios (with the exception of those works included in the programmes of the Lenten oratorio seasons at Covent Garden and, from 1770 onwards, Drury Lane) is tantalizingly limited, his *Judith* probably also received at least one later performance, as additional leaves in the score in Smith's own hand suggest. According to the watermarks, these interpolated leaves are of a later period and probably date from the mid-1760s (the watermarks for these sections are Hb and Hc, which Clausen dates as 1765).[11]

Thomas Arne's version, with a libretto by Isaac Bickerstaffe, was by far the most successful of the three Judith oratorios, if the number of performances is anything to go by: first performed in 1761, it was often revived in the following years, even outside the London oratorio season, and David Garrick chose to have this oratorio performed during his famous Shakespeare Memorial Festival in Stratford-upon-Avon in 1769. Some of the last complete performances in the eighteenth century were organized and directed by Arne's son Michael at the Little Theatre in the Haymarket in 1784 and 1785.[12] During its long performance life, the work was often revised. These changes are documented in the numerous librettos that have survived, as well as in the (mainly) autograph manuscript score of the work, held in the British Library (GB-Lbl MS Add. 11515–17), which served as the performing score on most (if not on all) of these occasions.[13]

---

[9] Barbara Small's doctoral thesis on the life and works of J.C. Smith is still in progress. I am very grateful to her for supplying me with information about the watermarks in the manuscript score of Smith's *Judith.*

[10] H.D. Clausen, *Händels Direktionspartituren,* (*Hamburger Beiträge zur Musikwissenschaft,* vol. 7) (Hamburg, 1972), p. 250.

[11] Apart from Hb and Hc, Barbara Small identified also a third (undatable) watermark in this additional section which she named F1a. According to Smith's later revisions, no fewer than nine recitatives were shortened and one aria ('When from the sacred paths of truth we stray') omitted. Other changes include alternative versions of two of the arias ('Inspire thine handmaid now' and 'Upon the God of Israel I'll call'), as well as the addition of a chorus ('Let pomp and triumph') to end the first scene of Act 3.

[12] Another, later performance of *Judith* took place on 22 November 1787, a benefit for Walter Clagget, proprietor of Apollo Gardens; see playbill GB-Lbl 937. c.5.

[13] E. Zöllner, 'English Oratorio after Handel' (PhD diss., University of Hamburg, 1997), pp. 97–8.

164 MUSIC IN EIGHTEENTH-CENTURY BRITAIN

The three oratorios have, surprisingly enough, very little in common, save their heroine and title. Even though they were created in relatively close proximity, there were no reciprocal influences between the individual works, not even in the case of the later two oratorios by Smith and Arne, separated by a mere three years. It has to be assumed, therefore, that all three composers and their authors were drawn to the subject independently.

The structural differences between the three oratorios can be seen from the list of scenes (see Table 6.1). In each of the three versions the scenes are arranged in noticeably different order. De Fesch includes a detailed account of Achior's sufferings, a minor character who is only briefly dealt with in Smith's version and does not appear at all in Arne's *Judith*.

Table 6.1: Three *Judith* oratorios

Willem De Fesch *Judith* (1733) (Libretto: William Huggins)	John Christopher Smith *Judith* (?1755–58) (Libretto: Robert Price)	Thomas Augustine Arne *Judith* (1761) (Libretto: Isaac Bickerstaffe)
ACT 1 *In the Assyrian camp:*	ACT 1 *In the Assyrian camp:*	ACT 1 *In Bethulia:*
Scene 1: Holofernes prepares for the attack on Bethulia Achior's protests	Scene 1: Holofernes prepares for the attack on Bethulia Achior's protests	Scenes 1 & 2: The Bethulians await the attack
Before the walls of Bethulia: Scenes 2–4: Achior is left to perish Achior is rescued by the Bethulians	*In Bethulia, Judith's house:* Scene 2: Judith prepares to go into the Assyrian camp	*Bethulia, in Judith's house:* Scene 2: Judith prepares to go into the Assyrian camp
	In Bethulia: Scene 3: Achior arrives in Bethulia	*In Bethulia:* Scenes 4 & 5: Judith leaves Bethulia
ACT 2 *In Bethulia:*	ACT 2 *In Bethulia:*	ACT 2 *In the Assyrian camp:*
Scenes 1 & 2 The Bethulians await the attack	Scene 1: The Bethulians await the attack	Scenes 1–3 Judith meets Holofernes, who invites her to the banquet Scene 4 Judith prepares for the murder
Scenes 3 & 4: Judith prepares to go into the Assyrian camp		
	In the Assyrian camp: Scene 2: Judith meets Holofernes, who invites her to the banquet	*In the Assyrian camp Holofernes' tent* Scenes 5 & 6 The banquet; Judith sings Holofernes to sleep

THE *JUDITH* ORATORIOS

(De Fesch)	(Smith)	(Arne)
ACT 3	ACT 3	ACT 3
In the Assyrian camp, Holofernes' tent:	*In the Assyrian camp, Holofernes' tent:*	
Scenes 1 & 2	Scenes 1 & 2:	
Judith meets Holofernes, who invites her to the banquet	The banquet; Judith prepares for the murder	
Scenes 3 & 4:		
The banquet		
Judith beheads Holofernes		
In Bethulia:	*In Bethulia:*	*In Bethulia:*
Scene 5:	Scene 3:	Scenes 1–5:
Judith is celebrated by the Bethulians	Judith is celebrated by the Bethulians	Judith is celebrated by the Bethulians

Furthermore, there are striking differences in the characterization of the heroine herself: De Fesch's and Huggins's Judith is a full-blooded heroine, who embarks on her mission in a fairly relaxed mood that borders on gleeful anticipation. She openly refers to the stratagems she is going to use in order to seduce Holofernes, 'Gayly smiling [...] with my falser soft caresses, I the tyrant will abuse' (Act 2, Scene 4), later declaring: 'My eyes, I dare believe, have executed their intended mischief' (2:2). She is contrasted with a Holofernes who is certainly no stranger to vice. When he first sets eyes on her, he can hardly restrain himself, asserting that 'the Hebrew Beauty has smote me to the Heart, and I'm in Rage to think I let a Jewel escape me' (3:1). Nor do Huggins and De Fesch spare us a full description of the murder, with every gory detail; placed near the end of the third and final act, it actually forms the high point of the oratorio, followed only by a concluding chorus in praise of God. After Holofernes has fallen into a drunken stupor, Judith not only cuts off his head with his own sword, but, as the numerous stage directions in the libretto indicate,[14] even comes forward with Holofernes's head in her hand to present it, before putting it into her basket to take away with her to Bethulia as proof of her deed.[15]

---

[14] The note in David Erskine Baker's (not overly reliable) *Biographica Dramatica* (London, 1764; 3rd edn, London, 1812), vol. 3, p. 445 that the work was 'performed with scenes and other decorations' should be taken with a pinch of salt; it is true that, according to an advertisement in the *Daily Journal* of 6 February 1733, it was 'to be performed in character', yet in later announcements this note was not repeated. In the light of the uproar that the proposal of a staged public performance of Handel's *Esther* had caused the previous year, it would seem improbable that Huggins and De Fesch should have tried to put on a staged performance of *Judith*. (See also F. van den Bremt, *Willem De Fesch (1678–1757?), Nederlands Componist en Virtuoos, Leven en Werk* (Louvain, 1949), pp. 53–4.) However, Huggins's detailed stage directions show that he envisaged the piece as a drama in the true sense.

[15] The basket is not a product of Huggins's overblown imagination but a detail included in the original Apocryphal legend and in many pictorial representations.

166 MUSIC IN EIGHTEENTH-CENTURY BRITAIN

Such bathetic bluntness was not for John Christopher Smith and his librettist Price, nor, indeed, for Arne and Bickerstaffe,[16] who were somewhat more cautious in their portrayal of Judith: in both oratorios she is shown as a virtuous and pious heroine, who tries to allay the fears and bolster the courage of her people, reminding them of their duty to be patient. The murder, described in every ghastly detail by Huggins and De Fesch, is only of minor importance to Smith and Arne: Smith introduces a sudden change of scene in Act 3, from the Assyrian camp, as Judith prepares for the murder, to Bethulia, where she is celebrated on her return. Arne follows a similar course by letting the murder take place in the interval between Acts 2 and 3, beginning Act 3 with a *recitativo secco* that gives a short account of the events in the Assyrian camp. (Roger Fiske, who otherwise favoured this work as one of the best of the repertory, commented disappointedly that Arne had handled this scene 'with no dramatic feeling whatsoever'.[17]) This notable difference between De Fesch's and Huggins's highly dramatic rendering of this part of the story and the versions by Arne and Smith, who resort to having a narrative description of the murder rather than the murderous deed itself, should not, however, be ascribed to uncommon bashfulness or to a failure to recognise the dramatic possibilities of the work. Rather, it seems that in all known *Judith* or *Betulia liberata* oratorios of the time, a change of scene was included at the crucial moment, and Judith appeared again only after having committed the murder;[18] this, of course, renders Huggins's *Judith* of 1733 an exceptional piece.

Smith's Judith could not possibly be more different from De Fesch's ferocious heroine: for a very large part of the later oratorio she is occupied either with scolding her people for losing their faith or with praying, in imploring arias, for the success of her mission. Never seriously in doubt about the happy ending of her mission, she exudes unshakeable confidence, preferably in simply-structured, melodious numbers, such as her 'With resignation let us wait the hour' (Ex. 6.1), or the duet with the Bethulian elder Ozias 'In the tremendous act I undertake', both from Act 2, Scene 1. Even in the scene before the murder, the dramatic high point of both oratorios, she merely expresses her fears and horror at what she is about to do in the aria 'What horrors now each sense alarm', accompanied by strings with the accustomed hectic, and in Smith's case rather wooden, semiquaver figurations (Ex. 6.2). Judith in her role as beautiful, scheming seductress, so much harped on by De Fesch and Huggins, is

---

[16] Both composers and their respective librettists might have had recourse to Metastasio's libretto on the same subject, *Betulia liberata* of 1734, which enjoyed enormous success on the continent and was set to music by Giuseppe Calegari (*c.* 1750–1812), Holzbauer (1711–83), Jommelli (1714–74), Mozart (1756–91) and many others. Yet the works are structured quite differently. With their tripartite layout they clearly adhere to the English oratorio tradition, and allow far more room for the chorus. Also, both oratorios include frequent changes of scene that run contrary to the principle of unity of time, place and action as observed in the Metastasian model (compare the list of scenes in Table 6.1).

[17] Johnstone and Fiske, *The Eighteenth Century*, p. 217.

[18] H. Geyer, 'Die Sterbeszene im Oratorium des 18. Jahrhunderts,' in *Opernheld und Opernheldin im 18. Jahrhundert*, (*Schriften zur Musikwissenschaft auf Münster*, vol. 1), (Hamburg, Eisenach, 1991), pp. 195–231.

Ex. 6.1 John Christopher Smith: *Judith*, 'With resignation let us wait the hour'
(Source: D-Hs MA/669)

Ex. 6.2 John Christopher Smith: *Judith*, 'What horrors now each sense alarm'
(Source: D-Hs MA/669)

168   MUSIC IN EIGHTEENTH-CENTURY BRITAIN

completely ignored by Smith and his librettist Price. It would seem that both were somewhat afraid of the dangerous charms of their heroine, who is denied a direct confrontation with Holofernes (Judith shares the oratorio's two duets, 'In the tremendous act I undertake' and 'He bragged that he would burn up my borders', with the Bethulian elder Ozias) and, as noted above, is only accorded a feeling of horror at the prospect of the terrible crime she is about to commit.

Arne's Judith on the other hand owes more to De Fesch's and Huggins's full-blooded virago than to Smith's ever-virtuous heroine: in the very demanding operatic aria 'Adventurous lo! I spread the sail', she is characterized as a daring character, fully prepared to meet and deal with whatever danger she may have to face (Ex. 6.3). Arne's more colourful characterization of Judith is also apparent in the scene before the murder. Arne, who is far less concerned with Judith's personal feelings at this point, introduces a slumber aria, the famous 'Sleep gentle cherub' (Ex. 6.4), with which she sings Holofernes to sleep, a more refined, toned-down version of Judith in her role as seductress than the very straightforward one presented by Huggins's Judith with her 'false tresses' (2:4) and flirtatious looks. Arne and Bickerstaffe very wisely steer a subtle course between Huggins's and De Fesch's 'smiling and beguiling' Judith (2:4) and her 'devout and pure' counterpart with her 'spotless innocence' in Smith's version (as she is described by Ozias in 2:1), thus avoiding both equally hazardous interpretations. 'At a time when the real energies were secular', writes Margarita Stocker, 'biblical heroines had only two kinds of appeal: official and sickly piety, or unofficial ribaldry. The success of Arne's oratorio was, in fact, owing to its ability to conflate the two.'[19] Furthermore, with Judith's maid Abra, a character omitted by Smith/Price and De Fesch/Huggins, Arne also provides a fitting counterpart for his heroine. Their duet 'On thy borders, O Jordan' before the final chorus ends the oratorio on a peacefully pastoral note.[20]

On the whole, Arne's *Judith* leaves a much more convincing impression than Smith's, not only because of the characterization of its heroine, but because of Arne's more varied orchestration and greater expertise in his handling of musical forms; whereas Smith uses *da capo* and *dal segno* structures almost throughout, there is a nearly even balance between binary and ternary patterns in Arne's work. Also, Arne is more confident in entrusting solo passages to the winds and strings (for instance in the Israelite's aria, 'No more the heathen shall blaspheme' (3:3) with its two solo cellos), and handles them with greater assurance.

Indeed, it may be no mere coincidence that Smith never put his *Judith* on the programme of the oratorio series at Covent Garden and (from 1770 onwards) Drury Lane, probably fearing direct competition with Arne. In all fairness to Smith, however, it should be observed that his (for modern observers) astonishingly tame reading of the heroine and her adventurous story may also

---

[19]   Stocker, *Judith: Sexual Warrior*, p. 141.

[20]   The duet, though discarded from the autograph manuscript some time after the première and omitted in later performances, was included in Walsh's printed score, entitled *Judith, As it is Perform'd at the Theatre-Royal in Drury Lane* (London, 1765); see also Zöllner, 'English Oratorio after Handel', p. 103.

THE *JUDITH* ORATORIOS 169

Ex. 6.3 Thomas Arne: *Judith*, 'Adventurous lo! I spread the sail'
(Source: *Judith, An Oratorio, As it is Perform'd at the Theatre-Royal in Drury Lane*, London: Walsh [1765])

Ex. 6.4 Thomas Arne: *Judith*, 'Sleep, gentle cherub'
(Source: *Judith, An Oratorio, As it is Perform'd at the Theatre-Royal in Drury Lane*, London: Walsh [1765])

have been influenced by the oratorio taste of his time. The new English oratorio repertory of the latter half of the eighteenth century included full-length works, almost entirely devoid of a plot, with equally virtuous characters, such as John Worgan's *Hannah* of 1764 and Felice Giardini's and Charles Avison's *Ruth* of

THE *JUDITH* ORATORIOS 171

1763; the latter was a very successful oratorio repeated annually in aid of the Lock Hospital. As Roger Fiske has observed: 'We today have been conditioned by stage performances of Handel's oratorios, and by Winton Dean's book *Handel's Dramatic Oratorios and Masques*, to regard the more dramatic ones as the more interesting, but this was hardly anyone's view in the latter part of the eighteenth century.'[21]

There can hardly be three more different oratorios on the same subject than the three settings of the Judith story by De Fesch, Smith and Arne. From the bloodthirsty protagonist in De Fesch's version, Arne's operatically minded Judith with her coloratura outpourings to the insipid scoldings of Smith's heroine, every imaginable interpretation of the Apocryphal lady is to be found. The appropriateness of Judith as a oratorio heroine was never called into question, however, not even by John Wesley who, after having attended a benefit performance of Arne's version for the Lock Hospital on 29 February 1764, thought only the 'singing of different words by different persons, at one and the same time' objectionable and not to his liking, but 'some parts of it exceedingly fine'.[22] There was no fixed eighteenth-century view of how the lady should be handled, but the popularity of Judith as an oratorio heroine during this time was never in any doubt.

---

[21] Johnstone and Fiske (eds), *The Eighteenth Century*, p. 212.
[22] Entry of 29 February 1764 in *The Journal of the Rev. John Wesley, A.M.*, ed. N. Curnock (London, 1909–16), vol. 5, p. 89.

CHAPTER SEVEN

A Reappraisal of Provincial Church Music

Sally Drage

Eighteenth-century provincial church music has an extremely poor reputation, and has been condemned by eighteenth-century commentators and twentieth-century scholars alike.[1] This essay attempts to re-examine the evidence and to consider whether derogatory comments about the repertoire and its performance are justified.

Most eighteenth-century provincial church music, usually termed 'psalmody', was written and performed by amateurs. It included not only psalms, but also anthems, service music, chants and hymns,[2] and could be heard in both Anglican parish churches and nonconformist chapels. Although this repertoire is often described as 'gallery music', this is an imprecise definition. It is true that eighteenth-century provincial choirs often claimed the west gallery of the church as their own special territory, but they also occupied special singing seats, and galleries, if they existed at all, could be privately owned. More pejoratively, 'gallery music' unfortunately evokes an image of elderly, musically inept country bumpkins. The term 'sacred folk song'[3] is also not accurate; and 'folk' is another emotive word with misleading connotations.[4] This music could, perhaps, be described as 'vernacular' – as opposed to 'art' – in the same way that architects distinguish between simple domestic homes and grand stately mansions, but it might be more accurate, and less controversial, to regard it as a separate genre, which absorbed elements of both styles. In England this sacred repertoire is largely unknown and, apart from the notable work of Nicholas Temperley,[5] has rarely been considered worthy of serious research. However, American musicologists have been producing academic studies and scholarly editions of American psalmody for many years, even though much of it originated in England.[6]

Before the music is examined in greater detail, it is necessary to consider the historical background and to chart the development of provincial choirs. England at the beginning of the eighteenth century was a rural society. Apart from London and about half-a-dozen large towns, most of the other 800 market towns

---

[1] S.H. Nicholson, *Choirs and Places where they Sing* (London, 1932); C.H. Phillips, *The Singing Church*, rev. edn (Oxford, 1979).

[2] The use of hymns was not officially sanctioned by the Church of England until 1820.

[3] As used in C.W. Pearce, 'English Sacred Folk Song of the West Gallery Period (c. 1695-1820)', *Proceedings of the Musical Association*, 48 (1921), 1–7.

[4] G. Boyes, *The Imagined Village* (Manchester, 1993), pp. 1–18.

[5] N. Temperley, *The Music of the English Parish Church* (Cambridge, 1979).

[6] See R. Crawford, *The Core Repertory of Early American Psalmody. Recent Researches in American Music*, vols. 11–12 (Madison, 1984); and A.P. Britton et al., *American Sacred Imprints: 1698-1810: A Bibliography* (Worcester, Mass., 1991).

PROVINCIAL CHURCH MUSIC

had only between 1000 and 2000 inhabitants; over half the population lived in the country, working in agriculture or cottage industries. Village parish churches were often poorly attended and many clergymen were pluralists or absentees; Anglican worship, in general, had become superficial and even irreverent.[7] Most churches lacked organs and the music was limited to a few metrical psalms, recited line-by-line by the parish clerk and sung extremely slowly and unrhythmically – if at all – by an apathetic congregation. Nevertheless the greatest changes to eighteenth-century church music occurred not in the cities and larger towns, where improvements usually consisted of acquiring an organ and maybe a choir of charity children, but in the country towns and villages, where changes eventually created a revolution in provincial psalmody.

In the late 1600s, High-Church reformers started religious societies for young men, who met regularly for prayer, discussion and the practice of psalmody, which they sang from the music rather than by ear. The plan was for the young men to learn a few simple tunes and then lead the psalm-singing by sitting with the congregation; it was hoped that any musical improvements would also encourage more devout worship. At first there was some success, as can be seen by examining contemporary accounts. One little-known source is the archive of the SPCK (the Society for Promoting Christian Knowledge) which was founded in 1698. It sent out regular circular letters recommending various ways to improve worship, and kept abstracts of the replies, which confirm the growing interest in psalmody and the development of country choirs. A circular letter of 24 September 1717 (now lost) apparently suggested that churches should make a 'Tryal of Psalmody' and generated a great deal of correspondence.[8] Many parishes were already successful in encouraging psalm-singing, and agreed that it was an excellent way to improve church attendance. At Box in Wiltshire over 160 young people, beginning with the charity children, had learnt to sing from music; by keeping to a few of the 'Oldest and most Grave' tunes most of the congregation now joined in the singing and, despite building a new aisle to seat another 100, the church was full.[9] In Loughborough they already had 'Psalmody performed in good Perfection';[10] and although slight bribery was necessary in order to obtain the desired results, William Shield at Saddington, Leicestershire had 'prevail'd with the great part of his P[ar]ish to learn to sing; had procur'd them a very good Master, and by promising them a small weekly allowance, they have contracted for a quarter of a year, and are to attend 8 a clock prayers before they part'.[11] The most negative comment came from Stoke Gabriel in Devon where the psalm-singing was excellent, but the rector found it harder to

---

[7] R. Porter, *The Penguin Social History of Great Britain – English Society in the Eighteenth Century* (London, 1982), pp. 174–5.

[8] The promotion of psalmody had been suggested by Robert Watts of Great Gidding, Hunts, as a suitable subject for a circular letter; *Abstract Letter Books, vol. 8 1717–18* no. 5288, 15 July 1777. The date of the consequent letter is given in ibid., no. 5438, 18 November 1717.

[9] Ibid., no.5213, 1 May 1717. This letter may have initiated the discussion that culminated in the circular letter of 24 September 1717.

[10] Ibid., no.5449, 30 November 1717.

[11] *Abstract Letter Books, vol. 15 1729–30*, no.10414, 22 September 1729.

174   MUSIC IN EIGHTEENTH-CENTURY BRITAIN

persuade the congregation to part with their money.[12] Later, in 1729, correspondents were still enthusiastic; at Creeke, Northamptonshire, the rector wrote how he had built at his own cost 'a commodious seat for the Singers, whose devout and orderly deportment in the church has been influential as 'tis Exemplary'.[13]

However, as singers improved they became bored with simple strophic psalm tunes and preferred more complex music worthier of their talents. At first new repertoire was limited to a few anthems, and so caused little controversy, but the introduction of more florid psalm tunes with melismas, dotted rhythms, and solo or duet sections was simultaneously condemned and condoned by many clergy: condemned because it effectively silenced any congregational participation, condoned because a performance by the choir of new, vigorous and tuneful music inevitably attracted larger congregations. As often in the history of religious music there was a conflict between worship in which everyone participated and elite performance that gratified the self-esteem of the performers.

More difficult music required regular rehearsals, and singers began to organize themselves into formal 'singing societies', as distinct from the original religious ones. Surviving articles of agreement show how they arranged membership, planned rehearsals, and even had a system of fines for absenteeism and bad behaviour such as drunkenness or swearing;[14] at Oldbury in Gloucestershire, two fishermen had special dispensation to miss rehearsals if they were working late on the Severn.[15]

When instruments were introduced during the second half of the century, initially to help singers maintain pitch, it was possible to perform more elaborate music. Most contemporary complaints about eighteenth-century church music focused on the increasing arrogance of the singers, and on the unsuitability of the repertoire, often noting that the singing of the Methodists was far preferable, since the whole congregation participated.[16] Beilby Porteus, Bishop of London, summed up the worst abuses of parochial psalmody:

> In country parishes it is generally engrossed by a select band of singers, who have been taught by some itinerant master to sing in the worst manner, a most wretched set of psalm tunes in three or four parts, so complex, so difficult and so totally void of all true harmony that it is altogether impossible for any of the congregation to take part with them, who therefore sit in silent admiration, or total inattention.[17]

But not all churches were totally dominated by their choir. In 1782 a young Prussian clergyman, Carl Philipp Moritz, was impressed by the psalm-singing at

---

[12]   *Abstract Letter Books, vol. 8 1717–18*, no. 5504, 31 January 1718.

[13]   *Abstract Letter Books, vol. 15 1729–30*, no. 10679, 2 March 1730.

[14]   Wysall, Nottingham 1774 (Nottingham Record Office PR790).

[15]   1742 (Gloucestershire Record Office D47642/1).

[16]   A. Bedford, *The Excellency of Divine Music* (London, 1733); *The Gentleman's Magazine* (February 1744), 82–3; E. Miller, *Thoughts on the present Performance of Psalmody* (London, 1791).

[17]   B. Porteus, 'A Charge Delivered to the Clergy of the Diocese of London... in 1790', *Works*, 6 (London, 1811), pp. 20–25.

PROVINCIAL CHURCH MUSIC

Nettlebed, Oxfordshire: 'I cannot well express how affecting and edifying it seemed to me, to hear this whole orderly and decent congregation, in this small country church, joining together with vocal and instrumental music in the praise of their Maker.'[18]

While many contemporary accounts of recalcitrant choirs and the dubious noises that emerged from west galleries were probably justified, bad news is always far more noteworthy than good; in the nineteenth century satirical descriptions of atrocious singing were used as propaganda by the Oxford movement, which was intent on replacing unruly choirs and bands with submissive surpliced choristers decently accompanied by a harmonium.[19] In fact, distinctive country psalmody was already in decline, as increased industrialization led to a migration of the workforce from the country to the fast-growing towns where, due to the shortage of urban parish churches, nonconformity flourished. Although a few country choirs and bands did survive until the end of the nineteenth century,[20] by 1861, when *Hymns Ancient and Modern* was published, provincial church music had become correct, conventional and less entertaining. The musicians vanished from the churches and, instead, acquired a rather doubtful immortality in English literature, thanks to such nineteenth-century authors as George Eliot, Thomas Hardy and Thomas Hughes.[21] Their nostalgic and sometimes patronizing accounts of musically incompetent but honest rustics, should be regarded with some scepticism as they are as much stereotype as the innocent maiden, the mad professor and the garrulous busybody that appear in such stories. Unfortunately, these tales are often all that is remembered about country church musicians today; they have become a rather comic addition to the national heritage. As recently as 1996 the author Alan Garner used a description of a church band to evoke memories of a Cheshire village.[22]

When examining music written mostly by amateurs it is not surprising to find some fairly incompetent compositions. Nevertheless much of this repertoire is worthy of performance as well as serious academic consideration. Nicholas Temperley has listed 756 English eighteenth-century psalmody books, and indexed 17,424 English and American strophic psalm and hymn tunes up to 1820,[23] and new books of psalmody are still being unearthed in local libraries and record offices. However, there is no real way of knowing how much of the repertoire was ever actually performed. Some pieces appeared in many different books, both printed and manuscript, and so must have been popular, but others may have been tried only once and then abandoned.

---

[18] C.P. Moritz, *Travels in England in 1782* (London, 1886), pp. 114–16.

[19] [W.P. Scargill], 'Village Choristers', *The Court Magazine and Belle Assemblee*, 6 (1835), 115–21; *The Parish Choir*, (1846–51), *passim*.

[20] J.S. Curwen, 'The Old Village Musicians', *Strand Musical Magazine*, 3 (1897), 137–9; F.W. Galpin, 'The Village Church Band', *Musical News*, 5 (1893), 31–2, 56–8.

[21] G. Eliot, *Scenes of Clerical Life* (1858); T. Hardy, *Under the Greenwood Tree* (1872); T. Hughes, *Tom Brown at Oxford* (London, 1897).

[22] A. Garner, *Strandloper* (London, 1996), p. 108.

[23] N. Temperley, *The Hymn Tune Index* (Oxford, 1998).

Much of the new repertoire was provided by peripatetic singing teachers who not only trained the country choirs but also peddled their own compilations of psalmody, freely borrowing material from each other. Some books included music from earlier sources, and it is quite common to find the 'Non nobis Domine' canon, usually attributed (spuriously) to Byrd, or Campion's 'Never weather-beaten sail' side by side with more modern compositions.

An itinerant teacher, William Anchors, included an anthem by John Weldon and some psalm tunes by John Bishop of Winchester in *A Choice Collection of Psalm-Tunes, Hymns, and Anthems, For the Delight and Improvement of all who are truly Lovers of Divine Musick* (1726?). He also added one of the newer tunes which would still have been singable by a congregation, 'Walsal', a strongly profiled melody in the aeolian mode (Ex. 7.1). Exact dating of early

Ex. 7.1 Walsal Tune, Psalm 103 v.13

unattributed tunes is not always possible, and it is unlikely that Anchors composed 'Walsal', as it is included in two books that may have been published slightly earlier.[24] It also reappeared in numerous later tune books: an early nonconformist compiler, Thomas Butts, improved the harmony and added a second part;[25] Abraham Adams, of Shoreham, Kent, set it in four parts to the funeral text, 'Since our good friend is gone to rest', making the bass move in thirds with the melody for notes two to four and sharpening the leading notes;[26] a manuscript version still kept one G natural in the treble and added a medius which creates some interesting dissonances (Ex. 7.2).[27]

One problem when considering musical quality is that lengthy, harmonically ambitious works composed by professionals will always be regarded as more significant than shorter, easier and predominantly melodic music written by

---

[24] M. Wilkins, *A Book of Psalmody* (Great Milton, c. 1723); M. and J. Broom[e], *Michael Broom's Collection of Church Musick* (1725).
[25] T. Butts, *Harmonia Sacra* (London, c. 1768), p. 11.
[26] A. Adams, *The Psalmist's New Companion*, 12th edn (Kent, c. 1775), p. 76.
[27] MS added to *Michael Broom's Collection*, GB-Lbl A.1231.t. The tune is found in a modern hymnbook: *Rejoice and Sing* (Oxford, 1991), p. 114.

Ex.7.2 A Funeral Hymn to be sung at the death of a Friend
[original version]

amateurs.[28] Another factor is that it is difficult to accept compositions that break the rules of textbook harmony. Some rural psalmody includes false relations, consecutive and open fifths, and strange dissonances, precisely because the melodic lines were considered to be more important than the harmonic implications. Country composers still used the Renaissance form of linear composition, and while the air and the bass may work well together, additional parts caused problems. Possibly the air and bass were so prominent in actual performance that the dissonances caused by the inner parts were inaudible, but, as Temperley points out, '18th-century psalmodists had as much right to change

---

[28] Vaughan Williams was an exception in that he admired much of this music: 'Shrubsole', unidentified article (*Manchester Guardian*, c. 1943?) in a collection of newspaper cuttings about hymns in Buxton Local Studies Library (782.27 NEW); an extract was published in *The Hymn Society Bulletin*, 25 (1943).

the conventions of musical style as 20th-century dodecaphonists'.[29] Certainly a piece that defies theoretical constraints, but which is resourceful and imaginative, may often be more rewarding than one which is academically correct and totally uninspired, and music which looks decidedly suspect on the printed page can work surprisingly well in performance.

A typical example is 'An Anthem taken out of the Psalm 150' from *The Psalm-Singer's Pocket Companion* by Uriah Davenport of Rushton Spencer, a tiny village near the edge of the Peak District on the Staffordshire–Cheshire border (Ex. 7.3). Little is known about Davenport, except that he produced this single volume of psalmody which was reprinted twice, in 1758 and, much later, in 1785, the year after his death; he may have been a carpenter and his ghost is still supposed to walk the banks of the River Dane. His initials, and the date 1719, are on one of the seats in the west gallery of the church, and when he died at the age of 94 the parish register noted that he had 'taught psalmody at Rushton for upwards of 60 years'. This may not be great music, but it is resourceful and extremely exhilarating to sing. It is a fairly typical parochial anthem from the middle of the century. Davenport wrote eight other similar ones, and there are many more in comparable psalmody collections. Most of them use some characteristics derived from English anthems of the Restoration period: dotted rhythms, changes of metre, verse sections for solo or duet, and a concluding alleluia. Some are totally unmemorable, but even these provide ample evidence that country psalm-singers must have been capable musicians, as they are all quite difficult to perform well. Davenport was one of the first country psalmodists to claim that he had composed all his own music, and he must have considered the abilities of his own pupils, as it would have been impracticable to provide music which was too complicated for them to sing with a reasonable degree of accuracy. Presumably they were also competent enough to perform unaccompanied, as no instruments are mentioned in Rushton parish records until 1765. Davenport wrote all his music in G major, A minor or E minor, but obligingly gave directions in his preface for setting the pitch in any suitable key.[30]

Although the harmony may be unconventional, Davenport's anthem is cleverly conceived with good textural variety; the part-writing is competent, the word-painting ingenious and the rhythms exuberant. A work such as this raises the important and still unanswered question: how did a country musician like Davenport learn to compose? It is recorded that two singing masters visited Leek, a nearby town, in 1716,[31] but they probably stayed for only a few weeks. Davenport may have seen the work of other psalmodists, such as John Chetham, John and James Green, and John and Robert Barber from Castleton in

---

[29] Temperley, *The Music of the English Parish Church*, p. 192.

[30] Pitching directions, based on the lowest comfortable note the bass could sing, are common in psalmody books from the early eighteenth century, as are instructions for ornamenting the music.

[31] N.J. Tringham, 'Uriah Davenport and the Psalm Singers of Rushton, Staffordshire', *The Newsletter of the West Gallery Music Association*, 5 (Summer 1993), 7–12.

PROVINCIAL CHURCH MUSIC 179

Ex. 7.3 An Anthem taken out of the 150th Psalm
The Psalm-Singer's Pocket Companion (London, 1755)

Uriah Davenport
of Rushton Spencer
(c. 1690–1784)
(ed. Sally Drage)

Ex. 7.3 *continued*

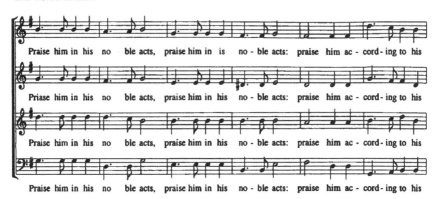

Ex. 7.3 *continued*

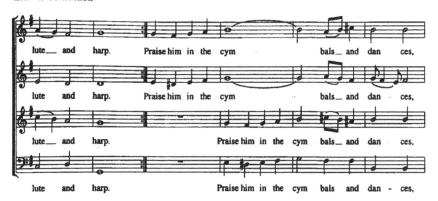

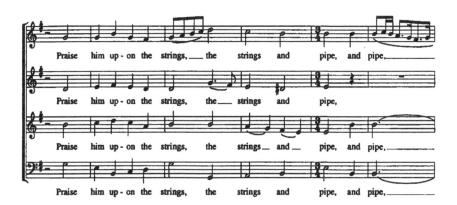

Ex. 7.3 *continued*

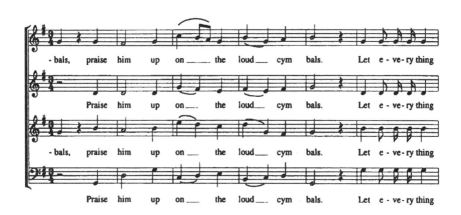

Ex. 7.3 *concluded*

Derbyshire,[32] and the treatises of Christopher Simpson (*c.* 1605–69) and John Playford (1623–86) were well-known. But he must have had leisure time in order to study; certainly his preface is well, if traditionally, written. This country musician was certainly not an illiterate peasant.

Another archaism connected with this music is the allocation of voices. Whereas the air in art music had long ago migrated from the tenor part to the treble, it remained in the tenor of country church music until the end of the eighteenth century, mostly because choirs were male-dominated, but also because women's and boys' voices were used to double the tenor part an octave higher.[33] This gives a much richer sonority to the music, especially when accompanied by instruments that also played at the higher octave. Tenor instruments were rare, and choirs were usually supported by a bass instrument, such as a bassoon or a cello, and two or three treble instruments, such as a flute, a clarinet or a violin.

Throughout the eighteenth century provincial psalmody continued to draw closer to the art music of the period. Professional musicians came to regard it as a financially attractive and artistically viable genre and published books designed specifically 'for the use of country choirs', often imitating the rural style of anthems and elaborate psalm-settings. For instance, John Alcock (the elder) published *Psalmody: or a Collection of Psalm Tunes... All set in a very easy Manner...* (*c.* 1745) when he was still organist at Reading; John Johnson published a collection of ten seventeenth-century anthems (*c.* 1760), which were republished about ten years later by Robert Bremner;[34] Capel Bond of Coventry wrote six anthems (1769); William Hayes's *Sixteen Psalms... set to music for the use of Magdalen College, Oxford* (1776), included a score without an organ part for country churches; and John Alcock (the younger) provided *A Collection*

---

[32] J. Chetham, *A Book of Psalmody* (London, [1718]); John and James Green, *A Book of Psalm-tunes* 2nd edn (London, 1713); Robert and John Barber, *A Book of Psalmody* (London, 1723).

[33] In America, Billings recommended doubling the treble with tenor voices as well. See D. Mackay and R. Crawford, *William Billings of Boston* (Princeton, 1976), pp. 232–3.

[34] The identity of the composers of three of the anthems and the sources for a further four are given in E.A. Wienandt and R.H. Young, *The Anthem in America and England* (New York, 1970), p. 125

of Anthems... and Parochial Harmony..., both published in 1777. Many other established composers, including Peter Hellendaal and his son (also Peter),[35] provided collections of psalm settings for general parish church use, and even Joseph Haydn (1732–1809) was persuaded to contribute six tunes to the second part of William Dechair Tattershall's extremely refined *Improved Psalmody* (1794). All these books provide further proof of the technical abilities of country choirs, and the growing market for this type of repertoire; the subscription list of John Valentine's *Thirty Psalm Tunes in Four Parts with Symphonies, Interludes, and an Instrumental Bass* (1784) includes the names of twenty-seven societies of singers from six counties, although most only bought a single copy.[36]

John Alcock (1715–1806), who was always extremely scathing about the state of cathedral music, provided a defence of provincial church music in the preface to his psalmody book, *The Pious Soul's Heavenly Exercise; or Divine Harmony* (1756), which he designed so that gentlemen could make 'Presents of them to the Singers of their Congregations'.

It has been my utmost Endeavour to preserve the original *Melody*, and likewise render the Whole as easy as possible to the Performers; for it wou'd be unreasonable to expect that such People, who seldom have proper Masters to instruct them, or regular *Music* to practise, and perhaps very little Time to spare, shou'd be so expert in singing their Parts as they who make Music their entire Study; and therefore great Allowances ought certainly to be made for all those Disadvantages which they labour under: But, on the other hand, as an Encouragement to all those who delight in *Psalmody*, I shall just mention the following Facts, and herein I hope I shall not be suspected of Flattery (a Crime which I fancy even my most inveterate Enemies will scarcely accuse me of), if I assure you that I have frequently had the Pleasure of hearing several *Psalm-Tunes, Hymns, Anthems, &c.* sung by Companies of Singers in the most exact Manner possible, particularly at Stockport in Cheshire, (at the Opening of the Organ) where I heard Mr Purcell's *Te Deum* and *Jubilate*, and two *Grand Anthems*, with all the Instrumental Parts, perform'd by Tradesmen (most of them from *Manchester*,) amongst which were only two Professors of *Music*: And at *Dudley* in *Worcestershire*, when that *Organ* was opened, the same *Te Deum, Jubilate* and a *Grand Anthem*, were perform'd when not more than two or three Masters assisted ... .[37]

Needless to say he managed to include a sarcastic comment about the authorities at Lichfield Cathedral where he was employed, complaining that he was not consulted when choirboys were chosen, and he also suggested that it would be better if country choirs performed new music before or after a service, especially as 'those Persons who sing worst are always fondest of singing'

---

[35] *A Collection of Psalms and Hymns for the Use of Parish Churches* (Cambridge, 1793).

[36] The high cost of printed music meant that many musicians made their own manuscript compilations; extant examples suggest that they acquired and adapted pieces from a wide variety of sources.

[37] A five-part 'Hallelujah', adapted from Purcell's Te Deum in D, was added as a conclusion to a number of anthems, e.g. 'Great is the Lord' in *Michael Broom's Collection*.

Plate 7.1 From *11 Anthems on General and Particular Occasions, Interspersed with Symphonies... Being particularly design'd for the Use of parochial Choirs* (Nuneaton, 1779)

186 MUSIC IN EIGHTEENTH-CENTURY BRITAIN

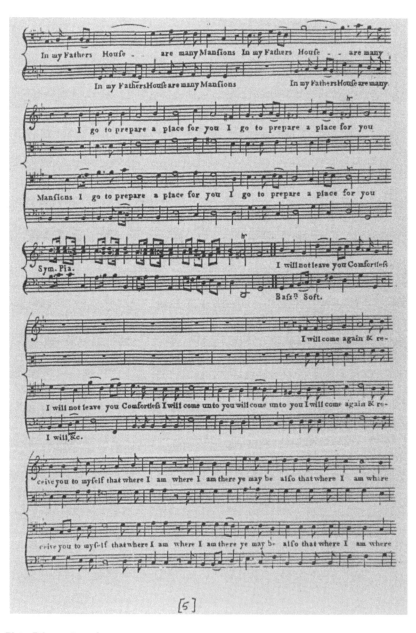

Plate 7.1 *continued*

PROVINCIAL CHURCH MUSIC 187

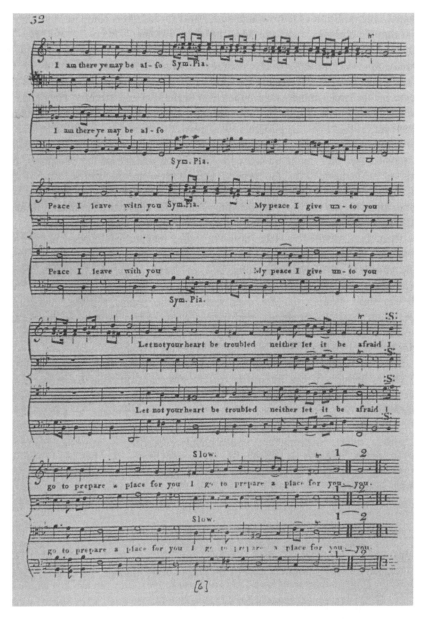

Plate 7.1 *concluded*

188 MUSIC IN EIGHTEENTH-CENTURY BRITAIN

Joseph Key of Nuneaton is another composer who deserves consideration. Again almost nothing is known about him except that at his death in 1784 he was described as an excise officer. Key's music is more urban and sophisticated, unlike Davenport's true country psalmody, but it raises the same intriguing and unanswered question as to how amateurs learnt to compose competently. One of his simpler anthems, 'Let not your heart be troubled' from *11 Anthems on General and Particular Occasions, Interspersed with Symphonies and Thorough Basses for two Hautboys and a Bassoon: Being particularly design'd for the Use of parochial Choirs* (Nuneaton 1779), is reproduced in Plate 7.1.[38] While some of his larger anthems are rather over-ambitious and slightly Handelian at times, this is much simpler but with strong melodic lines and assured harmony. However, in this book in particular, his music is marred by a preponderance of missing or totally misplaced accidentals, especially in the symphonies. Initially, it seemed that this might be caused by the incompetence of the composer, but this is at variance with the general skill shown in the music, and if the accidentals are corrected it works extremely well. It may merely be that there was some idiosyncrasy in Key's handwriting which the engraver, Thomas Williams, misinterpreted, or that the standard of proof-reading was particularly poor.[39]

There is a distinctive later style of more elegant psalmody, particularly observable in the work of Key and his Midland contemporaries, John Alcock (the younger) of Walsall and John Hill of Rugby, and of two even closer neighbours, Thomas Collins of Nuneaton and John Geary of Caldecote.[40] They all use short symphonies for even quite simple psalm settings, sometimes specifying the instrumentation, and their anthems again imitate art music and include elements of the Baroque 'full with verse' anthem, with solos, duets, or trios and symphonies alternating with passages for full choir.

Many mid-eighteenth-century composers wrote fuging tunes, a form beloved of choirs because of the interesting part-writing and detested by most clergy because it silenced congregations. 'Birmingham' (Ex. 7.4) is from *Sacred Harmony* (1784), compiled by Ralph Harrison, the minister at Cross Street Unitarian Chapel in Manchester, who is particularly important as an arranger of 'parody' tunes. 'Birmingham' was probably composed by Anthony Greatorex (1730–1814), organist at Burton on Trent and father of Thomas Greatorex (1758–1831), organist at Derby, and later conductor of the Concerts of Ancient Music and organist at Westminster Abbey, and shows yet again how an art composer adapted to the provincial style. When Victorian reforms banished such

---

[38] Other works consist of a first set of eight anthems (1773) and two books of anthems, psalms, canticles and carols that were published posthumously by his wife, Elizabeth (1785; *c.* 1790). Key's music is often given dates (in the British Library catalogue, for instance) that are too late. M. Foster, *Anthems and Anthem Composer* (London, 1901) even lists him as a nineteenth-century composer.

[39] Another unusual feature of Key's *11 Anthems* is that the music is not figured, despite the claim of 'thorough basses' on the title-page.

[40] The cluster of composers around Nuneaton, in particular, suggests a focus of musical activity, but research into local archives has so far been unproductive; Birmingham, Coventry and Leicester would seem to have been the nearest centres.

PROVINCIAL CHURCH MUSIC 189

extrovert music from parish churches, it was taken over by the nonconformists, and also continued to be used in local carolling traditions. These are still especially strong around Sheffield, where a visitor to local pubs just before

Ex. 7.4 Birmingham
R. Harrison, *Sacred Harmony* vol. 1 (London, 1784) Greatrix
text: Isaac Watts (ed. Sally Drage)

Ex. 7.4 *concluded*

Christmas will experience fuging tunes and eighteenth-century melodies sung with great enthusiasm, usually from memory. Greatorex's 'Birmingham' was sung round the village of Stannington (to the north-west of Sheffield) until the early 1950s; the notes were apparently identical but it had gained a short symphony and the text was changed to 'Joy to the World'.

Part 3
Sources and Resources

CHAPTER EIGHT

Handel's 1735 (London) version of *Athalia*

Donald Burrows

One of the most important dates in Handel's biography is 6 May 1732, when he introduced an English oratorio for the first time into his performing seasons at the King's Theatre, Haymarket, hitherto devoted solely to Italian opera. Six well-received performances of *Esther*, a much-expanded version of the oratorio written for Cannons, were followed by an adaptation of its companion-piece, *Acis and Galatea*, presented as a 'serenata' in a mixed English-Italian version. During the following season of 1732–33, Handel must have contemplated how he could match the success of the previous year by introducing similar works towards the end of the season. This meant producing at least one new score, and early in 1733 he composed the English oratorio *Deborah*, completing it on 21 February. The new oratorio duly came to performance on 17 March; six performances of *Deborah* were followed by a revival of *Esther*, and Handel closed his season on 9 June with a rather surprising revival of Bononcini's opera *Griselda*.

The end of the season was coloured by the announcement from Senesino, Handel's long-standing *castrato* soloist, that he would be leaving the company; he, and most of Handel's current cast, had been lured away to join the newly-founded Opera of the Nobility for the next season. No doubt Handel was disturbed by the prospect of the break-up of his current company, but his mind was also on other things. During the last weeks of the 1732–33 season he composed another oratorio score, *Athalia*, completing it on 7 June. While *Deborah*, also composed during the performing season, had been rather cobbled together using a considerable amount of pre-existing music from other works by Handel, *Athalia* was a more original score, and in many ways a much more carefully constructed work than *Deborah* or Handel's 1732 theatre version of *Esther*. The librettos for both *Deborah* and *Athalia* were written by Samuel Humphreys. Whether or not *Athalia* was intended as a formal 'exercise' for a doctorate that never happened, the new oratorio became the novelty in a series of performances that Handel gave at Oxford during the period of the *Encaenia* degree-giving celebrations there in early July. *Athalia* came to performance at the Sheldonian Theatre, Oxford on 10 July 1733. Thus, the work that is arguably Handel's first masterpiece of English theatre oratorio did not receive its first performance in London. Of his English oratorios, only *Athalia* and *Messiah* had their first performances away from London; both works, though written in London, were composed at crisis points in Handel's London career and were first presented in exceptional circumstances elsewhere.

194   MUSIC IN EIGHTEENTH-CENTURY BRITAIN

Athalia was nevertheless generically comparable to the London works, and there is no reason why Handel could not, in the right circumstances, have represented the work in London with only minor alterations. However, the circumstances were not right. For his next London season, 1733–34, Handel had to re-form his theatre company with new singers, since only the soprano Strada remained from the previous season. For a new leading man he gained the *castrato* Carestini. In the new company only Strada and the bass Waltz had sung in Handel's previous English oratorios (*Athalia* at Oxford, as it happens); the rest were Italians who would probably have had difficulties with performing in English. Nevertheless, towards the end of the season Handel revived *Deborah* (three performances) and *Acis and Galatea* (one performance), the former probably in a bilingual version, the latter presumably so.

Apart from the language problem, there was one critical reason why Handel did not attempt to include *Athalia* in his 1733–34 London season: he had reused a large amount of the music from the oratorio score in *Parnasso in Festa*, an Italian serenata (in three acts, and musically indistinguishable from an opera) that he performed just before *Deborah* as a theatrical contribution to the period of celebration surrounding the wedding of Princess Anne, the eldest daughter of King George II, and plausibly Handel's favourite pupil, which had taken place on 14 March 1734. Nineteen movements from *Athalia* went into *Parnasso in Festa*, either complete or as substantial independent sections, certainly enough for the music to be identifiable. Two of these movements, furthermore, were also used by Handel with new English texts in the anthem 'This is the Day that the Lord has made' which was performed at the royal wedding, and another two movements were included (with Italian texts) in *Terpsicore*, the prologue added to *Il pastor fido* at the revival of that opera later in 1734. In the nineteen movements Handel's musical alterations were minimal, concerned largely with adapting the music to Italian texts in *Parnasso in Festa* and to the styles of the new singers, for Carestini in *Parnasso in Festa*, for example, or for a Chapel Royal chorister in the wedding anthem. The extent of Handel's sensitivity to these self-borrowings will be discussed later but, for the moment, it is sufficient to note that Handel never performed *Athalia* and *Parnasso in Festa* in the same season, presumably because the quantity of music held in common between the two works was so large that it would have become obtrusive.

The 1734–35 season saw another major change in Handel's fortunes. With the close of the 1733–34 season, the five-year period that he seems to have negotiated for the use of the King's Theatre came to an end, and he was then apparently powerless to prevent the Opera of the Nobility from taking the theatre for their own performances. In consequence Handel had to look around for another venue and, in circumstances that are somewhat surprising, he came to an arrangement with John Rich for the use of his new theatre at Covent Garden.[1] The King's Theatre had been for more than thirty years the house for Italian

---

[1]   See R.D. Hume, 'Handel and Opera Management in London in the 1730s', *Music and Letters*, 67 (1986), 347–62.

opera in London. The opera-going public, and particularly the more serious or socially exalted part of it, would still tend to gravitate to this venue from habit, and possibly preference, since the King's Theatre was a large West End theatre, fully equipped for opera; it also seems likely that the capital equipment of the Royal Academy of Music, accumulated during 1719–29, was specifically attached to this venue, as was also the annual royal bounty of £1,000. Thus Handel needed to find ways of providing special attractions to lure regular opera-goers to Covent Garden, which was not in a prestigious location, and he had to broaden the appeal of his performances to a wider band of London audiences.

One of the attractions at Covent Garden at the beginning of the season was Madam Sallé's dancers. The dancers' company probably came as part of the deal with the theatre, and Handel may have had to commit himself to using them, or at least paying them, under the terms of his contract with Rich; but in practice he made excellent use of the dancers in his opera scores and their presence no doubt attracted one sector of the audience, since dancing was the sort of thing that was regularly associated with Rich's theatres. A second attraction lay in presenting good operas, in order to outdo the Opera of the Nobility on quality. There is hardly a better Handel opera than *Ariodante*, his new work for the season and a magnificent showpiece for Carestini. Indeed, the programme of the 1734–35 season as a whole was very attractive both musically and dramatically. However, there is no evidence that the work was particularly well received; audiences seem to have been more influenced by fashion, by rumour and by the arrival of Farinelli to perform with the Opera of the Nobility, than by the quality of the operas performed.

A third opportunity for Handel was that of bringing some life to the later part of the season by introducing English oratorios, something which was not likely to be attempted by the Opera of the Nobility and which, in any case, involved a genre with which Handel had recently had striking success. The Opera of the Nobility made an attempt at a pre-emptive strike with Porpora's Italian oratorio *Davide e Berseeba* (a revival from their programme of the previous season), performed on 28 February 1735 (second Friday in Lent); Handel began his oratorios with *Esther* the following Wednesday. In order to make his oratorios more attractive, he added another novelty: the advertisement for *Esther* promised 'several new Additional Songs; likewise two new concertos on the Organ'.[2] This was almost certainly the first time that he had introduced organ concertos into his London oratorio performances. He even seems to have had a new organ constructed for the purpose, though it was not quite finished in time for the *Esther* performances.[3] But, as a crowd-puller, the combination of English oratorio and organ concertos seems to have availed little against the performances of *Artaxerxes* by Hasse and Broschi, starring Farinelli, that the Opera of the

---

[2] Advertisement for the performance of *Esther*, 5 March 1735, in *The London Daily Post*, 4 March 1735.
[3] See the report of the organ in *The London Daily Post*, 1 March 1735, quoted in D. Burrows, *Handel* (Oxford, 1994), p. 186.

196   MUSIC IN EIGHTEENTH-CENTURY BRITAIN

Nobility was offering. On 20 March, after successive nights that had seen performances of *Artaxerxes* and *Esther*, one newspaper commented:

> In the flourishing state of this Opera, 'tis no wonder that the other Theatres decline. *Handel*, whose excellent Compositions have often pleased our Ears, and touched our Hearts, has this Winter sometimes performed to an almost empty Pitt. He has lately reviv'd his fine *Oratorio* of *Esther*, in which he has introduced two Concerto's on the Organ that are inimitable. But so strong is the Disgust taken against him, that even this has been far from bringing him crowded Audiences; tho' there were no other publick Entertainments on those Evenings.[4]

It is against this background that, after six performances of *Esther* and three of *Deborah* (accompanied by 'a New Concerto on the Organ' and the concertos from *Esther*, introduced in two stages), Handel for the first time performed *Athalia* in London on 1 April 1735, 'with a New concerto on the Organ [op. 4 no. 4, arguably his first entirely original organ concerto]; Also the first Concerto of Esther; and the last in Deborah'.[5] Handel played *Athalia* hard, with five performances beginning, most unusually, on three consecutive nights, the Tuesday to Thursday of Holy Week. It seems to have been at this moment that open warfare broke out between Handel and the Opera of the Nobility. Hitherto they had studiously avoided performing on the same nights, Handel generally performing on Mondays, Wednesdays and Fridays, the Opera on Tuesdays and Saturdays; Handel had offered no competition to the Friday performance of Porpora's oratorio on 28 February. Now, however, the Opera of the Nobility revived the Porpora oratorio on 1 and 3 April, in direct competition with Handel's first and third performances of *Athalia*. Handel presumably slipped in the extra performance on 2 April in order to have a performing night to himself.[6] After this gesture, however, things returned to normal and Handel performed *Athalia* twice more after Easter, before putting on his new opera *Alcina* for an amazingly successful run of eighteen performances to end the season late, on 2 July, outrunning the Opera of the Nobility's season by nearly a month.

The form of the work that Handel gave at the first London performances of *Athalia* has proved rather difficult to establish, and most of the evidence is fragmentary. The first modern investigation of this matter was undertaken by Winton Dean in the chapter devoted to the oratorio in *Handel's Dramatic Oratorios and Masques*.[7] Having dealt in some detail with the 1733 Oxford performing version of *Athalia*, Dean noted Handel's revival in 1735, identified a

---

[4]   *The Old Whig*, 20 March 1735.
[5]   *The London Daily Post*, 1 April 1735 (advertisement for the first performance of *Athalia*).
[6]   In previous weeks the Covent Garden actors had regularly performed on Thursdays, and indeed on the other available nights between Handel's Monday-Wednesday-Friday presentations, but they were probably not allowed to perform during Holy Week.
[7]   W. Dean, *Handel's Dramatic Oratorios and Masques* (London, 1959). pp. 247–64; the second edition (Oxford, 1990) did not make substantial changes.

HANDEL'S 1735 *ATHALIA*

likely cast, and listed nine additional or alternative musical items for the oratorio,[8] introduced as follows:

> No libretto for Handel's revival is known, but it is clear from scattered evidence that he recast the first two acts. Most of the following changes, none of which appears in any modern score, can be ascribed to this occasion. The list may not be complete; certain alterations to the conducting score ... may date from this period or 1743. They cannot have been made in 1756, when Handel was blind.

Since Dean wrote that in 1959, various advances in Handel source studies and one important discovery have provided the means to establish the nature of the 1735 London score of *Athalia* more precisely.

The re-investigation of Handel's 1735 version of *Athalia* involves four kinds of sources: autograph musical material, Handel's performing score (or, under its more conventional name, conducting score), secondary manuscript and printed musical sources, and relevant printed wordbooks containing the libretto. Most of the autograph material, as might be expected, relates to the original Oxford version of 1733. The principal 'autograph' volume (GB-Lbl RM 20.h.1) provides a fairly comprehensive picture of the work as drafted in 1733; a couple of leaves added at the end date from 1735, and other movements or fragments that may relate to the 1735 performances are spread around Handel's miscellaneous autographs (see Table 8.1). Rather perplexingly, these autographs come in three different shapes and sizes. Items **B** and **C** are written on large Format IV paper, the same size as Handel's main autograph and conducting score of the oratorio. Item **E** is on upright twelve-stave paper because that is the format that Handel used for his organ concertos; the presence of 'S.D.G.' among the annotations at the end is unusual for the concertos, and may suggest that the composer was here consciously marking the end of his new composition for the 1735 revival of the oratorio – the completion date of 25 March was, after all, less than a week before the *Athalia* performance. The remaining autograph items are on Handel's more usual Format I paper. There is no doubt that the aria in item **D** was composed in 1735 for *Athalia*. Item **A**, however, is a three-movement 'Ouverture' that Handel composed earlier, *c.* 1733–4;[9] he raided the first movement for *Parnasso in Festa* in March 1734 and the other two movements for the revival of *Il pastor fido* two months later.

---

[8] Ibid., pp. 259–61. The cast list on p. 261 is identical to that given in O.E. Deutsch, *Handel, A Documentary Biography* (London, 1955), p. 385.

[9] The autograph (GB-Lbl RM 20.g.13, ff. 33–6) appears to be an integral paper gathering, associating the three movements as a single composition. In Bernd Baselt's thematic catalogue of Handel's works, the entry for HWV 342 gives the first two movements but not the third (Bourée); *Händel-Handbuch* (Leipzig, 1986), vol. 3, p. 111.

Table 8.1: Musical sources relating to Handel's 1735 performances of *Athalia*

Autographs

A   GB-Lbl RM 20.g.13 ff. 33–6
Format I Watermark Cc (C30) Rastra 10 @ 2 29 to 29.5
3-movement F major *Ouverture* (q.v. HWV 342). Composed *c.* 1732–4;
first movement, transposed to G and horns omitted, used for overture to
Parnasso in Festa (1734) and then *Athalia* (1735)

B   GB-Lbl RM 20.h.1 ff. 56v–57r
Format IV Watermark C*c (C*60) Rastra 20 @ 2 30.5
Allegro [Gigue] for overture to *Athalia* (1735)

C   GB-Cfm MU MS 251 pp. 43–50, continuing GB-Lbl RM 20.h.1. f. 56r
Format IV Watermark C*c (C*60) Rastra 20 @ 2 30.5
Duet (Joad [B], Abner [B]) and Chorus (SATB + SATB) 'When storms
the proud / O Judah boast' HWV 52/Anhang (15). Ends with cue to
'Alleluja' at end of Part 1, HWV 52/16.

D   GB-Lbl RM 20.f.12 ff. 35–8
Format I Watermark Cc (C30) Rastra 10 @ 2 30.5
ff. 35r–38r Air 'Through the land' (Josabeth [S]), HWV 52/18b, with
second text 'Cease O Judah' added later by Handel for use in *Deborah*,
probably 1744.
On f. 38v, recitatives possibly added later by Handel:
(D1)   'What can the faithful fear' (Joad, S)
(D2)   'O Queen, now let your pow'r' (Mathan, T), to follow Athalia's Air
'Hence I hasten'.

E   GB-Lbl King's MS 317 ff. 21–37
Format IIa Watermark Cc (C30) Rastra 12 @ 2 32.5 to 33
Organ Concerto HWV 292 (later published as op. 4 no. 4), ending with
'Halleluja' choral movement, to conclude Part 3 of *Athalia*.
Dated on completion, 'March 25 1735', accompanied by 'S.D.G./GFH'.

Inserted Movements in the Conducting Score (D-Hs MC/264)
All Format IV Watermark C*c (C*60) Rastra 20 @ 2 30.5

F   f. 2 (Clausen E1) Ouverture (un poco allegro) (part-folio)

G   ff. 7–8 (Clausen E2) Allegro [Gigue] for Ouverture

H   ff. 34–5 (Clausen E4) Air (Mathan [T]) 'The Gods who chosen
Blessings shed', HWV 52/9b

HANDEL'S 1735 *ATHALIA*

Movements in the 'Aylesford' miscellany (GB-Lbl RM 18.c.8)
Format I Watermark Cd (C40) Rastra 10 @ 2 27

J   ff. 125–35 Ouverture (3 movements, as in *Athalia*, 1735).
Described by Jennens on 'Contents' fly-leaf as 'Overture of Parnasso in Festa, alter'd from Athaliah'.

K   ff. 136–42 Air (Joad [A]) and Chorus 'O Lord whom we adore', HWV 52/6b/ Jennens (Contents): 'new set'.

L   ff. 143–6r Air (Mathan [T]) 'The Gods who chosen Blessings shed'. Music as source **H**. Jennens (Contents): 'first a Chorus, now an Air'.

M   ff. 146v–52 Air (Josabeth [S]) 'Through the land'. Music as source **D**.

Items **K** and **D/M** were also printed in the Appendix to *Athalia An Oratorio Or Sacred Drama in Score*, in Arnold's edition of Handel's works [Nos. 1–4], 1787.

The conducting score of *Athalia* is, like most such sources that have been used (and altered) for successive performances, an informative but also a frustrating source.[10] Copied originally for the 1733 Oxford performances, it was amended at three subsequent periods: for the London performances of 1735, for a revival in Handel's 1743 season at Covent Garden which he prepared in detail but which never came to performance, and for a revival in 1756 at Covent Garden. Allowance also has to be made for markings relating to the use of the score as a quarry for movements for *Parnasso in Festa*, the 1734 wedding anthem and Handel's benefit oratorio in 1738. In the course of the alterations for revivals, new music was inserted, but obsolete music which was in the way was removed. Because the revivals of *Athalia* were relatively few and were well spaced out, it is possible to distinguish the dates of the various layers in the conducting score: the paper-types used in 1733, 1735, 1743 and 1756 are fairly distinct. For elucidation of the contents of the conducting scores scholars are particularly indebted to the work of Hans-Dieter Clausen;[11] in the present context, it was initially his analysis of the paper-types in Handel's conducting scores that enabled the identification of the 1735 insertions in the *Athalia* score by the manuscript paper with the C*c (C*60) watermark type.[12] Handel and his copyists used paper of this type only for a limited period in 1735–6, and so it neatly distinguishes the 1735 insertions from the original sections of the score copied less than two years previously. Three 1735 insertions are still to be found in the score: the opening and 'Gigue' movements for the overture, and Mathan's aria 'The Gods, who chosen blessings shed' (see Table 8.1). The overture to

---

[10]   D-Hs MC/264
[11]   H.-D. Clausen, *Händels Direktionspartituren ('Handexemplare')*, Hamburger Beiträge zur Musikwissenschaft 7 (Hamburg, 1972).
[12]   Watermark types are referred to by the sigla given by Clausen in *Händels Direktionspartituren* (e.g. C*c), accompanied where appropriate by the equivalent sigla (e.g. C*60) from D. Burrows and M. J. Ronish, *A Catalogue of Handel's Musical Autographs* (Oxford, 1994).

200   MUSIC IN EIGHTEENTH-CENTURY BRITAIN

Athalia in 1735 comprised movements that had been variously composed for, or presented in, other contexts (see Table 8.2). The aria, for which there is no direct autograph, was adapted with minimal musical changes from one in the composer's *Brockes Passion*.[13]

Table 8.2: Overtures to *Athalia*, and use of related movements

Athalia
1733 (Oxford)
[*'Sinfonia'*]   Allegro   Grave   Allegro

Ouverture in F
(q.v. HWV 342)
c. 1733–4
Overture (un poco allegro)   Allegro   A tempo
                                                           di Bouree

Parnasso in Festa
March 1734
Overture (un poco allegro)*   Allegro

Il pastor fido
May 1734
                              Overture   Allegro   A tempo
                              (Largo)   di Bouree

Athalia
1735 (London)
Overture (un poco allegro)   Allegro   Allegro
                                                                        [Gigue]

Parnasso in Festa
1736–7
Overture (un poco allegro)   Allegro   Allegro
                                                                        [Gigue]

    *Transposed to G major; horns omitted

Clausen also identified the conducting score copy of Athalia's air 'Hence I hasten' (one of Dean's nine 1735 'possibles') as a 1743 insertion,[14] thus increasing the probability that the recitatives added by Handel to autograph **D** were composed in 1743 (and not in 1735) on the empty staves of the verso at the end of the 1735 autograph of the aria. To 1743 also belongs the tenor aria 'The rising world', replacing the chorus to the same text; this movement seems to have eluded Dean, and indeed also eluded the entry for *Athalia* (HWV 52) in Baselt's thematic catalogue of Handel's works. In addition to the physically

---

[13] 'Dem Himmel gleicht sein buntgefärbter Rücken' (HWV 48/34) for soprano. The text for the *Athalia* movement included 'brighten all thy fear to joy', a phrase that may have suggested the re-use of this music from its original 'rainbow' context.

[14] Clausen, *Händels Direktionspartituren*, p. 119.

inserted movements, the conducting score has various additions and amendments to the music pages, and pencil annotations including cues and the names of singers, some of which are attributable to 1735.

The secondary copies of *Athalia* are in one sense disappointing. The manuscript full scores of the complete work follow the 1733 version, sometimes with minor variations, but provide nothing that helps to establish the form of the work in 1735. Nor is much help to be gained from John Walsh's publication of *The Most Celebrated Songs in the Oratorio Call'd Athalia*;[15] even though it was not published until early 1736 – presumably because Walsh or Handel did not consider that publication was worth the effort until the work had been heard in London – the musical contents all date back to 1733 (see Table 8.3).

Table 8.3: Contents of *The Most Celebrated Songs in the Oratorio Call'd Athalia* (Walsh, 1736)

Page(s)	Movement	Soloist(s) named	Comment
1	'Blooming Virgins'	Strada	*Dal segno* aria printed in full, but reduced to 'A' section only in 1735
2–6	'Cease thy anguish'	Carestini, Strada	Duet printed with English text, but sung in Italian in 1735
7	'Gentle Airs'	Beard	1733 and 1735
8–9	'Soothing Tyrant'	Strada	1733 and 1735
10–11	'Will God, whose mercies'	The Boy	1733 and 1735
12–15	'Through the land'	Strada	1733 version printed: different setting in 1735
16–18	'My vengeance'	Beard	For Athalia in 1733: probably sung by Beard (Mathan) in 1735
19–21	'Faithful cares'	Strada	1733 and 1735
22–4	'Softest sounds'	Young	1733 and 1735: obbligato instrument not specified by Walsh
25–7	'My spirits fail'	Strada, The Boy	1733 and 1735
28–9	'Oppression no longer'	Waltz	1733: shown as omitted in '1735' wordbook

The published movements comprised only eleven items, and it is not surprising

---

[15] W.C. Smith, *Handel. A Descriptive Catalogue of the Early Editions* (London, 1960; 2nd. edn Oxford, 1970), p. 97.

202   MUSIC IN EIGHTEENTH-CENTURY BRITAIN

that these were given in the 1733 versions, because Walsh's source was probably comparable to the known secondary manuscripts of the oratorio; the publisher had no doubt received (or acquired) his copy in 1733–4. As will be seen presently, the eleven items included several that in 1735 were omitted or not performed in their original versions. Nevertheless, Walsh added the names of the 1735 London soloists above the individual movements, presumably matching names and characters in the drama as performed in 1735.

There is, however, one useful secondary manuscript source for the 1735 music: a volume from the 'Aylesford' Collection, now GB-Lbl RM 18.c.8.[16] This is a miscellaneous volume of the type that Charles Jennens seems to have favoured in order to make his collection comprehensive: it provided variant movements from revivals of works for which he already owned one integral version of the score. Jennens wrote a list of contents on the fly-leaf, in which he attempted to relate individual movements to their relevant works. The volume comprises two manuscript sections copied at slightly different times, though about the same period. It opens with a complete score of Handel's 1737 version of his Italian oratorio *Il trionfo del Tempo e della Verità* in the hand of copyist S2;[17] the remainder, from f. 125 onwards, consists of miscellaneous movements from *Parnasso in Festa* and *Athalia* in the hand of copyist S1, with the last four folios (not relevant for the present purpose) copied by S4. The paper characteristics of this miscellaneous section (watermark Cd/C40, rastra 10 @ 2 27)[18] are the same as for the section of the volume containing the Italian oratorio, which of course cannot have been copied before 1737. The watermark and rastra in fact tie the date of the manuscript to a fairly narrow period: the C40 watermark is found in Handel sources from 1737–39, but the 27 mm. rastra only in 1737. In other words, the *Athalia* movements that are included in the volume, which are not taken from the 1733 score must relate to 1735, because they cannot have been copied as late as 1743. Dean had already noted the significance of this source as containing likely movements from the 1735 version. That dating can now be confirmed. The relevant contents are listed in Table 8.1 (pp. 198–9). This source provides one new 1735 movement for *Athalia*, the setting of 'O Lord whom we adore' for solo alto and chorus, and confirms two other airs as having originated in 1735. The overture appears in its three-movement form as in Handel's 1736–7 performances of *Parnasso in Festa*, but this was a repeat of the form of the overture from his 1735 *Athalia* performances.

That leaves one other kind of source to be evaluated: printed wordbooks giving the libretto. Dean, it will be remembered, began by saying that 'No

---

[16] See W.B. Squire, *Catalogue of the King's Music Library; Part I, The Handel Manuscripts* (London, 1927), p. 117; the descriptions of individual items are based on Jennens's list on the fly-leaf.

[17] Copyists are identified by the sigla given in J.P. Larsen, *Handel's 'Messiah': Origins, Composition, Sources* (London, 1957; 2nd ed. New York, 1972), pp. 262–74.

[18] Rastra types are referred to by codes indicating the number of staves per page, the composition of individual rastra sets, and the total span measurement (in mm.) of the rastra set; thus '10 @ 2 27' indicates ten-stave pages ruled with a two-stave rastra with a total span of twenty-seven millimetres.

HANDEL'S 1735 *ATHALIA*   203

libretto for Handel's revival is known', and, in the sense that no *Athalia* wordbook dated 1735 has yet come to light, this is still true. However, in 1993 the author discovered in the Gerald Coke Handel Collection a copy of the 1733 wordbook that had clearly been amended for use in 1735.[19] The amendments take two forms. A leaf is inserted at the beginning, printed on one side only, giving Italian texts for additional movements and cues for their insertion in the libretto; it is headed 'Part of SIGNOR CARESTINI in *Italian*'. At the bottom of the page is printed the rubric 'ADVERTISEMENT./ All those Lines mark'd down the Side with a Pencil, are left out in the Performance', and indeed there are extensive pencil brackets in the margins of the following text (see Plate 8.1).

To pursue the subject of Carestini's role first, the leaf in the *Athalia* wordbook indicates that he sang primarily, indeed possibly totally, in Italian; it also shows that the Italian arias listed on the leaf were being used by Handel for his oratorios by 1735. 'Bianco giglio', 'Cor fedele' and 'Angelico splendor' seem to have been part of a general stock of Italian arias that Handel periodically raided for his oratorios. Hitherto the movements have been primarily associated with *Esther*, partly on the strength of Jennens's ascription of them to that oratorio on the fly-leaf of another of his miscellaneous volumes, now GB-Lbl RM 18.c.5.[20] On the basis of information available at the time, Winton Dean had speculated that some, or possibly most, of these Italian movements might have been composed or adapted in 1737, when Handel had few English singers in his cast.[21] It is now clear, however, that the arias were in existence by 1735, and probably originated from the need to provide Carestini with a part on oratorio nights. Some of the Italian movements were adapted from music in Handel's Latin motet *Silete venti* (HWV 242), composed about ten years previously, though others, like 'Angelico Splendor' were newly composed, in this case on the basis of a thematic idea from Telemann. If they were performed in 1735, then it seems fairly certain that some had also been included in Handel's performances of *Deborah* in 1734, when Carestini had also been included in the cast. There is probably no need to go back any further since the author of a pamphlet described one of the features of Handel's 1732 performances of *Esther* thus: '*Senesino* and *Bertolli* made a rare work with the *English* tongue you would have sworn it had been *Welch*'.[22] No doubt Senesino did the same in 1733.

---

[19] The author gave preliminary thoughts on the significance of this discovery in a paper at the 1993 Handel Institute Conference; it was published as 'Handel's 1738 "Oratorio": A Benefit Pasticcio' in K. Hortschansky and K. Musketa (eds), *Georg Friedrich Händel – ein Lebensinhalt. Gedenkschrift für Bernd Baselt (1934–1993)* (Halle an der Saale, 1995), pp. 11–38. The original contents of the wordbook seem to be identical with those of other surviving exemplars: *Athalia. An Oratorio; or Sacred Drama. As Peform'd at the Theatre in Oxford* (London, John Watts, 1733).
[20] See Dean, *Handel's Dramatic Oratorios and Masques*, p. 211; also H. Serwer, 'The Italians in "Esther"' in Hortschansky and Musketa (eds), *Georg Friedrich Händel*, pp. 77–89.
[21] *Handel's Dramatic Oratorios and Masques*, pp. 211 and 239. There is now reason to question Dean's opinion (p. 239) that Carestini sang a significant amount of music in English.
[22] *See and Seem blind: or, A Critical Dissertation on the Public Diversions, &c* (London, [1732]), p. 16.

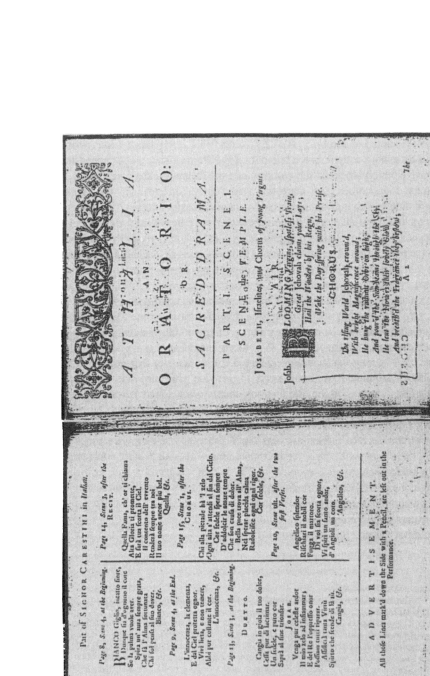

Plate 8.1 An opening from the '1735' wordbook for *Athalia*

HANDEL'S 1735 *ATHALIA* 205

Traces of the 1735 Italian insertions can be found in the conducting score of *Athalia*. Mostly these traces are pencil cues referring to the addition of movements that were subsequently removed again for the all-English version of the oratorio in 1743; in fact, the music copies may have been taken out long before 1743, in order to use the Italian movements in other oratorios. It is apparent from one of the pencil cues that Handel initially intended to use 'Bianco Giglio' at the end of Part 1 Scene 4, but then moved it back to the beginning of the scene, adding a second Italian aria at the end. The clearest trace of the insertions in the conducting score comes in Part 3 Scene 1, where Smith has written the recitative 'Chi alla pietade' (in ink) on some empty staves at the bottom of f. 91v. (See Plate 8.2). The following aria 'Cor fedele' was written on a leaf, subsequently removed, that was formerly stuck over f. 91v, but this leaf could not carry all of the music, and Smith continued the end of the aria on some empty staves at the bottom of f. 92r. (See Plate 8.3). Had not Smith written some of the music in the score at this point, the recitative would have been completely lost; this is the only source for 'Chi alla pietade'.

Most of the Italian movements whose texts are printed on the insert page of the wordbook are known from other sources. 'Quella fama' is an Italian text to 'Endless fame thy days adorning' from the 1732 score of *Esther*, and 'L'innocenza, la clemenza' is probably the movement that also turns up in different oratorio contexts from the 1730s with the texts 'Tua belezza' and 'La speranza, la costanza'.[23] The duetto 'Cangia in gioia' is an Italian version of the duet 'Cease thy anguish' in *Athalia* which, according to the pencil marks in the wordbook, it replaces at exactly the same point in the oratorio; Carestini and Strada had already sung the movement together in *Parnasso in Festa*, to an Italian text which began with the same two lines. There is no sign of the Italian text in the conducting score of *Athalia*, but the addition of the singers' names to the English text in Walsh's edition provides strong grounds for identifying the movement with Carestini and Strada.

The pencil marks in the left margins of the text are quite extensive throughout the wordbook, and the rubric on the insert page clearly gives authority to these indications of cuts in the text. Working from the marked-up wordbook, it is possible to follow through the conducting score and to see marks which correspond to most of the changes, at the same time taking into account the probability that the new music that Handel is known to have written for the 1735 revival was once inserted there. The resulting reconstruction of Handel's 1735 performing version (given in Table 8.4 pp. 208–11), is not perfect and there are alternative explanations for the few apparent anomalies. The wordbook may have been inaccurately marked, or perhaps did not amend the English part of the text by showing alterations from chorus to aria, or by giving any additional English texts; on the other hand, Handel may have composed movements in 1735 that he did not end up using in that year. There is also the

---

[23] See Burrows, 'Handel's 1738 "Oratorio"' p. 33. The surviving performing part for Handel's 1738 oratorio provides an important musical source for the Italian arias.

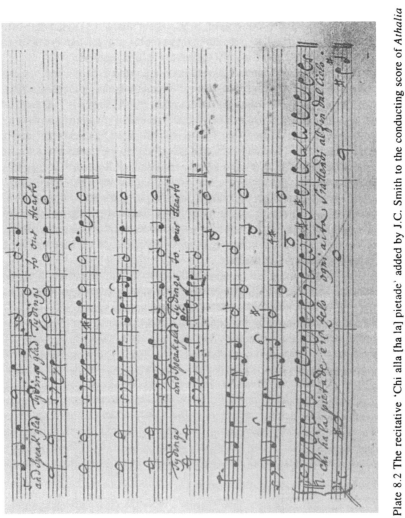

Plate 8.2 The recitative 'Chi alla [ha la] pietade' added by J.C. Smith to the conducting score of *Athalia*

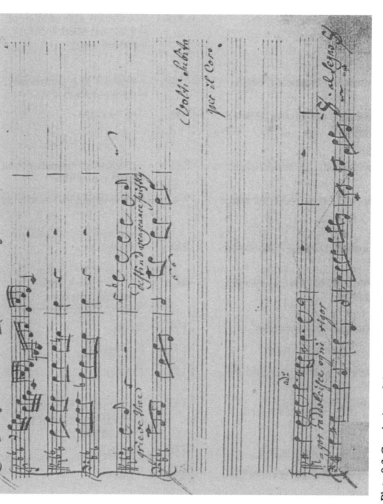

Plate 8.3 Conclusion of the aria 'Cor fedele' in the handwriting of J.C. Smith in the conducting score of *Athalia*

208 MUSIC IN EIGHTEENTH-CENTURY BRITAIN

possibility that Handel's five performances of *Athalia* in 1735 were not identical in the movements performed. The main uncertainty over musical content concerns the end of Part 1: the wordbook, if taken literally, indicates this as concluding with Carestini's aria 'L'innocenza, la clemenza', omitting both the 1733 air 'Gloomy tyrants' and the duet-and-chorus 'When storms the proud' which Handel composed to replace it in 1735, and probably omitting the final 'Hallelujah' as well.

Table 8.4: Handel's 1735 version of *Athalia*, based on the scheme from the 'Coke' wordbook

Movement	Sources †	Conducting Score
PART 1		
Overture/Allegro/Allegro [Gigue]	A, B, F, G	Amended with addition of F, G, and deletion of f. 1 (folded over)
Scene 1		
*Air (Josabeth), 'Blooming Virgins'	1733	Reduced to A section only: B section deleted f. 9r
*Air (Josabeth) and Chorus, 'Tyrants would/Tyrants'	1733	ff. 14v–19v
Scene 2		
Acc. Recit. (Joad), 'O Judah! Judah!'	1733	ff. 28v–29r: preceding recit. deleted on f. 28v
Air (Joad) and Chorus, 'O Lord, whom we adore'	K	[new setting: not now in score]
Scene 3		
Recit. (Athalia, Mathan), 'What scenes of horror'	1733	ff. 32v–33v
Air (Mathan), 'The Gods, who chosen blessings shed'	H, L	ff. 34–5 [new setting: wordbook heading 'Chorus' from 1733 not amended]
Recit (Athalia), 'Her form at this'	1733	f. 38v
*Chorus, 'Cheer her, O Baal'	1733	ff. 38v–41r
Recit (Athalia, Mathan), 'Amidst these Horrors'	1733	ff. 41r
Air (Mathan), 'Gentle Airs'	1733	ff. 41v–42r, for Mathan [wordbook: 'One of the Attendants']
*Air (Athalia), 'Softest Sounds'	1733	ff. 42r–43v
Recit (Mathan, Abner), 'Swift to the Temple'	1733	f. 43v
*Chorus, 'The Traitor'	1733	ff. 46r–47v

HANDEL'S 1735 *ATHALIA*

[Movement]	[Sources]	[Conducting Score]
Scene 4		
Air (Carestini), 'Bianco giglio'	?	f. 47v pencil cue 'Aria'
Recit (Joad, Josabeth, Abner), 'My Josabeth'	1733	f. 47r
*Air (Josabeth), 'Faithful Cares'	1733	ff. 48r–49r
Recit (Abner), 'O cease, fair Princess'	1733	f. 49v: recit reduced to 2 lines; cadence note added in pencil, remainder deleted
Air (Carestini), 'L'innocenza, la clemenza'	?	f. 9v original pencil cue, probably 'Aria/Ex G/bianco giglio', erased
[Duet (Joad, Abner) and Chorus, 'When storms/O Judah']	C	[not in score, nor any cue; no text in wordbook]
[Chorus, 'Hallelujah']	1733	[ff. 46 bis, 50–54r: unclear if included in wordbook cut, but no deletion in score]
PART 2		
Scene 1		
Chorus and Solo (Joad), 'The mighty Power/ He bids/Give Glory'	1733	ff. 54v–69v
Air (Josabeth), 'Through the land'	D, M	[not in score, which has only 1733 setting]
Recit (Abner, Joad), 'Ah! were this Land'	1733	f. 72v
*Air (Abner), 'Ah canst thou'	1733	ff. 73r–74r
Scene 2		
Recit (Athalia, Josabeth), 'Confusion to my thoughts'	1733	ff. 74v–75r
Air (Joash), 'Will God whose Mercies'	1733	ff. 75v–76v
Recit (Athalia, Joash), 'Tis my Intention'	1733	f. 76v
*Air (?Mathan), 'My Vengeance awakes me'	1733	ff. 78r–79v. Possibly transferred from Athalia to Mathan, though no change in wordbook: Beard's name written by Handel at begining of movement in conducting score.
Duet: (Josabeth, Joash), 'My spirits fail'	1733	ff. 79v–81r

210 MUSIC IN EIGHTEENTH-CENTURY BRITAIN

[Movement]	[Sources]	[Conducting Score]
Scene 3		
Duet (Carestini[Joad], Josabeth), 'Cangia in gioia' [= 'Cease thy anguish']	[1733]	[= ff. 81v–84r, no Italian text in score]
Recit (Abner), 'Joad, ere Day'	1733	f. 84r
Aria (Carestini), 'Quella Fama'	?	ff. 84v pencil cue 'aria C', and traces of music formerly stuck over page
*Chorus, 'The clouded Scene/When Crimes/Rejoice, O Judah'	1733	ff. 84v–89v
PART 3		
Scene 1		
Acc. Recit (Joad), 'What sacred Horrors'	1733	f. 90r
Chorus, 'Unfold, great Seer'	1733	ff. 90v–91r
Recit (Carestini), 'Chi alla pietade'	?	added f. 91r by Smith
Aria (Carestini), 'Cor fedele'	?	traces of music page formerly stuck over f. 91v, with continuation written by Smith on f. 92r
Recit (Joad, Joash), 'Eliakim'	1733	f. 93v
Chorus, 'With firm united Hearts'	1733	f. 94r–94v
Scene 2		
Recit (Josabeth, Mathan), 'O Princess'	1733	f. 94v
*Air (Josabeth), 'Soothing Tyrant'	1733	f. 95r–95
Scene 3		
Recit (Joad, Mathan), 'Apostate Priest'	1733	f. 95v
Scene 4		
Recit (Athalia, Joad), 'O bold Seducer!'	1733	f. 103r
*Chorus and Solo (Joad), 'Around let Acclamations ring/Reviving Judah/May God, from whom all mercies spring'	1733	ff. 103r–104v
Recit (Athalia, Mathan), 'Where am I?'	1733	f. 110r–110v
*Air (Mathan), 'Hark, hark'	1733	f. 111r–111v
Recit (Joad), Athalia), 'Yes, proud Apostate'	1733	f. 112r

[Movement]	[Sources]	[Conducting Score]
Scene 5		
Recit (Joad, Joash), 'Now Josabeth'	1733	f. 112v
Air (Carestini), 'Angelico Splendor'	?	f. 112v pencil cue 'aria angelico splendor'
Recit (Abner), 'Rejoice, O Judah'	1733	
Organ Concerto (HWV 292) and Chorus, 'Hallelujah'	E	f. 113v pencil cue 'Concerto Ex F'
[Chorus, 'Give Glory']	1733	[ff. 114r–119v, not deleted in score, or wordbook, but presumably omitted]

Notes:

 † '1733' indicates movements composed for the original 1733 score of *Athalia*. Letters refer to the sources listed in Table 8.1 (pp. 198-9).
 * Complete movements or sections also used in *Parnasso in Festa.*

Nevertheless, the overall form of the work that emerges is both clear and coherent enough to suggest that the annotations in the wordbook are correct; here, at last, is some sense of the form in which the oratorio was presented by Handel at its first London performances. The 1733 text was heavily cut to make way for the Italian movements, but retained the basic shape and incidents of the original drama. Handel's choices for the cuts do not seem to have been influenced by the fact that a large amount of the original *Athalia* score had appeared in *Parnasso in Festa*: he retained thirteen movements that had been used in the serenata. Table 8.5 lists the cast as proposed by Dean and Deutsch,[24] and the names of the singers who are known to have performed as soloists in the surrounding opera productions. Overall there is no problem with matching the

Table 8.5: Handel's 1734–35 casts

	Oreste	*Ariodante*	*Athalia**	*Alcina*
Strada	✓	✓	Josabeth	✓
Carestini	✓	✓	Joad	✓
Cecilia Young	✓	✓	Athalia	✓
Waltz	✓	✓	Abner	✓
Beard	✓	✓	Mathan	✓
Savage [treble]			Joash	✓
Maria Negri	✓	✓		✓
Stoppelaer		✓		

Note: * Cast as given by Dean and Deutsch, and in Walsh's collection of *Songs.*

---

 [24] See note 8 above. The cast-list was presumably based on the names printed above the arias in Walsh's publication of songs from *Athalia.*

212   MUSIC IN EIGHTEENTH-CENTURY BRITAIN

cast to the roles in *Athalia*, but did Carestini sing the role of Joad? Certainly in the duet 'Cangia in gioia' he sang the music that had been assigned to Joad in the English version of the movement. But does the heading to the insert page of the wordbook mean that Carestini sang this music in Italian, and the small residual part of Joad's role (including the solo at the beginning of the new setting of 'O Lord whom we adore') in English, or does it mean that these Italian texts represented the sum total of Carestini's part? It is not impossible that another singer took the (now small) dramatic role of Joad. The contralto Rosa Negri could have fulfilled this fairly undemanding duty; she apparently took English-language roles in previous seasons. On the other hand, Handel's specially-composed setting of 'When storms the proud' has Joad as a bass; perhaps the composer thought of using Stoppelaer as Joad, and perhaps he thought better of it before the performances, leading to the exclusion of this movement. In any case, during the 1734–35 season Handel had a number of spare singers in his company at Covent Garden who joined in the chorus movements; this much is apparent from the names that were added to the final *coro* of *Alcina*.[25] It would not have been difficult to find a singer for the role of Joad: apart from some *semplice* recitatives, his remaining part in 1735 consisted of the solo opening to 'O Lord whom we adore' and two short (though dramatically telling) accompanied recitatives, 'O Judah! Judah!' in Part 1 and 'What sacred horrors' at the beginning of Part 3. As far as Carestini's part fitted into any dramatic role, it was that of Joad; in Part 3, for example, his music was introduced by the chorus 'Unfold, great seer'. But the overall impression is that, while the cut version of the 1733 text preserved the bones of the drama in 1735, Carestini's role was ornamental rather than dramatic. He was there to draw the crowds with his singing, and it might not have been wise to let him loose in English. The 1735 *Athalia* offered the combined attraction to London audiences of an English oratorio which had not yet been heard in the capital, a new organ concerto, a 'Hallelujah' chorus as a rousing conclusion at the end of Part 3, and some lyrical interludes at stopping-points in the drama sung by one of Handel's most remarkable Italian soloists.

---

[25]   Between them the autograph (GB-Lbl RM 20.a.4) and conducting score (D-Hs MA/998) of *Alcina* add the names of [Mrs] Wright, Howard, Corfe, Thomson and Leveridge to the eight given in Table 8.5; these may not cover all the singers who contributed to the chorus.

CHAPTER NINE

The Mackworth Collection: a Social and Bibliographical Resource

Sarah McCleave

Background

The Mackworth Collection, comprising some 311 volumes, has a greater significance than its mere size might suggest, for the manuscripts and printed music therein contain a wealth of information about many understudied areas of musical endeavour.[1] The musical sources, which date from *c.* 1680 to 1790, offer the opportunity to assess the musical tastes and practices of four generations of a family of industrialists and politicians, rural gentlemen of both the 'landed' and 'monied' classes,[2] who enjoyed some links with London's thriving musical life, but whose family seat, in Gnoll Castle, Neath, lies in a part of Britain where our knowledge of musical life at that time is particularly sparse.[3]

This collection has a special value as it seems to have survived intact, a tribute to the organizational skills of Sir Herbert Mackworth (1737–91), who commenced dating and labelling volumes within it in 1761.[4] The development of the collection and its repertory suggest that Sir Herbert's father, also named Herbert (1689–1765), and his grandfather, Sir Humphry (1657–1727), made significant contributions, for most of the repertory found in the manuscripts

---

[1] Further writings on this collection include M. Boyd, 'Music Manuscripts in the Mackworth Collection at Cardiff', *Music and Letters*, 54 (1973), 133–41; ibid., 'The Mackworth and Aylward Collections at Cardiff', *Brio*, 28 (1991), 35–6; S. McCleave, 'Eighteenth-Century British Music in the Mackworth and Aylward Collections' (includes a handlist), in M. Burden and I. Cholij (eds), *A Handbook for Studies in 18th-Century English Music*, 8 (Oxford, 1997), 3–25. For catalogues of the collection, see S. McCleave, *A Catalogue of Published Music in the Mackworth Collection* (Cardiff, 1996); ibid., *A Catalogue of Manuscript Music in the Mackworth Collection* (Cardiff, 2000).

[2] See M. Ransome, 'The Parliamentary Career of Sir Humphry Mackworth, 1701–1713', *University of Birmingham Historical Journal*, 1 (1947–48), 232–54.

[3] Although Sir Humphry Mackworth, the founder of the collection, hailed from Betton, near Shrewsbury, he received property in Gnoll, Glamorganshire, upon his marriage to Mary, heiress of Sir Herbert Evans, in 1686. The earliest records pertaining to concert life in Swansea, the nearest urban centre to Gnoll Castle, date from 1792, the year after the younger Herbert Mackworth's death. See J.H. Thomas, 'Edward Edmund Ayrton. The Swansea Ayrton', *Morgannwg. The Journal of Glamorgan History*, 39 (1995), 30–49. None of the secondary sources cited below discusses musical life in Wales, nor does M. Tilmouth, 'The Beginnings of Provincial Concert Life in England', in C. Hogwood and R. Luckett (eds), *Music in Eighteenth-Century England: Essays in Memory of Charles Cudworth* (Cambridge, 1983), pp. 1–17.

[4] Many of the volumes, in addition to having their date of purchase or binding inscribed, are also labelled according to their genre. The collection remained with various members of the family until about 1916, when it was sold to a bookseller; it was subsequently purchased in 1919 by a Cardiff optician, Bonner Morgan, who presented it to Cardiff Public Library. The collection is now on permanent loan to Cardiff University.

predates 1760, as does a substantial portion of the printed volumes.[5] From time to time, the names of other family members, or connections through marriage, appear on the volumes. None of this pre-1760 music is signed or dated, so it is not possible to gauge the precise involvement of the individual elder Mackworths in forming this collection. Sir Herbert was definitely the main collector, for his signature, generally given as 'H. Mackworth', can be found on no fewer than 111 volumes. Of his generation, Mary Mackworth, his sister (b. 1745) also contributed three keyboard imprints and an ode by William Walond (c. 1725–70) while another sister, Juliana (b. 1733), seems to have begun copying a miscellaneous anthology of vocal music on 26 May 1761 (M.C. vol. 68). Sir Herbert's children, although praised for their 'elegant accomplishments' in their father's obituary,[6] do not seem to have been avid bibliophiles, for the collection contains few additions after his death in 1791, and this generation inscribed a mere two volumes: Robert (1764–94) owned a copy of William Shield's comic opera, *The Poor Soldier*, and his sister Eliza (b. 1769) was given a copy of Thomas Billington's *Gray's Elegy* by her brother Digby (b. 1766) in 1785.[7] Mary Anne Miers brought an imprint of William Shield's *Hartford Bridge* into the collection upon her marriage to Robert; the Hanburys, into whose family she later married (1797), inscribed three volumes, and were presumably responsible for purchasing the few nineteenth-century imprints now associated with this collection.

As Table 9.1 reveals, most of the seventeenth-century repertory is in manuscript, with a mere five printed works dating from this time, all issued in the last quarter of the seventeenth century. From 1700 through to the 1750s, the number of imprints purchased per decade remains fairly constant, with a rather irregular addition of manuscript material. The collection has the largest concentration of imprints issued in the 1760s, with seventy-four publications dating from that decade alone; it is doubtless no coincidence that young Herbert Mackworth, aged twenty-five, started to organize his library upon the year of his marriage in 1761, for this is the earliest purchase date found in the collection. From this point, the manuscript material added declines noticeably in quantity, which suggests the different generations had distinct methods of acquiring their materials. There is only a handful of additions to the collection after 1790, doubtless due to the death of the younger Herbert Mackworth, the chief collector, in 1791.

---

[5] Malcolm Boyd has suggested that Sir Humphry's diaries reveal no interest in music or the fine arts ('Music Manuscripts in the Mackworth Collection', p. 133), but the earliest repertory within the collection would certainly seem attributable to the collecting interests of someone from his generation.

[6] *Gentleman's Magazine*, October 1791, 970.

[7] The identity of 'Ensign Mackworth' of the '31 Regt Foot', who became the owner of a John Preston imprint, *New Instructions for the German-Flute*, on 24 December 1782, has not been determined, although Sir Herbert's elder son, Robert (b. 1764), is a plausible suggestion.

THE MACKWORTH COLLECTION   215

Table 9.1: Chronological development of the Mackworth Collection

The generation of Sir Humphry Mackworth (1657–1727)

1670s	0 MSS; 1 printed
1680s	1 MSS; 3 printed
1690s	14 MSS; 1 printed
1700s	2 MSS; 6 printed

? Herbert Mackworth (1689–1765)

1710s	3 MSS; 27 printed
1720s	14 MSS; 27 printed
1730s	4 MSS; 23 printed
1740s	6 MSS; 25 printed
1750s	6 MSS; 30 printed

Sir Herbert Mackworth (1737–91)

1760s	3 MSS; 74 printed
1770s	0 MSS; 51 printed
1780s	1 MSS; 32 printed

Sir Robert Mackworth (1764–94) and the Hanburys

1790s	0 MSS; 6 printed
post 1800	0 MSS; 4 printed

Note: For the purposes of compiling these statistics, the assigned date of publication has been used. The one exception is a volume of some 188 single sheet songs, a second-hand item which entered the collection in 1766, and has accordingly been entered as a single item from the 1760s. Dates such as '1720', '1720?' and 'c. 1720' have all been simplified as '1720s'. Undated manuscript repertory (most cantatas and instrumental works) has not been included, although theatrical repertory has. If a manuscript contains theatrical songs from the 1720s and the 1730s, one entry will be recorded in each of those decades. Most of the manuscript music not recorded in these statistics was composed by contemporaries of Sir Humphry (d. 1727) or his son, Herbert (d. 1765).

Dissemination

The collection includes sixty-eight manuscript volumes, which can be appreciated in a number of ways. In terms of provenance, they seem to fall into two broad categories, for most are copied by professional scribes, whereas a smaller number seem to have been copied by members of the family. The precise provenance of most of the professionally copied volumes remains undetermined at present, although studies of the paper-types and binding styles would certainly yield information of interest.[8] Three volumes featuring British vocal or theatrical

---

[8]   Intriguing possibilities for further study are suggested by copies of three Hasse operas: *Attilio Regolo* (M.C. vol. 13), *Didone abbandonata* (M.C. vol. 14) and *Cleofide* (M.C. vol. 19), each of which is bound in a gold-coloured board, further identification being provided by a distinctive cartouche on the title-page, featuring muskets that turn into branches.

216 MUSIC IN EIGHTEENTH-CENTURY BRITAIN

repertory *c.* 1680–1710 have inscriptions which lead us to previous owners, as do two volumes of instrumental music.[9]

Several professional copies of Italian operas and cantatas by composers such as Giovanni Bononcini (1670–1747) and Alessandro Scarlatti (1660–1725), and Spanish cantatas by Joseph de Torres (*c.* 1665–1738) raise interesting questions about the dissemination of such repertory, for there is no evidence to support the possibility that any of the Mackworths undertook a Grand Tour before the mid 1790s.[10] Nor is any of the family known to have entered diplomatic service, another obvious route for the introduction of foreign music.[11] It is possible these manuscripts were introduced into the collection by family friends such as the Dolbens, or that Mackworth family members who entered military service collected some music while serving abroad.[12] But when would the Mackworths as a family have had an opportunity to develop a taste for such repertory? Were performances of portions of operas and entire cantatas a commonplace occurrence in the homes of their acquaintances? If not, what was their motivation for collecting so many works which they are unlikely to have heard in performance? Moreover, the repertoire of both the manuscript and the printed music suggests that this was primarily a collection of music to be played, as there are many sets of instrumental parts, easy music for keyboard and guitar, and a plethora of pieces for the flute. The contents of this collection presumably reflect a repertory that was being performed in gentlemen's houses in South Wales during the

---

[9] Vol. 57, an anthology of British theatrical songs, is inscribed 'James Lovett his Book Aprill 27 1701'; vol. 64, some airs for the recorder, was formerly the property of 'John Forster in Bell Yard', whereas vol. 67, a miscellaneous anthology, may have belonged to 'Mr Deslormes'; vol. 32 (anonymous sonatas and minuets for keyboard) belonged to 'Sister Coningesby', while vol. 36 (two sonatas for violin and violoncello by 'Signor Sabbatini'), belonged to 'Revd. J. Joltham'. Preliminary research has failed to identify these people with any degree of certainty.

[10] Sir Herbert's widow, Elizabeth (Trefusis), is known to have travelled to Padua in 1796; see below for details concerning the travels of their daughter. For information concerning British travellers, see J. Ingamells, *A Dictionary of British and Irish Travellers in Italy, 1701–1800* (New Haven and London, 1997); I am grateful to Jane Clark for directing me to this source.

[11] Sir Herbert's daughter, Elizabeth Anne, married the diplomat Francis Drake in 1795, but there is nothing within the collection which would seem to have been purchased as a consequence of their subsequent sojourn in Italy.

[12] The Dolbens, who had considerable musical interests, were connected to the Mackworths by two marriages: the elder Herbert married Juliana, daughter of William, 5th Baron Digby in 1730 (Juliana's sister, Elizabeth, had married John Dolben, 2nd Bt., in 1720), while the younger Herbert Mackworth married Elizabeth Affleck, a granddaughter of the elder John Dolben, in 1761. Vol. 176 in the Mackworth Collection, an anthology of printed British songs, is inscribed, 'To Mrs. Robinson at Cransley near Kettering Northamptonshire Sr William Dolben'. For further information on the connection between the Dolbens and the Mackworths, see J.L.H. Bailey, *Finedon otherwise Thingdon* (Finedon, Northamptonshire, 1975); for Dolben as a collector, see D. Burrows, 'Sir John Dolben, Musical Patron', *Musical Times*, 120 (1979), 65–7 and Burrows, 'Sir John Dolben's Musical Collection', *Musical Times*, 120 (1979), 149–51. The elder Herbert's brother-in-law, the Hon. John Digby, travelled in Hanover and Italy in 1709–10. John Hanbury of Pontypool (into whose family the collection passed in 1797, see note d to Table 9.3, p. 219) travelled through Rome, Naples, Padua and Venice in 1724–5. Concerning the military connections of the Mackworths, a 'Major Mackworth' contributed a cantata, 'The Stocking', by one Thomas Stokes (issued *c.* 1765), while 'Ensign Mackworth' of the '31 Regt Foot' became the owner of a John Preston imprint, *New Instructions for the German-Flute* on 24 December 1782. The precise identity of these two gentlemen has not been determined.

THE MACKWORTH COLLECTION   217

eighteenth century; on the other hand, the collection would seem also to reflect a desire to be acquainted with a variety of music that could not easily be performed at home. Table 9.2 reveals some intriguing patterns in the collecting of serious operas in manuscript:[13] numbers 4–11 form a plausible group, while the Hasse operas (numbers 13–17) are the only examples of serious operas from the 1740s and 1750s in the collection.[14]

Table 9.2: Serious operas in the Mackworth Collection

1.	Rome, 1690	A. Scarlatti, *La Statira* (vols. 3–5)
2.	Rome, 1698	G. Bononcini's *Camilla* (vols. 6–8)
3.	Venice, 1726	N. Porpora's *Siface* (vol. 22)
4.	Rome, 1728	P. Auletta's *L'Ezio* (anthology, vol. 21)
5.	Rome, 1728	F. Feo's *Ipermestra* (anthology, vol. 21)
6.	Rome, 1728	L. Vinci's *Catone in Utica* (anthology, vol. 21)
7.	Rome, 1729	L. Vinci's *Semiramide* (anthology, vol. 21)
8.	Naples, 1729	L. Leo's *Arianna e Teseo* (anthology, vol. 21)
9.	Rome, 1730	L. Vinci's *Alessandro* (anthology, vols. 17 and 21)
10.	'1730'	J.A. Hasse's *Il Tigrane* (anthology, vol. 17)
11.	'1730'	G.M. Capelli's *Li fratelli riconosciuti* (vol. 15)
12.	Venice, 1738,1743	J.A. Hasse's *Cleofide* (vol. 19)
13.	Hubertusburg, 1742	J.A. Hasse's *Didone* (vol. 14)
14.	Dresden, 1745	J.A. Hasse's *Arminio* (vol. 1)
15	Dresden, 1750	J.A. Hasse's *Attilio Regolo* (vol. 13)
16.	Dresden, 1751	J.A. Hasse's *Il ciro riconosciuto* (vol. 24)

Note: Where possible, the dates of specific productions with which the Mackworth copy has been linked have been given. For further details see McCleave, *A Catalogue of Manuscript Music.*

An examination of the music by French composers in the Mackworth Collection (see Table 9.3) provides the tantalizing beginnings of an interesting case study on dissemination. Of the twenty-two 'French' imprints, five were published in London; at least two of these, a 1774 imprint of *The Maid of the Oaks* by François Barthélemon (1741–1808), and Purtin and Nicolas Lemaire's 1769 collection of French country dances, were composed by Frenchmen who were, at the time, actually based in London themselves. Of the sixteen Parisian imprints, the inscriptions on eleven of these reveal that they came into the collection as second-hand items; ten of these imprints had previously been owned by J. Brereton, while one collection of contredanses was the property of

---

[13] This table is confined to operas staged in Italy or Germany; manuscripts connected with the London operas obviously do not have the same implications for their dissemination.

[14] For those decades (1740s, 1750s), there is also no music from serious operas staged in London.

218 MUSIC IN EIGHTEENTH-CENTURY BRITAIN

Robert Sutton of the 75th Regiment of Foot, which was based in Belle-Isle in 1761.[15] A single London imprint, that formerly owned by one 'Miss Macoise', is evidently also a second-hand item. Most of the additional Parisian repertoire dates from 1730 or earlier, and includes a copy of the Ballard imprint of Lully's *Phaëton* dating from 1683 which would seem to have been purchased at an auction. It is not known whether the Aubert and Boismortier imprints came into the collection through a London dealer, or through friends who had travelled to the continent.[16] The manuscript collection suggests a more confined interest in Francophile music, with some dances by London-based Louis Grabu (*fl.* 1665–94) in a volume of instrumental airs (M.C. vol. 58), a handful of anonymous French songs (M.C. vol. 9, ff. 53v–51v), and a duo from Egide Duny's comic opera, *La Clochette* (1766), which is tucked away in a predominantly Italianate anthology (M.C. vol. 37, fols. 8r–10r).[17]

Table 9.3: French music in the Mackworth Collection

Date	Composer	Title	City of Publication	Owners[a]
1680?	Grabu, Louis	[Airs, instrumental]	MS	Mackworth
1683	Lully, J.B.	Phaëton	Paris, Ballard	'547'[b]
1700?	Anon.	[Airs, vocal]	MS	H. Mackworth
1719	Aubert, Jacques	Premier livre de sonates	Paris, Author	H. Mackworth
1725	Chaboud, Pierre	Solos for a German Flute	London, Walsh +[c]	H. Mackworth
1729	Boismortier, J.B.	Six sonates (op. 25)	Paris, Author +	–
1730	Boismortier, J.B.	Six sonates (op. 29)	Paris, Author +	–
1731	Anon.	Tons de chasse	Paris, Boivin +	J. Brereton
1738	D., ———	Fanfares nouvelles	Paris, Chevardière	J. Brereton

---

[15] The possibility that Brereton was connected to the ancient Cheshire family of that name is suggested by the identity of the friend, 'Thomas Assheton Smith Junr.' (1752–1828), who gave him the imprints now in the Mackworth Collection. *The Dictionary of National Biography* (London, 1917) indicates that the senior Assheton Smith was of Ashley Hall, near Bowden in Cheshire. Although inscriptions in this collection attest that Mackworth family members saw military service (see discussion above, and notes 7 and 12), no connection with Robert Sutton has yet been established.

[16] S. Sadie affirms that the music of French composers rarely appeared in London publishers' catalogues of this time; S. Sadie, 'Music in the Home II' in H.D. Johnstone (ed.), *Music in Britain, The Eighteenth Century* (Oxford, 1990), p. 337.

[17] Duny's serious opera, *Demofoonte*,was performed in London during his visit of 1737.

THE MACKWORTH COLLECTION

[Date]	[Composer]	[Title]	[City of Publication]	[Owners]
1758	Bordet, Toussaint	Méthode Raisonnée	Paris, Author +	Mr Hanbury[d]
1759	Taillart, Pierre	Pieces Françoises (I)	Paris, Author	J. Brereton
1760	Taillart, Pierre	Pieces Françoises (II)	Paris, Author	J. Brereton
1760	Various	Suite de Contredanses	Paris, various	Robt. Sutton
1760	Davesnes, Pierre	Suite de Contredanses	Paris, Chevardière	J. Brereton
1762	Granier, François	Pieces Françoises (I)	Paris, Chevardière	J. Brereton
1762	Granier, François	Pieces Françoises (II)	Paris, Chevardière	J. Brereton
1763	Granier, François	Pieces Françoises (III)	Paris, Chevardière	J. Brereton
1764	Granier, François	Pieces Françoises (IV)	Paris, Chevardière	J. Brereton
1766	Duny, Egide	La Clochette (duo)	MS	–
1770	Lemaire, Nicolas	14 New Cottillons	London, Author +	Miss Macoise
1773	Davesnes, Pierre	Suite de Menuets	Paris, Chevardière	J. Brereton
1774	Barthélemon, F.	Maid of the Oaks	London, Longman +	–
1780	Du Monchau, C.	A Collection of Airs	London, Welcker	H. Mackworth
1780	Anon. adaptation	Senses (= La lumière)[e]	London, J. Fentum	–
1790	Montlivaut,Chev.	Rondo, Canzonetta...	London, Author +	–

Notes:

[a] As indicated by the inscriptions.
[b] This would seem to be an auctioneer's slip.
[c] Space constraints preclude listing all publishers where more than one is named.
[d] Robert Mackworth's widow married into the Hanbury family in 1797.
[e] The title-page of this single-sheet song, which includes an arrangement for the guitar, reads, 'The Senses. Adapted to the favorite French Air La Lumiere. The words by R.D. Esqr.' (M.C. vol. 309).

220   MUSIC IN EIGHTEENTH-CENTURY BRITAIN

Notably, most of the French repertory listed in Table 9.3 is suited or designed for performance on the flute. The predominance or absence of certain genres within the collection reflects, as one might expect, the relative levels of achievement that individual family members attained on their respective instruments. The Mackworths display markedly catholic tastes in their selection of flute repertoire, which includes purpose-written repertory such as solo sonatas by Lewis Christian Austin Granom (c. 1725–91) as well as the remarkable Walsh and Hare imprint of 1730, *The Bird Fancyer's Delight*, 'with Lessons properly compos'd within the compass and faculty of each bird'. As one would expect, the Mackworth Collection also contains many flute adaptations of songs, particularly opera arias.[18] Perhaps the most interesting example of this marketing ploy is the manuscript volume of arias from J.A. Hasse's opera, *Il Tigrane* (1729), which bears the title 'Arie nel Tigrane del Signr Hasse per il Flauto' (M.C. vol. 17). Were any of the other operatic scores in manuscript perhaps collected to add to the Mackworth flute repertory?

Evidence of the eclecticism of the collection is provided when examining the dated inscriptions supplied by Herbert Mackworth the younger on some of his flute music. William Gould's *Six Sonatas or Duets* was bought shortly after it was published in 1775,[19] while other repertory, such as an anthology of flute publications which Mackworth had bound for preservation in 1780, contained music published as early as 1725 and no later than 1762.[20] Although a significant proportion of Herbert Mackworth's flute repertoire was therefore of a quasi-antiquarian nature, his balanced selection, which also included composers such as Lewis Granom (c. 1725–91), John Hebden (fl. 1740–50) and James Hook (1746–1827) suggests a collector of modest performing abilities who was seeking to preserve and re-use the repertory already purchased by his father and grandfather (neither of whom seem to have dated or labelled their purchases), rather than someone with exclusively conservative tastes. If it is recalled that the younger Herbert Mackworth was cataloguing and collecting at a time when the musically fashion-conscious seemed divided between a passion for antiquarian repertory and a marked enthusiasm for 'the new', the apparently rather different concerns of a musical gentleman in the provinces is striking.[21]

---

[18] See, for example, the 1709 Walsh, Randall and Hare imprint of Francesco Conti's *The Most Celebrated Aires and Duets in the Opera of Clotilda: Curiously Fitted and Contriv'd for Two Flutes* (M.C. vol. 295) and Walsh's 1711 issue of Handel's *The Most Celebrated Aires and Duets in the Opera of Rinaldo Curiously Fitted and Contriv'd for Two Flutes and a Bass* (M.C. vol. 294).

[19] *Six Sonatas or Duets for Two German Flutes or Violins... Opera Terza* (Edinburgh: printed for the Author... , [c. 1775]), was inscribed 'H. Mackworth Octbr. 1776' (M.C. vol. 182).

[20] The contents of this anthology (M.C. vol. 115) are as follows: Pierre Chaboud, *Solos for a German flute* (London: I. Walsh and Ino. & Ioseph Hare, [1725?]); Jacques Aubert, *Premier livre de sonates a violin seul* (Paris: author, 1719); Carlo Tessarini, *Easy and familiar airs for the violin* (London: John Cox, 1751); Lewis Christian Austin Granom, *XII sonate per flauto traversière solo* (London: s.n., [c. 1745]); John Hebden, *Six solos for a German flute* (London: John Johnson, [c. 1745]); Various, *VI sonate a flauto traversa solo* (London: John Cox, [c. 1762]); John Frederick Ranish, *XII solos for the German flute* (London: Jno. Walsh, [1744]); and Thomas Davis, *A second collection of VI solos for a German flute* (London: H. Waylet, [1745]).

[21] See also the discussion of 'Antiquarian Issues', pp. 225–6 below.

THE MACKWORTH COLLECTION

Most of the genres present in the printed collection – quantities of solo music for flute, guitar, keyboard and voice, instrumental duets, and trio sonatas – conform to the accepted norms of eighteenth-century domestic music-making.[22] The predominance of an admirable variety of types and kinds of vocal repertoire, from simple single song sheets to the more intricate textures of William Jackson's *Twelve Songs* (op. 4, published *c.* 1765), which featured two violins, viola and continuo in the accompaniment, suggests that the English composer's predilection for vocal genres alluded to in Peter Holman's essay[23] held a strong appeal for the Mackworths. Indeed, many of the generic labels which Mackworth used in organizing his collection, namely 'Canzonets', 'Scotch Songs', 'Catches and Glees', 'English Songs' and 'Airs', reflect his recognition of the variety of contemporary vocal genres.

Apart from Handel (22 imprints, 32 MS items), Hasse (11 imprints, 9 MS) and Corelli (5 imprints, 3 MS), most composers are represented, in the printed collection, by a mere one to three works,[24] while the manuscript collection favours some composers not found in the imprints, including Alessandro Scarlatti and Pietro Sandoni (1685–1748), the latter of whom was active in England for part of his career. Other composers who feature prominently in the manuscript collection include British-born Henry Purcell (1659–95), John Eccles (*c.* 1668–1735), Jeremiah Clarke (*c.* 1674–1707), Thomas Arne (1710–78), John Stanley (1712–86), and Robert Bremner (*c.* 1713–89). Although modest in size, the collection is eclectic in scope, with some 190 named composers sharing 503 imprints, plus an additional fifty-one composers who are represented in the manuscript collection only.

Taste and Influences

What considerations, apart from the purely practical concerns of collecting a performing repertory, shaped the tastes of the musical Mackworths? As three generations of Mackworths were Tory Members of Parliament, and also served at various Inns of Court, one presumes there was a family base in London.[25] Indeed, it is known that the Mackworth males were usually educated at Westminster, and Sir Herbert's second son, Digby, was born in Marylebone in 1766. Musical events and fashions in the capital would therefore have had a certain influence on Mackworth purchasing and performing patterns.

---

[22] See H.D. Johnstone, 'Music in the Home I', in Johnstone (ed.), *Music in Britain*, pp. 159–204, and S. Sadie, 'Music in the Home II', ibid., pp. 313–56.

[23] See Chapter 1 above.

[24] Composers such as Henry Carey (*c.* 1689–1743) and Samuel Howard (1710–82) are represented by nine and ten imprints respectively, but most of these are found in an anthology of vocal music (M.C. vol. 176) that entered the collection as a single item in 1766.

[25] Sir Humphry entered the Middle Temple on 10 June 1675, subsequently serving Cardiganshire and later Totnes as MP (1701–13); Herbert senior entered the Temple in 1708, he was MP for the Cardiff boroughs from 1739 to 1765; the younger Herbert entered Lincoln's Inn in 1759, later serving the Cardiff boroughs as MP from 1766 to 1790.

222   MUSIC IN EIGHTEENTH-CENTURY BRITAIN

When examining possible influences on the Mackworth family's musical tastes, there are some obvious trends in the development of the theatrical collection, trends which suggest the Mackworths were fairly avid theatrical connoisseurs, whose tastes, nonetheless, experienced a marked shift between generations.[26] The manuscript collection best represents the interests of the eldest collecting generation, for it includes an anthology of British theatrical songs by composers such as Henry Purcell (1659–95), John Eccles (c. 1668–1735), and Jeremiah Clarke (c. 1674–1707), taken from stage works which were performed in London in the 1680s and 1690s (M.C. vol. 57). The second Mackworth generation, that of the elder Herbert, continued to demonstrate an interest in theatre music, as attested by a burgeoning number of operatic imprints and selected arias in manuscript (e.g., M.C. vol. 41) reflecting the repertory of serious operas staged in London from about 1708 to 1730, as well as a Walsh and Hare imprint of John Galliard's *Calypso and Telemachus* issued in 1712. This generation was more cosmopolitan, however, for there is now a larger proportion of manuscripts representing foreign productions, featuring composers such as Nicolà Porpora (1686–1768) and J.A. Hasse (1699–1783), both of whom were undoubtedly known to London audiences,[27] as well as operas by more obscure composers such as Giovanni Maria Capelli (1648–1726), whose work would not have circulated as widely (see Table 9.2, p. 217).

In theatrical terms, the 1740s and 1750s are sparsely represented, apart from some Hasse operas in manuscript; when the Mackworths again turned to the theatre in the late 1760s, the tastes of the family had altered significantly, for the only serious Italian opera collected after 1751 is Venanzio Rauzzini's *La Regina di Golconda*, issued by Longman and Broderip in 1784. Imprints by composers of popular English comic operas, such as Charles Dibdin (1745–1814) and William Shield (1748–1829), now take precedence, while manuscript copies of overseas repertory are confined to one or two arias in miscellaneous anthologies. Some writers would argue that the later generations of Mackworths (Sir Herbert and his children) were evincing 'bourgeois' tastes.[28]

---

[26] Perhaps this change reflected the 'decline' in taste which Sadie ('Music in the Home', 314) suggests occurred in the later part of the eighteenth century. Sadie attributes this phenomenon to a 'rapid spread of wealth among a public that was culturally inexperienced and [therefore?] lacking in discrimination'; this suggestion would scarcely seem to fit the profile of Sir Herbert, or his children.

[27] See Table 9.2 (p. 217), 'Serious operas in the Manuscript Collection'. The Mackworth Collection includes one Porpora opera in manuscript, *Siface* (Kurt Markstrom has suggested to the author that this copy represents the 1726 Venetian production). That none of Porpora's five London operas (1733–36) is found in this collection presumably reflects the evident change in family tastes, discussed below; his chamber output, which might have appealed to the Mackworths' practical inclinations, was extremely modest. Hasse was widely performed and circulated in London at this time; his popularity is reflected by the eight complete operas and two smaller items in manuscript, and the twelve imprints (chiefly chamber music), now in the Mackworth Collection.

[28] R. Hoskins, 'Theatre Music II', in Johnstone, *Music in Britain*, pp. 261–312.

THE MACKWORTH COLLECTION 223

Thus theatrical productions in London had some influence on the development of the collection. When the instrumental repertory is considered, however, the Mackworth taste seems more independent of London concert life, for although most of the concert series in London were dominated by the music of foreigners during the latter half of the eighteenth century,[29] the Mackworth Collection is almost half British in content,[30] with Italians comprising just under a third of the collection, French and German composers weighing in nearly equally at just over ten per cent each, and Handel taking up approximately five percent of the shelf space. The Collection also notably lacks fashionable German and Austrian composers from the latter half of the eighteenth century: the only music by Joseph Haydn (1732–1809) is that in the anthology *Twelve Duets for Two German-Flutes*, issued by Harrison & Co. in 1784, while J.C. Bach (1735–82) is merely represented by op. 4 and op. 6 of his canzonets. Many popular composers and styles are sparsely represented: Carl Friedrich Abel's music, for example, is confined to his contribution to the 1770 J. Longman imprint, *Eight Italian Sonatas, For two Violins or Flutes, with a Thoro' Bass for the Harpsicord or Organ*, while the galant style is represented by one or two compositions each from composers such as Felice de Giardini (1716–96), Lewis C.A. Granom (c. 1725–91) and James Hook (1746–1827).

A recently published calendar of keyboard concerts in London in the latter half of the eighteenth century provides an opportunity to compare this particular repertory with that found in the Mackworth Collection, seeking to isolate an influence on the development of that facet of the collection.[31] Unfortunately, the composers featured in these London entertainments are not always specified, so only limited conclusions can be drawn. Of the thirty-four named composers in this calendar, only seven are found in the Mackworth Collection; of these, a mere two, Niccolo Pasquali (c. 1718–57) and Georg Christoph Wagenseil (1715–77), are represented by actual keyboard repertory (the former by his treatises, *The Art of Fingering* and *Thorough-Bass Made Easy*, the latter by *Six Sonatas for the Harpsichord*, op. 1). Indeed, the Mackworth keyboard music, as

---

[29] 'Nationality' is admittedly a concept fraught with ambiguities. For the purposes of providing a statistical breakdown, I have generally defined nationality according to the composer's birthplace, with further qualifying factors, such as the place where the composer lived and where the work was published, being taken into account in the discussion which follows. For further information on London's concert life, see S. McVeigh, *Concert Life in London from Mozart to Haydn* (Cambridge, 1993); foreign dominance of British musical life at this time is alluded to by R. Fiske, 'Music and Society', in Johnstone, *Music in Britain*, pp. 3–4 and by S. Sadie, 'Concert Life in Eighteenth Century England', *Proceedings of the Royal Musical Association*, 85 (1988), 17–30. Sadie has elsewhere suggested ('Music in the Home II', p. 321) that this foreign dominance extended also to publishers' lists, which favoured foreign composers in a 5:1 ratio, a phenomenon which is certainly not reflected in the Mackworth Collection
[30] An examination of S. McCleave's *Catalogue of Published Music* may suggest a higher percentage of British content but, for the purposes of this calculation, an anthology containing over 180 single-sheet songs (M.C. vol. 176) has been counted as one item only, as it was bought by Mackworth second-hand, as a single item.
[31] N. Salwey and S. McVeigh, 'The Piano and Harpsichord in London's Concert Life, 1750–1800: A Calendar of Advertised Performances', in M. Burden and I. Cholij (eds), *A Handbook for Studies in 18th-Century English Music*, 8, (Oxford, 1997), 27–72.

224   MUSIC IN EIGHTEENTH-CENTURY BRITAIN

does the operatic repertory, shows a change in taste between generations, for the elder Mackworths relished the works of composers such as Pietro Sandoni and Johann Mattheson (1681–1764) – the former represented in manuscript, the latter by I.D. Fletcher's 1714 imprint of *Pieces de clavecin*; while the younger generation was content with less inspirational material, such as Gartini's *Six Easy Lessons* (published by C. & S. Thompson in 1773) and D.A.L. Smiths' *Six Sonatas* (published in 1793 by Preston and Son). Indeed, the modest abilities of the Mackworth family, suggested by much of the instrumental music in the collection, presumably also accounts for the absence of certain difficult genres, such as Handelian trio sonatas or string quartets. Popular new genres from the second half of the eighteenth century are fairly rare as well, for the collection contains only three sets of accompanied keyboard sonatas.[32]

Despite a certain insularity in the development of the instrumental repertory, the presence of various imprints representing London theatrical repertory, songs performed at the pleasure gardens, collections of court minuets, and pieces stemming from topical theatrical events (such as *Miss Dawson's New Hornpipe as Perform'd at Drury Lane*), nevertheless suggests a family which was *au courant* with certain fashionable developments in the capital.[33] The eight imprints in the collection which were available only at the composer's address provides a further link between the Mackworths and London musical life,[34] as do those imprints which appear to have been bought fairly soon (i.e. within two years) after they were published (See Table 9.4).

---

[32]   Felice (de) Giardini, *Sei sonate di cembalo con violino o' flauto traverso... opera terza* (London: John Cox, [1751]), M.C. vol. 277; Georg Christoph Wagenseil, *Six Sonatas for the harpsichord with an accompaniment for a violin... opera prima* (London: A. Hummel, [c. 1760]), M.C. vol. 160; and Ferdinando Pellegrini, *Three sonatas for the harpsichord with accompaniment for a violin...* (London: A. Hummel, [c. 1765]), see M.C. vol. 310.

[33]   M.C. vol. 304. This hornpipe, 'by means of which Nancy Dawson danced into fame ... became a popular household tune', and was even cited in the Epilogue of Oliver Goldsmith's *She Stoops to Conquer*. See 'Dawson, Nancy', in vol. 4 of P. Highfill et al. (eds), *A Biographical Dictionary of Actors, Actresses, Musicians, Dancers, Managers, and other Stage Personnel in London, 1660–1800* (Carbondale and Edwardsville, Ill., 1975), p. 239. See also M.C. vol. 309, the *Minuet de la Duchesse de Devonshire, As Danced by Sigr. Vestris at the Opera House*, a single-sheet imprint capitalizing on performances of this dance by Gaëtan Vestris and Mme Simonet during the 1780–81 season at the King's Theatre.

[34]   John Lenton, *The Gentleman's Diversion, or the Violin Explain'd* (London: Sold by the author, 1693); William Croft, *Musicus Apparatus Academicus* (London: Printed for the Author, and to be had at his House in Charles-Street Westminster), [1720]; Giovanni Bononcini, *Divertimenti da Camera* (London: Sold onely at Mrs: Corticelle's House, 1722); William Walond, *Mr. Pope's Ode on St Cecilia's Day* (London: Printed for the Author, [1760?]); Joseph Tacet, *Second Collection of Italian French and English Favorite Airs* (London: Printed & sold by Mr. Tacet in Mears Court, Dean Street, Soho, [1765]); Stephen Paxton, *Eight Duets for a Violin and Violoncello... Opera Seconda* (London: To be had of the Author No 29 Great Titchfield Street, [1780?]); Stephen Paxton, *Six Easy Solos for a Violoncello or Bassoon... Opera III* (London: Printed for the Author, No 82, Great Titchfield Street, [c. 1780]); and Thomas Billington, *Gray's Elegy* (London: Printed for the Author, and to be had at his house No. 24, Charlotte Street Rathbone Place, [1785]).

THE MACKWORTH COLLECTION

Table 9.4: New publications bought by the Mackworths (ordered by inscribed date)

Composer	Title	Published	Inscribed
Zuccari, Carlo	The... Method of Playing an Adagio	1762	1762
Anon.	Minuets... 1763 (pub. Thompson)	1762	1762
Cocchi, Gioacchino	Six Duets for two Violoncellos	1764	1765
Broderip, John	Six Glees for three Voices (op. 5)	1770	1770
Light, Edward	Six English Songs (op. 1)	1774	1774
Real, Joseph	Twelve Duets for Two German Flutes	1775	1775
Alcock, John	A Favorite Duett for two Bassoons	1775	1775
Barthélemon, F.	The Maid of the Oaks	1774	1776
Giordani, Tommaso	Six Duettos for two Violoncellos	1780	1780
Paxton, Stephen	Eight Duets (op. 2)	1780	1781
Paxton, Stephen	Six Easy Solos (op. 3)	1780	1781
Du Monchau, Charles	A Collection of Airs	1780	1782
Fischer, Johann	Ten Sonatas for a Flute	1780	1782
Anon.	New Instructions for the German-Flute	1780	1782
Arnold, Samuel	The Castle of Andalusia	1782	1783

Antiquarian issues

Despite a certain influence exerted by London's cultural life, in particular its theatrical events and pleasure garden concerts, further examination of the repertory within this collection reveals a detachment from fashionable concerns. Herbert the younger's development of the collection suggests that he had a fairly relaxed attitude towards the relative currency of a given work: although he purchased many items within two years of their publication date, other items were bought or bound together in anthologies well over a decade after they were first issued (see Table 9.5).

The gaps between publication and purchase or binding, which range from eight to forty-eight years, confirm that the Mackworths were far from fashion conscious in their choice of performance repertory. It is perhaps of significance that the longer gaps tend to occur with works bound together in anthologies, which suggests Mackworth had a particular interest in preserving some of this older repertory. Mackworth's most antiquarian purchase, a copy of *Mace's Monument*, was added to the collection in 1766, some ninety years after publication. The presence of this work within the Mackworth's collection is difficult to explain, for all the other treatises relate closely to repertory within the

226 MUSIC IN EIGHTEENTH-CENTURY BRITAIN

collection (instruction books for figured bass, guitar, voice and flute). Mace's treatise, which treats psalm singing, lute and viol technique, would seem to have had little or no practical relevance, for Mackworth's collection of psalms was negligible, and that of music for lute and viol non-existent.

Table 9.5: 'Unfashionable' items in the Mackworth Collection (ordered by inscribed date)

Composer	Title	Published	Inscribed
Mace, Thomas	Musick's Monument	1676	1766
Johnston, Arthur	Psalmi Davidici	1741	1766
Holmes, Valentine	Six Sonatas for Two German Flutes	1766	1775
De Fesch, Willem	Thirty Duets for two German Flutes	1747	1776
Burney, Charles	VI Sonatas or Duets For... Flutes	1754	1776
Bryan, Joseph	The Muses Choice (vol. II)	1758	1776
Dothel, Nicolas	Six Trios for Two German Flutes	1764	1776
Florio, Pietro Grassi	Six Sonatas for Two German Flutes	1767	1776
Dibdin, Charles	Shakespear's Garland (vol. I)	1769	1776
Marcello, Benedetto	Six Solos for a Violoncello (op. 2)	1732	1780
Galliard, John	Six Sonatas for the Bassoon	1733	1780
Flackton, William	Six Overtures (op. 3)	1771	1784
Gartini	Six Easy Lessons or Sonatinas	1773	1784

A relaxed attitude towards fashionable concerns is also revealed in the manuscript collection, for an anthology begun by the younger Herbert in 1766 contains Handel cantatas dating from 1707–18,[35] movements from the overture to that composer's *Alcina* (1735), as well as some pieces copied from John Stanley's *Eight Solos for a German Flute* (1740). Many of the pieces within this anthology were copied from items found in the printed music in the collection, chiefly publications issued in the 1740s, 1750s and 1760s. The broad chronological spread demonstrated in this manuscript, and indeed the information revealed by the inscriptions on the imprints, suggests a family that was neither resolutely antiquarian nor relentlessly fashion conscious.

---

[35] The Handel cantatas, found at the beginning of the manuscript (M.C. vol. 9, fols 1r–28r), include HWV 151, 100, 168, 129, 162, 127a, 121b.

Networking

Did various contemporary musical societies play any role in forming the Mackworths' tastes? Did the Mackworths, as provincial gentlemen creating their own oasis of culture in remote Neath, join various clubs to establish contacts when they were in London? Despite the proliferation of imprints dating from the Royal Academy years in the 1720s, no Mackworth can be found amongst its known directors or subscribers.[36] A search through certain documents connected with The Academy of Vocal Music (1725–30), The Concert of Antient Vocal and Instrumental Music (1776) and The Noblemen's and Gentlemen's Catch Club (1779–1861) failed to yield any Mackworths among their respective lists of subscribers.[37] The repertory within the Mackworth Collection does not suggest a strong link with any of these institutions, in any case. Indeed, the overlap in repertoire between the Mackworth Collection and The Concert of Antient Music is remarkably modest, when one considers their strong family connection to those notable antiquarians, the Dolbens,[38] and the fact that all the Mackworth males matriculated at Magdalen College, Oxford, an environment which would have fostered any latent antiquarian interests. A shared interest in Corelli (1653–1713) and Handel (1685–1759) is offset by the poor representation of the types of vocal music favoured by the Academy of Vocal Music, which is confined to part of one manuscript anthology in the Mackworth Collection which includes a few anonymous motets as well as one motet each by Giacomo Carissimi (1605–74) and Giovanni Battista Bassani (c. 1657–1716).[39] Moreover, despite the marked British slant to the Mackworth repertory, this collection notably lacks the Arne overtures which featured in the programmes of The Concert of Antient Music. In any case, much of the earlier repertory was presumably added by the older generations of Mackworths: none of the Corelli or Handel imprints has an inscription which links them to Sir Herbert (the younger) or to his children, while Handelian imprints issued in the latter half of the eighteenth century are notably lacking from the collection. Indeed, the Handel material found here is largely confined to his earlier serious operas and their overtures. The Mackworth tastes are best seen as eclectic rather than institutionally inspired.

---

[36] E. Gibson, *The Royal Academy of Music 1719–1728: The Institution and Its Directors* (London, 1989).

[37] 'The Academy of Vocal Music 1725–1730' (GB-Lbl Add. MS 11732); 'Concert of Antient Vocal and Instrumental Music. Established AD 1776. With a Catalogue of The Several pieces Performed since its Institution' (GB-Lbl King's MS 318); the directors of the 'Concert of Antient Music' are listed in H. Reynell's *Concerts of Antient Music, As Performed at the New-Rooms, Tottenham-Street, MDCCLXXXIII* and in the dedication of W. Jones, *A Treatise on the Art of Music* (Colchester: Printed for the author, by W. Keymer, 1784). The list of 'Honorary Members, Candidates, etc.' from 1779 to 1861 for the Catch Club (GB-Lbl H.2788.bbb) also fails to list any Mackworths.

[38] Burrows, 'Sir John Dolben's Musical Collection', p. 149. See also note 12 above.

[39] M.C. vol. 10, which is inscribed 'H Mackworth Gnoll'. Bassani is also represented in the printed collection by op. 8 and op. 13 of his *Harmonia Festiva... Divine Motetts...* (London: Printed by William Pearson for John Cullen and John Young, [1708] and [c. 1710]).

228   MUSIC IN EIGHTEENTH-CENTURY BRITAIN

Publishers patronized

It has been seen that this collection suggests a family with fairly wide musical tastes; it remains to be seen whether their patronage of publishers was as widespread. The 503 imprints within the collection were the product of some ninety-two publishers,[40] with a mere fourteen firms (represented by some twenty-five individuals) being represented by five or more imprints. Most of these firms were based in London. Some seventeen imprints are inscribed with the names of previous owners and one (Lully's *Phaëton*) has an auctioneer's label.[41] The salient points concerning some of the principal publishers within this collection are summarized in Table 9.6.

Table 9.6: Publishers' profile, Mackworth Collection

Name	Total[a]	Comments[b]
Bland, John	5	Glees and operas yes; no republished Handel nor Haydn.
Cooke, Benjamin	5	Pirated editions (Ariosti, Bononcini, possibly Geminiani).
Hummel, A.	5	A fairly obscure firm?
Johnston, John	5	Including one Stratford Jubilee publication (Dibdin).
Roger, Estienne	5	Examples of this firm's Italian bias.
Frères Legoux, Les	6	Second-hand flute music.
Oswald, James	6	Several of his own compositions.
La Chevardière	6	Second-hand flute music, fashionable rather than serious repertory.
Bremner, Robert	8	Guitar yes; no Periodical Overtures.
Johnson, John	8	A very prominent firm, here well represented.
Kearsly, George	8	Monthly Melody.
Thompson	18	A very prominent firm, here well represented.
Longman & Broderip	19	Strong profile of foreign repertory, not here represented.
Walsh	72	Supplier of 11 of the 23 Handel imprints, a very prominent firm.

Notes:

[a]   Representing the total number of imprints within the Mackworth Collection issued by the named publisher.

[b]   Most of this information has been derived from D.W. Krummel and S. Sadie (eds), *Music Printing and Publishing, The New Grove Handbooks in Music* (London, 1990); further information from C. Humphries and W.C. Smith, *Music Publishing in the British Isles* (London, 1954).

---

[40]   Here individual names of publishing partners have been counted, rather than firms.

[41]   Many of the imprints in the Aylward Collection, also housed in Cardiff University, have auctioneers' labels, so it is possible that this item has strayed into the wrong collection.

THE MACKWORTH COLLECTION   229

The Mackworths must have been fairly *au fait* with the publishing world, for they patronized a considerable number of firms, and seemed well aware of where to acquire particular types of music. Although the bulk of the repertory was supplied by three very major firms (Thompson, Longman & Broderip, and Walsh), more obscure firms, such as A. Hummel, receive a fair representation. The Mackworths were fairly regular patrons of Longman & Broderip, yet they were not tempted by any of that firm's considerable foreign repertory, a fact which throws their evident commitment to British music (discussed earlier) into relief.

Contexts of performance

Apart from collecting repertory, how did the Mackworth enthusiasm for music manifest itself? Although it is known that provincial gentlemen frequently formed their own concert societies,[42] information about concert life in Wales at this time is sadly lacking, so any information which can be extracted from the Mackworth Collection is of particular value. Since many of the sets of parts are now incomplete, it is possible to assume that the Mackworths shared some of their music-making with neighbours. An intriguing question is raised about the possible context in which the music was played by the presence of concertos by composers such as Robert Woodcock (d. 1734), Antonio Vivaldi (1678–1741) and J.A. Hasse (1699–1783); opera overtures, chiefly by Handel, represent further repertory for larger ensembles. Although these works could have been played in an informal family-type setting, the inclusion of music for larger forces suggests that more formal concerts may have been part of the Mackworth music-making routine.

This selection of chamber and concerted music[43] suggests some interesting trends in the music making of the Mackworths (see Table 9.7). It is notable that all the concerted repertory was published between 1710 and 1745, which suggests that any neighbourhood 'gentlemen's concert' was most likely formed around this time. As can be seen, only five of these larger works exist in complete sets, there is no particular pattern as to which parts are missing amongst the remainder. Whether the gentlemen of Sir Herbert's generation continued to play the same repertory, someone else took charge of purchasing, or the group (supposing one existed) disbanded, is not clear. In the 1770s, a small but interesting set of martial works for medium-sized ensemble were assembled (see Anon. and Dobney in Table 9.7, as well as John Reid's *A Set of Marches for Two Clarinets... Two Horns, & a Bassoon*, issued in score by Robert Bremner in 1778).[44] Possibly a closer examination of the family papers may

---

[42] E.D. Mackerness, *A Social History of English Music* (London and Toronto, 1964), pp. 115–16; Sadie, 'Music in the Home II', pp. 317–20.

[43] Of necessity, the former (chamber) is selective, the latter (concerted) more comprehensive.

[44] See the previous discussion of the family's known military connections in note 12 above.

230   MUSIC IN EIGHTEENTH-CENTURY BRITAIN

reveal more about the performance context of these works.[45]

Table 9.7: Chamber and concerted music in the Mackworth Collection (ordered by published date)

Composer	Title	Date	Missing parts
Conti, Francesco	... Clotilda... for Two Flutes	1709	1st fl
Corelli, Arcangelo	Sonatas of Three Parts (op. 1–4)	1710–15	1st+2nd vn
Vivaldi, Antonio	L'estro armonico (op. 3)	1710	1st va
Various	Six Overtures for Violins	1724	Complete[a]
Handel, G.F.	Six Overtures (2nd, 3rd, 4th Coll.)	1725–27	complete
Woodcock, Robert	XII Concertos in Eight Parts	1727	2nd fl
Anon.	Musica Bellicosa	1730	continuo
Vinci, Leonardo	Overture in Elpidia	1730	complete
Geminiani, Francesco	Concerti Grossi	1732	1st+2nd vn
Handel, G.F.	Six Overtures (7th Collection)	1738	va, 3rd vn
Handel, G.F.	Six Overtures (5th Collection)	1740	va, vc, hn
Hasse, J.A.	Six Sonatas or Trios	1739	1st+2nd vn/fl
Hasse, J.A.	Sei sonate a tré (op. 2)	1740	vc, continuo
Hasse, J.A.	Sei concerti (op. 1)[b]	1740	2nd vn
Hasse, J.A.	Six Concertos in Eight Parts (op. 4)	1741	complete
Handel, G.F.	Six Overtures (8th Collection)	1743	1st ob, 1st hn
Felton, William	Six Concerto's for the Organ	1744	continuo
Hasse, J.A.	Twelve Concertos in Six Parts (op. 3)	1745	va
Anon.	XXIV Marches in Five Parts	1770	1st+2nd vn/fl
Dobney, Michael	... Marches in Five Parts	1770	1st+ 2nd vn, 1st hn
Hook, James	Six Sonatas for Two German Flutes	1775	1st fl/vn

Notes:
   [a] All string parts and the continuo are present, although the GB-Lbl has additional manuscript parts for first and second oboe, and for bassoon; see h.3211.(1.).
   [b] This set of parts is inscribed 'Mackworth Praed', and thus would have belonged to William Morgan Mackworth, younger brother of the elder Herbert (b. 1689).

---

[45] Sir Humphry's diaries are divided between the National Library of Wales, Aberystwyth (MS 14362D) and the archives of the Neath Antiquarian Society; the Royal Institution, Swansea, has further family records (including MSS 886 and 1379). Malcolm Boyd has examined some of the family papers, see 'Music Manuscripts in the Mackworth Collection', 133–4.

THE MACKWORTH COLLECTION   231

Bibliographical issues

In addition to its value as a social document, the Mackworth Collection contains considerable information for the music bibliographer. Sadly, there is only a handful of dated manuscripts, confined to the years 1761–77. These inscribed dates tell us when certain repertory was being circulated, but there are no apparent revelations about the genesis of any of this music, for most of the inscribed repertory was copied well after it would have been composed.

The value of the inscribed dates in the printed collection is considerable, for they establish a *terminus ad quem* for many imprints. The date of '*circa* 1780' which the British Library's *Catalogue of Printed Music*[46] assigns to Stephen Paxton's self-published *Six Easy Solos for a Violoncello or Bassoon* (op. 3) is confirmed, and Mackworth's inscribed purchase date of '14th. April 1781' further refines the probable date of publication for these identical imprints. It should be remembered, however, that the inscription date applies only to the specific issue or state to hand.[47] For example, the Mackworth copy of Johann Christian Fischer's *Ten Sonatas for a Flute* (Longman & Broderip) differs from the British Library copy (g.72) in some typographical details on the title-page. Although the Mackworth copy may well have been published between 1779 and 1781 (the date range suggested by '1780?' in the British Library's *Catalogue of Printed Music*), it is also possible that the Mackworth inscription date of '1782' sets a new *terminus ad quem* for the specific issue in the collection.

In other instances, the Mackworth inscription reveals that a work was available earlier than had previously been thought. Thomas Billington's own publication, *Gray's Elegy*, which has been assigned a date of 1786 in two reference works[48] was in fact published no later than 1785, as Digby Mackworth's thoughtful dating of a present to his sister Eliza attests.[49] In other instances, the Mackworth inscription considerably refines knowledge concerning a particular imprint: Edward Light's *Six English Songs* (op. 1), which is variously dated *c.* 1780 in the *British Union Catalogue of Early Music* (vol. 2, p. 620) and *c.* 1800 in the *New Grove*, (vol. 10, p. 856) was actually available no later than 11 May 1774, in an imprint issued by the composer himself. Thus this collection informs our understanding of the publication and dissemination of specific pieces of repertory within this period.

The Mackworth inscriptions remind modern scholars not to accept anything at face value on the title-page of an eighteenth-century music publication. A case

---

[46] *Catalogue of Printed Music in the British Library to 1980* (London, 1981); g.500.(9.).

[47] For the purposes of cataloguing the Mackworth Collection, issues were differentiated by typographical details found on the title-page, whereas states were distinguished by variations of the actual content, such as the addition of a publisher's catalogue or a dedicatory page.

[48] *Catalogue of Printed Music in the British Library* and E.B. Schnapper (ed.), *British Union-Catalogue of Early Music Printed before the Year 1801*, (London, 1957).

[49] 'Eliza Mackworth the gift of her Affectionate Brother Digby Mackworth Bath May 4th 1785'. Thus we learn that musical events at this fashionable resort could have had some influence upon the development of this collection. For further on musical life in Bath, see K.E. James, 'Concert Life in Eighteenth-Century Bath' (PhD diss., University of London, 1987) and K. Young, *Music's Great Days in the Spas and Watering-Places* (London, 1968).

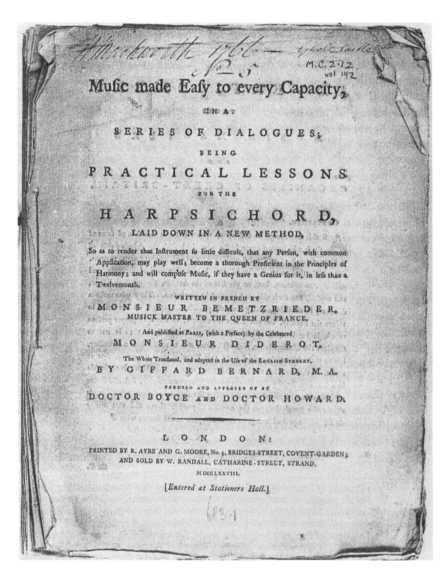

Plate 9.1 Title-page of Bemetzrieder's *Music made Easy to every Capacity* (London, c. 1766).

THE MACKWORTH COLLECTION   233

in point is Anton Bemetzrieder's harpsichord treatise, *Music made Easy to every Capacity*, which was issued in London by R. Ayre and G. Moore in an English translation. According to Albert Cohen's article on Bemetzrieder in *New Grove* (1980 edition), this work was first published as *Leçons de clavecin, et principes d'harmonie* in Paris in 1771.[50] Mackworth's inscription of '1766' not only throws into question the date clearly presented in the English imprint (see Plate 9.1), but also suggests that the first issue of this work in French has not yet surfaced. According to Cohen, Bemetzrieder was known for issuing 'new editions, translations or expansions' of his earlier pedagogical publications, so the Mackworth inscription suggests that the evolution of this particular work needs to be carefully re-examined. The complications arising from Mackworth's inscription do not stop here, however, for the title-page of the English edition claims that the work was 'perused and approved of by Doctor Boyce and Doctor Howard'. Although William Boyce was awarded his doctorate in 1749, according to Roger Fiske, Howard did not become 'Dr' until 1769.[51]

Conclusion

This analysis of certain facets of the Mackworth Collection demonstrates its value as a social document and a bibliographical resource. In total four generations of a particular family built an eclectic musical library which drew upon various aspects of their background and experience, although a certain portion of the foreign manuscripts are of more uncertain origin. Indeed, the composition of the collection suggests that the Mackworths were fairly resourceful; there are some second-hand items (both imprints and manuscripts), professionally-copied manuscripts (which presumably entered the collection through the efforts of various family connections) and volumes compiled by family members themselves. The fact that later generations of this undeniably upper-class family seem to have developed what some writers would describe as 'bourgeois' tastes suggests that modern understanding of the formation of taste at the time is uncertain, not least because of the further work that remains to be done on the dissemination and performance of music in this period. The examples presented above by no means exhaust the potential of what can be learned from this valuable collection.

---

[50] A. Cohen, 'Anton Bemetzrieder' in *New Grove Dictionary of Music and Musicians*, ed. S. Sadie (London, 1980), vol. 2, pp. 460–61.

[51] R. Fiske, 'Samuel Howard' in *New Grove Dictionary*, vol. 8, p. 744. The discussion above concentrated on the value of the inscribed dates found within the collection; obviously valuable information concerning scribes and the dissemination of certain repertory remains to be extracted. A small number of autobiographical imprints (Thomas Billington, Giovanni Battista Cirri, Thomas Curtis, Joseph Tacet) may also be of interest.

CHAPTER TEN

The Papers of C.I. Latrobe: New Light on Musicians, Music and the Christian Family in Late Eighteenth-Century England

Rachel Cowgill

There is very good opportunity of hearing good Music & exquisite performances in this City; but it is all managed by a set of mercenary animals, who will be well paid & are otherwise, few excepted, not fit Companions for any man regarding his own character. I find however now and then suitable occasions to hear their Doings.[1]

Musicologists working on the eighteenth century come across the Revd Christian Ignatius Latrobe (1758–1836) in a variety of contexts: he was a friend of the Burney family, and of Haydn's whilst he was in London, and he is generally credited with having introduced new continental church music to England through the publication of his *Selection of Sacred Music from the Works of some of the most eminent Composers of Germany & Italy* (6 volumes, London, 1806–25). For all this, however, he has remained a peripheral figure; most of what is known of 'this benevolent Moravian minister' derives from the eloquent tribute penned by Edward Holmes for the *Musical Times* in 1851.[2] A

---

[1] Letter from C.I. Latrobe, London, to his brother, J.F. Latrobe, Dorpat, Livonia (Russia), 14 November 1802. Private collection of Dr John Henry de La Trobe, Hamburg (quoted with kind permission).

Christian Ignatius spelt his surname in three different ways: 'Latrobe', 'LaTrobe', and 'La Trobe'. He was of Huguenot descent, his great-grandfather having left Languedoc for Britain shortly after the Edict of Nantes was revoked in 1685; yet he did not like to hear his name pronounced in the French manner, partly because of his horror at the French Revolution and his profound dislike of Napoleon. For this reason, he is referred to as 'Latrobe' throughout this paper.

For their invaluable assistance during the research for this essay I would like to thank John Mason, historian and missiologist, and Janet Halton, Archivist of the British Province of the Moravian Church, Moravian Church House, Muswell Hill, London.

[2] E. Holmes, 'The Rev. Christian Ignatius Latrobe', *Musical Times*, 3 (1851), 249–50, 255–6. Latrobe's friendship with Burney is discussed in R. Lonsdale, *Dr. Charles Burney: A Literary Biography* (Oxford, 1965), *passim*; Lonsdale's sources for his observations are limited to the Burney–Latrobe correspondence in the Burney Family Collection, in The James Marshall and Marie-Louise Osborn Collection, Beinecke Rare Book and Manuscript Library, Yale University.

On Latrobe's contact with Haydn, see J. Boeringer, 'Haydn's Herrn Hutters', *Moravian Music Journal*, 29 (1984), 14–20. Haydn, as he himself recorded in his First London Notebook, was the dedicatee of Latrobe's Three Piano Sonatas op.3: see H.C. Robbins Landon (ed.), *The Collected London Correspondence and London Notebooks of Joseph Haydn* (London, 1959), p. 263. Latrobe reminisced about his friendship with Haydn in a letter to Vincent Novello, 22 November 1828, GB-Lbl Add. MS 11730, ff. 112–13. Novello published this letter in the preface to his new edition of Haydn's Stabat Mater in vocal score (dedicated to Latrobe); and Holmes also printed a transcription of it (op. cit., pp. 225–6). For more on Latrobe's relations with Haydn, see this author's 'Latrobe, Christian Ignatius', in D.W. Jones (ed.), *Oxford Composer Companions: Joseph Haydn* (forthcoming).

THE PAPERS OF C.I. LATROBE   235

substantial corpus of Latrobe's printed and manuscript writings has survived, held principally in the Osborn Collection at the Beinecke Library, Yale University (New Haven); John Rylands Library (Manchester); Bodleian Library (Oxford); British Library (London); and in various private collections. Yet, whilst Latrobe's musical compositions have received some attention in recent years, his papers have, to date, been largely overlooked by musicologists.[3] As this essay will show, a close reading of this material – much of it discussed here for the first time – yields not only a fresh perspective on musical life in late Georgian London, but also a more detailed impression of Latrobe's significance – a figure who, as Holmes recalled, exercised a quiet yet profound influence on the musical life of his generation.

Latrobe's reputation as a fine musician was emphasized by the artist Thomas Barber, who painted his portrait during the 1820s (see Plate 10.1). A chamber organ with an open music book is clearly visible in the background but, as his clerical black coat and folder of letters symbolize, Latrobe's life was in all respects given over to the work of the Moravian Church. The Moravians (or United Brethren) are a Protestant denomination renowned for their global outlook and missionary zeal. Their faith originated in one of the earliest, pre-Lutheran dissents from Roman Catholicism, the ancient church of the Bohemian Brethren (or Unitas Fratrum), which was founded around 1457 by disciples of the martyr Jan Hus. Enduring ruthless suppression by the Counter-Reformation, the faith survived as a 'hidden seed' in Bohemia and Moravia, whilst some Brethren left their homeland in search of a more tolerant regime. In 1722, three refugee families from Moravia were given sanctuary by the devout Lutheran Pietist, Count Nikolaus Ludwig von Zinzendorf, who allowed them to found a settlement, Herrnhut ('The Lord's Protection'), on his estate at Berthelsdorf, near Zittau, in Saxon Upper Lusatia.[4] Under Zinzendorf's aegis the Church revived and flourished, and, in what is now referred to as the 'Moravian diaspora', intrepid 'messengers' issued forth from Herrnhut to spread the faith among the heathen, and to seek fellowship with other Christians. Moravian missions were established as far afield as Ceylon, South Africa, Surinam, the Danish West

---

On the *Selection of Sacred Music*, see N. Temperley, 'Latrobe [La Trobe], Christian Ignatius', in S. Sadie (ed.), *New Grove Dictionary of Music and Musicians* (London, 1980), vol. 10, p. 535. W.H. Hadow still considered this collection 'valuable' enough to append a full list of its contents to his article on Latrobe for the first edition of *Grove*: W.H. Hadow, 'Latrobe, Rev. Christian Ignatius', in G. Grove (ed.), *A Dictionary of Music and Musicians*, (London, 1878–90), vol. 2 (1880), pp. 102–3.

[3]   Only those papers that contain material relating to music are cited here. For discussion of Latrobe's musical compositions, see C.E. Stevens, 'The Musical Works of Christian Ignatius Latrobe' (PhD diss., University of North Carolina at Chapel Hill, 1971). Stevens's study includes a thematic catalogue of Latrobe's compositions and selected transcriptions of his correspondence with Burney. Modern editions of Latrobe's music have recently been published by Boosey & Hawkes in 'The Moramus Edition', under the auspices of the Moravian Music Foundation.

[4]   On Zinzendorf see: J.R. Weinlick, 'Zinzendorf, Nikolaus Ludwig von', in Sadie (ed.), *New Grove*, vol. 20, pp. 695–6; A.J. Lewis, *Zinzendorf, the Ecumenical Pioneer* (London, 1957); C. Podmore, *The Moravian Church in England, 1728-1760* (Oxford, 1998), *passim*. Nikolaus Ludwig (1700–60), who became the leader of the Moravian church, was the uncle of Karl von Zinzendorf (1739–1813), the Viennese diarist and socialite.

Plate 10.1 Reverend Christian Ignatius Latrobe

Indies, Latin America, North America, Greenland, and Labrador. Congregations began to spring up in England too, largely as a by-product of the missionaries' interest in the British colonies (initially, the new American colony of Georgia); the first of these, the Fetter Lane congregation in London, became the headquarters of the British Province. Three Moravian settlements were also founded in England during the eighteenth century (Fulneck at Pudsey, near Leeds, 1744; Ockbrook, west of Derby, 1752; Dukinfield, 1755, moving to Fairfield, Droylsden, near Manchester in 1785). Designed, like those on the continent, as earthly counterparts of the heavenly Jerusalem, these were communities centred on worship, prayer and music, cherishing simple living and a devotion to Christ. But they also earned a reputation for hard work, achieving self-sufficiency by a variety of 'diaconies', or communal businesses; sisters and brethren at Fulneck, for example, were engaged in branches of the textile industry, including spinning, weaving and embroidery.[5]

Based in London from 1784, Latrobe lived with the community of Moravians in Fetter Lane, for whom he undertook the spiritual charge of the Single Brethren.[6] In January 1787, he was appointed Secretary of the Moravian Society for the Furtherance of the Gospel among the Heathen, a voluntary religious society (henceforth referred to as the SFG). He was ordained Deacon in December of the following year, aged thirty; but rather than being engaged to lead a specific congregation, he continued as Secretary of the SFG, a role he would fulfil for almost fifty years, before passing it on to his son. In 1795, Latrobe succeeded Burney's friend James Hutton as Secretary of the Unity of Brethren in England, thereby becoming the supreme representative of the Moravian Church in the British Isles. Six years later, Latrobe was appointed *senior civilis*, a high and ancient office, which he was the last to hold.[7]

These honours were granted in recognition of Latrobe's dedication to the cause of the Moravian missions. With Moravians scattered across the globe, the

---

[5] J.T. Hamilton and K.G. Hamilton, *History of the Moravian Church*, 2nd. edn (Bethlehem PA and Winston Salem NC, 1983). *The Moravian Atlas [...] compiled [...] by the Teachers of Fulneck Academy* (n.p., 1853). C. Podmore, *The Moravian Church in England, 1728–1760*. G. Stead, *The Moravian Settlement at Fulneck 1742–1790* (Leeds, 1999). By 1760 there were twelve Moravian congregations in England, which equalled the number of congregations active in Germany at that time. For analysis of the appeal of Moravianism to the English see Podmore, *The Moravian Church*, pp. 120–58.

[6] The nexus of buildings occupied by the Moravians in Nevil's Court and Fetter Lane, north of Fleet Street (a stone's throw from Dr Johnson's house), was destroyed by bombing during the Second World War. For a history of the Fetter Lane community, see C. Podmore, *The Moravian Church and The Fetter Lane Moravian Congregation, 1742–1992* (London, 1992). Latrobe was to stay with this community until his retirement to the Moravian settlement at Fairfield, near Manchester, in 1834.

[7] J. Mason and L. Torode, *Three Generations of the Latrobes in the Moravian Church* (Newtownabbey, 1997), pp. 16–28. J. Mason, 'La Trobe, Christian Ignatius', in D.M. Lewis (ed.), *Blackwell Dictionary of Evangelical Biography* (Oxford, 1995), vol. 2, p. 664. J.C. H[adden], 'Latrobe, Christian Ignatius', in *Dictionary of National Biography*, ed. by Stephen Lee (London, 1885–), vol. 32, p. 183. 'Historical Sketch of the Latrobe Family', *Periodical Accounts Relating to the Missions of the Church of the United Brethren*, 25 (1863), 79–84. Latrobe was appointed minister of the Fetter Lane congregation in August 1792; but the Elders relented when he expressed his commitment to the work of promoting the missions.

Church depended heavily on effective communication to maintain its unity, and to ensure that even the most isolated member was kept informed and supported. Once a month, each community would put aside a whole day to listen to letters and diaries exchanged with other congregations and emissaries. Hence, Latrobe acted as a conduit for information, circulating news in a steady stream of correspondence between the Moravian missionaries, settlements, and the mission-board in Germany. As Secretary of the SFG, his specific function was to promote and raise funds for the work of the Moravian missions, particularly the Labrador mission, established in 1771, for which the SFG was directly responsible. Latrobe, therefore, became a crucial advocate for the Moravians in English society, attracting financial, practical and spiritual aid for the missionaries, by establishing and nurturing personal 'connexions' with fellow Christians and sympathizers. Support came from the upper strata of English society, including prominent clerics, academics, politicians and the nobility, many of whom attended meetings of the SFG at Fetter Lane. Those associated with the Society received the *Periodical Accounts Relating to the Missions of the Church of the United Brethren*, which Latrobe initiated in 1790 and compiled each quarter, by collating, translating and editing the reports of missionaries. Circulation eventually reached 3,000, and many denominations, both Established and Nonconformist, were represented in the membership of the Society; as Latrobe himself declared, their donations and goodwill proceeded 'from a spirit of true Brotherly Love, which, setting aside all opinions on particular Systems or points of doctrine & practice, embraces all those who love the Lord Jesus Christ in sincerity'.[8] By these means, Latrobe helped to secure a pivotal role for the Moravian Church in the burgeoning evangelical movement of late eighteenth-century England.[9]

Latrobe's success in winning support in England for the Moravian missions was to a large extent due to his personal qualities: he was well read, widely travelled, and a talented musician, all of which endeared him to polite company. But Latrobe was no autodidact: these accomplishments had been fostered by the

---

[8]   Latrobe, to Rev John Rippon, 20 December 1796, GB-Lbl Add. MS 25387, ff. 432–3. Rippon was a Baptist minister, hymnologist and evangelical leader. This letter records a donation he had made on behalf of the Particular Baptist Missionary Society for Propagating the Gospel among the Heathen. Ecumenicalism was a central concept in Zinzendorf's vision for the Moravians (see Podmore, *The Moravian Church, passim*) and Latrobe's father had been particularly loyal to this ideal.

[9]   The influence of the Moravian Church during the great Evangelical Revival in eighteenth-century England has been throughly re-examined and documented in two recent studies: C. Podmore, *The Moravian Church* and J.C.S. Mason, 'The Role of the Moravian Church during the Missionary Awakening in England, 1760–c. 1800' (PhD diss., University of London, 1998). Latrobe's father, Benjamin, had been a Baptist before converting to Moravianism, and there were already close links with the early Methodists: it was at a meeting of the Moravian-style Fetter Lane Society, under Peter Böhler's influence, that John Wesley had felt his heart 'strangely warmed' in 1738. Furthermore, in 1749 the British Parliament, with the support of its bishops, had passed an act recognizing the Moravians as 'an antient Protestant Episcopal Church'; although this would soon provoke controversy, resulting in the crisis of 1753.

The records of the SFG and Latrobe's *Periodical Accounts* are held in the archives of the British Province of the Moravian Church, London.

THE PAPERS OF C.I. LATROBE   239

rigorous but enlightened Moravian education system, within which he had spent the first twenty-six years of his life.[10] By 1800, Moravian schools were considered to be among the best in the Western World, because of the Church's emphasis on formal education as the backbone of faith. Since these institutions were vital in shaping Latrobe's musical tastes, experiences and values, they merit consideration here.

By modern standards, Latrobe began his education at a young age. Born on 12 February 1758 at the Moravian settlement of Fulneck near Leeds, where his father Benjamin was minister, Latrobe had entered the boy's 'œconomy' by the time he had reached his third birthday.[11] In 1771 he travelled to Germany, aged thirteen, to continue his studies at the prestigious Moravian Pædagogium at the settlement of Niesky, north-west of Görlitz in Upper Lusatia; and he was to remain in Germany for the next thirteen years. At Niesky, Latrobe was received into the Moravian Church, and was first admitted to Holy Communion a year later, on 8 July 1775, a profoundly moving experience which, as he later recalled, set the tone of his faith for the rest of his life: 'This world lost part of its hold upon me; I had tasted something of the powers of the world to come, besides the sweets of a preparation for it here on earth.'[12] In 1776, he was enrolled at the seminary of Barby in Saxony, the jewel of the Moravian education system, situated on the Elbe, between Magdeburg and Dessau. This was virtually a closed community, one that stressed the development of personal piety in its training of future ministers, missionaries and teachers.[13]

Music appeared on the curriculum at each of these institutions, alongside a broad range of subjects, including Latin, Greek, Hebrew, French, German, English, geometry, arithmetic, history, natural history, geography and drawing.[14] At Niesky, as Latrobe recalled, any boy who declared sufficient interest could learn to play a musical instrument, and three 'exercise-concerts' were given each week. As in most Moravian communities, the Brethren formed

---

[10] Nicholas Temperley's statement that Latrobe was 'apparently self-taught' needs correction; see 'Latrobe [La Trobe], Christian Ignatius', in *New Grove*, vol. 10, p. 535.

[11] 'Lists of Boys, 1760–1814', Boys' School Archives, Fulneck School. Latrobe's father, Benjamin La Trobe (1728–86), was minister at Fulneck from 1757 until 1767, and became a Moravian leader in Britain, see: J. Mason and L. Torode, *Three Generations of the Latrobes*, pp. 3–15; J. Mason and C. Podmore, 'La Trobe, Benjamin' in Lewis (ed.), *Blackwell Dictionary of Evangelical Biography*, vol. 2, pp. 663–4; 'Historical Sketch of the Latrobe Family', pp. 79–80.

[12] C.I. Latrobe, *Letters to my Children; written at sea during a voyage to the Cape of Good Hope, in 1815, containing a Memorial of some occurrences of my past life*, ed. by J.A. La Trobe (London, 1851), p. 34. These autobiographical letters were not written for publication; they were issued after Latrobe's death by his son John Antes Latrobe, whose eldest brother Peter furnished explanatory notes on the text.

[13] Latrobe, *Letters to my Children*, pp. 26–45. J.C. Van Horne and L.W. Formwalt (eds), *The Correspondence and Miscellaneous Papers of Benjamin Henry Latrobe, Vol. I: 1784–1804* (New Haven, 1984), pp. 3–10 (Benjamin Henry Latrobe, the celebrated American architect, was the brother of Christian Ignatius; he also attended Niesky and Barby, from 1776 until 1783). Further information kindly supplied by Janet Halton.

[14] Horne and Formwalt describe the course of study at Niesky Pædagogium, 1779, in *The Papers of Benjamin Henry Latrobe, Vol. I*, pp. 3–10. See also: 'Examination Papers for 1794 and 1795', Boys' School Archives, Fulneck; H.H. Hall, 'Moravian music education in America, ca.1750 to ca.1830', *Journal of Research in Music Education*, 29 (1981), 225–34.

240   MUSIC IN EIGHTEENTH-CENTURY BRITAIN

orchestras, or *collegia musica,* that would meet during the week to rehearse and perform; hence, at Barby, Latrobe acquired a working knowledge of most instruments, and of orchestral and chamber repertory, that would later prove invaluable to him in his own compositions.

> As it had pleased God to give me a genius for music, I learnt with great facility, to play such instruments as were wanting to make our little band more complete; and successively took up the violin, viola, violoncello, oboe, French-horn, trumpet, trombone, bassoon, clarionet, and double bass. Nor was much time required to gain skill sufficient for common use in accompanying others, which was all I aimed at; in most cases, discontinuing my performance on them, as others stepped in to take my place. The clarionet, however, I learnt to play tolerably well.[15]

The orchestra also played for worship. Typically, accompanied hymns and concerted anthems composed by fellow Brethren, past and present, were sung; but, according to Latrobe, sacred music by non-Moravian composers such as C.H. Graun (1703/4–59) and J.A. Hasse (1699–1783) could also be included in services.[16] Thus, music played a central role in the education, recreation and spiritual development of a young Moravian such as Latrobe.

Latrobe was already proficient on the organ by the time he left Fulneck; but at Barby he encountered some of the finest musicians in the Moravian Church, most notably Christian Gregor (1723–1801) who encouraged him further.[17] One of only eight student-organists who took turns to play during services at Barby, Latrobe became a particular protégé of the venerable Bishop August Gottlieb Spangenburg, a friend of his father. At that time, Latrobe recalled, it was the practice for Moravian organists to ornament and improvise around the hymn tunes and anthems they accompanied:

> our taste at that time was bad. The noble simplicity of our church-music and hymn-tunes was lost in flourishes and ill-placed decorations, and deformed by long straggling interludes. Little attention was paid to that agreement between

---

[15] Latrobe, *Letters to my Children,* pp. 35–6. Latrobe underplays his abilities on the clarinet; he was, it seems, an excellent player. At Barby, he made such rapid progress on the instrument that he quickly exhausted the available repertory. He composed a series of concertos of his own, which according to his son, contained 'obligato passages of so difficult a character, that [Latrobe] could scarcely believe in after-life, that he had ever been able to execute them' (ibid., p. 36). These concertos do not appear to have survived, although Latrobe certainly brought them with him to London: he showed them to one of the Mahon brothers, 'the first [i.e. best] Clarinet player in England', on 21 May 1788, according to his journal (GB-Mu English MS 1244, f. 20). Shortly after this, however, Latrobe seems to have laid his clarinet aside, presumably for lack of suitable performing opportunities in England.

[16] ibid., pp. 26–45. For more on music in the Moravian communities, see K. Kroeger, 'Moravians, American, in *New Grove,* vol. 12, pp. 562–4; K. Kroeger, 'A Preliminary Survey of Musical Life in the English Moravian Settlements of Fulneck, Fairfield, and Ockbrook, during the 18th and 19th Centuries', *Moravian Music Journal,* 29 (1984), 20–26 (also in *Unitas Fratrum: Zeitschrift für Geschichte und Gegenwartsfragen der Brüdergemeine,* 14 (1983), 95–100).

[17] See J.R. Weinlick, 'Gregor, Christian Friedrich', in *New Grove,* vol. 7, pp. 691–2; J. Boeringer, 'Christian Gregor', *Journal of Church Music,* 24 (1982), 5–6, 9. The organ at Fulneck had been built by the Swiss John Snetzler in 1748, a year after his completion of an organ for the Fetter Lane chapel. On Snetzler's work for the Moravians, see A. Barnes and M. Renshaw, *The Life and Work of John Snetzler* (Aldershot, 1994), pp. 284–300 and *passim.*

THE PAPERS OF C.I. LATROBE

music and words, by which they are made to speak the same language, and to convey, each in their degree, the same feeling to the mind.[18]

Spangenburg corrected this fault in Latrobe's playing, who henceforth held fast to the tenets of 'plain hymn-accompaniment', and a simplicity and humility of style.[19] As Holmes recalled, although the mature Latrobe was a gifted extemporizer and improviser, 'he much disliked the coxcombry of performance. Some young man having in his presence executed a fugue of Handel with much display, Mr. Latrobe told him that Handel would have thrown his wig at him, if he had heard him play it.'[20]

Towards the end of 1779, Latrobe returned to Niesky as a tutor of piano and organ. In later years, he thought of Niesky as his 'favourite place', and much of his happiness there stemmed from the activities of the orchestra, 'a most musical party', with whom he spent his leisure hours.

> As we had a good leader [Johann Ludwig Freydt (1748–1807)], our little band became more and more perfect, and our performances more correct and pleasing. This was particularly the case in the years 1783 and 1784,. when, with the addition of all hands, both in the Institution and in the settlement, we could muster thirty-two vocal and instrumental performers.[21]

Although much research has still to be done to identify the repertory peculiar to each of the Moravian settlements, it is certain that music by Joseph Haydn (1732–1809) was known and played by Latrobe and his musical brethren at Niesky. The Osborn Collection at Yale University houses a holograph musical manuscript book from Latrobe's library, whose date (1783) suggests it was probably copied by him in Niesky. It contains the following Haydn works, put into score: 'Quartet V from Op. XVI; Minuet from Quartet I, Op. XVI; Affettuoso from Quartet I, Op. XVI; Quartet II from Op. XVI'.[22] Haydn never published a set of string quartets as 'op. 16', but Hoboken and Jones both mention a publication of the op. 20 quartets, brought out as 'Op. XVI', by Hummel in Berlin and Amsterdam, in 1779, and Blundell in London, between 1778 and 1780: Hummel's edition would seem to have been the most likely

---

[18] Latrobe, *Letters to my Children*, pp. 36–41.

[19] ibid., p. 40. Latrobe published his ideas on 'plain hymn-accompaniment', in the preface to his *Hymn-Tunes Sung in the Church of the United Brethren* (London: John Bland, 1790); and in L.B. Seeley (ed.), *Devotional Harmony* (London, 1806). The instructions he gives to organists are a useful indicator of performance practice in the Moravian church during this period. See Stevens, 'The Musical Works of Christian Ignatius Latrobe', pp. 95–9; C.D. Crews, 'Latrobe on Harmony in the Church', *Moravian Music Journal*, 35 (1990), 1–4. Latrobe returned to this theme after attending a church service in Capetown, in his *Journal of a visit to South Africa, in 1815, and 1816, with some account of the Missionary Settlements of the United Brethren, near the Cape of Good Hope* (London, 1818), pp. 299–301.

[20] Holmes, 'The Rev. Christian Ignatius Latrobe', p. 250.

[21] Latrobe, *Letters to my Children*, p. 42. Latrobe's band gave 'two exercise-concerts' each week.

[22] Osborn Music MS 517, The James Marshall and Marie-Louise Osborn Collection, Beinecke Rare Book and Manuscript Library, Yale University. For the date of this manuscript, see the list of contents on f. 2.

242 MUSIC IN EIGHTEENTH-CENTURY BRITAIN

source for Latrobe's score.[23] Also copied into this volume are four choruses by Latrobe himself, inscribed 'Condemned by the Composer for too much fiddling' on the title-page, and two choruses from Gluck's *Alceste*.

It was probably also at Niesky that Latrobe first encountered Haydn's Stabat Mater. In his letter to Vincent Novello of 1828, he described how in 1779 he had borrowed the parts for the work from a friend, who had procured them at Dresden, the nearest city to Niesky. As with the op. 20 quartets, Latrobe scored these up in order to study the piece at the keyboard; and, as he later told Haydn himself, he judged that this, 'more than [...] any other Work, helped to form my taste, & make me more zealous in the pursuit of this noble science'.[24] In the same letter, Latrobe also highlighted Graun's *empfindsamer* passion cantata *Der Tod Jesu*, published at Leipzig in 1760, as having played a key role in his musical development, also probably encountered by him during his years at Niesky. No doubt the subject matter of these works enhanced their appeal to the Moravians, whose heartfelt spirituality centred on the blood and wounds of Christ. Indeed, this could partly account for Latrobe's interest in the op. 20 quartets. We know from Holmes that Latrobe would often play at the piano 'the whole of the beautiful violin quartett in F minor, with the fugue'; clearly, this was op. 20 no. 5, copied at Niesky in 1783, the 'learned' fugal finale of which is built on a theme similar to that of Handel's chorus, 'And with His stripes we are healed', from *Messiah*.[25]

On his return to England in the summer of 1784, Latrobe presumably brought these and other German instrumental and sacred works from the Niesky repertory with him. Indeed, the appearance of John Bland's first edition of the full score of Haydn's Stabat Mater in 1784, 'as performed at the Nobility's Concerts', combined with the fact that by 1788 at the latest, Latrobe considered him a close friend, suggests that Latrobe may have influenced his decision to publish the work. In this way, Latrobe may have already begun to play what would become a major role in the dissemination of Haydn's music within months of his arrival in London in 1784.[26]

Despite his German education, faith and accent, Latrobe regarded himself as an Englishman, and his return to England was, therefore, something of a homecoming.[27] He arrived a well-educated, companionable young man, high-

---

[23] A. van Hoboken, *Joseph Haydn: Thematisch-bibliographisches Werkverzeichnis, Band I* (Mainz, 1957), pp. 391–2; D.W. Jones, 'Haydn's Music in London in the Period 1760–1790, Part One', *Haydn Yearbook*, 14 (1983), 160, 172.

[24] Latrobe to V. Novello, 22 November 1828, GB-Lbl Add. MS 11730, ff. 112–13 (f.113).

[25] Holmes, 'The Rev. Christian Ignatius Latrobe', p. 250. I am grateful to Christina Bashford for drawing this connection to my attention. Similarly, the first Haydn work Latrobe selected for inclusion in his *Selection of Sacred Music* was *The Seven Last Words of our Saviour on the Cross* (Hob.XX/2). On Moravian spirituality, see Podmore, *The Moravian Church*, pp. 132–6.

[26] *The Celebrated Stabat-Mater as Performed at the Nobility's Concert* (London: John Bland, [1784]). On the Nobility's Concerts, see S. McVeigh, *Concert life in London from Mozart to Haydn* (Cambridge, 1993), pp. 47–8. Latrobe had hopes that Bland might 'one day become a child of God' ('Journal', English MS 1244, f. 122).

[27] See Holmes, 'The Rev. Christian Ignatius Latrobe', p. 249; also Fanny Burney to Charlotte Burney, 7 December 1784, quoted in T. Hamlin, *Benjamin Henry Latrobe* (New York,

THE PAPERS OF C.I. LATROBE   243

principled and dedicated to spirituality and evangelism. As such, he was welcomed by his father, now Leader of the English Moravians, into a circle of friends that extended way beyond the Moravian Church into many corners of London society. Latrobe began to expand on these acquaintances, who would eventually include Sir Charles Middleton (1726–1813), later Baron Barham and First Lord of the Admiralty, a known evangelical, comptroller of the British navy from 1778 until 1790, and MP for Rochester; William Legge, second earl of Dartmouth (1731–1801), statesman and Calvinistic Methodist, nicknamed 'the psalm-singer', who was profoundly influential in the development of English evangelicalism; Sir Richard Hill (1732–1808), the ardent, controversial evangelical, who entered parliament as MP for Shropshire in 1780; his brother Rowland Hill (1744–1833), the Anglican clergyman who preached as a roving evangelist, and in 1783 founded Surrey Chapel, Blackfriars, which he opened to all denominations; Bielby Porteus (1731–1809), Bishop of Chester, and, from 1787, of London, who supported the Evangelicals (within the Church of England), was an early patron of the Church Missionary Society, and whose diocese included the British colonies in the West Indies; Charles Wesley (1707–88), Methodist leader, hymn-writer, brother of John Wesley, and father of the musical prodigies Charles and Samuel Wesley.[28]

Latrobe was soon deeply involved in church affairs, and the nature and extent of his activities in London can be surmised from a private journal, now housed in the John Rylands Library, which he began to keep just over a year after the death of his father. Running to 125 folios, written on both sides almost throughout, it begins on 2 January 1788, and continues until the end of August 1789. After a gap of three years, it resumes on 29 September 1792, but breaks off again only two months later; the final entry is dated 2 December 1792.[29] Sadly, therefore, the journal falls silent during the period of Haydn's visits to London, and at best it documents only a thin slice of Latrobe's life; nevertheless its pages afford valuable and unique insights into the musical world of London during the late 1780s and early 1790s, and Latrobe's place within it.

In January 1788, now living with his brother Benjamin Henry at 6 Roll's Buildings, Holborn, Latrobe was working closely with a committee of Brethren to prepare the first English edition of the Moravian hymn-book, which John

---

1955), pp. 9–10. Latrobe styled himself 'a warmhearted lover of England', whilst unleashing a searing diatribe against the French and Americans, in a letter to John Frederick Latrobe, 26 October 1813, private collection of Dr J.H. de La Trobe. His other brother described him as 'a thoroughbred Englishman! & a Pittite with a vengeance'; see Benjamin Henry to Christian Ignatius Latrobe, 5 January 1807, in *The Correspondence and Miscellaneous Papers of Benjamin Henry Latrobe, Volume 2: 1805-1810*, ed. by J. C. Van Horne (New Haven, 1986), p. 350
   [28] D. Lewis (ed.), *Blackwell Dictionary of Evangelical Biography*. S. Lee (ed.), *Dictionary of National Biography*. The Earl of Dartmouth's son was the dedicatee of Vol. I of Latrobe's *Selection of Sacred Music* (London, 1806).
   [29] 'Journal Written in the Year 1788 and beginning of 1789 [*sic.*] by Chr. Ig. La Trobe', GB-Mu English MS 1244. Latrobe probably gave up writing his journal because of lack of time; in 1790 he took on the preparation of the quarterly *Periodical Accounts* for the SFG, which added to the already immense volume of correspondence he dealt with each week. Subsequent references to this journal will be given in the main body of the text.

244   MUSIC IN EIGHTEENTH-CENTURY BRITAIN

Bland would publish as *Hymn-Tunes Sung in the Church of the United Brethren* in 1790.[30] At the same time, Latrobe was also representing the Moravians in covert discussions with William Wilberforce MP over the abolition of the slave trade and the conversion of blacks to Christianity.[31] For present purposes however, the most significant thread to trace though the journal is his contact with Charles Burney, which helps to determine the nature of Latrobe's involvement with the *General History of Music*, a subject about which musicologists have often speculated.

It was probably James Hutton, a founder member of the Fetter Lane Society, who introduced Burney to Latrobe. Hutton had become a close friend of Burney's after writing to him in July 1773, initially to object to the remarks about poor travel conditions in Germany made in Burney's *The Present State of Music in Germany, the Netherlands, and the United Provinces* (London, 1773).[32] Christian Ignatius and his brother became house guests of the Burney family almost as soon as they arrived in London, and Burney was quick to appreciate how useful they could be in his research. Unable to read or write German fluently, he was experiencing great difficulty with the German treatises that he needed to consult for the *General History*, as the following letter illustrates.

> My dear Friend
> I am now so surrounded & bewildered with *Charman* books of all kinds, that I shall fret myself to Sauer=Kraut if you do not come & disentangle me soon. But, seriously, if it is impossible or inconvenient for you to give me a long day while these matters are in hand, c^d. you tell me of any honest, Idle German, who w^d. come hither for a few days to explain & translate bits & scraps of German books, wch. I want to quote or mention? For poking out their meaning with a Dict^y. in my hand is so slow & unsure, that I can neither spare the time, nor venture to use what I may make out this way, if I c^d. – Do ye, therefore, kind Soul! take a little compassion on Yours Affectionately
>   Chas. Burney.
> Chelsea College
> Friday Morn^g.
> If the German body, sh^d. know a little ab^t. Music & German Musicians, & musical politics, he w^d. be a *Charmin* man *inteet!*[33]

Not only was Latrobe able to assist Burney with his translations, he could also answer some of his queries about Protestant hymnody. Burney lent him an unspecified volume (probably a collection of psalms or hymn tunes, with a

---

[30] Latrobe used as a starting point Christian Gregor's *Choral-Buch enthaltend alle zu dem Gesangbuche der Evangelischen Brüdergemeinen vom Jahre 1778, gehörige Melodien* (Leipzig, 1784). The importance of this task should not be underestimated; the publication of some rather idiosyncratic Moravian hymn texts in translation had played a part in discrediting the Moravians in England in 1753; see Podmore, *The Moravian Church*, pp. 228–89.

[31] On Latrobe's contact with Wilberforce and his links with the Abolitionists see J. Mason and L. Torode, *Three Generations of the Latrobe Family*, pp. 20–21.

[32] See Lonsdale, *Dr. Charles Burney: A Literary Biography*, pp. 124–5.

[33] Burney to Latrobe, [1788], Burney Family Collection, The James Marshall and Marie-Louise Osborn Collection, Beinecke Rare Book and Manuscript Library, Yale University. Docketed by Fanny Burney, 'XV'.

THE PAPERS OF C.I. LATROBE

preface) that he had borrowed from a Moravian three years earlier to copy some extracts, asking Latrobe to 'run it over, & extract from it any anecdote or Chronological information concerning the share wch. Luther, & his pious predecessors John Huss & Gerome of Prague had in establishing Psalmody in the Vulgar Tongue, as a Part of Divine Service.'[34] As their correspondence also indicates, Latrobe furnished the examples of hymn tunes attributed to Luther that appear in the first chapter of Burney's Volume III, and details of the Lutheran Easter hymn given in a footnote.[35] He ordered books from German-speaking parts of the continent for Burney, and the Latrobes made items from their own libraries available to him; in 1784, Burney asked Latrobe to present his 'comp^{ts}. & thanks to your Brother for the sight of Mattheson['s] old *gibberish*' – probably a copy of *Der vollkommene Capellmeister.*[36]

Latrobe contributed also to the chapter on 'the Progress of Music in Germany, during the present Century' in the fourth volume of the *General History*, which took Burney's *magnum opus* up to modern times (1789). The entry for 14 January 1788 in Latrobe's journal reads: 'went to D^r. Burney to breakfast. and spent, contrary to my intention the greater part of the forenoon with him, looking over several paragraphs in his History of Music. He is an indefatigable man.' (f. 3). Latrobe drank tea with the Burneys again in April and May, enjoying 'musical chat', and his visits became more frequent in July and August. On 26 August 1788, he records: 'went in the F[ore] N[oon] to Chelsea & spent the day till 6 oclock with Dr Burney looking over old German Music books & Music – to assist in his History of Music.' (f. 40). Again, on 5 September, Burney notes that 'Having rec^d. a letter from Mrs Burney, I was against my inclination obliged to go to Day to Chelsea'; from one until six o'clock he assisted Burney 'in his musical researches' (f. 41v). Burney must have been tying up the loose ends of his German coverage at this point, for on 27 September Latrobe writes, 'went to D^r. Burney to Chelsea. I read the Chapter conc^g. German Music in this Century thro' and staid with him' (f. 44v).

Thanks to Latrobe's journal therefore, we know that Burney was still writing the German chapter of the fourth volume of the *General History* as late as September 1788, and that he was doing so in consultation with Latrobe, who not only had close links with Germany, but had lived there until recently, and

---

[34] Burney to Latrobe, 14 June [1786/7], Burney Family Collection, The James Marshall and Marie-Louise Osborn Collection, Beinecke Rare Book and Manuscript Library, Yale University. Docketed by Fanny Burney, 'XIV'.

[35] Burney to Latrobe, 18 July [1787], Burney Family Collection, The James Marshall and Marie-Louise Osborn Collection, Beinecke Rare Book and Manuscript Library, Yale University (docketed by Fanny Burney, 'XXXII'); F. Mercer, ed., *A General History of Music, From the Earliest Ages to the Present Period (1789) by Charles Burney* (New York, 1957), vol. 2, pp. 38 and 39–40.

[36] 'I fear this long & severe Frost will impede all intercourse wth. Germany by water, & that the books you kindly ordered from Hamburgh will for some time remain Stationary', Burney to Latrobe, 29 December 1784. Burney to Latrobe, 1 February [1786?], Burney Family Collection, The James Marshall and Marie-Louise Osborn Collection, Beinecke Rare Book and Manuscript Library, Yale University. Docketed by Fanny Burney, 'XXXV' and 'XXXVII' respectively. Benjamin Henry recalled his translation of 'Mathesons's Musical rainbows' for Burney, in a letter to Charlotte Broome, 13 August 1816, quoted in Hamlin, *Benjamin Henry Latrobe*, pp. 20–21.

MUSIC IN EIGHTEENTH-CENTURY BRITAIN

had heard and played music by modern German composers. Whilst it would be difficult to identify with certainty those passages in the fourth volume of Burney's history that reflect Latrobe's views, the extent to which Burney valued his friend's opinion is apparent from the following letter:

> I rec^d. yesterday a letter from Carl. Ph. Em. Bach, with advice that he had sent me 13 Copies of his Sixth Collection of Sonatas; & tells me of other works that he has just published – his *Resurrection, Ascension, & Litany* [Wq.204 and 240], in Score; *'qui meritent d'etre parcouru par un Docteur de Musique'* – concerning all these I want to talk with you.[37]

One could also, for example, attribute to the Moravian's influence Burney's criticism of the Protestant/Catholic divide in German musical life, and the footnote which adds the organ at Görlitz, near Niesky, to the list of major German organs given by Marpurg in Vol III of his periodical *Historisch-kritische Beyträge zur Aufnahme der Musik* (Berlin, 1754–62, 1778).[38] Clearly, however, his contact with Latrobe was not sufficient to redress Burney's predilection for Italian music over German: the space allotted to German composers in the fourth volume of the *General History* was a fraction of that devoted to his discussion of the Italians and, with the exception of Haydn and C.P.E. Bach, few German composers received anything more than a passing mention.[39]

As a prominent member of an international church, with its headquarters in Germany, Latrobe had plenty of opportunity to refresh his musical library when called abroad on church business. According to his journal, only three weeks after reading the draft of Burney's chapter on German music, Latrobe was summoned to attend the Unity Conference of Elders at Gnadenfrei, in Silesia (now Piława Górna, south-west Poland). Such trips would become more frequent as his seniority within the Moravian Church progressed. *En route* to Gnadenfrei, he visited other Moravian settlements, meeting his youngest brother John Frederick at Barby, where he was caught up once again in the musical life of the community: 'I supped with Freddy & was afterwards treated with some Quartettos by Haydn. Vietinghof jun^r. plays a good Violin. Then followed some Pieces of [Johannes] Sörensen & Freddys Comp. for Clar. Ob. & Basson. (f. 52).[40] Revisiting Barby on his journey back to London, on 13 January 1789,

---

[37] Burney to Latrobe, 18 July [1787], Burney Family Collection, The James Marshall and Marie-Louise Osborn Collection, Beinecke Rare Book and Manuscript Library, Yale University. Docketed by Fanny Burney, 'XXXII'. This letter probably dates from July 1787, because C.P.E. Bach had written the following to Breitkopf on 30 June 1787: 'I am sending Burney the 6th collection tomorrow', i.e. vol. VI of the Sonatas 'für Kenner und Liebhaber', quoted in *The Letters of C.P.E. Bach*, trans. and ed. by S.L. Clark (Oxford, 1997), p. 265. Bach was assisting Breitkopf in his search for subscribers for his *Die Auferstehung* (H.777) of which Burney eventually took two copies.

[38] F. Mercer (ed.), *A General History of Music [...] by Charles Burney*, vol. 2, pp. 950–51 and p. 953.

[39] This national bias in Burney's musical tastes – by no means entirely the result of his difficulty with the German language – is examined in more detail in the author's doctoral thesis: 'Mozart's Music in London, 1764–1829: Aspects of Reception and Canonicity' (PhD diss., University of London, forthcoming).

[40] The Moravian love of wind instruments is evident in many of the entries concerning music in this German phase of Latrobe's journal: at Herrnhut, for example, 'Aft. supper we played

THE PAPERS OF C.I. LATROBE

247

Latrobe wrote out in score 'a fine new Quartetto of Hayd^n.' (f. 88). This may have been one of the 'Tost I and II' quartets, opp.54 and 55, which Haydn had completed during the previous September. But since these quartets were not published until the summer of 1789 the op. 50 set is a more likely possibility. William Forster's edition of the op.50 quartets was on sale in London by November 1788 (followed immediately by Artaria's in Vienna), so Latrobe would still have considered them 'new' in early 1789. Latrobe kept up this enthusiasm for Haydn's chamber music, almost keeping pace with the composer's quartet output; by the time Burney introduced him to Haydn in 1791, as Latrobe recalled, he had already made 'scores of about 25 of his Quartettos, from the printed parts, & continued to play them on the pianoforte with tolerable accuracy'.[41]

Stopping in Leipzig, 7–10 January 1789, Latrobe called on the publisher Breitkopf, with whom he had probably established a friendship during his years as a piano tutor at Niesky. Although Latrobe seems only to have bought '*Bachs* Choral tunes' on this occasion, Breitkopf would later supply him with many of the works that appeared in his *Selection of Sacred Music* (see Table 10.1, pp. 257–8).[42] In the absence of extensive formal relationships between continental publishers and their English counterparts, Latrobe and his musical acquaintances in England would find his connection with Breitkopf a valuable one, particularly when the military campaign against Napoleon began to disrupt trade links with Germany. On 15 July 1803, for example, Latrobe penned the following to Burney:

> The [Haydn] Masses I have rec^d: are one in B flat sharp 3^d [i.e. B flat major; Missa S^{ti} Bernardi von Offida 'Heiligmesse' Hob.XXII/10] the other in C sharp 3^d. [i.e. C major; Missa in tempore belli 'Paukenmesse' Hob.XXII/9]. They are in a full score & delight me, especially the latter, exceedingly. There are some heavenly strains of true devotional music in them. I hope Breitkopf will treat us with more of them. I have written to Boehme at Hamburg to send me [Haydn's] Te Deum Laudamus in score [Hob.XXIIIc:2], Mozarts Requiem adapted for the Pianoforte & Voices, and a *Missa Spartizione* by Mozart [Missa brevis in F (K.192, KE. 186f)] which I find in his Catalogue. What that means I

Suites 2 bassons, 2 horns, 2 Clarinets and I was forced to exhibit on the Clarinet' (f. 78v). For more on this, see R. Hellyer, 'The Harmoniemusik of the Moravian Communities in America', *Fontes Artis Musicae*, 27 (1980), 95–108.

[41] Latrobe to Vincent Novello, 22 November 1828, G-Lbl Add. MS 11730, ff. 112–13 (f. 112). For details of the publication of the op.50 quartets, see W.D. Sutcliffe, *Haydn: String Quartets, Op.50*, (Cambridge, 1992), pp. 33–6.

The catalogue from the sale of Latrobe's library, preserved in the Harding collection in GB-Ob, lists only 'Six Violin Quartetts' by Haydn (lot 185). However, the auction did not take place until 2 May 1842 – six years after Latrobe's death – by which time the library may have been far from complete. Furthermore, Latrobe himself was generous in lending his scores to friends, and bequeathed prized scores to his children; Frederick, for example, was invited to select 'Some book containing Vocal or Instrumental Music that he may choose', Public Record Office, PROB11/1876.

[42] *Joh. Seb. Bachs vierstimmige Choralgesänge*, ed. J.P. Kirnberger and C.P.E. Bach, 4 vols (Leipzig, 1784–7). Latrobe also bought 'a book conc.^{g} Struensee and Brandt' (f. 85v), which his brother would later publish in an English translation: Johann Friedrich, Count Struensee, *Authentic elucidation of the history of Counts Struensee and Brandt, and of the revolution in Denmark [...] in 1772*, trans. B.H. Latrobe (London, 1789).

248 MUSIC IN EIGHTEENTH-CENTURY BRITAIN

don't know, but suppose it to be a *mass*. Neither of Haydn's two Masses has an obligato part for the Organ, so Yours must be a different one. You gave me directions to get Don Giovanni for You, when I was last with You. It is a comic Opera & reported to be his best work of that kind. I made my memorandum about getting it for You & wrote for it immediately.

The worst is, that the Elbe is now blockaded by our Men of War. This is a spirited measure, for which I give our Government credit, but I only wish they would let my Music slip thro'.[43]

Latrobe enjoyed good relations with Breitkopf & Härtel throughout the Napoleonic period; when Latrobe was not able to visit in person, or when letters might otherwise have gone astray, the Moravian network would have offered an alternative means of making contact, perhaps with one of the Niesky or Barby Brethren acting as his agent. Even with the conflict at its height, the Moravians were able to sustain a limited correspondence by a 'costly and circuitous route via Copenhagen and Gothenburg'.[44] This goodwill between Latrobe and the Leipzig publishers also meant that rarities occasionally came his way; for example, Latrobe wrote the following to Vincent Novello on 17 July 1817, in answer to his questions about the origin and authenticity of several Mozart masses in Latrobe's library, and about the music he had brought back with him from a recent trip abroad.

I obtained them thro' Breitkopf & Haertel at Leipsic, who would have published them, had their other publications of Mozart's works proceeded better in the way of profit. M'. Haertel told me himself, (when I was at Leipsic last May [1817]), that he had been obliged to stop – for want of a sufficient number of purchasers – which is a great disgrace to the present Generation. [...] I have bespoke several good old morsels, but did not bring much with me of what has been lately published. What I have brought is

A *Requiem* by Neukom. –
A Mass by Schneider.
A Miserere by Haeser.
& some smaller pieces – printed –
& a whole wheelbarrow full of MSS music scores & some very good German oratorios which I bought for a trifle.[45]

Thus, it seems that Breitkopf & Härtel, who were forced to abandon their publication of Mozart's 'Œuvres complettes' (1798–*c*. 1808) because of a lack of demand, were content to sell copies of unpublished material to Latrobe.

---

[43] Latrobe to Burney, 15 July 1803, Burney Family Collection, The James Marshall and Marie-Louise Osborn, Beinecke Rare Book and Manuscript Library, Yale University. The 'Boehme' Latrobe mentions here is Johann August Böhme, of the publishing firm Günther and Böhme, based in Hamburg and Vienna; it issued the first edition of Mozart's Symphony in C (K.162) in 1798, as well as several other important early Mozart prints. The Haydn mass in Burney's possession was the Missa in honorem beatissimæ Virginis Mariæ ('Great Organ Solo Mass') (Hob.XXII:4). Haydn gave Burney a copy of this mass, as far as the Credo, and Burney allowed Latrobe to copy it in 1805; see Latrobe to Vincent Novello, 21 August 1824, GB-Lbl Add MS 11730, ff. 110–11.

[44] J.T. Hamilton and K.G. Hamilton, *History of the Moravian Church*, p. 314.

[45] Latrobe to Vincent Novello, 17 July 1817, GB-Lbl Add. MS 11730, ff. 108–9. The Mozart masses in question, were probably those represented by extracts in vols. III and IV of *Selection of Sacred Music*, published in 1814 and 1818 respectively (see Table 10.1, pp. 257–8)

THE PAPERS OF C.I. LATROBE 249

Besides renewing his connections with continental publishers, and participating in Moravian musical life, Latrobe also attended public concerts whilst abroad on church business. In January 1789, according to his journal, he visited the Gewandhaus in Leipzig for a 'Great Concert', which included performances of symphonies by Pichl (1741–1805), Vanhal (1739–1813) and Kozeluch (1747–1818), and a scene from Martín y Soler's *L'arbore di Diana*. Yet, despite his love of instrumental music, Latrobe did not regularly attend concerts in London, partly, it seems, because of the perceived lack of attentiveness of the audience; as he observed in his journal, following his visit to the Gewandhaus, 'Between the Acts was a most stunning noise of prating, which I easily pardoned for the Sake of the Silence during the performance so much wanted in English Auditories.' (ff. 86v–87). Among the London concerts he did support were the Annual Benefit for the New Musical Fund at the King's Theatre, 13 April 1789, and the third of Gertrud Mara's concerts at the Pantheon on 6 March 1788, when he 'had much Conversation' with the German composer Friedrich Hartmann Graf (1727–95), and thought the 'magnificent saloon [...] too large, tho' they had covered the Dome' (ff. 11v–12). Doubtless Latrobe also attended Haydn's London concerts, but in general, he confessed a dislike of the professional music-making scene in London, as he wrote to his brother John Frederick in 1807.

> music in England in general is at a low Ebb. There is very good opportunity of hearing good Music & exquisite performances in this City; but it is all managed by a set of mercenary animals, who will be well paid & are otherwise, few excepted, not fit Companions for any man regarding his own character. I find however now and then suitable occasions to hear their Doings.[46]

As this damning pronouncement suggests, Latrobe objected to the commercialism of public musical entertainment in London and, in particular, the increasingly entrepreneurial activities of musician-impresarios. But his words also cast doubt over the moral and social standing of professional musicians in the capital, a prejudice characteristic of many of the 'highborn' at the time. He made exceptions, to judge from his journal and correspondence, in the case of 'gentleman' musicians, such as Salomon, Burney and Charles Wesley's sons Samuel and Charles Jun., who were well educated, at ease in polite society, and shared Latrobe's cultivated musical tastes. However, when Samuel Wesley moved to Ridge, Hertfordshire, in October 1792, and set up house with Charlotte Martin, whom he declared he had no intention of marrying, Latrobe considered him 'lost to the World & good society' (f. 119). Haydn also proved an exception; indeed, Latrobe told Novello that his conversations with Haydn had often turned to matters of spirituality: 'He appeared to me to be a religious character, & not only attentive to the forms and usages of his own Church, but under the influence of a devotional spirit.'[47]

---

[46] Latrobe, London, to his brother, John Frederick, Dorpat, Livonia (Russia), 14 November 1802. See note 1 above.

[47] Latrobe to Novello, 22 November 1828, GB-Lbl Add. MS 11730, ff. 112–13 (f. 113).

250   MUSIC IN EIGHTEENTH-CENTURY BRITAIN

For Latrobe, London's musical world was spoilt by a baseness and vulgarity brought on by 'the almost total annihilation of Church music [which] has destroyed all musical taste in the generality of our fellow craftsmen'.[48] Opera he considered to be an immoral art-form, particularly comic opera, and although Burney sometimes offered him the use of his ticket, Latrobe seems to have boycotted the Italian opera house altogether.[49] His criticisms of the genre were levelled mainly at the ostentatious 'caterwauling' of the principal singers, and at the setting of unchaste words to sumptuous music, like the 'gilding of a poison pill'. As he later warned his daughter Agnes:

> Never suffer yourself to be deceived by the plausible sophistry of persons, who would try to give you a relish for music, which is employed to make vice more palatable [...] Whenever you employ your voice on earth, remember, that it is soon to be employed in heaven, in singing the song of the redeemed; and that your musical talent was given to you, that you might in this state of trial and preparation have, for your encouragement, the means of enjoying a foretaste of that eternal bliss.[50]

Just as the Moravians designed their settlements as earthly reflections of the heavenly Jerusalem, the act of singing was, for Latrobe, a rehearsal for the *ultimate* concert, in which souls would unite in the afterlife to sing praises eternally to God. It is not surprising, therefore, to discover that Latrobe's journal records numerous attendances at the Drury Lane oratorios, and other performances of predominantly sacred music.

Clearly, Latrobe's rather jaundiced view of the professional music scene in London resulted from his experience of community music in Moravian settlements on the continent, and his conviction that music-making should be for spiritual rather than financial profit: 'it is intellectual, and Spiritual Enjoyment', he declared, and even 'the practice of instrumental music, by which we are introduced to a more extensive acquaintance with the infinite, various, & delightful details of this noble science, than, in general, can be obtained by vocal, may be equally conducive to our spiritual profit, if it is accompanied by a grateful sense of the bounty of the Giver of so precious a gift'.[51] Though an amateur, Latrobe could certainly hold his own as a performer and composer in the company of London's professional musicians. He was also relatively cosmopolitan in his musical tastes; in contrast to the Handel fixation exhibited by many English amateurs of his day, Latrobe favoured the 'chordy and chromatic', words synonymous with the 'modern' Austro-German instrumental

---

[48]   Latrobe to Novello, 17 July 1817, GB-Lbl, Add. MS 11730, ff. 108–9 (f. 108v).
[49]   For example: 'The Subscriber's Ticket will be kept for you on *Saturday* next, as it is the *Serious* Opera, & it is *reported* you think the *Comic* opera *vorcsher arsh de oder!* [*sic*.]', Burney to Latrobe, 9 February [1785], The James Marshall and Marie-Louise Osborn Collection, Beinecke Rare Book and Manuscript Library, Yale University. Docketed by Fanny Burney, 'XXXIII'. See also 'Journal', f. 8.
[50]   Holmes, 'The Rev. Christian Ignatius Latrobe', p. 250; Latrobe, *Letters to my Children*, p. 44.
[51]   Latrobe to John Frederick, Dorpat, Livonia, 7 March 1828, private collection of Dr J.H. de La Trobe.

THE PAPERS OF C.I. LATROBE 251

idioms.[52] Among the English Moravians, he found few musicians who could match the experience and calibre of his German brethren; in his journal Latrobe is sometimes preoccupied with the problem of producing music fit to praise God, with the assistance of amateurs who might be poorly-trained and hopelessly unmusical: 'Wrote a long letter to Hartley about Musical Performances in our Chapels chiefly insisting that our performers, being weak, should content themselves with easy pieces – both for their own Comfort & that of the Cong."' (f. 116v).

While it seems that Latrobe experienced a degree of musical frustration in England, a chance meeting with the Jowett family did much to relieve this sense of isolation. For Latrobe, the Jowetts realized an ideal: they were the epitome of the devout, Christian family, who sang sacred music together in the home, for their own recreation, enjoyment and spiritual well-being. Not only did this recapture the ambience of Moravian communities like Barby, it also chimed with Latrobe's aspirations as a spiritual father within the Church, and as the father of a young family (his initial acquaintance with the Jowetts coinciding with the birth of his first children). By the mid-nineteenth century, the concepts of parlour worship and the Christian family would evolve as defining features in the self-image of the English middle classes, a cultural trend that accounts for the longevity of Latrobe's *Selection of Sacred Music*, and, to a large extent, the commercial success of related publishing ventures by Novello.[53] At the head of the family was John Jowett, whose father, Henry Jowett of Leeds, had been converted through the evangelism of John Wesley in 1749. John ran a fellmongery in Newington Butts, Southwark, and would be active in the early days of the Church Missionary Society. Latrobe first met him and his brother, the Revd Henry Jowett, of Magdalene College, Cambridge, in around 1791, at the house of Revd Gambier, Rector of Langley in Kent and cousin of Admiral James Gambier. During conversation, as Latrobe recalled, John Jowett had expressed a rather provoking musical conservatism, asserting 'that there was no music to be compared to Handel's, [and] expressing his opinion rather severely respecting all *foreign* music'. Frederick, Latrobe's brother, challenged this, arguing that 'the old obsolete compositions of Handel and his associates were unworthy of the present improved state of music on the Continent, and could

---

[52] See Latrobe, *Letters to my Children*, p. 28. Latrobe uses this phrase when describing (with approval) the musical tastes of his daughter Charlotte; Latrobe, to John Frederick, Dorpat, Livonia, 26 October 1813. When Latrobe's ability to play the piano was hampered by a stroke, in 1828, his children afforded him 'much pleasure by 4 handed adaptations of Haydn's, Mozart's & Beethoven's Quartets & Sinfonias, &c'; Latrobe to John Frederick, Dorpat, Livonia, 24 November 1828, private collection of Dr J.H. de La Trobe.
[53] On the role played by domestic worship in the evolving identity of the middle classes, see '"The one thing needful": religion and the middle class', in L. Davidoff and C. Hall, *Family Fortunes: Men and women of the English middle class, 1780–1850* (London, 1987), pp. 76–106. Latrobe's *Selection of Sacred Music* was a useful model for Vincent Novello, who consulted Latrobe closely during the preparation of his vocal scores of, for example, Haydn and Mozart masses. Latrobe's musical library often supplied the sources for Novello's editions; and in the preface to the final volume of his *Selection*, Latrobe recommended his subscribers to pursue their interest in sacred music via Novello's publications.

252 MUSIC IN EIGHTEENTH-CENTURY BRITAIN

only be pleasing to such as knew no better'. This exchange escalated into a heated debate, but rather than engendering enmity between the two families, the foundations were laid for a mutual respect and affection.[54]

John Jowett introduced Latrobe to another of his brothers, Dr Joseph Jowett of Trinity Hall, Cambridge, Regius Professor of Civil Law. Joseph had a particularly fine alto voice, which Latrobe considered 'the sweetest and richest of the kind *I* have ever heard, either in public or private'.[55] Joseph and his brother Henry joined John Jowett's family at Southwark as often as they could, when they would sing 'all Handel's oratorios, or rather select portions of them, with great precision', accompanied by Latrobe, score-reading at the keyboard.[56] Latrobe often walked from Fetter Lane to Newington Butts after evening service, to join the Jowetts in their family worship, 'which was conducted with solemnity, and the singing of an hymn in parts in a very superior style'.[57] Since Marcello's psalms were the only continental music in the Jowetts' repertory, Latrobe introduced them to Haydn's Stabat Mater and a series of other 'foreign' compositions from his own library, namely 'the old Italian composers, with Graun, Haydn, and Mozart'.[58] Latrobe, in turn, developed a new interest in Handel under the guidance of the Jowetts, particularly in *Samson*, *Jephtha* and one of the settings of the Te Deum. As a child at Fulneck, Latrobe had heard individual numbers by Handel, such as 'He was despised' from *Messiah*, but the majority of his oratorios had remained unknown to the Moravian, perhaps because of their Old Testament bias.[59]

Joseph Jowett remained 'a most sincere and cordial friend' of Latrobe's for twenty-three years, and his sudden death in 1813 affected the Moravian deeply. A member of the Bible Society at Cambridge, he shared Latrobe's commitment to evangelism and personal piety. The Jowett brothers had been awarded the livings of Little Dunham (Norfolk) and Wethersfield (Essex), and together had established a network of Anglican Evangelicals at Cambridge. Latrobe therefore began to make annual visits to Cambridge, which yielded rich pickings in the form of donations for the Moravian missions, besides providing ample opportunity for music-making among like-minded friends.[60]

It was apparently Joseph Jowett's encouragement, perhaps during one of these Cambridge sojourns, that persuaded Latrobe to embark on the publication of his *Selection of Sacred Music*.[61] Eventually running to seventy-two numbers,

---

[54] See D. Lewis (ed.), *Dictionary of Evangelical Biography*. Latrobe recalls his encounters with the Jowetts, in the first of his *Letters to my Children*, pp. 1–12 (quotations taken from p. 5); he penned a further tribute to Joseph Jowett, and the Jowett family, in the preface to vol. 3 of his *Selection of Sacred Music* (London, 1814).

[55] Latrobe, *Letters to my Children*, p. 8.

[56] ibid., p. 7.

[57] ibid., p. 8.

[58] ibid., p. 6.

[59] ibid., pp. 7 and 29–30. 'Journal', ff. 116, 118v, and 122.

[60] See: Latrobe, *Letters to my Children*, pp. 8–11 (quotation from p. 9); J.B. Cutmore, 'Jowett, Henry', and T.C.F. Stunt, 'Joseph Jowett', in D. Lewis (ed.), *Dictionary of Evangelical Biography*, vol. 1, p. 628; *Cambridge Chronicle*, 19 November 1813.

[61] Preface to Vol. III of the *Selection of Sacred Music* (London, 1814).

THE PAPERS OF C.I. LATROBE 253

published in six volumes, representing more than 230 works by over fifty composers, the *Selection* was a major achievement in itself. But, when viewed in context, it was nothing short of a movement for the reform of English musical taste, a scaled-up version of the Jowett–Latrobe fracas. Latrobe sought to disseminate the finest Italian and German sacred music from his own extensive library, much of it Roman Catholic in origin, in easy arrangements designed for performance around the parlour piano, in the homes of Christian families. By issuing excerpts in such an accessible format, Latrobe hoped to create sufficient public demand for publishers to risk editions of the complete works in full score. This, he hoped, would go some way towards redressing the current neglect of church music, with the ultimate goal of breaking the Handelian monopoly over sacred music repertory in England. Latrobe's intention was not to oust Handel entirely, as he confided to his brother John Frederick, but simply to place other composers alongside him in the lists: 'I published [... these] specimens of foreign Music, to drag my Countrymen out of the ruts of Handel. Not that I despise Handel; I love him dearly & consider him a most gigantic Genius, but others deserve also some Attention'.[62]

The *Selection* was not only a collaboration between Latrobe and Jowett, however. As is evident in the following letter addressed to Joseph Foster Barham MP, one of the major benefactors of the Moravians' Jamaican mission, Latrobe was content for his subscribers and friends to make their own suggestions about works to be included.

At last I have undertaken to put forth my *adaptations* for the P.forte, of Sacred Music &c as in the advertisement enclosed. It gives me more trouble than I thought it would, but I enjoy it much as I go along. The first number is printed & contains the whole first Chorus of Graun's Te Deum, & a Song of Ciampi. The second will be engraved this week & will contain a greater variety – a *Chorus* by Hasse – a Terzetto by Astorga, a Duetto by Astorga – and a charming little scena from a Salve Regina of *Pergolesi* not known in general, but which I am sure you will like. Of course I have entered your name as a subscriber – and if there is any favourite piece of yours that you wish to be inserted, I shall gladly do it. I think it will be a choice Collection of musical Tit-bits, & *ought* to find many purchasers even in this degenerate age.[63]

In the Preface to Volume II, published in 1809, Latrobe also singled out the following for thanks, in addition to Jowett: Dr Henry Harington, the physician and amateur musician from Bath; Charles Burney; the violinist Salomon; the music publisher Robert Birchall; the Moravians H. Hase and Christian Frederick Hassé (organist at Fulneck); and the amateur artist and writer William Young Ottley, who owned a small collection of mainly Italian music.[64] They probably earned his gratitude by offering advice on the selection of works, or for

---

[62] Latrobe to John Frederick, Dorpat, Livonia, 26 October 1813, private collection of Dr J.H. de La Trobe.
[63] Latrobe to Joseph Foster Barham MP, 13 February 1805; GB-Ob Clarendon MS c.378, bundle 1.
[64] Two copies of the sales catalogue for Ottley's library are preserved in GB-Lbl: S.C. Sotheby 220. (8.) and Hirsch 479. (1.). On Ottley as a collector, see A. Hyatt King, *Some British Collectors of Music, c. 1600–1960* (Cambridge, 1983), pp. 38–9.

254 MUSIC IN EIGHTEENTH-CENTURY BRITAIN

supplying biographical information about the composers represented in the anthology. That Charles Burney was a prime mover in this project should come as no surprise. A long-standing friend he shared Latrobe's frustration at criticism of Haydn's *Creation* from die-hard Handelians within the ranks of English musical amateurs.[65] Indeed, in 1805 (the same year in which the *Selection* was initiated) Burney clashed with Lord and Lady Darnley, fellow guests of the Duke of Portland at Bulstrode Park, over the respective merits of ancient and modern music. The earl was one of the Directors of the Concerts of the Ancient Music, and therefore a formidable adversary.[66]

As Latrobe and his associates realized, for the *Selection* to achieve its aims, they would have to employ stealth to overcome the prejudices of these devotees of 'ancient' music. George Legge, the third earl of Darmouth was chosen as dedicatee, a calculated decision since he was a friend of Latrobe, a favourite of George III, and the son of a respected evangelical and a long-standing subscriber to the Concerts of Ancient Music. With advice from Burney, Latrobe also produced a preface that began reassuringly by paying homage to the King and to Handel, but, cunningly, went on to highlight the 'works of Foreign Composers [...] of different styles' already being featured in the Royal Institution musical lectures given by William Crotch, an influential spokesman for the Handelians at this time. Thus Latrobe encouraged wary readers by seeming to cast the *Selection of Sacred Music* in the same mould as the musical 'specimens' played by Crotch in his lectures; in reality, however, there was a marked difference.

Crotch was Professor of Music at Oxford University, but Burney, Jowett and Latrobe had all been close to him during his years as a child prodigy, and now began to use their influence to soften his stance against the 'moderns'. For example, Jowett wrote to Crotch in December 1804, broaching the subject of the *Selection* on Latrobe's behalf, to which Crotch responded positively, offering to lend Latrobe items from his own library if necessary. But, Crotch confessed, he could not share Jowett's enthusiasm for Haydn's masses, and even Mozart's Requiem was 'inferior to Hasse & so much so to Handel', although he promised Jowett that he was speaking 'a little more favourably of Mozart as a vocal comp[r]. than I did'.[67] In December 1804, according to Crotch's memoirs, he was also offered copies of some Haydn and Mozart masses, and Mozart's accompaniments to Handel's *Messiah*, by one Samuel Fripp of Worcester

---

[65] See, for example, Burney to Latrobe, [April, 1800], The James Marshall and Marie-Louise Osborn Collection, Beinecke Rare Book and Manuscript Library, Yale University, New Haven. Docketed by Fanny Burney, 'VIII'. On the reception of Haydn's *Creation* in early nineteenth-century England, see H. Irving, 'William Crotch on "The Creation"', *Music and Letters*, 75 (1994), 548–60.

[66] Howard Irving discusses this incident in *Ancients and Moderns: William Crotch and the Development of Classical Music* (Aldershot, 1999), pp. 98–9.

[67] Crotch to Jowett, 17 December 1804, Norfolk Record Office, MS 11214, f. 5. Crotch had met Jowett whilst at Cambridge (1786–8), and in his Memoirs he described him as 'my warmest and most intimate friend at Cambridge. Thru' him I know Mr Henry Jowett of Magdalen College – an excellent perf[er]. on the harpsichord; & afterwards all his family; all most good', Norfolk Record Office, MS 11244, p. 53. Jowett had encouraged Crotch to prepare for a career in the church, a plan that was scotched by the death of Crotch's patron Alexander Crowcher Schomberg.

THE PAPERS OF C.I. LATROBE   255

College, Oxford, 'an acquaintance of Mr Latrobe'.[68] The well-known letters Burney exchanged with Crotch in 1805, which reprimanded him for his treatment of the 'moderns', principally Haydn and Mozart, in the Royal Institution lectures, are seen in a new light, when Burney's involvement with Latrobe's *Selection of Sacred Music* is taken into consideration.[69] And similarly, the fact that Crotch applied to the Royal Institution for permission to publish 'Specimens of the various Styles of Music referred to in his Lectures' in March 1806 adds further weight to the argument that Latrobe's and Crotch's anthologies were published in a spirit of rivalry, from opposite sides of the Ancient/Modern divide in English musical taste.[70]

Volume I was deemed a sufficient success for Latrobe to continue with the project, but a second volume was not to emerge from the press until 1809, when it was specifically requested by Princess Charlotte of Wales, then thirteen years old. The reason for this delay was probably lack of time; but an unsigned letter containing an account of Latrobe's life sent to John Sainsbury for inclusion in his *Dictionary of Musicians*, suggests that despite Latrobe's tact and stealth, Volume I of the *Selection* had come up against considerable resistance from the supporters of Ancient music.

> An idea has been entertained by some persons, that this work was published in a spirit unfavourable to the reputation of Handel, as if admiration of the compositions, which have assisted to form the taste of the most Musical nations of Europe were inconsistent with the full enjoyment of the works of that sublime composer. – So far from this being correct, it may be affirmed without hazard, that few among our country men, even of the most rigid Handelians, have viewed with more regret and surprize, the increasing neglect, which seems to be the lot of some of the finest monuments of Handel's genius. – One performance of the Messiah and one of the Dettingen Te Deum, in the course of the year, is indeed a meagre tribute from a metropolis like London, to the memory of the greatest composer, of whose residence England could ever boast.[71]

Since the handwriting of this anonymous letter bears a distinct resemblance to that of Latrobe himself, this may well have been his own apologia for his perceived affront to the supporters of Handel. Latrobe's concern for the feelings

---

[68] Crotch to Jowett, 17 December 1804, and Crotch, 'Memoirs', p. 98. The Mozart and Haydn masses mentioned here probably included those that were featured in the early volumes of the *Selection of Sacred Music* (see Table 10.1).

[69] Frank Mercer published these letters as an appendix to his edition of Burney's *A General History of Music*, vol. 2, pp. 1032–9. Jamie Croy Kassler discusses this spat between Burney and Crotch in 'The Royal Institution Music Lectures, 1800–1831: A Preliminary Study', *Royal Musical Association Research Chronicle*, 19 (1983–5), 1–30. See also Irving, *Ancients and Moderns: William Crotch and the Development of Classical Music* and Part II of Cowgill, 'Mozart's Music in London'.

[70] Crotch finally began to publish his Specimens two years later: *Specimens of Various Styles of Music*, 3 vols (London, c. 1808–15). The delay was, according to Kassler's findings, largely a result of Burney's resistance to his project. See, for example, Burney's letter to Latrobe, [1806], The James Marshall and Marie-Louise Osborn Collection, Beinecke Rare Book and Manuscript Library, Yale University. Docketed by Fanny Burney, 'I'

[71] Anonymous letter [from Christian Ignatius Latrobe] to John H. Sainsbury [1823–4], GB-Gu R.d.87/122.

256 MUSIC IN EIGHTEENTH-CENTURY BRITAIN

of the Handelians is easy to explain. As William Weber has shown, a taste for 'ancient' music represented a powerful complex of ideas relating to English Protestantism, nationhood, morality and the monarchy; as such, a veneration for Handel was still a potent factor in the identity of the Established Church.[72] As the principal representative in England of a foreign church, dependent on the support of English Christians and the goodwill of the Church of England's episcopate in order to maintain the work of the Moravian missions in the British colonies, Latrobe had to think very carefully indeed about the consequences of offending the lovers of Ancient music.

Because of his position, high moral character and pious altruism, however, Latrobe's name was sufficient endorsement to ensure the ultimate success of the *Selection of Sacred Music*. Summing up his character, Holmes described him as 'a musical Dr. Johnson': 'a non-professional gentleman, of position, accomplishments, and high connections, who afforded an example of the enthusiastic pursuit of music for its own sake alone.'[73]

Having courted English society since his arrival in London, in order to promote the work of the Moravian missions, Latrobe had already established a network of contacts sympathetic to his complementary interests of spirituality and music, who were willing to subscribe to the *Selection of Sacred Music* or to purchase each volume as it was published. Thus the channels of communication laid down to spread the Moravian gospel were also those he would use to transmit the musical 'good news', awakening the English to a wealth of sacred music by a variety of composers other than their revered Handel. Indeed, for Latrobe, the circulation of news from the missions, and the dissemination of new hymns, choruses and anthems, ultimately served the same purpose; Moravians believed that sung worship not only focused the faith of a single congregation, but also had the power to harmonize the Church of the United Brethren throughout its geographically scattered provinces, and to create fellowship between Christians of different faiths.

---

[72] W. Weber, *The Rise of Musical Classics in Eighteenth-Century England: A Study in Canon, Ritual, and Ideology* (Oxford, 1992), *passim*.
[73] Holmes, 'The Rev. Christian Ignatius Latrobe', pp. 249 and 255.

THE PAPERS OF C.I. LATROBE

Table 10.1: Sacred works by Haydn and Mozart featured in Latrobe's
Selection of Sacred Music

Volume One (1806):

Hob.XX/2, 2
K.192 (KE.186f) 'Benedictus'
K.626 'Recordare'
K.317 'Agnus Dei'

Volume Two (1809):

Hob.XXI: 11 ''Gloria, Qui tollis, Quoniam'
Hob.XXII: 5 'Agnus Dei'
Hob.XXII: 9 'Qui tollis'
Hob.XXII: 10 'Sanctus, Osanna' and 'Et incarnatus est'
Hob.XXII: 11 'Et incarnatus' and 'Agnus Dei'
K.345 (KE.336a), 1
K.317 'Sanctus' and 'Benedictus'

Volume Three (1814):

Hob.XXbis, Nos. 3 and 5
Hob.XXII: 5 'Et incarnatus est'
Hob.XXII: 6 'Kyrie Eleison', 'Et incarnatus est', 'Sanctus', and 'Benedictus'
K.125 'Panis vivus'
K.243 'Kyrie' and 'Dulcissimum convivium'
K.257 'Gloria'
K.275 (KE.272b) 'Benedictus'
K.321 'Laudate Dominum'
K.469, 8

Volume Four (1818):

Hob.XXbis, Nos. 1, 6, and 13
Hob.XXI: 1, No.2
Hob.XXII: 7 'Sanctus, Osanna, Benedictus'
K.192 (KE.186f) 'Agnus Dei'
K.194 (KE.186h) 'Agnus Dei'
K.259 'Benedictus'
K.275 (KE.272b) 'Kyrie'

Volume Five (*c.* 1822):

Hob.XXII: 5 'Quoniam'
Hob.XXII: 10 'Kyrie' and 'Gloria'
Hob.XXIIIb: 2, I and III
Hob.XXVc: 8

Table 10.1 *concluded*

K.125 'Panis omnipotentia'
K.243 'Verbum caro factum'
K.345 (KE.336a) 'Ne pulvis et cinis'

Volume Six (1825):

Hob.XX/2, 1
Hob.XXbis, Nos. 11 and 12
Hob.XXI: 1, Nos. 9b–c and 11b
Hob.XXII: 4 'Kyrie'
K.125 'Kyrie eleison' and 'Agnus Dei'
K.275 (KE.272b) 'Agnus Dei'

Part 4
Individuals and Style

CHAPTER ELEVEN

Maurice Greene's Harpsichord Music: Sources and Style

H. Diack Johnstone

As Organist of St Paul's Cathedral, Organist and Composer of the Chapel Royal, Master of the King's Musick and honorary Professor of Music at Cambridge, Maurice Greene (1696–1755) was not only the most eminent, but also the most naturally gifted, of Handel's English contemporaries. In his late teens, he had the good fortune to become acquainted with the great man himself, and to strike up a friendship which evidently flourished until, some time in the mid-1720s, the two fell out, so violently in fact that, to quote Burney, Handel never again spoke of Greene 'without some injurious epithet'.[1] According to Hawkins, it was on learning that his young English admirer was also courting the attention of his rival, Giovanni Bononcini (1670–1747), that Handel (1685–1759) decided he would no longer be at home when Greene came to call on him. But this, it appears, was only one of several factors involved. That Greene was on terms of some intimacy with Bononcini during the 1720s and early 1730s is clear from other sources, and that both men, Bononcini no less than Handel, played a key role in the development of his own compositional style will soon become apparent to anyone who takes the trouble to consider his creative output as a whole.

Though now remembered chiefly for his church music, Greene also produced a substantial amount of secular vocal music, and has to his credit not only two pastoral operas and a masque – the latter now lost – but also a great many chamber cantatas and songs, some of which (including several settings of Italian verse) have been recorded.[2] A large body of keyboard music also survives, most of it for the harpsichord, and most of it apparently written chiefly for teaching purposes. Among his pupils were three outstanding English musicians of the next generation: William Boyce (1711–79), John Travers (c. 1703–58) and the blind John Stanley (1712–86). Unlike Stanley, Greene himself seems to have had no particular reputation as a player, and it is somewhat surprising therefore that Johann Mattheson, in his *Vollkommene Capellmeister* (1739), should include him in a list of the foremost organists in Europe. For a cathedral organist with a daily need of such pieces, the number of voluntaries that he actually committed to paper is surprisingly small: just twenty-two in all (and none of those published during his lifetime), with a further eighteen short single-movement pieces seemingly written for the instruction of the young Jonathan

---

[1] C. Burney, *A General History of Music*, ed. F. Mercer (New York, 1935), vol. 2, p. 489. For a detailed discussion of their relationship see H. Diack Johnstone, 'Handel and his bellows-blower (Maurice Greene)', *Göttinger Händel-Beiträge*, 7 (1998), 208–17.

[2] By Emma Kirkby and Lars Ulrik Mortensen (Columns Musica Oscura, 070978, 1995).

Battishill (1738–1801) in 1753.[3] Much the same is true of William Croft (1678–1727), and John Blow (1649–1708) also, of course. Presumably they all relied almost entirely on extemporization, as Purcell, to judge by a mere half-dozen surviving organ works, must obviously have done.

Of Greene's published harpsichord music, much the most substantial items are the *Six Overtures ... Being proper Pieces for the Improvement of the Hand* printed by John Walsh in October 1745, and arranged, seemingly by the composer himself, from the orchestral originals published six months earlier. The phrase 'Being proper Pieces for the Improvement of the Hand' is no particular indication of compositional intent, however, for it was also used by Walsh on the title-pages of the first nine of his eleven collections of Handel overtures 'fitted to the Harpsicord or Spinnet' and issued over a thirty-year period (1726–58).[4] All six kick off with a bipartite first movement whose opening section, sometimes heavily dotted, leads on in every case to a spirited

Ex. 11.1 Greene: Overture I

fugal Allegro. Nos. 1, 4, 5 and 6 are especially interesting in that their initial overtures proper are separated from the concluding fast movement by a self-

---

[3] See *Maurice Greene: Complete Organ Works*, ed. H. Diack Johnstone (Oxford, 1997).

[4] For details, see W.C. Smith, *Handel: A Descriptive Catalogue of the Early Editions*, 2nd edn (Oxford, 1970), pp. 280–87; also T. Best, 'Handel's Overtures for Keyboard', *Musical Times*, 126 (1985), 88–90. Most of these are the work of a publisher's hack, and it could be that the Greene items are too; if so it might explain why Greene published nothing else with Walsh after 1745. Certain changes of detail, however, seem more likely to have been made by the composer than by anyone else.

contained and somewhat slower central movement which, in the case of nos. 4 and 5, is set in the opposite (minor) mode of the prevailing tonic: a curiously hybrid form, common also in Boyce, which verges on that of the pre-Classical symphony. And so too with the style which, though obviously Italianate, is distinctly un-Handelian at times (see Ex. 11.1). No. 4 began life as the overture to an ode for the King's birthday in 1739, and it may well be that the other five have similar origins: of the thirty-five court odes that Greene is known to have written as Master of the King's Musick, however, only thirteen are still extant. Technically, the *Six Overtures* are all quite demanding, and were they available in a reliable modern edition they would make a useful addition to the repertoire.

Five years later, in November 1750, Greene published a rather more substantial volume of original keyboard music entitled *A Collection of Lessons for the Harpsichord*, and this was printed not by Walsh (who had hitherto been the composer's main publisher), but by his rival, John Johnson at the Harp & Crown in Cheapside. From the fact that very few manuscript copies of any of these later lessons survive, and that none appears to be textually independent of the print, we may perhaps infer that all forty-eight of the pieces it contains had been only fairly recently composed, and that the volume itself was most probably engraved from the autograph. Though savagely dismissed by Burney in his *General History of Music* (1789) as a mere 'boarding-school book' which displayed 'no great powers of invention, or hand' and whose contents, being 'neither so elaborate as those of Handel, nor difficult as Scarlatti or Alberti's, ... gave but little trouble either to the master or scholar'; they seem, he said, 'to have been occasionally produced for idle pupils ... with whom facility was the first recommendation'.[5] Nevertheless, the volume was sufficiently successful to have run to a third edition by the spring of 1752.[6] By no means all the pieces are technically straightforward, however, and if eighteenth-century schoolgirls

Ex. 11.2 Greene: A Collection of Lessons, No. [II]

---

[5] Burney, *History*, vol. 2, pp. 491–2.
[6] See *The General Advertiser*, 18 March 1752. A second edition 'corrected by the Author' was announced in *The General Advertiser* of 28 March 1751. Modern facsimile edition with introduction by D. Moroney published by Stainer & Bell (London, 1977).

could rattle them off without much effort, then the general level of musical accomplishment must have been rather higher than the evidence might otherwise lead one to assume.

As with the *Six Overtures*, the music in this volume is thoroughly modern and stylistically up-to-date. As Davitt Moroney remarks in his introduction to the Stainer & Bell facsimile, Greene here 'speaks a language which anticipates the *rococo* accents of J.C. Bach and his generation' (see Ex. 11.2). The obvious catalyst in this, for Greene as for several other of his native contemporaries, most notably Arne (1710–78) and Nares (1715–83), was Domenico Scarlatti (1685–1757) whose *Essercizi per Gravicembalo* had made its first appearance in London in January 1739, and to the expanded Roseingrave edition of which (*XLII Suites de Pièces Pour le Clavecin*) Greene himself had subscribed.[7] One lesson, indeed, actually borrows its opening thematic idea from an *Essercizi* sonata (K. 16) in the same key (see Ex. 11.3), and there is also some affinity between the opening of the F minor Andante in Greene's sixth set (pp. 34–5) and the sonata in F minor (K. 19). Though Greene makes no use of those

Ex. 11.3 (a) Scarlatti: Essercizi, K.16

Ex. 11.3 (b) Greene: A Collection of Lessons, No. [VI]

grindingly dissonant *acciaccature* or of the elaborate hand-crossings and other virtuosic features which are so characteristic of the *Essercizi*, the influence of the Italian master is apparent on almost every page, and not least, as we shall see, in matters of form. This is most clearly evident in what is, by comparison with Handel, a generally more 'open', harmonically conceived texture, basically two-part, with much use of arpeggiated figuration, Alberti basses in particular; also a fondness for occasional chromatic appoggiaturas and sudden changes of harmonic direction, augmented sixths, triplets in the context of what is otherwise a

---

[7] See R. Newton, 'The English Cult of Domenico Scarlatti', *Music and Letters*, 20 (1939), 138–56.

GREENE'S HARPSICHORD MUSIC

prevailingly binary division of the beat, and generally rapid tempi (with Andante the slowest marking anywhere in the collection). One movement – the first of the second set (see Ex. 11.2) – is actually a diminutive but perfectly proportioned example of sonata form, complete with rudimentary development and a tonic recapitulation not only of the opening, but also of a figuratively distinctive secondary idea first stated in the dominant.[8]

Though the Galuppi sonatas were not yet published, the sonatas of Domenico Alberti had been available since November 1748, and it is abundantly clear that Greene was familiar with them.[9] Another Italian composer of the period who almost certainly influenced him (and with whom Greene was quite possibly personally acquainted) was Giovanni Battista Pescetti (c. 1704–66), who came to London as a harpsichordist in April 1736, and replaced Porpora (1686–1768) as director of the Opera of the Nobility later in the year. His *Sonate per Gravicembalo* published in London in 1739 are little known, but, like the *Essercizi* and the Alberti op. 1, show many traces of that incipiently pre-Classical style which is one of the most immediately striking features of the Greene 1750 collection.[10]

In arranging his collection of lessons in threes and fours by key, seven groups on either side of a central Aria con Variationi in D minor, Greene conspicuously avoids any mention of the word suite. Except for a single Tempo di Gavotta in group 3 and a Minueto [*sic*] Allegro in group 6, neither does he allude to any of the dance titles normally associated with it; the movements are distinguished only by their tempo markings which, as has already been observed, are all on the fast side of Andante. Some movements are obviously dances in disguise (as, for example, are all four movements in the first set), but with the nine three-movement groups in particular it is the word sonata rather than suite which springs most readily to mind. And this chimes in quite nicely with Marpurg's definition as published in his collection of *Clavierstücke* (Berlin, 1762) where sonatas, he says, 'are pieces in three or four movements, marked merely *Allegro, Adagio, Presto* etc., although in character they may be really an *Allemande, Courante* and *Gigue*'.[11] Except for three simple rondos (ABACA) and a couple of movements that make use of a somewhat ritornello-like design, the 1750 Greene lessons are all in binary form, some in 'closed' or 'rounded' binary form, but with most featuring that distinctively Scarlattian rhyming of cadences whereby the concluding dominant-oriented bars of the first half are reproduced in

---

[8]   In the US-Ws copy of the 1750 collection (M 22 G79 C4 cage), this movement (pp. 8–9) is liberally sprinkled with additional ornaments which are wrongly said (by Moroney) to be in Greene's hand; the 'signature' on the title-page also is false. The ornaments are interesting, but have no special authority.
[9]   According to Burney (*History*, vol. 2, p. 1008), Alberti's sonatas had already been circulating in England as the work of the Italian castrato, Giuseppe Jozzi (c. 1710–c. 1770), a former pupil, for some three or four years prior to their publication by Walsh.
[10]   For a discussion of Pescetti's sonatas, see W.S. Newman, *The Sonata in the Classic Era* (Chapel Hill, 1963), pp. 684–6; also F. Degrada, 'Le Sonate per cembalo e per organo di Giovanni Battista Pescetti', *Chigiana*, 23 (1966), 89–108.
[11]   See J.S. Shedlock, *The Pianoforte Sonata: its origin and development* (London, 1895), pp. 2–3; also Newman, *The Sonata in the Classic Era*, p. 22 on the origins of Marpurg's comment.

266 MUSIC IN EIGHTEENTH-CENTURY BRITAIN

the tonic key at the end of the second, the point of 'crux' (to use the term invented by Ralph Kirkpatrick)[12] generally lying well in advance of the terminal cadence itself. This structural use of extended tonal parallelism – an obviously important ingredient in the evolution of sonata form proper – is also very evident in Pescetti's harpsichord sonatas. An occasional isolated case (such as the concluding Giga of Corelli's op. 5 no. 7) can be found as early as 1700, and there are four fairly extended examples in Handel's first set of suites (1720), with one rather more extended example still in the Courante of Suite VIII in the second set which, though not published until 1733, seems, like much of the music in this volume, to have been composed some time prior to 1706.[13] By the mid-1740s, this kind of extended cadential parallelism was becoming quite common on the continent, as can be seen from the 'Prussian' and 'Württemberg' sonatas of C.P.E. Bach (1714–88), for example, but among earlier keyboard composers like J.S. Bach (1685–1750) and Couperin (1668–1733), any such cadential rhyming seldom amounts to more than a bar or two at most. In England, on the other hand, it was being quite frequently used by such native composers as Thomas Chilcot (1707?–66), organist of Bath Abbey, as early even as 1734. And so too as it happens by Maurice Greene in a good deal of his harpsichord music not so far discussed, and apparently written at very much the same time – that is, at least five years in advance of the publication of Scarlatti's *Essercizi*.

So where then does the idea come from? One possible source, as Deiniol Morgan pointed out in an unpublished paper given at the 1996 Cardiff conference on music in eighteenth-century Britain, is Bononcini's *Divertimenti da camera pel violino, o flauto* published in London in 1722 and also issued in a version 'tradotti pel cembalo'.[14] That Greene must have known this work goes without saying. The contents are grouped, by key, in two three-movement sonatas and six four-movement sonatas. The music itself is unremarkable, but, of the thirty pieces in this collection, no fewer than fourteen feature dominant/tonic rhyming of between two and fifteen bars in the approach to the two main structural cadences; another three involve extended cadential rhyming within the second half of the movement. Bononcini's poised and polished (but mostly short-breathed) phraseology is unmistakably echoed in a good many of Greene's early keyboard pieces (see Ex. 11.4a and 4b). So too are the tonal

---

[12] See R. Kirkpatrick, *Domenico Scarlatti* (Princeton, 1953), pp. 251–79; also K.F. Heimes, 'The Ternary Sonata Principle before 1742', *Acta Musicologica*, 45 (1973), 222–48.

[13] See T. Best, 'Handel's harpsichord music: a checklist', in C. Hogwood and R. Luckett (eds), *Music in Eighteenth-Century England: Essays in Memory of Charles Cudworth* (Cambridge, 1983), p. 181. The relevant movements in the 1720 set are the Allegro in Suite II, the concluding Presto in Suite III, the Courante in Suite IV and the Gigue of Suite VIII. Not entirely surprising, perhaps, in view of the Scarlattian input (see A. Silbiger, 'Scarlatti Borrowings in Handel's Grand Concertos', *Musical Times*, 125 (1984), 93–5), there are also three interesting examples in the op. 6 concertos: the second and last movements of no. 1 and the Polonaise of no. 3 (where, by a more extensive use of parallelism together with a thematically distinctive secondary idea, Handel manages to create, almost inadvertently, a diminutive but fully-fledged sonata form).

[14] Except for the title-page, the two are, in fact, the same. Modern edition by H. Ruf published by Schott (Mainz, 1964); also edition by I. Máriássy for Editio Musica Budapest (1988).

Ex. 11.4 (a) Bononcini: Divertimento VI

Ex. 11.4 (b) Greene: Allmanda (as in GB-Lbl Add MS 31467)

268 MUSIC IN EIGHTEENTH-CENTURY BRITAIN

parallelisms. With the exception of twenty-eight pieces included in a doubly-pirated edition of 1733 (of which more anon), none of Greene's early harpsichord music – a total of some eighty-odd individual movements – was published in the composer's lifetime, and much of it still survives only in manuscript.[15]

Autographs apart, much the most important source of Greene's early harpsichord music (as it is also of Croft's) is GB-Lbl Add. MS 31467 copied by John Barker, a former chorister of the Chapel Royal, in 1735 or thereabouts, and quite likely therefore to be fairly reliable in its attributions to these two composers at any rate.[16] In Greene's case, no fewer than twenty-nine of the forty-three pieces it contains are confirmed as his by other surviving sources. Here they are grouped, mainly in fours, by key, to form eleven suites, the first of which, rather interestingly, is actually headed 'Sonata per il Cembalo'.[17] Two have introductory preludes, but otherwise the constituent movements are distinguished by dance titles used as additional to (or sometimes instead of) tempo markings. Nearly all contain a Minuet (and/or an Aire), and most feature the standard Almand-Corant pair by way of starters. The style is essentially Baroque, but, as previously remarked apropos of Bononcini, is also rather shortwinded, and thus quite distinctively different from that of Handel in most of his suites;[18] it is also thoroughly Italianate in its prevailingly thin textures and clear, relatively simple, melodic outlines, and shows no sign of those obviously galant traits which are apparent in so many pieces in the 1750 collection. The opening bars of the first movement of a suite first printed piratically in 1733 and still sufficiently well known twenty-five years later, it seems, to justify its separate publication by Thompson & Son in 1758 as *A Favourite Lesson for the Harpsichord or Organ Compos'd by the Late Dr. Green* will serve as well as any other by way of illustration (see Ex. 11.5).

A further three suites copied by John Alcock sometime in the 1740s are also to be found in a manuscript now in the library of the Royal College of Music (MS 1057), and another four, two of which are otherwise unknown (but almost certainly by Greene), survive in a manuscript recently discovered by Deiniol Morgan in the National Library of Wales, Aberystwyth (GB-AB)[19] The latter, a manuscript dated 1732 and formerly in the Verney collection at Claydon House, was evidently compiled for the instruction of Mary Nicholson (who married into the family in 1736) by a group of three copyists who may be identified as Maurice Greene and his two articled pupils, William Boyce and Martin Smith

---

[15] For a complete listing (with sources), see Appendix 11.1 (pp.273–81).
[16] Add. MS 31467 also contains music by Handel, Bononcini, Pepusch, Loeillet, Dean, Weldon and Jeremiah Clarke. One Handel item, an Air in C minor (HWV 458), is peculiar to this source.
[17] Modern edition, ed. G. Beechey, in *Recent Researches in the Music of the Baroque Era*, 19 (Madison, [1975]), pp. 85–8.
[18] This curious shortwindedness has been noted also by John Caldwell in relation to Ex. 11.4(b) in his book, *English Keyboard Music Before the Nineteenth Century* (Oxford, 1973), p. 223.
[19] MS 10929 D. For full details, see D. Morgan, 'The Mary Nicholson Manuscript: its copyists, contents and provenance' (MMus diss., University of Manchester, 1994). The copying of this MS evidently began some time before 1732, and went on until the end of 1734 at least.

Ex. 11.5 Greene: Allmand (as in Walsh, 1733)

(father of John Stafford Smith). One suite (no. XIV) is the autograph of a work hitherto known only from Add. MS 31467; the other three are all in the hand of Smith who, though active earlier (as this manuscript shows), served as Greene's principal copyist from January 1737 until his appointment as organist of Gloucester Cathedral in June 1740. At much the same time – early to mid-1730s – these same three men (together with another person not yet identified) were also involved in the production of another keyboard manuscript once owned by (and presumably put together for) one 'Mary Grevile' who may (or may not) have been the sister of Burney's patron, Fulke Greville. This volume, now in the collection of the late Gerald Coke,[20] consists mainly of operatic arias, mostly by Handel, arranged for the harpsichord, but it also contains several genuine keyboard pieces by Greene, one of which also turns up in the Nicholson MS. Another five have concordances in Add. MS 31467. Four comprise a suite in G major whose first movement (as copied here) has been supplied with basso continuo figuring in the hand of the composer, and a concluding 'Siciliana' not otherwise known (but using an opening harmonic gambit very similar to that of the D major Allegro printed as the first movement of group 2 in the 1750 *Collection of Lessons*). The other is an autograph copy of the 'Aria con variationi' later included by Thompson in his 'Favourite Lesson' of 1758. Two other pieces also copied by Greene (and likewise peculiar to this particular source) must surely be his as well, while at the very end of the volume (reversed), and likewise in Greene's hand, are four pages of elementary instructions in figured bass playing.

---

[20] MS Miscellanies C. 11. The collection, formerly to be seen in the library at Jenkyn Place, is currently housed in the Hampshire Records Office in Winchester. Coke MS Miscellanies C. 10 also contains, though not in Greene's hand, five movements in F which, in Add. 31467, are spread over two suites and are here given an arpeggiated semibreve prelude that is otherwise unknown. The last of these five movements, a Siciliana, is to be found also in one of the Stoneleigh Abbey MSS sold at Christie's in 1985, where it is attributed to 'Mr Green' (thus implying a date of composition some time prior to July 1730); this too is now in the Coke collection.

270 MUSIC IN EIGHTEENTH-CENTURY BRITAIN

Until the discovery of the Nicholson manuscript in 1992, these were the only keyboard pieces which were known to have survived in the hand of the composer.[21] Then, just two years later, the British Library purchased from Ms Lisa Cox (the Devonian antiquarian book dealer) another manuscript (now Add. 71244), most of which is in the hand of Greene's good friend, the violinist Michael Christian Festing (1705–52), and contains, in addition to the early versions of three of his op. 4 violin sonatas (1739), his ornamented playing versions of several movements from Corelli's op. 5.[22] Also included, but not hitherto identified, are eleven keyboard pieces all of which are in Greene's hand, and may perhaps have been intended for the instruction of a junior member of the Festing family, conceivably the eldest son, Michael, who subsequently married Greene's daughter and only surviving child. Two of these are arrangements of arias from operas by Ariosti (1666–c. 1740) first performed in London in 1723; they are also to be found copied by Travers, the first of Greene's articled pupils, in GB-Ob MS Mus. Sch. d. 224, while the C major piece on f. 2 (together with an explanation of the gamut, and table of relative note-values etc.) also turns up, again in Greene's hand, in Mus. Sch. d. 262 and is there called a 'Trumpet Tune'.[23]

One other movement, also in C (ff. 5v–6), is likewise concordant with Add. MS 31467 where it appears (f. 104v) a tone higher in D, while the F major suite on ff. 7–10 (its last movement incomplete) is not only the same as the first of the suites in Add. MS 31467 (the afore-mentioned 'Sonata per il cembalo') but is also to be found (in Martin Smith's hand) in the Nicholson MS where it is provided with a short introductory prelude otherwise unknown. The remaining three pieces, also autograph, are to be found only in this manuscript, and seem most likely therefore to be authentic. Comparison of the Barker copies of the F and A major suites (in Add. MS 31467) with the surviving autographs is interesting, and clearly shows that he was not copying from the originals (as one might perhaps have supposed) but from sources at least one stage removed. To a potential editor, such information is obviously useful in that the sort of errors they regularly contain (chiefly wrong or misplaced ornaments, occasional octave displacement of the bass, and varied left-hand figuration at major cadences) will

---

[21] The six pieces in GB-Ob MS Mus. Sch. d. 262, also in Greene's hand, may perhaps be discounted in that none of them, save the keyboard arrangement of the song 'The sun was sunk beneath the hill' (1729), is known to be by Greene himself.

[22] For further discussion of this source, see the author's article, 'Yet more Ornaments for Corelli's Violin Sonatas, op. 5', *Early Music*, 24 (1996), 623–33.

[23] For Mus. Sch. d. 262, still in its original eighteenth-century binding, and evidently written for Elizabeth Child c. 1730, see note 21 above. From the fact that it contains only six short pieces, the last of which is incomplete, it may perhaps be inferred that Miss Child's lessons with Greene did not go on for very long. The same Greene song as appears here is also be be found as the first item in MS Mus. Sch. d. 224, a volume of songs and operatic arias (mainly by Handel) arranged for the harpsichord by John Travers (pp. 1–30) and Greene (pp. 31–45) at much the same time. (The Greene song, 'Ye happy swains', copied by the composer himself on p. 45, was likewise published for the first time in 1729.) Only two untexted movements are included in the MS; the G minor minuet on p. 10 is almost certainly by Bononcini, and so too is the G major minuet on p. 11.

GREENE'S HARPSICHORD MUSIC 271

need to be borne in mind when dealing with the text of those suites for which Add. MS 31467 is still the only known source.

Of the several sources so far mentioned, all are in one way or another connected either directly, or at one remove, with the composer and his circle. Among those which are not (and were seemingly copied somewhat later), the most important is a manuscript in the US-NYp (Mus. Res. MN*) which, in addition to several pieces ascribed to Greene – two of them unique – also includes, anonymously, a further pair of movements which are known to be his, and two pieces which are quite likely on grounds of style and their placement in the manuscript to be by Greene as well. Other apparent *unica* such as the two-movement 'Sonata by Dr. Green' in GB-Cfm MS 668, and a single Gavot in the Dolmetsch collection at Haslemere (MS II.C.26) have no strong claims to authenticity.

In April 1733, Greene enjoyed the dubious distinction of having an entire volume of his keyboard pieces pirated by Daniel Wright, a publisher who, said Hawkins,[24] 'never printed anything that he did not steal'. This, in an announcement first published in *The Whitehall Evening-Post* of 19–21 April, Greene hotly denied having any responsibility for, while at the same time acquainting the public that not only were these lessons 'publish'd without my Knowledge or Consent', but also that 'those which are mine, were composed many Years ago, and are very uncorrect'.[25] Only one copy of the Wright edition survives (now in GB-Lbl), but within just over a month of its appearance, it too had been re-pirated by Walsh as the first nineteen pages of Book 2 in a series of six keyboard anthologies entitled *The Lady's Banquet* and sold at a price undercutting Wright by a shilling per copy.

As published by Wright, the volume contains twenty-eight pieces, twenty-three of which are grouped together to form four suites; at least half of these are also to be found in Add. MS 31467. One movement, the final Aire of the suite in B flat (no. XVIa), had evidently been composed by June 1722 (as appears from a copy of the tune only in GB-Lbl Add. MS 47446), but there is only one piece which can be shown to be by someone other than Greene (in this case, Bononcini). In *The Lady's Banquet*, the order is slightly altered, and the notation modernized (with trill signs replacing the old-fashioned double-stroke shake of the Wright edition). Walsh's engraver also corrects a few of the more obvious of his predecessor's errors, whilst at the same time creating several others of his own devising. By the time he came to publish his official *Collection of Lessons* in 1750, Greene had, as previously remarked, severed his connection with the house of Walsh. In January 1758, however, just ten days after the publication by Thompson of *A Favourite Lesson*, and three years after

---

[24]   J. Hawkins, *A General History of the Science and Practice of Music*, modern edn (New York, 1963), vol. 2, p. 884.

[25]   For full details, see H. Diack Johnstone, 'Greene and The Lady's Banquet: a case of double piracy', *Musical Times*, 108 (1967), 36–9. At this stage, not a note of Greene's music had appeared in print, except for one cantata and a few simple ballad songs such as those cited in notes 21 and 23 (which may or may not have been published with the consent of the composer).

272   MUSIC IN EIGHTEENTH-CENTURY BRITAIN

the composer was safely in his grave, Walsh brought out another version of the second book of *The Lady's Banquet* which he now entitled *A Collection of Lessons for the Harpsichord Compos'd by Dr. Greene. 2d. Book*. This is simply a reprint from the same plates of his earlier piracy with the contents juggled yet again, and the addition of that curious (and terribly feeble) early Handel Sonata in C (HWV 577) first published by Witvogel in Amsterdam in 1732 and then two years later by Walsh himself as the last of four anonymous harpsichord pieces at the beginning of *The Lady's Banquet*, Book 5. What it is doing here in a collection of lessons ostensibly by Greene (and including still at least one piece known to be by Bononcini taken over from the original Wright edition), heaven only knows. Most probably it was added simply as ballast, to turn what would otherwise have been a twenty-one-page volume into one of twenty-four.

GREENE'S HARPSICHORD MUSIC

Appendix: A Checklist of Maurice Greene's harpsichord music

Printed Sources:

1733 *Choice Lessons For the Harpsichord or Spinnet. Compos'd by Dr. Green Organist of the Cathedral Church of St. Paul's &c. Carefully corrected by himself and never before publish'd.* Printed for and sold by Daniel Wright next the Sun Tavern in Holbourne, and D. Wright, jun. at the Golden Bass in St. Paul's Church-yard, and Tho. Wright at the Golden Harp on London Bridge. (Only known copy now GB-Lbl g. 679.) Publication announced in *Fog's Weekly Journal* of 14 April 1733, but any responsibility for it was denied by Greene in *The Whitehall Evening-Post* of 19–21 April. Also re-pirated by John Walsh as *The Lady's Banquet 2d Book* on 19 May 1733, and subsequently reissued by Walsh as *A Collection of Lessons for the Harpsichord Compos'd by Dr. Greene. 2d. Book* in January 1758.

1745 *Six Overtures for the Harpsicord or Spinnet Compos'd by Dr. Maurice Greene Being proper Pieces for the Improvement of the Hand.* Printed for I. Walsh in Catherine Street in the Strand, and issued on 26 October 1745.

1750 *A Collection of Lessons for the Harpsichord Compos'd by Dr. Greene.* Printed for John Johnson at the Harp & Crown in Cheapside on 22 November 1750. Second edition 'corrected by the Author' published on 28 March 1751, and third edition 'on a fine Imperial Paper', 18 March 1752. Modern facsimile, with an introduction by Davitt Moroney, published by Stainer & Bell (London, 1977).

1758 *A Favourite Lesson for the Harpsichord or Organ Compos'd by the Late Dr. Green* published by Thompson & Son on 7 January 1758.

Manuscript Sources:

A   GB-Lbl, Add. MS. 31467, copied by John Barker, a former chorister of the Chapel Royal, *c.* 1735. Contains 43 pieces by Greene, 29 of which are confirmed as his by other sources. Among these are Suites I-III, VI-VIII, X, XIV, and XVI(b).

B   GB-AB, MS 10929 D, copied by Maurice Greene, William Boyce and Martin Smith in early 1730s. Contains autograph of Suite XIV, together with copies of Suites VII, XI and XIII in the hand of Martin Smith.

C   MS in the Gerald Coke Collection (Miscellanies C. 11), copied by Greene, Boyce, Smith and one other unidentified hand in early 1730s. Contains autograph of the concluding Minuet and variations from Suite II; also two other pieces in Greene's hand and likely to be by him, together with four pages of elementary instructions in figured bass playing. Suite X is the hand of the unidentified copyist, and so too is an unattributed piece in G minor which is also to be found in B and is almost certainly by Greene (as is the Siciliana here added to Suite X).

D   GB-Lbl, Add. MS 71244, largely in the hand of Michael Christian Festing (d. 1752), but with an initial two-page explanation of the gamut and table of relative note-values etc. plus sixteen pages of keyboard music copied by Maurice Greene. Among these is the autograph of Suite VII, plus five other pieces; one of these is to be found in A and 1733, and it may well be that the other four are his also.

E   GB-Lcm, MS 1057, owned by John Alcock in 1763. Contains three suites (nos. I, IV and IX) copied by Alcock on paper which, elsewhere in the same volume, he was using in 1740.

F   US-NYp, MS Music Reserve *MN, contains keyboard music in several different hands (but none recognized), and was seemingly compiled in the 1740s. The ten Greene pieces to be found here (two of them unique) are all the work of the same copyist, but not all are attributed, and there are another two in the same hand which may possibly be his as well.

G   MS in the Gerald Coke Collection (Miscellanies C. 10), formerly owned by William Walond Jun. of Chichester (in 1778) but the contents are considerably earlier. 'Sonata [in F] by Dr: Green' as given here combines movements from Suites VI and VIII and adds an arpeggiated prelude which is peculiar to this source. The concluding Siciliana (pp. 85–6) also appears in one of the Stoneleigh Abbey MSS sold at Christie's in 1985 and is there attributed to 'Mr Green'. This too is now in the Coke Collection.

H   GB-Cfm, Mus. MS 668, contains a two-movement 'Sonata [in G] by Dr. Green' which is otherwise unknown and probably spurious.

I   GB-Cpl, MS 24 (now in GB-Cu as MS 9127), contains an early (pre-1730) copy of the Allemanda of Suite II.

J   GB-H, MS 30.B.XII, contains a mid-eighteenth-century copy of Suite II. Last movement lacks the variations, but first two are fully fingered (in the right hand).

K   GB-Ob, Tenbury MS 752, contains a mid-eighteenth-century copy of the first movement only of Suite VII.

L   GB-Lcm, MS 1120, contains eight lessons copied from Greene's 1750 Collection: groups 1–3, 5, 9, 11, 8 and 10.

GREENE'S HARPSICHORD MUSIC   275

Table 11.1: Greene: The Suites

The grouping of pieces by suite follows that of Add. MS 31467 and the other principal sources, but the ordering of suites by key (and hence the numbering) is purely editorial.

No.	Key	Movements	Autog.	MS copies	Prints
I	c	Allmand		A, E, F	1733
		Corant		A, E, F	1733
		Gavot*		A, F	1733
		Minuet		A, E, F	1733

* Gavot appears separately in **F**.

No.	Key	Movements	Autog.	MS copies	Prints
II	D	Allemanda		A, I, J	1733 and 1758*
		Corrente		A, J	1733 and 1758
		Minuet and 2 vars.	C	A, J	1733 and 1758

* In 1733 edns, the Minuet from Suite III is placed between the Allemanda and Corrente here. **J** lacks the concluding variations. Last movement headed 'Aria con Variationi' in autograph.

No.	Key	Movements	Autog.	MS copies	Prints
III	D	Preludio	D*	A	1733
		Aire		A	
		Minuet**		A	1733

* Autograph is in C major (and so too are 1733 edns).
** Keyboard arrangement of the song 'The Pangs of Forsaken Love' [1731].

No.	Key	Movements	Autog.	MS copies	Prints
IV	E♭	Almand		E	
		Corant		E	
		Minuet		E, F	
		Untitled mvt in 3/8 [Minuet]		E, F	

No.	Key	Movements	Autog.	MS copies	Prints
V	F	Prelude	A*		1733
		Gavot			1733
		Aire			1733
		Minuet			1733
		Jigg			1733
		Minuet			1733
		Hornpipe			1733

* As given in **A**, the Prelude forms the first movement of Suite VI.

276 MUSIC IN EIGHTEENTH-CENTURY BRITAIN

Table 11.1 *continued*

No.	Key	Movements	Autog.	MS copies	Prints
VI	F	Prelude*		A	
		Allemande		A, G	
		Corante		A, G	
		Gavotta		A, G	

* Source G provides a quite different Prelude, and there the Gavotta is followed by the last two movements of Suite VIII in reverse order.

No.	Key	Movements	Autog.	MS copies	Prints
VII	F	'Arpeggio' [Prelude]		B	
		Allegro*	D	A, B, K	
		Courant	D	A, B	
		Minuetto	D	A, B	
		Giga	D**	A, B	

* Headed 'Sonata per il Cembalo' in A.
** Autograph of last mvt (here called a Siciliana) is incomplete; in B the piece is headed 'Siciliani' [*sic*].

No.	Key	Movements	Autog.	MS copies	Prints
VIII	F	Aire		A	
		Sciciliana [*sic*]		A, G*	
		Aire		A, G	

* A further copy (ex-Stoneleigh Abbey) now in the Coke Collection calls this a 'Ceciliana' and ascribes the piece to 'Mr Green'.

No.	Key	Movements	Autog.	MS copies	Prints
IX	f	Almand		E	
		Corant		E	
		Minuet		E	
		Gigg		E	

No.	Key	Movements	Autog.	MS copies	Prints
X	G	Allmanda*		A, C	
		Sarabanda		A, C	
		Minuetto [1 & 2]		A, C	
		Siciliana		C	

* Suite is anonymous in C, but first mvt has basso continuo figuring in Greene's hand. The second minuet is in G minor.

No.	Key	Movements	Autog.	MS copies	Prints
XI*	G	[Almand]		B	
		[Corant]		B	
		Sarabanda Largo		B	
		[Minuet]		B	

* Anonymous in source, but B copied by Martin Smith and is almost certainly authentic.

GREENE'S HARPSICHORD MUSIC

Table 11.1 *continued*

No.	Key	Movements	Autog.	MS copies	Prints
XII	g	Allemanda		A	
		Courant		A	
		Aire		A	
		Minuett		A	
		Giga		A, F	
XIII*	g	'Arpeggio' [Prelude]		B	
		[Almand]		B	
		[Corant]		B	
		[Minuet]		B, C	
		[Gigue]		B	

* Anonymous in source, but copied by Martin Smith and almost certainly authentic; mvt 4 also anonymous in C.

No.	Key	Movements	Autog.	MS copies	Prints
XIV	A	Allemand	B	A	
		Courant	B	A	
		Aire	B	A	
		Minuett (+7 vars.)	B	A	
XV	a	Allemanda		A	
		Courant		A	
		Minuett		A	
		Jigg		A	
XVIa*	B♭	Prelude			1733
		Allmand			1733
		Corrent			1733
		Gavott**			1733
		Aire			1733
		Jigg		F	1733
		Slow Aire			·1733
		Aire+			1733

* In both Wright and Walsh edns, the first two mvts are printed in reverse order, and the Allmand (in Wright) is called an Overture. The titles given here are those of the Walsh edn.

** Also published as a song 'The Happy Shepherd' [1733], but it is not clear which version is the earlier of the two.

+ Tune only is included in GB-Lbl Add. MS 47446 where it appears to have been copied some time prior to 12 June 1722, and is thus the earliest known keyboard piece attributed to Greene.

MUSIC IN EIGHTEENTH-CENTURY BRITAIN

Table 11.1 *concluded*

No.	Key	Movements	Autog.	MS copies	Prints
XVIb*	B♭	Aire		A	
		Aire		A	
		Aire		A	
		Jigg		A	

* First two and last mvts are the same as the Prelude, Corrent and Jigg of Suite XVIa; the third mvt also appears separately (in G) in 1733 edns.

GREENE'S HARPSICHORD MUSIC

Table 11.2: Greene: Miscellaneous harpsichord pieces

No.	Key	Movement	MS copies	Print
1	C	Trumpet Tune	D*	

* Another autograph copy in GB-Ob MS Mus. Sch. 262, but it may be that the piece is not by Greene.

| 2 | c | Untitled mvt in 3/8 [Minuet] | D* | |

* Seems likely to be authentic.

| 3 | c | Jigg | F* | |

* Unattributed, but is in the same hand as other Greene pieces in this source, and could well be authentic; if so, it might usefully serve as a final mvt to Suite I.

| 4 | D | Jigg | F* | |

* Attributed to Greene by copyist whose other attributions in the same source seem mostly to be accurate.

| 5 | D | 'Gavot by Dr Green'* | | |

* Only known copy in Dolmetsch MS II.C.26; seems unlikely to be authentic.

| 6 | e | Lento Siciliano | F* | |

* Attributed to Greene by copyist whose other attributions in the same source seem mostly to be accurate.

| 7 | F | Slow Aire* | | 1733 |

* Keyboard arrangement of the song 'Charming Silvia' [1731].

| 8 | G | 'Sonata by Dr Green'* | H | |

* Has two mvts: Andante Allegro and Minuetto, and is probably spurious.

| 9 | G | Aire* | | 1733 |

* See Suite XVIb.

| 10 | G | Untitled mvt in 3/8 [Minuet]* | | |

* Keyboard arrangement of the song 'The sun was sunk beneath the hill' [1729]. Autograph copy in GB-Ob MS Mus. Sch. d. 262; also copied (with words) by Travers in GB-Ob Mus. Sch. d. 224.

280   MUSIC IN EIGHTEENTH-CENTURY BRITAIN

Table 11.2 *concluded*

No.	Key	Movement	MS copies	Print
11	G	Untitled mvt in common time*		

* Autograph copy (9 ½ bb. only) in GB-Ob Mus. Sch. 262; may well be a keyboard arrangement of a vocal original as yet unidentified.

| 12 | G | Untitled mvt in 3/8 [Minuet]* | | |

* Copied by Travers in GB-Ob Mus. Sch. d. 224; unattributed, and almost certainly not by Greene. The G minor [Minuet] which precedes it is attributed elsewhere to Bononcini.

| 13 | g | Slow Aire* | | 1733 |

* Keyboard arrangement of the song 'Robin's Complaint' [1729].

| 14 | A | Untitled mvt in 3/8 [Minuet]   **D*** | | |

* Autograph; seems likely to be authentic.

| 15 | A | Untitled mvt in 3/8 [Minuet]   **D*** | | |

* Autograph; seems likely to be authentic.

| 16 | A | Untitled mvt in 3/8 [Minuet]   **C*** | | |

* Autograph (incomplete); seems likely to be authentic.

| 17 | a | Untitled mvt in 3/8 [Minuet]   **C*** | | |

* Autograph; seems likely to be authentic.

| 18 | a | Untitled mvt in 3/8 | **F*** | |

* Of doubtful authenticity, but follows on from a piece (no. 6 above) which is attributed to Greene (and is in the same hand).

| 19 | a | Untitled mvt in 3/8* | | |

* Only known copy (in Greene's hand) in GB-Ob MS Mus. Sch. d. 262, but like no. 1 above, it may or may not be authentic.

The E major piece attributed to 'Dr. Greene' in GB-Ckc, Rowe MS 251, is actually the Gavot from no. 5 of Henry Symonds's *Six Setts of Lessons* [1734], a work to which Greene himself subscribed.

GREENE'S HARPSICHORD MUSIC

Table 11.3: Greene: *Six Overtures* (1745)

No.	Key	Movements
I	D	Allegro assai: Andante: Allegro
II	G	[Moderato]: Allegro: Allegro
III	C	[Moderato]: Allegro assai: Allegro ma non troppo
IV	E	Con Spirito: Allegro: Moderato (in e): Allegro
V	D	Allegro: Andante (in d): Presto
VI	B♭	Con Spirito: Allegro: Andante: Presto

All are arrangements, presumably by the composer, of orchestral originals, and no manuscript copies are known to survive. In its original form, no. IV was the Overture to the royal Birthday Ode for 1739 (GB-Ob MS Mus. d. 39).

Table 11.4: Greene: *A Collection of Lessons for the Harpsichord* (1750)

No.	Key	Movements
I	G	Allegro: Allegro: Vivace: Allegro (MS copy in L)
II	D	Allegro: Andante: Allegro (MS copy in L)
III	g	Vivace: Allegro: Tempo di Gavotta (MS copy in L)
IV	c	Presto: Vivace: Allegro: Allegro
V	F	Allegro: Andante vivace: Allegro (MS copy in L)
VI	B♭	Allegro: Minueto Allegro: Vivace (repeat Minueto Allegro)
VII	F	Molto Allegro: Allegro: Andante (in f): Allegro
–	d	Aria con Variationi
VIII	F	Allegro: Andante: Allegro (MS copy in L: also in GB-Lam MS 166)
IX	a	Allegro: Vivace: Molto Allegro (MS copy in L)
X	A	Aria con Variationi: Andante: Allegro: Allegro (MS copy in L; first mvt. only also in GB-Cpl MS 26, and in GB-DRc Bamburgh MS 69)
XI	E	Allegro: Vivace: Aria con Variationi (MS copy in L)
XII	B♭	Allegro: Vivace: Allegro: Allegro
XIII	C	Allegro: Vivace: Allegro (all three mvts in GB-Cpl MS 26)
XIV	F	Allegro: Allegro: Allegro

CHAPTER TWELVE

Viotti's 'London' Concertos (Nos. 20–29): Progressive or Retrospective?

Robin Stowell

Giovanni Battista Viotti (1755–1824), 'pupil of the celebrated Pugnani', came to London in July 1792. His Parisian debut in one of his own concertos at the Concert Spirituel, on 17 March 1782, and his numerous subsequent appearances at those prestigious concerts had quickly established him as one of the foremost violinists of his time. Various sudden changes in career direction had resulted in his temporary retirement from the public concert platform in September 1783, his subsequent employment as violinist in the service of Marie Antoinette at Versailles, and his establishment in 1788 of a new opera house, the Théâtre de Monsieur (re-named Théâtre Feydeau in July 1791). His ambitious plans as a theatre manager, which also included public concert performances of some of his own works, had been wrecked by the revolutionary uprisings – and at quite some personal financial cost. By mid-1792, his royalist associations had made his position in Paris untenable and he fled to London to rebuild his personal fortunes.

With its buoyant economy, active concert life, flourishing publishing activity and numerous opportunities for aristocratic patronage and other private employment, London was a financially attractive cultural centre, particularly for foreign musicians. The capital proved an especially popular refuge for French émigrés towards the end of the eighteenth century. One reporter commented, 'Music as well as misery has fled for shelter to England',[1] while Friedrich Wendeborn observed: 'Many foreign singers, fidlers [sic], and dancers, are extravagantly paid; and, if they are the least frugal, they are enabled to retire to their own country, where they may live in affluence, enriched by English money.'[2]

In London, Viotti revived his solo career and first made his mark at Johann Peter Salomon's Hanover Square Concerts on 7 February 1793. He became the featured violinist for two seasons and eclipsed established London favourites such as Giovanni Giornovichi (c. 1740–1804) and Wilhelm Cramer (1746–99). A correspondent of the *Berliner Musikzeitung* (1794) considered him 'probably the greatest violinist in Europe. A strong, full-bodied tone, incredible agility, accuracy and precision ... are characteristic, and his concertos surpass all others known to me ... He is equally irresistible as composer and performer.'[3]

---

[1] *Morning Chronicle*, 15 February 1793.
[2] F. A. Wendeborn, *A View of England towards the Close of the Eighteenth Century* (1785–), trans. author, 2 vols (London, 1791), vol. 2, p. 237. See also 'Zustand der Musik in England', in *Allgemeine musikalische Zeitung*, 15 December 1802, cols. 193–5.
[3] Cited in B. Schwarz, *Great Masters of the Violin* (London, 1984), p. 140.

VIOTTI'S 'LONDON' CONCERTOS

Viotti's association with another popular distinguished visitor to London, Joseph Haydn, throughout the 1794 season offered him a springboard to further success. But the impresario in him again proved a distraction, and he was appointed 'acting manager' of London's King's Theatre in October 1794. Following the termination of Salomon's Hanover Square Concerts in that year, Viotti started a prestigious new series of nine subscription concerts at the King's Theatre between February and May 1795, known appropriately as the 'Opera Concerts'. This series represented the capital's grandest concert enterprise, providing an orchestra of at least sixty members. As director of the series, Viotti undertook to 'furnish new pieces of music', and he also figured prominently as soloist there until 1798.[4]

An ironic twist in his circumstances led to his expulsion from England by the British government in March 1798, on suspicion of revolutionary activity.[5] There is some uncertainty regarding the date of his return to this country from his German retreat near Hamburg,[6] but it is clear that he resolved largely to devote his energies to running a wine business. Apart from appearing as a leader and chamber musician at the Royal Philharmonic Society between 1813 and 1815 – he later served as one of its directors – he largely withdrew from the concert platform.[7] He continued composing, however, and re-established links in 1802 with the Parisian publishing firm in which his friend Luigi Cherubini (1760–1842) was a partner. The eventual failure of his wine business and of his subsequent opera directorships in Paris resulted both in his financial ruin and his final return to London, where he died on 3 March 1824.

Reports of Viotti's playing consistently pay tribute to his assertive style, full tone, singing legato, accuracy, expression and his mastery of the bow. A review of Salomon's Fifth Concert at Hanover Square (10 March 1794) records that

> The masterly performance of Viotti exceeded all former sample; his power over the instrument seems unlimited. The grand mistake of Musicians has been a continued effort to excite amazement. Viotti, it is true, without making that his object, astonishes the hearer; but he does something infinitely better – he awakens emotion, gives a soul to sound, and leads the passions captive.[8]

Such acclamation is in keeping with his technical credo,[9] his championing of the violins of Antonio Stradivari,[10] and his possible connection with the

---

[4] See M. Scott, 'The Opera Concerts of 1795', *Music Review*, 12 (1951), 24–8.
[5] According to *The Times* (5 March 1798) Viotti was expelled 'under the authority of the Alien Bill'.
[6] Chappell White believes that Viotti returned to England in the autumn of 1799. See E.C. White, 'Toward a more accurate chronology of Viotti's Violin Concertos', *Fontes Artis Musicae*, 20 (1973), 112.
[7] G. Hogarth, *The Philharmonic Society of London ... .1813–1862* (London, 1862), pp. 6 and 145. Details of the Society's varied concert programmes are provided in M.B. Foster, *History of the Philharmonic Society of London 1813–1912* (London, 1912). See also C. Ehrlich, *First Philharmonic. A History of the Royal Philharmonic Society* (Oxford, 1995).
[8] *Morning Chronicle*, 12 March 1794.
[9] See P. Baillot, *L'art du Violon* (Paris, 1835), Eng. trans. L. Goldberg (Evanston, Ill., 1991), p. 261, regarding Viotti's expressive approach to fingering.
[10] A Stradivari violin is listed in Viotti's will amongst his most valuable and prized possessions. See A. Pougin, 'Le Testament de Viotti', *Le Ménestrel*, 68 (1902), 371.

284 MUSIC IN EIGHTEENTH-CENTURY BRITAIN

development of the 'modern' bow, synthesized c. 1785 by François Tourte (1747–1835).[11]

Viotti's playing style is faithfully reflected in his twenty-nine violin concertos, which are generally conceived on a larger scale than those of his predecessors and contemporaries. All consist of three movements, a formal tradition much stronger for the violin concerto of the time than for the newer keyboard concerto, which commonly comprised only two movements. His first twelve 'Paris' concertos adopt a quasi-galant style; but the following seven (Nos. 13–19) treat the orchestra more symphonically, thanks doubtless to his familiarity with Haydn's symphonies, particularly the six 'Paris' symphonies premièred at the French capital's Loge Olympique concerts in 1787. Furthermore, Viotti's later concertos for Paris (Nos. 13–19) incorporate more elaborate solo parts, perpetuate the Italian cantabile tradition and draw dramatic traits from the operas of Cherubini and other contemporaries.

Viotti's last ten concertos are products of his London years and are his most polished and mature. According to Chappell White, Nos. 20–27 were composed between 1793 and 1798, while watermarks date No. 28 and, possibly, No. 29 from the early 1800s[12] (see Table 12.1). Although some of the 'Paris' concertos probably formed part of his early London repertory, Viotti had good reason for introducing new works, not least because, as director, he had committed the Opera Concerts to such novelties. Competition in the capital from virtuoso pianists and other well-established violinists, the richer orchestral resources available, and the influence of Haydn also inspired him to develop further the scope and content of his compositions. Consequently, the 'London' concertos generally expand upon the expressive language of his 'Paris' works, and their lyrical melodic qualities, particularly of the last two concertos, foreshadow the Romantic ideal. Extracts from works by Mendelssohn and Schumann, for example, have been likened to the opening of Viotti's Violin Concerto No. 29 (Ex. 12.1),[13] while an 'excellent, beautiful and melodious phrase' ('ausgezeichnete, schöne und melodiose Stelle') from No. 21. (Ex. 12.2a) was especially remarked upon by one contemporary reviewer.[14] Introduced during the development section in the first movement, it is clearly derived from a theme presented at the beginning of that section. (Ex. 12.2b)

---

[11] François-Joseph Fétis's claim (in *Antoine Stradivari...suivi d'analyse théorique sur l'archet et sur François Tourte* (Paris, 1856), p. 119) that Tourte benefited from Viotti's advice in making this synthesis is not corroborated by any other source. Furthermore, David Boyden (in S. Sadie (ed.), *The Violin Family* (London, 1989), p. 31) refers to a pen and wash portrait by an unknown artist, housed in London's British Museum, representing Viotti late in his career but holding a bow of Baroque design and dimensions; this portrait is reproduced in *The New Grove Dictionary of Music and Musicians*, ed. S. Sadie (London, 1980), vol. 19, p. 864.

[12] See E.C. White (ed.), *Four Concertos by Giovanni Battista Viotti*, vols. 4–5 in *Recent Researches in Classical Music* (Madison, 1976), p. viii. Readers should be warned of the inaccuracies and ambiguities in Remo Giazotto's dating of the violin concertos in *his Giovan Battista Viotti* (Milan, 1956), pp.289–368.

[13] *Die Musik in Geschichte und Gegenwart*, vol. 13 (Kassel, 1966), opp. cols. 1743 and 1744.

[14] *Allgemeine musikalische Zeitung*, 7 September 1803, col. 829.

Table 12.1 Viotti's 'London' concertos

No.	Key	Approx. date of composition	1st edn pf. trans.	1st edn original	Evidence for dating	Instrumentation (strings +) fl	ob	cl	bn	hn	tpt	timp
20	D	1793[1]	1795	1799[2]	Title-page	–	2	–	–	2	2	–
21	E	1793–4	1796–7	1803	Instrumentation	1	2	–	2	2	–	–
22	a	1795–8	–	1803	Instrumentation	1	2	2	2	2	2	1
23	G	1794	1796	1804	Title-page	2	–	–	1	2	–	–
24	b	*c.* 1794	–	1805	Concert review	2	2	–	2	2	2	1
25	a	1795	1796	1807	Publication	1	2	2	2	2	2	1
26	B♭	1795–7	*c.* 1797	1808	Instrumentation	1	2	2	2	2	–	–
27	C	1794	1813	1815	Watermark	1	2	–	2	2	–	–
28	a	1803–04	–	1823	Watermark	1	2	2	2	2	–	–
29	e	1801[3]	–	1824	Watermark[3]	2	2	2	2	2	2	1

Sources: This table is a collation of information provided in the following: E.C. White, 'Toward a more accurate chronology of Viotti's Violin Concertos', *Fontes Artis Musicae*, 20 (1973), 11–23; E.C. White, *From Vivaldi to Viotti: a History of the Early Classical Violin Concerto* (Reading, 1992), pp. 332–6; and T.B. Milligan, *The Concerto and London's Musical Culture in the Late Eighteenth Century* (Ann Arbor, Mich., 1983), pp. 134 and 137.

[1] slow movement later, probably 1798

[2] However, there was probably an earlier publication which has yet to be discovered; for the piano transcription made by Hüllmandel (London, 1795) records the availability of the work for violin. See E.C. White, 'Did Viotti write any Original Piano Concertos?' *Journal of the American Musicological Society*, 22 (1969), 275–84.

[3] The surviving parts can be dated 1801, but their status is uncertain; it is possible, therefore, that the work dates from the mid-1790s.

Ex. 12.1
(a) Viotti: Violin Concerto No. 29, first movement

(b) Mendelssohn: Violin Concerto op.64, first movement

(c) Schumann: Piano Concerto op.54, first movement

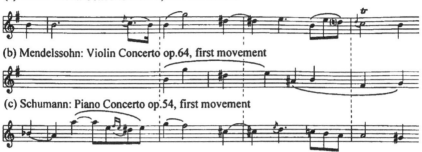

Ex. 12.2 Viotti: Violin Concerto No. 21, first movement

By the turn of the century, Viotti had not only raised the violin concerto to new heights but had also introduced into his fundamentally Classical approach modifications of structure and style sufficiently progressive to justify the description of some of his later works as 'pre-romantic'. The slow introduction, which had become a feature of most of Haydn's later symphonies, including eleven of his 'London' works, also forms part of Viotti's scheme in Concertos Nos. 25 and 27.[15] Apart from the Adagio solo introductory passage in the first movement of Mozart's A major violin concerto (K.219, 1775), there are few precedents for the formal, pertinent relationship of Viotti's brief, slow introduction to the first theme of the ensuing Allegro of No. 27. (Ex. 12.3) In No. 25, however, no direct relationship between the orchestra's pastoral, siciliano-like introductory Andante and the ternary Allegro vivace assai is distinguishable. Instead, Viotti appears to opt for diversity of approach, following the two opening orchestral sections with an expressive Andante in A

---

[15] One of Viotti's 'Paris' concertos, No. 16 in E minor (to which Mozart added trumpet and timpani parts in 1785), also has a slow introduction.

minor, featuring an expressive solo cantilena, prior to a lively, major-mode solo section proper, which introduces unrelated thematic material.

Ex. 12.3 Viotti: Violin Concerto No. 27, first movement

The opening ritornellos of Viotti's first movements normally incorporate at least one of the following characteristics: a 'military' theme, characterised by a march-like pulse, dotted rhythms and often by repeated notes; a chordal theme based on the tonic triad and usually succeeded by a similar figure on the dominant; or a lyrical, sustained melody. Although these characteristics are not as sharply defined in the 'London' as in the 'Paris' concertos, Ex. 12.4a–c clearly demonstrates Viotti's perseverance with such thematic traits. Unlike

Ex. 12.4

(a) Viotti: Violin Concerto No. 28, first movement

(b) Viotti: Violin Concerto No. 22, first movement

(c) Viotti: Violin Concerto No. 21, first movement

Mozart in his piano concertos, Viotti normally effects a modulation for the second theme within the first ritornello. His manner of re-establishing the tonic key before the first solo entry is also unusual. Instead of the customary addition of a brief concluding passage, he normally recalls the opening theme, thereby giving the first ritornello a rounded ternary design. He also enlarges the first solo section and, like some of his predecessors, frequently introduces more than one melody in each of the two keys, as well as solo passage-work. The longest section of passage-work regularly follows the (usually new) second theme. Viotti increases its overall significance by varying the figuration, implementing occasional passing modulations and often repeating the entire section, sometimes with subtle elaboration. The second ritornello is generally concluded in a suitably climactic manner.

Viotti's first thirteen concertos are exclusively in major keys, but ten of the remainder are in the minor mode, including five of the 'London' group. Many contemporary London musicians may have considered this shift of emphasis towards minor keys to be a reversion to the 'ancient' style, somewhat like the phrygian cadence and the imitative passage in Ex. 12.5, from Viotti's Concerto No. 24;[16] but the tonal scheme in many of the first movements of these minor-key works is nothing but progressive. Instead of modulating to the expected secondary key area, the mediant, the A minor Concerto No. 22, for example, modulates to the dominant major in both the opening ritornello and the first solo section, preceded in both cases by a change of mode from tonic minor to major. Viotti also commonly dispenses with the usual dominant and submediant keys for his re-statement in the second solo section of thematic material from the first ritornello or first solo. Instead, he favours, for major-key movements, the mediant (as in No. 27), the flattened mediant (as in No. 20), the submediant (as in No. 23) or the flattened submediant (as in No. 25). His minor-key concertos demonstrate similar unorthodoxy, No. 22 in A minor modulating to C sharp minor for the second solo, while No. 24 in B minor exploits the Neapolitan relationship at that juncture.

Ex. 12.5 Viotti: Violin Concerto No. 24, first movement

The first-movement developments of Viotti's 'Paris' concertos normally comprise a new melody (in the dominant or relative major), modulating solo passage-work, another melody (in a different key), and further passage-work. However, his 'London' concertos demonstrate greater freedom of treatment, especially as regards tonality. No. 22 (in A minor), for example, substitutes the dominant minor for the more commonly employed relative major, and No. 24 (in B minor) adopts the parallel minor of the relative major. Viotti only rarely modulates by fifths beyond the dominant or sub-dominant, showing a preference for modulation by thirds. Modulation to the relative major of either the tonic, dominant, or subdominant parallel minor is common.

---

[16] T.B. Milligan, *The Concerto and London's Musical Culture in the Late Eighteenth Century* (Ann Arbor, Mich., 1983), p. 147.

Genuine symphonic development of thematic material is rare, but the 'London' concertos show a marked increase in the proportion of development material that is related to either the first ritornello or the first solo section. The opening theme of the first movement of No. 23 dominates to a larger extent than usual. Varied only slightly for the first solo section, it also receives a complete statement in the development, where Viotti normally re-introduces the second theme. But the first movement of No. 26 is the most outstanding for its unity of conception, especially its progressive approach to developmental technique. Its opening ritornello theme (Ex. 12.6) is pregnant with developmental potential

Ex. 12.6 Viotti: Violin Concerto No. 26, first movement

and Viotti soon indulges in some simple imitation featuring its four-note rhythmic pattern; he then substitutes for the customary second theme a brief development of that four-note figure, which later serves as an accompaniment to solo passage-work and plays a prominent part in both the rigorous development and the brief transition to the surprisingly regular recapitulation.

As signalled by No. 20, most of the recapitulations of the first movements of Viotti's 'London' concertos are truncated. The second theme is commonly omitted, the first being followed by a transposition of the passage-work that originally succeeded the first solo section's second theme. In some of his mature concertos, however, Viotti sometimes begins the recapitulation with a brief tutti which incorporates both themes. The free organization of No. 24 is exceptional; using a secondary *semplice* melody from the opening ritornello as its cornerstone, it recalls this melody first in the development and again later as the only melodic material of the recapitulation. The solo cadenza is an inconsistent feature of Viotti's first movements, but a short orchestral coda generally rounds off the movement with reference to the first solo section's closing tutti.

The central slow movements of Viotti's 'London' works are largely founded on the instrumental romance, although not so titled (see, for example, the Adagio of No. 22);[17] most adopt a ternary design, feature a short, simple cantabile melody and require a more prominent orchestral contribution in the contrasting central section. Viotti normally assigns the soloist a sustained, lyrical and expressive role – the free lyricism of the slow movement of No. 27 is especially remarkable – and he exercises restraint in the addition of written ornamentation, acknowledging the London taste for slow music of unadorned but profound expression. Baillot, discussing the more progressive dramatic music of late-eighteenth-century composers such as Gluck, Haydn, Mozart and Beethoven, claimed that

---

[17] For a detailed description of a typical Romance, see E.C. White, 'The Violin Concertos of Giornovichi', *Musical Quarterly*, 58 (1972), 33–5.

290 MUSIC IN EIGHTEENTH-CENTURY BRITAIN

> Les Concertos de Viotti introduisirent cette marche dramatique dans la musique de Violon; leur caractère soutenu, leurs chants nobles et expressifs, qui semblent avoir été faits sur des paroles, firent connaître que le premier des instruments n'est jamais plus beau que dans les compositions dictées par un sentiment profond et par le besoin d'émouvoir plutôt que par le simple désir de briller.

> Viotti's concertos introduced this dramatic direction into the violin literature; their sustained character, their noble and expressive melodies, which seem to have been composed with words in mind, made it clear that the foremost of instruments is never more beautiful than in compositions inspired by profound sentiment and by the need to affect the emotions rather than the simple desire to shine.[18]

Viotti's additional solo ornamentation at the end of the slow movement of No. 21, the elaborately ornamented initial solo statement of No. 22 or his suggested ornamented version of the slow movement of No. 27 [19] could thus be considered retrospective in style. But many of his slow movements are progressive for their introduction of distant tonal relationships, the increased prominence they give to the orchestra, and the occasional use of the fashionable, so-called 'chordal' texture (for example, in No. 22) popularized by Haydn in, for example, the slow movement of his 'Rider' quartet, op. 74 no. 3, and the Largo section of his Scena di Berenice. Especially unusual is the key of the slow movement of No. 23 in G: the submediant (E major). No. 27 in C also exploits a distant relationship: the mediant (E major). Interestingly, this relationship is anticipated in the first movements of both these concertos, the distantly related key being exploited as the second tonal centre in the second solo section. Similar unusual key relationships apply, of course, in Haydn's London works, as for example in the Symphony No. 99 in E flat major (1793), which has a slow movement in G major (the mediant), and the 'Rider' Quartet in G minor, which has a Largo assai in E major (the submediant).[20]

Viotti's somewhat freer treatment of concerto form extends to linking the slow movement and finale of three of his 'London' concertos. In No. 20, the dominant chord which concludes the dark, dramatic second movement leads straight into the finale. Similar linking of movements is made in No. 26, in which the G minor Andante modulates towards its end to the relative major, again closing on the dominant chord in preparation for the finale; and No. 29 anticipates Mendelssohn's Violin Concerto in E minor (1844), its nineteen-bar slow 'Introduzione' for orchestra serving as a transitional modulatory passage between the C major of the slow movement and the Allegretto finale in E minor. (Ex. 12.7) Furthermore, the similarity between this 'Introduzione' and the opening of Haydn's 'Drum Roll' Symphony No. 103 (Ex. 12.8) can scarcely pass unnoticed.

---

[18] See Baillot, *L'art du violon*, Eng. trans., p. 287.
[19] In this movement, Viotti wrote various decorated versions on an empty stave above the solo violin part.
[20] Milligan, *The Concerto*, p. 159

Ex. 12.7 Viotti: Violin Concerto No. 29, third movement

Ex. 12.8 Haydn: Symphony No. 103 ('Drum Roll'), first movement

Viotti generally favoured a format of three refrains and two episodes for his rondo finales, but many of his 'London' concertos are extended to incorporate a brief fourth refrain as part of the coda, again probably reflecting Haydn's progressive influence. Viotti preserved the traditional light and often witty character of the genre and incorporated sufficient variety and structural interest to counterbalance his first movements, most notably in terms of the tonalities exploited, in the character of the episodes, and in the diversity of his transitions back to the refrain. He generally allows the soloist to begin the refrain, but, unlike many predecessors and contemporaries, he never restricts it to the common, simple formula of an eight-bar solo statement with tutti repetition. At the very least he adds a closing section, and sometimes extends the refrain to embrace up to three solo and three tutti subdivisions. This more complex arrangement enables him to vary the remaining refrains; he usually shortens the second considerably and the third somewhat less. The finale of No. 20 is unusual in that it incorporates a change of tempo within the rondo refrain. It begins with an Allegretto, followed by an Allegro vivo, both in 6/8 metre, and these dual tempos are maintained wherever the refrain appears later in the movement.

Viotti's first episodes are typically in the dominant or relative major key. In his major-key concertos, however, the episode in the new tonality is usually preceded by a short section of melodic material in the tonic, or passage-work or both (sometimes with an additional section in another related key). Viotti's second episodes, like Haydn's, often display elements in common with the developmental techniques of his first movements, as, for example, in the content of their passage-work, in their freedom of modulation, or in their restatement in a different key of a theme from the first episode. Viotti normally avoids using the refrain theme within an episode, but Nos. 21 and 22 are significant exceptions, the use of the refrain here approaching genuine thematic development. His tendency to modulate by thirds to the flat side of the tonic, mentioned earlier in respect of his first movement developments, is also evident in the rondos, but modulations tend to be more sudden and the flattened sixth degree is especially emphasized, as in the finale of No. 23.

Viotti's final codas constitute almost another episode in length and significance. The greater portion is customarily devoted to a re-statement, in the tonic, of the material from the first episode. In the middle and late Paris concertos, the passage-work alone is customarily used; but Viotti aims for greater coherence in his 'London' concertos, generally re-stating both the melody and the passage-work. A brief tutti, using material from the closing section of the refrain, usually brings the end.

Viotti's adoption of a drone idea in the finales of Nos. 20, 23 and 27 reflects the popular style cultivated in London and perpetuated by Haydn and his contemporaries (for example, in the finale of Haydn's 'London' Symphony No. 104). In No. 20 the simple solo melody of Ex. 12.9, the repeated pattern of the

Ex. 12.9 Viotti: Violin Concerto No. 20, third movement

accompaniment and the drone bass suggest some inspiration in popular folk idioms, an impression confirmed by the orchestra's dance-like allegro vivo, also with drone. (Ex. 12.10) The finale of No. 23 incorporates a similar effect. The

Ex. 12.10 Viotti: Violin Concerto No. 20, third movement

polonaise finale of No. 29 also reflects this 'popular' approach and had significant implications for the genre in the nineteenth century.[21]

---

[21] The polonaise finales of, for example, Viotti's Concertos Nos. 2, 13 (headed Tempo di Menuetto) and 29 were among the first uses of this dance in the genre.

Some of Viotti's 'London' concertos include innovatory accompanied cadenzas in their finales. Those in the finales of Nos. 22, 27, 28 and 29 are especially noteworthy, particularly the 'Cadenza con sentimento' before the coda in No. 28. More lyrical and more economically accompanied is the cadenza in the finale of No. 29, derived from the E major portion of the second episode, while the opening cadenza material for No. 22 is derived from the first episode, to which it returns at the end of its ternary design.

Thematic interrelationships play a significant part in integrating the content of most of Viotti's outer movements, whether this involves deriving further melodic material from themes already introduced (as in the first movement of No. 27), recalling the material of the opening in the passagework of an episode (as in the finale of No. 26), or cultivating important thematic links between episode and refrain (as in the finale of No. 21). No. 22 is perhaps the most concentrated of Viotti's rondo finales, three elements of its refrain being used almost continuously throughout: anacrusic rhythm (Ex. 12.11a); the dotted rhythm which follows a contrasting passage in C (Ex. 12.11b); and the demisemiquaver figure of the tutti closing section (Ex. 12.11c). These three elements are incorporated into new melodies and employed as the basis of solo passage-work, giving a further sense of unity to the movement.

Ex. 12.11 Viotti: Violin Concerto No. 22, third movement

Viotti once extended his quest for unity to a whole concerto through thematic recall. In No. 21, that unusual *minore* melody (Ex. 12.2a, p. 286), derived from earlier material and featured in the first movement's development, is twice recalled in the rondo finale, first in G minor and then in G major. Despite such progressiveness, some will regard Viotti's straightforward 'literal' recollection of the theme as a missed opportunity, because it is required to undergo neither development nor 'transformation'; nor does it play any other significant structural role in either movement.

The technical demands of Viotti's 'London' concertos are generally more conservative than in the later 'Paris' concertos and faithfully reflect contemporary

294   MUSIC IN EIGHTEENTH-CENTURY BRITAIN

British taste. Thomas Twining believed that emphasis on 'trick, caprice and the difficulté vaincue' undermined expression,[22] and Viotti appears to have moderated the virtuoso element accordingly. 'His execution is not more astonishing by its difficulty, than it is delightful by its passion', wrote one reviewer;[23] another commented thus regarding Concerto No. 26:

> ... jedoch bemerkt man in demselben, so wie überhaupt in seinen spätern Werken, einen mehr vervollkommneten Geschmack und einen Grad der Kunstvollendung, der sich von dem blos Rauschenden, und von dem, was nur durch Ueberwindung mechanischer Schwierigkeiten glänzen will, immer mehr entfernt, und dagegen mehr das Gediegnere, Gehaltvollere, um das, was tiefer eingreift, wählt, ohne dabey weder den Allegrosätzen die angenehme und reizende Munterkeit, noch dem Instrumente das Brillante, zu entziehen.

> ... however, in this, as is generally the case in his [Viotti's] later works, a more perfect taste and a degree of artistic maturity can be observed which is far removed from mere noise and from the desire to impress by overcoming mechanical difficulties, and which on the contrary chooses the simpler and deeper in content and makes a greater impression, without thereby sacrificing either the brilliance of the instrument or the pleasing and attractive liveliness of the allegro movements.[24]

Solo passage-work is often justified musically by serving as counterpoint or embellishment for thematic material played by the orchestra. It rarely requires exceptional virtuosity, but the proportion, as opposed to the extent, of technical difficulties prescribed shows a significant increase. The use of high melodic passages, double stops with occasional tenths and frequent octave passages, and rapid, varied passage-work may demand of the soloist a remarkable left-hand facility, but rarely preoccupies him with technical obstacles. Viotti consciously avoided awkward leaps and double stopping in the high reaches of the instrument, preferring the security of the lower registers and the use of open strings for greater resonance. His conservative approach to position changing involved him in avoiding shifts whenever possible and opting for fullness of sonority and expression.[25] However, his predilection for sonorous passages on the G string did not always find favour with English audiences, one critic remarking that Viotti's 'power on the fourth string is indeed great; but, like power in general, it is liable to abuse. To speak proverbially, "He harps a little too much on one string".'[26]

Viotti's orchestra for his 'Paris' concertos comprises essentially the basic ensemble of two oboes, two horns and strings.[27] His use of these forces is conservative, particularly his unimaginative treament of the woodwind instruments, which are included only in tutti passages and rarely undertake a

---

[22] Cited in S. McVeigh, *Concert Life in London from Mozart to Haydn* (Cambridge, 1993), p. 145.
[23] *Morning Chronicle*, 15 February 1793.
[24] *Allgemeine musikalische Zeitung*, 12 October 1808, col. 28.
[25] See Baillot, *L'art du Violon*, Eng. trans., pp. 261–2.
[26] *Morning Chronicle*, 19 February 1794.
[27] Nos. 1, 9 and 19 add flutes, while No. 19 also includes clarinets in its slow movement.

VIOTTI'S 'LONDON' CONCERTOS 295

melodic role. The resultant simple texture involves the first violins in shouldering the principal melodic interest, while the cellos generally supply a simple bass-line and the second violins and violas offer appropriate harmonic support. As is evident from Table 12.1 (see p.285), Viotti took advantage of the larger orchestral forces at his disposal in London, and he gradually exploited to great effect his first-hand experience of the latest symphonic techniques of instrumentation and development. His 'London' concertos thus demonstrate a growing interest in texture, a gradual expansion in the sonority of his accompaniments, an enrichment of the tutti–solo relationship, greater independence for the woodwind (as, for example, in the first movement of No. 27), and the emancipation of the violas from doubling either the bass-line or the second violin part. As one might expect, the parts for trumpets and timpani are confined solely to tutti passages and, save for their very use, are not especially significant.

The gradual development of Viotti's instrumentation skills is most clearly evident in the contrasting middle sections of many of his slow movements, especially Nos. 23, 24, 27 and 28, where the role of the orchestra is enlarged to significant and dramatic effect. The flute has an unusually important and individual role in Nos. 23 and 24. However, the orchestration of No. 25 may be regarded as representing a backward step, the woodwind instruments largely being unimaginatively and sparingly employed, except in the finale. Like the finale of No. 28, this movement is interesting for its imitation of 'Turkish' music; more significantly, it includes a part for triangle, suggesting some possible cross-influence between this concerto and Haydn's Symphony No. 100 ('Military') composed the previous year.[28]

Haydn probably also influenced Viotti's more advanced instrumentation in No. 26. The outer movements of this concerto are outstanding for their variety of texture, their superior integration of tutti and solo, and their skilful and independent use of the wind instruments, the woodwind and horns sometimes playing a part in the solo sections. The greater independence of the violas is also noteworthy; so, too, is that of the woodwind, the two voices of the various pairs of which are often granted rhythmic and melodic freedom from each other. The flutes are favoured with the most melodic interest, but the first bassoon is occasionally allotted thematic material in combination with others. The slow movement of No. 27 displays Viotti's greater concern for subtleties of timbre and balance; a solo quartet is exploited to great effect (as in the slow movement of Haydn's Symphony No. 93), while the finale features the principal orchestral violinist and the soloist virtually as a solo duo.

The general trend of development through Viotti's 'Paris' concertos had been towards an expansion of overall structure and a greater concentration of expressive content. But the first of his 'London' concertos (No. 20) is relatively small in scale and of predominantly lyrical rather than impassioned or dramatic

---

[28] Viotti's Concerto No. 17 provides a slightly earlier example of a 'Turkish' rondo finale.

296 MUSIC IN EIGHTEENTH-CENTURY BRITAIN

character. Despite the progressive influence of Haydn, Viotti sometimes continued to write entire movements in such a retrospective style; the slow movement of No. 23, nicknamed 'John Bull',[29] is a notable example, Baillot even drawing parallels between it and the idiom of Handel. Sometimes stylistic differences are juxtaposed in the same movement, the opening theme of the first movement of No. 24, for example, contrasting markedly with the graceful, quasi-Mozartian second theme. Although much of Viotti's mature contribution to the concerto may justifiably be deemed progressive, various retrospective features can thus be readily identified, in keeping with a composer who belonged to the great eighteenth-century tradition of Italian violin playing. Indeed, one reviewer summarized this stylistic antithesis neatly in his account of a Viotti concerto: 'In style it was neither perfectly ancient nor modern, though it partook of the beauties of both.'[30] Less than two months later, a review in the same newspaper of Salomon's Ninth Concert (7 April 1794) confirms that there were differing opinions as to the merits of Viotti's mixture of old and new in his works.

> Some of the conoisseurs profess to like the playing of Viotti better than his Music. Judgements differ; we will not pretend to affirm they are mistaken; we can only say, though his Compositions partake of the old French School, yet there is a richness, unity and grandeur in them, that in our opinion place them far beyond the jigs, quirks and quackery, in which modern music is so apt to indulge.[31]

Although the 'London' concertos lack some of the boldness, brilliance and drama of the later works written for Paris, together with Mozart's last three violin concertos (K.216, 218 and 219) they constitute the finest violin concertos of the period. That Viotti believed them to be forward-looking is verified by his revisions to the last Paris concerto (No. 19) in about 1818. As Chappell White observes, Viotti shortened the work drastically, removing its most daring and unusual tonal relationship, and he brought its texture and orchestration into conformity with late eighteenth-century symphonic conventions.[32] Daniel Steibelt arranged this concerto for piano and orchestra (Paris, Naderman, 1797) and both Simrock and Janet et Cotelle later published a very different arrangement for string quartet (1816), believed to have been made by Viotti himself.[33] In its revised form, Viotti's concerto approximates more closely the tighter, more refined structures, style characteristics and Classical maturity of his 'London' concertos than the more Romantic works of its time.

The favourable reception of Viotti's 'London' concertos around the turn of the century was scarcely matched in the publishing world. Market forces in London so favoured the publication of works for the piano that many of these violin

---

[29] A. Pougin, *Viotti et l'école moderne de violon* (Paris, 1888), pp. 123–4.
[30] *Morning Chronicle*, 19 February, 1794.
[31] Ibid., 9 April 1794.
[32] E.C. White, *From Vivaldi to Viotti: a History of the Early Classical Violin Concerto* (Reading, 1992), p. 349.
[33] See E.C. White, 'Viotti's Revision of his Concerto in G minor', in *Essays on J.S. Bach and other Divers Matters: A Tribute to Gerhard Herz* (Louisville, 1981), pp. 223–34.

VIOTTI'S 'LONDON' CONCERTOS

concertos were first issued in print as arrangements for piano with or without orchestra. Piano versions of Viotti's Concertos Nos. 20, 21, 23, 25 and 26 appeared in London between *c.* 1795 and 1797, long before the publication of the original violin versions of Nos. 21 to 26, which were eventually issued by the Magasin de Musique in Paris between 1803 and 1808. No. 27 experienced even greater delay. Written in 1794 and intended for the Opera Concert series, it was first published in 1813 in a piano arrangement by J.B. Cramer; the original violin version appeared some two years later. Similarly, the violin versions of Nos. 28 and 29 were published respectively in 1823 and 1824, some twenty years or so after their composition.[34]

Because of such a remarkable delay in their public dissemination, Viotti's 'London' concertos were considered outdated by the time they became widely known, and they were soon relegated to the status of pedagogical works or competition pieces.[35] Paradoxically, they appear to have commanded less significance in real terms in Viotti's oeuvre than the concertos of the late Paris years; yet their historical importance in the development of the structural, symphonic, instrumentational, textural, tonal, expressive and, to some extent, technical aspects of the genre lead them justly to be described as the summit of the Classical, and the starting point of the Romantic violin concerto. Newspaper critics were struck by the expressive power of his works, one reviewer commenting on No. 27 as follows:

> Der um das Violinspiel so hochverdiente Veteran fährt frischen Geistes fort, i n seiner Weise, wie Jedermann sie kennet, thätig, erfreulich, nützlich zu seyn. Auch dieses, sein neuestes, vor kurzem zuerst in London producirtes Concert ist Zeuge davon; ja, man findet sich darin durch eine Lebendigkeit des Ausdrucks, selbst durch manche wahrhaft neue Wendungen, mehr als i n verschiedenen seiner frühern Concerte überrascht.

> The so highly revered veteran of violin playing continues, with fresh spirit and in his own well-known fashion, to be active, pleasing and useful. Even this, his newest concerto recently produced in London, is testimony to it; indeed, by a vitality of expression and even by truly new developments, it is more surprising than many of his earlier concertos.[36]

Viotti's corpus of violin concertos thus ranks him as arguably the most important transitional figure between Mozart and Beethoven in the history of the genre. His influence may be traced in most symphonically conceived violin concertos of the first half of the nineteenth century, whether by Rode, Kreutzer, Baillot, Spohr, David or Mendelssohn; it is still evident thereafter in the music of Brahms, who considered Viotti's Concerto No. 22 as his 'own special passion' ('ganz besondere Schwärmerei')[37] and alluded to it in his own Violin

---

[34] See White, 'Toward a more accurate chronology', 111–24.

[35] Viotti's concertos were used annually as competition pieces at the Paris Conservatoire until 1844.

[36] *Allgemeine musikalische Zeitung*, 22 May 1816, col. 359.

[37] Letter to Clara Schumann, June 1878; cited in A. Einstein's preface to the Eulenburg score of Viotti's Violin Concerto No. 22 in A minor (London, 1939).

298   MUSIC IN EIGHTEENTH-CENTURY BRITAIN

Concerto and, allegedly, other works.[38] Much of Beethoven's Violin Concerto in D may be legitimately viewed as an individual and advanced interpretation of Viotti's conception.[39] Compare, for example, the majestic character of the first movement, march-like yet lyrical, with many of Viotti's first movements; Beethoven's broad, singing passage-work, some of which displays close violinistic similarities to Viotti's models; the accompanied first-movement cadenza of Beethoven's piano transcription of his concerto (op. 61a) and the precedents in Viotti's finales; Beethoven's simple, romance-like second movement and the parallels of its concluding section with that of the equivalent movement of Viotti's Concerto No. 22; the link forged between Beethoven's second and third movements and its precedents with Viotti; the relation of Beethoven's rondo themes to those of Viotti's sixth concerto; and the more striking similarity of the end of Beethoven's work to Viotti's Concertos Nos. 20 and 24. Although nowhere near examples of full-blown Romanticism, Viotti's 'London' concertos demonstrate in melodic, tonal, harmonic, technical and textural characteristics, a progressive movement in the direction of the following century, and it is difficult to refute Alfred Einstein's claim that 'Viotti does not stand, in the development of concerto form, behind Mozart, but beside him, at least in its bearing on the next generation of musicians and especially Beethoven'.[40]

---

[38]   Bars 235–7 of the first movement of Brahms's Violin Concerto have been likened to bars 119–21 of the first movement of Viotti's Violin Concerto No.22. Some scholars, notably Max Kalbeck (in *Johannes Brahms* 3rd edn (Berlin 1912–21/R1976), vol. 4, p. 62), have even traced connections between this concerto and Brahms's Concerto for violin and cello (op. 102) and Clarinet Trio (op. 114) far beyond their common A minor tonality. See S. McVeigh, 'Viotti's Concerto No. 22', *The Strad*, 105 (1994), 343–7.
[39]   See B. Schwarz, 'Beethoven and the French Violin School', *Musical Quarterly*, 44 (1958), 431–47.
[40]   A. Einstein, in his preface to his edited score of Viotti's Violin Concerto No. 22 published by Ernst Eulenburg Ltd (London, 1939).

Index

Abel, Carl Friedrich 80, 81, 85, 94, 97, 125, 223
Abell, John 154
Aberystwyth (National Library of Wales) 230n, 268
Abingdon, Earl of 88, 98
Academy of Ancient Music 9, 72, 74, 86, 89, 98, 99, 100, 160n
Academy of Vocal Music 227, 227n
Achiapati, Lelia 33
Ackermann, Rudolf 104
Adams, Abraham 176
Adler, Guido 1
Adriano in Siria 44
Affleck, Elizabeth 216n
Agus, Giuseppe 96
Agutter, Ralph 129
Aisne 135n
Alberti, Domenico 263, 265, 265n
Albinoni, Tomaso Giovanni 2
Alcock, John (Sen.) 183, 225, 268, 274
Alcock, John (Jun.) 183, 188
Alessandria 24, 44
Alessandri, Felice 21, 22, 23, 32, 56, 26n
    Il re alla caccia 24, 56
    La moglie fedele 24, 69
Algarotti, Count Francesco 17, 18
Alkmaar 135n
Allone 43
Altieri, Angela 45
Amadei, Filippo (Pippo) 126, 128–9, 131, 132, 133n, 140
Amati, Andrea 125
Ambrosini 41
America 183n, 237
Amervoli, Francesco 37, 39
Amor fra gl'inganni 48
Amsterdam 126, 128, 144, 150, 156, 241, 272
Ancaster and Kesteren, Duke of (Peregrine) 157
Anchors, William 176
Andreani, Luigi 59
Andreoli, Giuseppe 53, 55
Anelli, Brigida Lolli 61, 63
Anfossi, Pasquale 58

Anjou, Duke of (became Louis XV) 140
Anne, Princess 194
Anne, Queen 139
Antoinette, Marie 282
Antoniotto, Giorgio 128, 143, 144, 145
Antwerp 159
Archari, Giovanni Battista 49
Arianna e Teseo 17
Ariosti, Attilio 140, 159, 228, 270
Arnaboldi, Cristofolo 65
Arne, Michael 163
Arne, Thomas Augustine 11, 95,109, 109n, 221, 227, 264
    Artaxerxes 11
    Comus 6, 10
    Judgement of Paris 10
    Judith 6
    Love in a Village 11
    O saluatris hostia 109n
    Requiem Mass 109n
Arnold, Samuel 7, 79, 82, 84, 85, 86, 92, 96, 97, 98, 100, 225
Artaria 7
Ashby, John 72n
Ashley, Charles 96, 132, 133n
Assheton Smith, Thomas (Sen.) 218n
Assheton Smith, Thomas (Jun.) 218n
Astarita, Gennaro
    Armida 66
    L'astuta cameriera 62
    La contessa di Bimbimpoli 62, 64
    La Dama immaginaria 66
Asti 146
Astorga 253
Aubert, Jacques 218, 220n
August, Edward (Duke of York) 133, 134, 147
August, George Frederic (Prince of Wales/George IV) 122, 133, 135
Auletta, Pietro 19, 217
    Il Marchese Sgrana 36
    Orazio 27
Avison, Charles 133n, 170
Aylward, Thomas 92
Ayre, R. 223
Ayrton, Edward 92, 96

300   MUSIC IN EIGHTEENTH-CENTURY BRITAIN

Bach, Johann Christian 11, 20, 24, 27, 31, 78, 80, 81, 82, 84, 85, 92, 97, 134n, 223, 264
    Concerto for two violins and a cello 134
    Endimione 58
    Orione 27n
    Vauxhall songs 5
    Zanaida 27n
Bach Johann Sebastian 2, 114, 266
Bach, Carl Philipp Emanuel 5, 246, 246n, 266
Badini, Carlo Francesco 21, 21n, 32, 33, 35, 57, 59, 63, 69
Bagliacco, Pietro Antonio 67
Bagliona, Anna Maria 51
Bagliona, Clementina 49, 51, 53
Bagliona, Francesco 37
Bagliona, Giovanna 49, 51, 53
Baglioni, Constanza 55
Baglioni, Francesco 51
Baglioni, Vincenza 49, 51, 53
Baillot, P. 289, 296, 297
Balestra, Giuseppe 51
Bambini, Anna (Tonelli) 47, 49
Ban(n)ister, Henry Charles 92
Bararini, Ottavia 41
Baratti, Cat(t)erina 39, 41
Barbandt, Charles 107–8, 108n, 111
Barbarossa, Giuseppe 47, 49
Barber, John 178
Barber, Robert 178
Barber, Thomas 235
Barby 239–40, 239n, 240n, 246, 248, 251
Barchetti, Anna 39
Baretti, Giuseppe (Marc Antonio) 18, 19, 19n, 142, 143, 144
Barham, Joseph Foster 253, 253n
Barker, John 268, 270, 273
Barlocci, Francesco 37
Barlocci, Giovanni Gualberto 37
Barsanti, Francesco 5, 73
Barthélemon, François-Hippolyte 31, 56, 86, 97, 98, 99, 217, 219, 225
Barthelemon, Mrs. 55, 57, 59, 61, 99
Bartleman, James 74, 93, 99
Bartolini, Caterina 41, 51, 67
Bartolozzi, Francesco 81, 94
Baruffi, Rosa 43
Baselt, Bernd 197n, 200
Bashford, Christina 242n
Bassanese, Giovanni Battista 32, 57
Bassani, Giovanni Battista 227, 227n

Bassano family 4, 60
Bassini, Anna 51
Basteris, Gaetano Pompeo 43
Bastiglia, Anna 39, 41
Bath 11, 12, 144, 145, 231n, 253, 266
Battaglia, Maria 61
Battishill, Jonathan 261–2
Battisti, Francesco 53
Baumgarten, Karl Friedrich 96
Beard, John 201, 209, 211
Beccari, Antonio 63
Becheroni, Gaspera 37
Bedford, Duke of 138
Bedford, Arthur 9
Bedini, Domenico 67
Beethoven, Ludwig van 11, 251n, 289, 287, 298
Bellamy, Thomas (Jun.) 93
Belle-Isle 218
Beltrami, Geltrude 59
Bemetzrieder, Anton 283
Benedetti, Pietro 45
Beni, Isabella 49, 51, 53
Benini, Nicola 51
Benjamin and Flight 88
Bennett, T. 153
Bentinck, Count William 145
Benvenuti, Giovanni 37
Berardi, Niccola 39
Berera, Giuseppe 61
Berkeley, George (Bishop of Cloyne) 143
Berkeley, Rowland 83, 98
Berlin 23 25, 26, 70, 140, 146, 241, 246, 265
Bernardi, Rosa 59
Bertati, Giovanni 63, 65
Berthelsdorf 235
Bertles, Miss 100
Bertoldino alla corte del re Alboni 42
Bertoldo Bertoldino e Cascasenno 23, 26, 40, 70–71
Bertolli 203
Bertoni, Ferdinando
    Aristo e Temira 64
    L'anello incantato 62
    Le pescatrici 44, 68
    La Vedova accorta 38
    Orfeo ed Euridice 66
Betton 213n
Bianchi, Benedetto 33, 57, 63
Bianchi, Giovanni Battista 37
Bickerstaffe, Isaac 163, 164, 166, 168
Bigari, Francesco 31, 32, 33

INDEX

301

Biggs, John 132
Bigiogero, Pietro 41, 43, 45, 47
Billings, William 183n
Billington, Thomas 96, 98, 214, 224n,
  231, 233n
Birchall, Robert 78, 93, 155, 253
Birmingham (hymn tune) 188–90
Birmingham 188n
Bishop, John 176
Bland, John 78, 79, 93, 155, 228, 242,
  242n, 243–4
Blow, John 3, 262
Blundell, James 241
Boccabianca, Girolama 37
Bocchi, Lorenzo 124, 132, 140–41,
  150
Boehm, Theobald 247
Bohemia 235
Böhler, Peter 238n
Böhme, Johann August (Günter &
  Böhme) 248n
Boini, Francesca 47
Boismortier, Joseph Bodin de 218
Bologna 36, 46, 48, 50, 68, 69, 124,
  138, 140, 141
Bombari, Carlo 47
Bonafini, Caterina 61
Bonaveri, Paolo 63
Bond, Capel 183
Bondichi, Verginio 67
Bonn 144
Bonomo, Carlo 45
Bononcini, Giovanni 9, 130, 141, 152,
  216, 217, 228, 261, 268, 268n, 270n,
  271, 272, 280
    Camilla 127, 137
    Divertimentos 266, 224n
    Griselda 193
Bordet, Toussaint 219
Borghesi, Ambrogio 37, 39
Borghesi, Tommaso 49
Borghi, Giuseppe 67
Borghi, Luigi 80, 94, 96, 99
Boroni, Antonio 64
Borselli, Anna 53
Boschetti, Mengis 59
Boscoli, Antonio 55
Bossi, Agostino 41
Bottarelli, Francesco 21, 24, 27, 28,
  30, 31, 32
Bottarelli, Giovanni Gualberto 20, 31,
  32, 33, 45, 55, 57, 59, 61, 63, 69
Bottari, Alberto 67
Botticelli 158

Bovina, Mattio 47
Bovini, Francesca 47
Bowden (Ashley Hall) 218n
Boyce, William 78, 233, 261, 263,
  268, 273
    Cathedral Music 8
    *David's Lamentations over Saul
      and Jonathan* 6
    Eight Symphonies in Eight Parts
      (op. 2) 12
    Peleus and Thetis 10
    Secular Masque 10, 12
    Solomon 12
Boyd, Malcolm 214n, 230n
Boyden, David 284n
Bracci, Luigi 53
Brahms, Johann 11, 297, 298n
Brandt, Count 247
Brascaglia, Laura 41
Breitkopf, Johann Gottlob Immanuel
  246n, 247, 248
Bremner, Robert 78, 89n, 133n, 154,
  183, 221, 228, 229
Brereton, J. 217, 218–19, 218n
Brescia 24 44, 46, 66
Bréval, Jean-Baptiste Sébastien 135n
Bristol 144
Broadway, Richard 90n
Brocchi, Giovanni Battista 67
Broderip, Francis 86
Broderip, John 225
Brogi, Caterina 37
Broome, Charlotte 245n
Broschi, Riccardo 195
Brusa, Francesco 46, 52
Brusa, Giovanni Battista 47, 53
Brussels 29, 144
Bryan, J. 226
Buckland, Brother 82
Buini, Francesca Santarelli 47, 55
Buini, Matteo 47
Bulkeley 96
Bulstrode Park 254
Burckhardt, Jacob 2
Burlington, Earl of 140
Burney, Charles 5, 7, 8, 10, 17, 18, 20,
  121–2, 121n, 125, 125n, 133, 142,
  143, 146, 159, 159n, 226, 234, 234n,
  235n, 237, 244–6, 244n, 245n, 246n,
  247, 248n, 249, 250, 250n, 253,
  254–5, 255n, 261, 265n, 269
    A General History of Music 122,
      244, 245, 263
Burney, Charlotte 242n

Burney, Fanny 242n
Burton, John (Sen.) 96
Burton, John (Jun.) 96
Bussani, Francesco 61, 63
Butler, Charles 109n, 116
Butler, James (2nd Duke of Ormonde) 138
Butts, Thomas 176
Buxton (Local Studies Library) 177n
Byrd, William 108, 176

Cadiz 24
Cajo Fabricio 36
Calandra, Nicola 46
Calcine, Nicodemo 45, 63, 65
Caldalora, Nicoló 45
Caldecote 188
Caldinelli, Giacomo 49, 51, 59
Caldinelli, Margarita 51, 53
Caldwell, John 268n
Calegari, Giuseppe 166n
Calori, Angiola 30, 45
Calzabigi, Ranieri de 67
Cambridge 145–6, 153, 252, 254n, 261
  Fitzwilliam Museum 115
  Magdalene College 251, 254n
  Trinity Hall 252
Campioni, Carlo Antonio 33
Campion, Thomas 176
Campollini, Luisa 32
Candi, Angiola 47
Canzon Novissima 54
Capelli, Giovanni Maria 217, 222
Capetown 241n
Caporale, Andrea 130–31, 132, 142, 143, 151, 152
Capua, Rinaldo di 36
Caputi, Ant 152
Carattoli, Francesco 39, 49, 51, 55
Carbonelli, Stefan 131
Cardiff 213n, 221n, 228n
Cardini, Elisabetta 61
Carestini, Giovanni 194, 195, 201, 203, 203n, 205, 208, 209–11, 212
Carey, Henry 221n
Caribaldi, Gioachino 51
Carissimi, Giacomo 227
Carlani, Carlo 39
Carmignani, Giovanna 31
Carnarvon, Earl of 127, 150
Carolan, Nicholas 150
Caroline, Princess 139
Carrattoli, Francesco 49

Caruso, Luigi 66, 124, 132, 145
Casaccia, Giuseppe 49
Casanova 28
Castelli, Anna 41
Castelli, Catterina 37
Castelli, Maria Eleonora 41
Castle Society 72, 73
Castleton 178, 183
Castrucci (brothers), 79, 140
Cattaldi, Giovanni Fabbri 59
Cattanei, Alessandro 37, 39
Cavalli, Margherita 37, 39
Cecconi, Francesco 51
Celesti, Giuseppe 47
Celle 135n
Ceni, Francesco 61
Cerri, Ferdinando 63
Cerri, Giacomo 45
Cerruti, Felice 59
Cervetto, Giacobbe Basevi (Sen.) 122n, 124, 129, 130, 132, 142, 146, 151, 152, 153
Cervetto, James (Jun.) 122, 124, 129, 132, 146, 154, 155
Cesena 58
Ceylon 235
Chaboud Pierre (Pietro) 124, 128, 129, 138, 218, 220n
Champness 97
Chandos, Duke of 138, 139
Chard 96
Charles II, King 3
Charlotte, Princess of Wales 255
Chatterton, Thomas 10
Chelleri (Keller), Fortunato 124, 128, 141–2
Cherubini, Bartolomeo 37
Cherubini, Luigi 283, 284
Chetham, John 178
Chiabrano, Gaetano 148, 154, 155
Chiabrano, Francesco 149
Chiari, P. 53, 57, 61, 63, 65, 67, 69
Chiaveri, Caterina 37
Chilcot, Thomas 6, 49, 266
Child, Elizabeth 270n
Chimenti, Margherita 37
Ciacchi, Giuseppe 37
Ciampi, Vincenzo (Legrenzio) 253
  Bertoldo, Bertoldino e Cacasenno 20, 22n, 25, 27n, 38, 68, 70
  Bertoldino alla corte del rè Alboino 27n, 44
  Il chimico 48
  I tre gobbi rivali 40

INDEX

Ciampi, Vincenzo (Legrenzio)(*cont.*)
  La favola de' tre gobbi 38
  La maestra di scola 40
  La scuola moderna 38
Ciardini, Domenico 31, 43
Cicognani, Giuseppe 47
Cioffi, Francesca 49
Cipriani, Giovanni Battisata 81, 94
Cirri, Giovanni Battisata 129, 132,
  133–4, 133n, 135, 146, 153, 155,
  156, 233n
Clagget, Walter 163n
Clark, Jane 216n
Clark, William 133n
Clarke, Jeremiah 221, 222, 268n
Clausen, Hans Dieter 163, 199, 199n,
  200
Clawson, Mary Ann 73
Cocchi, Gioacchino 20, 22, 30, 44,
  130, 153
  Il mondo della luna 22n
  La famiglia in scompiglio 24, 44
  La mascherata 22, 22n
  Le donne vendicate 22, 46, 70,
  22n
  Li matti per amore 22
  Six duets (op. 3) 225
Coghlan, J.P. 106–7
Cohen, Albert 233
Coke, Gerald 203, 208, 269, 269n,
  273, 274, 276
Colchester 9
Collins, Thomas 74, 188
Colliva, Chiara 51
Cologne 23n
Cologne, Elector of 144
Colonna, Giuseppe 61
Compassi, Ferdinando 47, 61
Compassi, Pietro 37
Compstoff, Giuseppe 39
Concert of Ancient Music 7, 188, 227,
  227n, 254
Concert Spirituel 282
Conclin, Maria 47
Coningesby, Sister 216n
Conti, Francesco 220n, 230
Conti, Vincenzo 31, 32
Cooke, Benjamin 74, 79, 86, 92, 97,
  98, 150, 157, 228
Coopere, Jean Baptiste 105n
Copenhagen 248
Coppola, Giuseppe 65, 67
Corbett, William 4
Cordicelli 96

Cornaggia, Emanuel 37, 39
Corelli, Arcangelo 8, 9, 82, 96, 127n,
  221, 227
  Sonate a tre (op. 1) 7
  Sonate da camera a tre (op. 2) 7
  Sonate a tre (op. 3) 7
  Sonate a tre (op. 4) 7
  Sonate (op. 5) 7, 126n, 266, 270
  Concerto Grossi (op. 6) 6, 9
Cosimi, Giuseppe 39, 47
Cosimi, Nicola 137, 126
Cosino, Giuseppe 39
Costanza, Giovanna Battista 130, 134,
  152, 156
Cöthen 125
Cotte, Roger 88
Cotton, Robert 82
Couperin, F. 266
Coventry 183, 188n
Cowgill, Rachel 72n
Cox, Lisa 270
Cramer, John 93, 297
Cramer, William (Wilhelm) 80, 82, 85,
  86, 88, 94, 97, 98, 99, 282
Cranach 158
Cransley 216n
Crawford, Peter 21, 31, 33
Creeke 174
Cremona 125
Cremonini, Clementina 31
Cremonini, Domenico 67
Crespi, Teresa 43, 47
Croce, Giacomo 45
Croft, William 5, 224n, 262, 268
Crosa, Dr Francesco 19
Crosdill, John 82, 85, 96, 97, 99,
  122n, 132, 146, 155
Crotch, William 99, 254–5, 254n,
  255n
Cudworth, Charles 2
Cumberland, Duchess of 85
Cumberland, Duke of 77
Curioni, Rosa 30, 45
Curtis, Thomas 233n

Dacquini, Giovanna 51
Dagge, Henry 98
Dal Fuoco, Elisabetta 59
Dall'Abaco, Giuseppe Clemente
  Ferdinando 124, 142, 144
Danby, John 79, 92
Dante, Alighieri 159
Darnley, Lady 254
Darnley, Lord 254

Dartmouth, Earl of 243
Davenport, Uriah 178–83, 188
Davesnes, Pierre 219
David, Giacomo 65
David, Paolina 65
Davis, Thomas 220n
De Amicis, Anna 17, 20, 22, 23, 25, 26, 26n, 27, 28, 29, 31
De Amicis, Domenico 22, 23, 25, 26, 26n, 28, 29, 31
Dean, Winton 171, 196–7, 200, 202–3, 203n 211
De Cristoferi, Carlo 49
De Fesch, William 5, 131, 135, 135n, 157, 165n, 226
De Fesch, Mrs 131
De Hè, Anna Chiari 43
De la Faye, Charles 138
De Michele, Leopoldo 31, 32
Del Zanca, Michele 22, 47, 53, 57, 59
Della Nave, Agnese 45
Delpini, Giovanni 51
Demena, Marianna 57, 59
Denbigh 96
Derby 188, 237
Desaguliers, John 78
Des Mullins 99
Dessales, Filippo 41
Dessau 239
De Torres, Joseph 216
Deutsch 211
Dibdin, Charles 82, 90–91, 90n, 222, 228
   Shakespear's Garland 226
   The Lyrist 90n
Didone abbandonata 28
Dieupart, Charles 5
Digby, 5th Baron of (William) 216n
Dighton, Robert 92, 92n
Dignum, Charles 93
Di Marzis, Pasqualino 130, 132, 142, 143, 144, 152
Dittersdorf, Carl Ditters von 9
Dobney, Michael 229–30
Dodd, William 84
Dolben family 216, 216n, 227
Don Calascione 19, 36
Dondi, Giuseppe 43, 47
Dorpat 234n, 249n, 250n, 251n, 253n
Dors, Louis 105n
Dothel, Nicolas 226
Drage, Sally 4
Draghi, Giovanni Battista 3
Drake, Francis 216n

Dresden 135, 217, 242
Dryden, John 10
Du Monchau Charles 219, 225
Dublin 23, 23n, 26, 26n, 27, 27n, 29, 68, 90n, 131, 140, 143, 144, 150
Dubourg, Matthew 81
Ducci, Giuseppe 39
Duckford, J. 155
Duckinfield 237
Dundas, Thomas 155
Dudley 184
Duni, Egidio (Romualdo) 145, 218, 218n, 219
Dunstable, John 8
Dunvault 96
Duport, Jean-Pierre 98, 132
Dupuis, Thomas Sanders 79, 86, 92, 97
Durante, Francesco 114
Dyne, John 92

Eberardi, Teresa 23, 23n, 30, 45, 55
Eccles, Henry 156
Eccles, John 4, 5, 221, 222
Edinburgh 129, 133n, 140, 141, 144, 145
Egmont 122n, 127, 143
Einstein, Alfred 297n, 298, 298n
Elbe 239, 248
Elgar, Edward 2
Elisi, Filippo 17, 30, 39
Eliot, George 175
Emiliani, Sebastiano 41
Essex 252
Evans, Sir Herbert 213n

Fabri, Luca 51
Faenza 50
Fanti, Eugenia Mellini 37
Farinelli (Broschi, Carlo Farinello) 59, 195
Farnassi, Gaetano 53
Fasciatelli, Antonia 47
Federico, Gennaro Antonio 37
Felice, Evaristo 124, 144
Felloni, Lodovico 53
Felton, William 6, 79, 230
Feo, F. 217
Fentum, J. 219
Ferrabosco, Alfonso I 3
Ferretti, Agata 49
Festing, Michael Christian 143, 270, 274
Fétis, François-Joseph 284n

INDEX

305

Field, John 93
Finger, Gottfried/Godfrey 5
Fini, Michele 36
Finzi, Gerald 133n
Fischer, Johann Christian 81, 85, 88, 97, 98, 99, 25, 231
Fisher, Johann Abraham 79, 84–5, 92, 95, 96, 97, 99
Fischietti, Domenico 70
    Il mercato di Malmantile 44, 48, 52, 56, 68, 70
    Il signor dottore 25, 48, 50, 52, 54, 60, 69
    La fiera di Sinigaglia 48
    La ritornata di Londra 46
    Lo speziale 52, 69
Fiske, Roger 160–63, 166, 171, 233
Flackton, William 226
Flemming (Fleminiani), Francis 124
Fletcher, I. D. 224
Florence 21, 22, 36, 38, 40, 42, 66
Florio, Pietro Grassi 226
Focchetti, Vincenzo 59, 63
Folicaldi, Sebastiano 63, 65
Forster, John 216n
Forster, William 155, 247
Foschi, Alessandro 59
Fought, Henry 156
Frankfurt 146
Frederick, William II (Prince of Wales) 77, 86, 122n, 127, 131, 134, 146, 150, 151
Freemasons Society 85, 88
Freydt, Johann Ludwig 241
Frezza, Girolamo 126n
Fripp, Samuel 254
Fryer, William Victor 118
Fulneck 237, 239, 239n, 240, 240n, 252, 253
Fumagalli, Caterina 39

Gabri, Luca 51
Gabrieli, Caterina 43
Gaggiotti, Pellegrino 37
Galeazzi, Giuseppe 51, 53
Galeotti, Stefano 129, 130, 153, 154, 155
Galeotti, Vittoria 47
Gallia, Maria Margarita 148
Galliard, John Ernest 9, 90, 130, 131, 135, 135n, 151, 157, 222, 226
Gallo, Anna 45, 61
Galuppi, Antonio 51, 53, 55, 57, 69

Galuppi, Baldassare 5, 24, 265
    Gli amanti ridicoli 56, 59
    I bagni d' Abano 70
    Il caffè di campâgna 52
    Il conte Carmella 27n, 46
    Il filosofo di campagna 20, 42, 44, 46, 48, 50, 54, 68
    Il mondo della luna 25, 44, 68
    Il re alla caccia 69
    La calamita de cuori 68
    La diavolessa 46
    La donna di governo 50
    La Lavandra (Il marchese villano) 62
    Le Arcifanfano re de'mati 48
    Le nozze 25, 46, 48, 52
    Le nozze di Dorina 68, 70
    L'Ipermestra 42
    Li tre amanti ridicoli 50, 54
Gambier, Admiral James 251
Gambier, Rev 251
Ganassetti, Bartolo 49, 51
Garcia, Manuel 117
Garibaldi, Giovacchino 67
Garner, Alan 175
Garrick, David 10, 163
Garth, John 133–4, 133n
Gartini 224, 226
Gaschi, Ann 37
Gass, Jacques 105n
Gassmann, Florian Leopold 21, 56
Gates, Bernard 159
    L'isola di Alcina 62
    Il calandrano 64
Geary, John 188
Geminiani, Francesco 5, 9, 73, 73n, 78, 79, 82, 130, 139, 151–2, 228
    Concerti Grossi (op. 2) 5, 6
    Concerti Grossi (op. 3) 5, 6
    Concerti Grossi (op. 7) 5
George I, King 139, 141
George II, King 194
George III, King 77, 146, 254
Gerber, Ernst Ludwig 121n
Gerome 245
Gheradi, Giovanni Battista 67
Ghezzi, Ambrogio 41, 43
Giacomazzi, Teresa 32, 57
Giardini, Domenico 43, 45
Giardini, Felice 80–81, 94, 99, 145, 170, 223, 224n
Giazotto, Remo 284n
Gibbons, Edward 10

306   MUSIC IN EIGHTEENTH-CENTURY BRITAIN

Gibetti, Margherita 31, 32, 55, 57, 61
Giordani, Maria 59
Giordani, Tommaso 5, 23, 56, 58, 130
    Six duets for two cellos 155, 225
    Il padre e il figlio rivali 25, 56,
      62, 69
Giorgi, Anna 49, 53
Giornovichi, Giovanni 282
Giovacchina, Maria 65
Giovannola, Alessandro 61, 63
Giraudoux, Jean 158
Giuliani, Massino (Mauro) 63, 65
Giustinelli, Giuseppe 31, 49, 51
Glee Club 75, 79
Gli intrighi per amore 23n, 27n
Gli stravaganti 54, 60
Gli uccellatori 24n
Gloucester 269
Gloucester, Duke of 133n, 134, 146,
    153, 154
Gluck, Christoph Willibald 242, 289
Gnoll 213n
Goldoni, Carlo 20, 21, 22, 24, 39, 43,
    45, 47, 49, 51, 53, 55, 57, 59, 61, 68,
    69, 70
Goodsens, Francisco 124, 128, 138
Gordon, Alexander 140
Gordon, John 20, 21 31, 32, 33, 132,
    142
Gore, Israel 92
Goresi, Vincenzo 45, 63, 65
Gori, Anna 32, 57
Görlitz 239, 246
Gorri, Nicola 39
Gothenberg 248
Gould, William 220
Gozzi, Carlo 47
Grabu, Louis 218
Gradati, Carlo Ambrogio 43
Graf, Frederich Hartmann 249
Grandatis, Ambrogio Gian 43
Granier, François 219
Granom, Lewis Christian Austin 220,
    223, 253
Grassi, Cecilia 33, 59
Graun, Carl Heinrich 240, 242, 252,
    253
Gray, Thomas 20, 96
Graziani, Carlo 146
Great Gidding 173n
Greatorex, Thomas 188
Greatorex, Anthony 188–90
Green, James 178
Green, John 178

Green, Samuel 89
Greene, Maurice 6, 78, 159
Greenland, Augustus 80
Gregor, Christian 240
Grevile, Fulke 269
Grevile, Mary 269
Grosse, Samuel 94
Guadagni, Angela 53
Guadagni, Gaetano 18, 33, 67
Guadagni, Giuseppe 47
Guadagni, Lavinia 21, 23n, 32, 33, 47,
    51, 53, 55, 57, 63
Guarducci, Tomasso 31, 32
Guerini, Francesco 153
Guglielmi, Lelia 59
Guglielmi, Pietro 21, 22, 32, 33, 56,
    62
      I viaggiatori ridicoli 24, 24n, 25,
        26n, 69
      *I viaggiatori ridicoli tornati in
        Italia* 21, 56, 58
      *Il carnovale di Venezia (o sia La
        virtuosa)* 58
      Il disertore 24, 58, 62, 66, 69
      Il ratto della sposa 22, 23n, 54,
        60, 69
      L'assemblea 58
      L'impresa d'opera 64
      *La costanza di Rosinella (La
        sposa fedele)* 56, 62, 69
      La sposa fedele 22, 22n, 62, 64
      Le pazzie di Orlando 56, 58
      Lo spirito di contradizione 60
Guichard, John 93
Gwilt, Joseph 116

Hadow, W. H. 235n
Haeser, Miserere 248
Hallet, Benjamin 132
Halton, Janet 234n, 239n
Hamburg 163, 234n, 247, 248n, 283
Hamill, John 72n
Hamilton and Brandon, Duke of
    (James) 150
Hammersley, Thomas 86
Hanbury family 214, 215, 216n, 219,
    219n
Handel, George Frideric 2, 4, 5, 6–8, 9,
    10, 77, 78, 79, 82, 83, 84, 116, 143,
    158, 160, 171, 188, 221, 223, 226,
    226n, 227, 228, 229, 241, 250, 251,
    252, 253, 254, 255–6, 261, 262, 263,
    264, 266n, 268, 268n, 269, 270n

INDEX

307

Handel, George Frideric (*cont.*)
  Acis and Galatea (HWV 49) 88,
    143, 193, 194
  Alcina (HWV 34) 196, 226
  Alexander's Feast (HWV 75) 10,
    134
  Ariodante (HWV 33) 195
  Brockes Passion 200
  Concerti Grossi (op. 3) (HWV
    312–17) 5, 6
  Concerti Grossi (op. 6) (HWV
    319–30) 5, 6
  Deborah (HWV 51) 193, 194, 196,
    198, 203
  Dettingen Te Deum (HWV 283)
    252, 255
  Esther (HWV50) 159–60, 159n,
    165n, 193, 195–6, 195n, 203,
    205
  Il Parnasso in festa (HWV 73)
    194, 197, 198, 199, 200, 202,
    211
  Il pastor fido (HWV 8) 194, 197,
    200
  Il trionfo del Tempo e della Verita
    (HWV 46) 202
  Jeptha (HWV 70) 252
  Keyboard Concerto (op. 4) (HWV
    318) 6
  *L'Allegro, il Penseroso ed il
    Moderato* (HWV 55) 5
  Messiah (HWV 56) 85, 97, 193,
    242, 252, 254, 255
  Ode for St Cecilia's Day (HWV
    76) 10
  Overture in F (HWV 342) 200
  Rinaldo (HWV 7) 220n
  Samson (HWV 57) 252
  Silete venti (HWV 242) 203
  *Six fugues for organ (HWV
    605–10)* 6
  Six Overtures (2nd, 3rd, 4th coll)
    230
  Six Overtures (5th collection) 230
  Six Overtures (7th collection) 230
  Six Overtures (8th collection) 230
  Solo/Trio Sonatas (op. 1, 2, 5) 7
  Sonata in C (HWV 577) 272
  Terpsichore (HWV 8) 194
  'This is the Day which the Lord
    hath made' (HWV 262) 194, 199
  Wake the Lute 84
  'Zadok the Priest' (HWV 258) 84,
    85, 95, 96, 97

Hanover 139, 141, 216n
Hanover, Electress of (Sophia) 139
Hardy, Thomas 175
Harington, Dr Henry 253
Harrison & Co. 223
Harrison, Ralph 188
Harrison, Samuel 79, 92, 92n, 96, 98,
  99
Harrop, Miss 99
Hartley 251
Harvard University 131n
Hase, H.,253
Hasse, J. A. 217, 221, 222, 222n, 229,
  240, 253, 254
  Artaxerxes 195–6
  Attilio Regolo 215n, 217,
  Cleofide 215n, 217
  Didone abbandonata 215n, 217
  Il Ciro riconosciuto 217
  Il Tigrane 217, 220
  Sei Concerts (op. 5) 230
  Sei Sonate a tré (op. 2) 230
  Six Concertos in 8 parts (op. 4)
    230
  Six Sonatas or Trios 230
  Twelve Concertos in Six Parts
    (op.3) 230
Hawkins, John 10, 140, 241, 271
Haydn, Joseph 2, 5, 8, 81,81n, 89, 97,
  114, 115, 116, 133, 184, 223, 228,
  234n, 239, 241, 242, 243, 246,
  247–8, 249, 251n, 252, 254, 255,
  255n, 283, 284, 289, 290, 291, 292,
  296
  Aus dem Danklied zu Gott
    (Hob.XXVc:8) 257
  Il ritorno di Tobia (Hob.XXI:1)
    257, 258
  'London' Symphonies (Nos.
    93–104) 286
  Missa brevis Sancti Joannis de
    Deo ('Little Organ Solo Mass')
    (Hob.XXII:7) 257
  Missa Cellensis in honorem
    B.V.M (Missa Sanctae Caeciliae)
    (Hob.XXII:5) 257
  Missa in angustiis ('Nelson
    Mass') (Hob.XXII:11) 257
  Missa in honorem Beatissimae
    Virginis Mariae ('Great Organ
    Solo Mass') (Hob.XXII:4) 248n,
    258

308 MUSIC IN EIGHTEENTH-CENTURY BRITAIN

Haydn, Joseph (*cont.*)
  Missa in tempore belli
    ('Paukenmesse') (Hob.XXII:9)
    247, 257
  Missa Sancti Bernardi de Offida
    ('Heiligmesse') (Hob.XXII:10)
    247, 257
  Missa Sancti Nicolai
    (Hob.XXII:6) 257
  'Paris' Symphonies (Nos. 82–7)
    284
  Quartets (op. 20) 241, 242
  Quartets (op. 50) 247, 247n
  'Rider' Quartet (op. 74, no. 3) 290
  Stabat Mater (Hob.XXbis) 234n,
    242, 252, 257, 258
  Symphony No. 99, 290
  Symphony No. 100 ('Military')
    295
  Symphony No. 103 ('Drumroll')
    290
  Symphony No. 104 ('London')
    292
  Te Deum (Hob.XXIIIc:2) 247
  The Creation (Hob.HXXI:2),524
  The Seven Last Words (Hob.XX:2)
    242n, 258
Hayes, William 75, 183
Haym, Nicola Francesco 124, 126–7,
  126n, 131, 137
Hebbel, Friedrich 158
Hebden, John 220, 220n
Hellendaal, Peter 5, 184
Henry VII, King 3
Henry VIII, King 3, 4
Hereford 6
Heron, Claudius 153
Herrnhut, 235, 236n
Herschel, Sir William 5, 133n
Hesse-Kassel 141
Hill, John 188
Hill, Rowland 243
Hill, Sir Richard 243
Hill, Thomas 125n
Hindle, John 92, 92n
Hindmarsh 98
Hinner 99
Hobart, George 21, 33
Hobler, John Paul (Jun.) 92
Hoboken, Antony van 241
Hogarth, William 160, 160n
Holland, Henry 86
Holman, Peter 10n, 11n, 12n, 221

Holmes, Edward 234, 234n, 235, 241,
  242, 256
Holmes, Valentine 226
Holzbauer, Ignaz (Jakob) 166n
Honegger 158
Hook, James 220, 223, 230
Horace 88
Horne 239n
Howard, Dr Samuel 221n, 233
Hubertusberg 217
Huggins, William 159–60, 159n,
  160n, 164, 165n, 166, 168
Hughes, Thomas 175
Hüllmandel 285n
Humane Society 99
Hume, Robert 131n, 140n
Hummel, A. 154, 228, 229
Hummel, J. 155, 241
Humphreys, Samuel 193
Huntingdon Library 160n
Huss, John 245
Huttley 100
Hutton, James 237, 244

I francesci in Corsica 21
Il disertore 26
Il filosofo di campagna 23, 26, 27n,
  28, 29, 69
Il farnace 44
Il mercato di Malmantile 23n, 69
Il mondo alla roversa 42, 46
Il mondo della luna 25, 27n, 42, 46,
Il signor dottore 50
*Il tutor burlato (Il filosofo di
  campagna)* 23n, 24n, 26n
Il tutore e la pupilla 24, 26, 26n, 27,
  27n, 28, 68
Il virtuose ridicole 27n
Imer, Mariana 37
Imer, Teresa 37
Irving, Howard 254n
Isaurence, Alcindo 53, 55, 68
I tre gobbi rivali 44
I viaggiatori ridicoli 23, 26, 58

Jackson, William 221
Jacob, Margaret 73
Jacques, Jean Baptist 104
James I, King 3
James II, King 104, 138
Janson, Jean-Baptist 104
Jazzi, Domenico 43
Jennens, Charles 202, 202n, 203
Johnson, Dr 237n, 256,

INDEX

309

Johnson, John 133, 144, 150, 151, 152, 153, 154, 157, 183, 228, 263, 273
Johnston, Arthur 226
Johnston, John 228
Joltham, Revd. J. 216n
Jommelli, Niccolò 17, 160
  Don Trastullo 54
  L'uccellatrice 46, 56
Jones, David Wyn 241
Joseph I 140, 141
Jowett, Dr Joseph 252, 252n, 253, 254, 254n, 255n
Jowett, Henry 251–2, 254n
Jowett, John 251–2
Jowett, Rev Henry 251
Jozzi, Giuseppe 265n

Kalbeck, Max 298n
Kammel, Antonín 81, 94
Karl, Landgrave 141
Kaas, Baron 88, 98
Kassler, Jamie Croy 255n
Kearsly, George 228
Kelly, Earl Thomas Alexander Erskine 94
Kettering 216n
Key, Elizabeth 188n
Key, Joseph 188, 188n
Kirchhoff, J. A. 94, 99
Kirkby, Emma 216n
Kirkpatrick, Ralph 266
Knyvett, Charles 79, 92, 92n
Kozeluch, Leopold 249
Kreutzer, R 297

La Betulia liberata 64
La buona figliuola 19, 23, 26, 28, 56, 58, 62
La campagna 60
Labrador 237
La calamità de' cuori 23
Lacey [Lacy], Willoughby (Lacy, Michael Rophino) 93
La cascina 23n, 26n
La Chevardière 218–19, 228
La commedia in commedia 19
La costanza di Rosinella (La sposa fedele) 28
La Didone abbandonata 44
La facendiera 23, 38, 40, 42
La favola de' tre gobbi 23, 40
La fiammetta 36
La finta sposa 23n, 27n

Lambertini, Giacomo 45, 61
Lamotte, Franz 97
Lampe, John Frederick 5
Lamperini, Domenico 61
Landi, Artemisia 39
Landi, Margherita 39
Lanetti, Gaetano 37, 39
Lang 96
Languedoc 234n
Lanzetti, Salvatore 129, 130, 132, 135, 142, 143, 150, 151, 153
Lapis, Santo 153
L'Arcadia in Brenta 40, 42
La schiava 23
Laschi, Filippo 37, 49, 51, 55, 63, 67
Laschi, Giuseppe 37
Laschi, Gaetano 37
La semplice spiritosa 38
La serva padrona 28
Latilla, Gaetano 19, 36, 38, 68
Latrobe, Benjamin Henry 80, 238n, 239, 239n, 243, 243n, 245n
Latrobe, Charlotte 251n
Latrobe, Christian Ignatius 80
Latrobe, John Antes 239n
Latrobe, John Frederick 243n, 246, 247n, 249, 249n, 250n, 251, 251n, 253, 253n
Latrobe, John Henry 234n, 243n, 250n, 251n, 253n
Latrobe, Peter 239n
La vedova accorta 42
La vedova spiritosa 38
La vilanella 48
La virtuosa moderna 38
Le Cène, Michel Charles 128, 142, 156
Le Clerc, Charles Nicolas 135, 148, 151, 152, 153, 155
Leeds 103n, 237, 239, 251
Leek, 178
Legge, George (3rd Earl of Dartmouth) 254
Legge, William (2nd Earl of Dartmouth) 243
Leghorn, Livorno 36
Leibniz 140
Leicester 188n
Leiffler 96
Leipzig 242, 247, 248, 249
Lemaire, Nicolas 217, 219
Lenton, John 224n
Leo, Leonardo 36, 217
Leonardi, Giovanni 41, 43, 47, 51
Leonardi, Pietro 30, 43, 45

310 MUSIC IN EIGHTEENTH-CENTURY BRITAIN

Leonhardi, Johann 81, 88, 98
Leoni, Pietro Maria 42
Leopold I 141
Le pescatrici 23n
Le serve rivali 26, 26n
Leveridge, Richard 212n
Le vicende della sorte 56
Lewis, Frederick (Prince of Wales) 122
Library of the United Grand Lodge 84, 95
Lichfield Cathedral 184
Liesem, R. 153
Light, Edward 225, 231
Lindeleim, Joanna Maria 148
Lindley, Robert 121, 122, 132, 133, 148
Lindley, William 121n
Linley, Thomas (Jun.) 6, 10, 11, 12, 97
L'innamorate del cicisbeo 60
Linton 96
Lisbon 24, 62, 64, 141
Lodi, Francisco 42, 138
L'Olimpiade 36, 44
Lombardi, Giuseppa 45
London 3, 4, 5, 6, 9, 121, 122, 122n, 124, 125, 125n, 126, 126n, 127, 129, 131, 132, 133n, 135, 135n, 137, 138, 139, 140, 141, 142, 143, 144, 145, 146, 147, 148, 149, 159, 163, 172, 213, 217, 217n, 218–19, 218n, 221, 222, 222n, 223, 223n, 224, 225, 227, 228, 233, 234, 235, 237, 240n, 241, 242, 243, 244, 246, 247, 249, 250, 255, 256, 265, 266, 270
  Apollo Gardens 163n
  Blackfriars (Surrey Chapel) 243
  British Library 35, 163, 235, 270
  Chapel Royal 128, 128n, 138, 194, 261, 268, 273
  Cheapside 263
  Chelsea 245
  Christie's 269n, 274
  City of London Lying in Hospital 99
  Covent Garden Theatre 79, 81, 90, 117, 160, 163, 168, 194–5, 199, 196n
  Crown and Anchor Tavern 89, 159
  Drury Lane Theatre 83, 131, 142, 144, 163, 168, 224, 250
  Duke Street 104
  Fetter Lane 237, 237n, 238, 238n, 240n, 244, 252

London (*cont.*)
  Fleet Street 235n
  Freemasons Hall 73, 74, 81, 82, 83, 88–9, 95, 96
  Freemasons Tavern 79, 83
  General Lying-In Hospital 100
  Golden Square 103–4
  Great Queen Street 83
  Grosvenor Chapel 103, 103n
  Hanover Square (Rooms) 88, 282, 283
  Haymarket (Little)Theatre 90, 163
  Haymarket 145
  Hickford's 131, 143, 152
  Holborn 243
  King's Theatre (Queen's Theatre / Haymarket / Opera House) 4, 54, 134, 138, 139, 143, 146, 147, 193, 194–5, 224n, 249, 250, 283
  Kingsway 104
  Lincoln's Inn Fields 104, 159, 221n
  Lock Hospital 171
  Marybone Gardens 90
  Marylebone 221
  Middlesex Hospital 99
  Mitre Tavern 82
  Muswell Hill 234n
  National Gallery 122n
  Nevil's Court 237n
  Pantheon Theatre 147, 249
  Parliament 126, 221
  Queen Square 76n
  Royal College of Music 268
  Royal Cumberland Freemasons' School 85, 97
  South Audley Street 103
  Southwark, Newington Butts 251–2
  South Street 103, 117
  St Anselm and St Cecilia, Kingsway 104
  St George's Fields 86
  St James Street 81
  St Pauls 84, 96, 261
  The Strand 145
  Thatched House Tavern 81
  Twickenham 10
  Vauxhall Gardens 81, 142
  Warwick Street 103–4
  Westminster 221
  Westminster Abbey 7, 188
Longazo, George 150

INDEX

311

Longini, Lucrezia 37
Longman and Broderip 155, 156, 219, 222, 223, 228, 229, 231
Longoni, Maria 37
Lonsdale, R. 234n
Lo speziale 26, 26n
Lottini, Antonio 37
Loughborough 173
Louis, Frederick 135
Lovattini, Giovanni 18, 21, 22, 23, 25, 31, 32, 33, 46–59, 61, 63
Lovett, James 216n
Lovicina, Signora 148
Lucca 38, 73, 125, 140
Luciani, Domenico 32, 57
Lucio Silla 17
Ludwig, Nikolaus 235n
Lully, Jean-Baptiste 218, 228
Lungi, A.,51
Lupo family 4
Luther, John C.,92, 96, 245

Mace, Thomas 225–6
Machon 96
Macklin 10
Mackworth, Digby 214, 221, 231, 231n
Mackworth, Eliza 214, 231
Mackworth, Elizabeth 216n
Mackworth, Elizabeth Anne 216n
Mackworth, Herbert (Sen.) 213, 215, 216n, 218, 221n, 222
Mackworth, Sir Herbert (Jun.) 213–15, 220, 213n, 216n, 221, 221n, 222, 222n, 225, 226, 227, 229
Mackworth, Humphrey 213, 213n, 214n, 215, 221n, 230
Mackworth, Juliana 214
Mackworth, Mary 213n, 214
Mackworth, Robert 214–15, 214n, 219n
Mackworth, William Morgan 230
Macoise, Miss 217, 219
Macpherson, James 10
Madrid 141
Madrigali, Domenico 59
Magdeburg 239
Maggini, Maria 39
Maggioni, Gaetano 37
Maggiore, Francesco 36
Maggiore, Angelica 32, 55
Magito, Alexis (Sen.) 124, 132
Magito, Alexis (Jnr.) 124, 144, 145, 153

Maguire, Mrs 99
Mahon 98, 240n
Mainwaring, John 7
Mallet, John 82
Manchester 184
    Cross Street Unitarian Chapel 188
    Droylsden 237, 237n
    Fairfield 237, 237n
    John Rylands Library 235, 243
Manchester, Duke of 88, 98
Manfredini, Francesco Onofroi / Vincenzo 32
Mannheim 147
Mann, Horace 22, 22n
Mantua, Duke of 140
Manzoletto, Angiolo Monani 65
Manzuoli, Giovanni 18
Mara, Johann Baptist 132
Mara, Getrude 249
Marcello, Benedetto 130, 150, 226, 252
Marchesi, Antonio 63, 65
Marchesi, Luigi 59
Marchetti, Baldassare 59
Mareschi, Marco Antonio 41, 65
Markstrom, Kurt 222n
Marlborough, Duchess of (Henrietta) 141
Marmaduke, J. 106n
Marpurg, Friedrich Wilhelm 246, 265, 265n
Marrochini, Giuseppe 53
Marsh, John 9
Martin, Charlotte 249
Martinelli, Gaetano 55, 61, 69
Martinenghino, Carlo 43
Masi, Violante 39
Masi-Tibaldi, Angela 53
Mason, John 234n
Mason, Robert 132, 133n
Mattei, Colomba 20, 21, 24, 30, 31
Mattheson, Johannn 224, 245, 261
Mawhood, William 108–9, 108n, 109n, 111
Mazzinghi, Joseph 96
Mazzola, Teresa 43
Mazzoni, A. 50
McVeigh, Simon 149
Megrino, Giuseppe 48
Meighan, Thomas (Sen.) 106n
Meisner Giuseppe 41
Melini, Grazia 37
Meloni, Antonio 126n

312   MUSIC IN EIGHTEENTH-CENTURY BRITAIN

Mendelssohn, Felix 11, 284, 290
Mercier, Philippe 122n
Metastasio, Pietro 39, 41, 43, 59, 63, 65, 71, 158, 166n
Micheli 55, 57, 59, 61
Michelon, Mlle 152
Middleton, Sir Charles 243
Migliavacca, Giann'Ambrogio 67
Miers, Mary Anne 214
Milan 17, 40, 42, 44, 46, 48, 50, 52, 70, 144, 147
Milhous, Judith 131n, 140n
Milton, John 5, 89
Mocci, Francesca 47
Modena 141
Monari, Maria 47
Mondina, Ippolita 43
Money, John 76, 77, 83
Mongeri, Francesco 63
Mongis, Teresa 45
Montanari, Teresa 63
Monteverdi, Claudio 2, 8
Moore, G. 233
Morati, Vincenzo 53
Moravian Society for the Furtherence of the Gospel (SFG) 237, 238, 238n, 243n
Morelli, Giovanni 63
Moreschi, Lucia 55
Morgan, Bonner 213n
Morgan, Deiniol 266, 268
Morigi, Andrea 31, 32, 33, 55, 57, 59, 61, 63
Moritz, Carl Philipp 174
Morone, Francesco 49, 51
Moroney, Davitt 264, 265n, 273
Mortellari, Michele 64
Mortensen, Lars Ulrik 261n
Moser, Francesco 31, 32
Mozart, Wolfgang Amadeus 8, 12, 17, 114, 115, 116, 146, 147,166n, 248, 251n, 252, 255, 255n, 286n, 289, 296, 297
   Davidde penitente (K.469) 257
   Don Giovanni (K.527) 248
   Incidental Music: King Thamos (K.345/KE.336a) 257, 258
   Litaniae de Venerabili (K.125) 257, 258
   Litaniae de Venerabili (K.243) 257, 258
   Mass in C ('Coronation Mass') (K.317) 257
   Mass in C (K.257) 257

Mozart, Wolfgang Amadeus (*cont.*)
   Missa brevis ('Organ Solo Mass') (K.259) 247
   Missa brevis ('Sparrow Mass') (K.220) 247
   Missa brevis (K.192/KE.186f) 257
   Missa brevis (K.194/KE.186h) 257
   Missa Brevis (K.275/KE.272b) 257, 258
   Piano concertos 287
   Requiem (K.626) 118, 247, 254, 257
   Symphony in C (K.162) 248n
   Vesperae de Dominica (K.321) 257
   Violin concertos 12, 286, 296
Mozart, Leopold 124, 145, 147
Mozart, Nannerl 118, 146
Munich 1, 124, 144
Muschietti, Giuseppe 59

Naldi, Giuseppe 117
Nanes 263
Naples 20, 28, 141, 143, 145, 216n, 217
Napoleon 234n, 247
Napolioni, Antonio 61, 63
Nas(z)olini, Antonio 61
Neal, John 150
Neal, William 150
Neath 213, 227, 230n
Negri, Pasquale 37
Negri, Rosa 212
Negro, Maria 211
Nelson, Claire 72n
Nestroy, Johann 158
Nettlebed 175
Neukomm, Sigismund 248
Newcastle 95
Newman, W. S. 130n
Nicholson, Mary 268, 269–70
Nield, Jonathan 93
Niesky 239, 239n, 241–2, 246, 247, 248
Nobleman and Gentlemen's Catch Club 75, 79, 227, 227n
Nofere 96
Non nobis Domine 176
Noorthouck 93
Noris, Matteo 37
Norman, Edward 104
Norris, Thomas 84, 85, 95, 96, 97

INDEX

313

North, Roger 9, 126n
Notari, Angelo 3
Novara 42
Novelli, Felice 47
Novello, Mary 117
Novello, Vincent 103n, 107, 111, 112, 113, 113n, 114, 116n, 117, 118, 234n, 242, 242n, 247n, 248, 248n, 249, 249n, 250n, 251, 251n
Nuneaton 188, 188n

Ockbrook 257
Oldbury 174
Old Field 96
Olleson, Philip 80n
Opera Concerts 283, 284, 297
Opera of the Nobility 193, 194, 195–6, 265
Orazio 19, 27n, 36,
Orlandi, Appolonia 61
Orlandini, Giuseppe Maria 41
    Arsace 40
    Catone in Utica 40
    Lo scialacquatore 42
    Lo scialacquatore alla fiera 36
Orti, Giuseppe 49
Osmond, Thomas 92, 92n
Oswald, James 76, 76n, 228,
Ottani, Bernardo 60, 64
Ottley, William Young 253, 253n
Oxford 175, 193, 194, 196, 197, 199, 200
    Bodleian Library 235
    Magdalen College 227
    Sheldonian Theatre 193
    University 84, 97, 254
    Worcester College 254–5

Padua 38, 40, 46, 70, 216n
Paganini, Carlo 20, 22, 22n, 23, 24, 25, 26, 27n, 30, 37, 39, 41, 43, 45, 71
Paganini, Maria Angiola 20, 22, 23, 24, 25, 26, 27, 27n, 30, 36–45, 71
Page, John 93
Pagnanelli, Luigi 63
Paisible, Jacques/James 5, 128
Paisiello Giovanni
    Le due contesse 66
    Le nozze disturbate 60
Palermo 44
Palestrina, Giovanni Pierluigi 8, 9
Pallavicini, V. 52, 69
Palomba, Antonio 37, 39, 51, 53
Papendiek, Christoph 81, 94

Pardini, Charles 139–40, 140n
Pardini, Father Pier Vincenzo 124, 133n, 140
Parigi, Maria Maddalena 39
Paris 135, 135n, 140, 141, 148, 149, 151, 155, 218–19, 233, 282, 283, 284, 296, 297, 297n
Parisina, Margarita 47, 51
Parma 141
Parry, Hubert 2
Parsons, William 93
Pasquali, Francis 144
Pasquali, Niccolò 131, 131n, 132, 144, 151, 223
Pasqualini, Giuseppe 53
Passia, Angela 67
Passionei, Carlo 128
Pavia 42
Paxton, George 111
Paxton, Stephen 109, 224n, 225, 231
Paxton, William 132
Pearmain, Andrew 85n
Pellegrini, Ferdinando 224n
Pellerino 43
Pellicioni, Eusebio 67
Pemberton, J. 96
Pembroke, Earl of 154
Penachi, Anna 45
Penni, Serafina 47
Pepusch, Johann Christoph 9, 268n
Percy, Thomas 10
Peretti, Nicola 41
Perez, David 116
Pergolesi, Giovanni Battista 28, 36, 114, 253
Perillo, Salvatore 60
Persichino, Giovanni, Battista 49
Pertici, Pietro 37
Peruzzi, Luiggia 39
Peruzzi, Luisa 37
Pescetti, Giovanni Battista 265, 265n, 266
Pesci, Antonio 61, 63
Pessina, Rosa 47
Petre, Lord 78
Petri, Niccola 43
Petrosellini, Giuseppe 53, 57, 65, 67
Philidor 88, 98
Piantanida, Francesco de 154
Piatti, Lorenzo 33, 57, 63, 67
Piatti, Teresa 31, 32, 33, 45, 51, 55, 57, 61, 63
Piazza, Gaetano 42
Pichl, Václav 249

314   MUSIC IN EIGHTEENTH-CENTURY BRITAIN

Piccinni, Niccolì 17, 24, 56
   Gli stravaganti 52
   Il cavaliere per amore 52
   Il perucchiere 52
   L'amante ridicolo deluso 50
   La baronessa riconosciuta 52
   *La baronessa riconosciuta e
     maritata* 52
   La buona figliuola 21, 24n, 26n,
     48, 50, 52, 54, 60, 69
   La buona figliuola maritata 50,
     52, 54, 60, 69
   La buona figliuola zitella 50, 58
   La donna di spirito 58
   La molinarella 64
   La Scaltra spiritosa 64
   La schiava 21, 24n, 25, 54, 58, 69
   Le contadine bizzarre 56, 62, 69
   Le donne vendicate 52, 54, 56, 69
   Le finte gemelle 64
Pieri, Francesco 49
Pilotti, Elisabetta 139, 139n, 141
Pinto, Thomas 30
Pirazzini, Santo 67
Pirovana, Madalena 41, 43
Pisa 36, 38
Pisento, Madalena 61
Pitt, George 33
Pizza, Giovacchino 57, 65
Playford, John 183
Poggi, Domenico Giovanni 51, 61
Pohl, Carl Ferdinand 122, 122n
Poleraine, Lord 155
Pontypool 216n
Pope, Alexander 135
Pope Pius V 112
Popplewell 96
Porpora, Nicola (Antonio) 130, 134,
   217, 222, 265
   Davide e Berseeba 195, 196
   Siface 222n
   Six sonatas for two violoncellos
     and two violins 134, 156
Porta, Giovanni 152
Porteus, Beilby (Bishop of London/
   Chester) 174, 243
Portland, Duke of 254
Portugal, Elizabeth of 105
Posci, Antonio 61
Potenza, Michele Angelo 49
Potsdam 42, 146
Preston, John 224, 214n, 216n
Preston, William 79–80, 82, 83, 93
Price, Curtis 11

Price, Robert 160, 164, 166, 168
Priorino, Antonio 43
Professional Concert 86
Prona, Giuseppe 41
Puccinelli, Gioaccino 49, 51
Pucini, Giuseppe 61
Pucinni, Rosa 47
Pugin, Augustus Charles 104
Pugnani, Gaetano 23, 24, 32, 56, 69,
   282
Pullini, Antonio 55
Purcell, Henry 2, 3, 8, 10, 82, 115, 221,
   222, 262
   Grand Anthems 8, 184
   Jubilate 184
   Te Deum 184, 184n
Purdie, E. 159n

Quaglia, Giuseppe 43
Quercioli 55
Querzoli, Anna Laschi 37
Querzoli, Vittoria 32
Quilici, Gaetano 24, 30, 31, 45

Ramsey, Allan 150
Randall, W 96, 154
Ranish, John Frederick 220n
Rauzzini, Venanzio 53, 222
Ravena 46
Reading 183
Real, Joseph 96, 225
Rees 99
Regis, Catterina 47, 49
Reid, John 229
Reiley 96
Rembrandt 158
Reynolds, E. E. 108n
Reynoldson 96
Rheinhold, Frederick 84, 85, 93, 95,
   96, 97
Riboldi, Angiola Cattarina 43
Riboldi, Bianca 47, 49
Ricci, Agato 47
Ricci, Francesco Pasquale 109, 115,
   147
Ricci, Maddalena 63
Ricciardi, Domenico 32
Rich, John 194, 195
Rigacci, Anna 27
Rippon, Rev. John 238n
Ristorini, Catterina 22, 49, 53, 57, 59
Ristorini, Giovanni 53, 57, 59
Ristorini, Giuseppe 37
Ristorini, Luigi 37

INDEX

315

Ritti, Patrizio 49
Rizzoli, Giacomo 61
Roccaforte, Gaetano 65
Rocchetti, Gaetano 141
Rochester 243
Rode 297
Roderghel, Marianna 61
Rodney, Admiral 88
Rodrigues, Prof Garça Almeida 105n
Roger, Estienne 126, 128, 155, 228
Rolli, Giovanni 142
Rolli, Paolo Antonio 142
Rome 48, 50, 52, 58, 69, 71, 112,
  131n, 137, 138, 140, 141, 142, 155,
  216n, 217
Ronchetti, Andre 55
Ronchetti, Elisabetta 37, 39
Ronchetti, Regina 43
Rosignoli, Costanza 37
Rosingrave 264
Rossi, Antonio 47, 49, 53
Rossini, G.,117
Rotherham 121
Rotterdam 145
Rowlandson, Thomas 104
Royal Academy of Music 128, 137,
  138, 139, 140, 141, 195, 227
Royal Philharmonic Society
  159n–60n, 283
Royal Society of Musicians 82,
  139–40
Rugby 188
Ruspini, Chevalier Bartholomew 86,
  94
Russell, Wriothesley (Marquess of
  Tavistock) 137
Rushton Spencer 178
Rutini, Gio Marco 44
Ryder, Dudley 126n

Sabbatini, Luigi Antonio 216n
Sacchini, Antonio 56
  Il Cidde 64
  La contadina in corte 58
  L' isola d'amore 64
Sachs, Curt 2
Sachs, Hans 158
Saddington 173
Sadie, Stanley 218n, 222n, 223n
Saggione, Giuseppe Fedeli 148
Sainsbury, John 255, 255n
Sale, John Bernard 92, 93
Salisbury 124
Sallé, Madam 195

Salomon, Johann Peter 81, 88, 89, 94,
  98, 100, 249, 253, 282, 283, 296
Salvadori, Leonora 151
Salvi, Antonio 40
Sammartini, Giuseppe 2, 5, 10
Sanders, Thomas 79, 92, 97
Sandoni, Pietro 221, 224
Sani, Agata 37
Santarelli, Francesca 47
Santoro, Marianna 59
Sardinia, King of 104, 143
Sarti, Giuseppe 31, 64
Sartori, Angiola 30, 41, 45
Sartori, Elisabetta 63
Savoi, Gaspare 32, 49, 51, 53, 55, 57,
  59, 61
Scarlatti, Alessandro 216, 217, 221
Scarlatti, Domenico 6, 263, 264, 266,
  266n
Scarlatti, Giuseppe
  Artaserse 38
  Gli stravaganti 52, 68
Scartabelli, Nunziata 37
Schener, J. B. 154
Schenk, Giovanni 127
Schettini, Innocenzo 65
Schiavonetti (Zanetti), Giovanni 139,
  141
Schirolli, Bartolomeo 45, 61
Schmitz, Oscar 1
Schneider, Johann Christian Friedrich
  248
Schomberg, Alexander Crowcher 254n
Schönborn, Prince Bishop Johann
  Philipp Franz von 134, 139, 141,
  142
Schubert, Franz 11
Schumann, Clara 297n
Schumann, Robert 11, 284
Schütz, Heinrich 8
Scola, Adamo 124, 145
Scola, Charles 124, 145
Scolari, Giuseppe
  La buona figliuola maritata 60
  La cascina 20, 26, 46, 68, 70
  La donna stravagante 54
  La fata meravigliosa 36, 38
  La sciava riconosciuta 54
  I viaggiatori ridicoli 50, 58
Scovel 96
Sechioni, Giuseppe 45
Sedatti, Filippo 43
Sedgwick, Thomas 93
Segantini, Livia 31, 39

316 MUSIC IN EIGHTEENTH-CENTURY BRITAIN

Selhof, Nicolas 141
Senesino (Bernardi, Francesco) 193, 203
Seni, Giovanni Battista 67
Serafin, Carolina 39
Serov, Alexander Nikolayevich 158
Sestini, Anna 59, 63, 65
Sestini, Giovanni Stogler 59, 65
Sforzini, Giovanni 63, 65
Shakespeare, William 10, 89, 163
Sharp, Samuel 96
Shaw, Thomas 12
Sheffield 189, 190
Sheridan, W. 1n
Shield, William 173, 214, 222
Shoreham 176
Shrewsbury 125
Shrewsbury, Duchess of 139
Shropshire 243
Sibilla, Paolo 61
Silva, Alberto Giuseppe Gomes da 64
Simoni, Francesco 51
Simpkinson 96
Simpson, A.127n
Simpson, Christopher 183
Simpson, J. 152
Simpson, Redmond 79, 81–2, 85, 86, 92, 96, 97
Siprutini, Emanuel 130, 132, 145, 153, 154
Smith, Ruth 78
Small, Barbara 163, 163n
Smart, Sir George 86, 96, 97
Smith D. A. L. 224
Smith, John Christopher (Sen.) 205, 206, 210
Smith, John Christopher (Jun.) 126n
Smith, John Stafford 92, 96, 269, 276, 277
Smith, Martin 268–9, 270, 273
Smith, Theodore 133
Snetzler, John 240n
Society for Promoting Christian Knowledge 173
Society for the Encouragement of Arts, Manufactures and Commerce of Great Britain 156
Society of the Temple of Apollo 76
Soler, Martín y 249
Sorbelloni, Pietro 30, 45
Sörensen, Johannes 246
Spangenburg, Bishop August Gottlieb 240–41
Sperati, John 121, 124, 148

Spiletta 59
Spofforth, Reginald 79, 93
Spohr, Louis 297
Spourini, Wenceslaus Joseph 152
Stahmer, Klaus 134
Stamitz, Carl 88, 97, 99
Stanford, Charles Villiers 2
Stanley, John 160, 221, 226, 261
Stannington 190
Steibelt, Daniel 296
Stevens, C. E. 235n
Stoke Gabriel 173
Stocler, Giovanni 65
Stocker, Margarita 168
Stokes, Thomas 216n
Stockport 184
Stonleigh Abbey 269n, 274, 276
Stoppelaer 211, 212
Strada del Pò, Anna Maria 194, 201, 205, 211
Stradivari, Antonio 283, 283n
Strambi, Orsola 41
Stratford-upon-Avon 163
Strohm, Reinhard 11
Stuttgart 139
Surinam 235
Sutton, Robert 218, 218n, 219
Swansea 213n, 230n
Symonds, Henry 280

Tacet, Joseph 224n, 233n
Tagliavini, Rosa 37
Talliart, Pierre 219
Tanara, Angiola 41
Tattershall, William Dechair 184
Taylor, William 94
Tearelli, Girolama 37
Tedeschi, Antonio 63, 65
Tedeschi, Catterina 43
Tedeschini, Christiano 30, 45
Telemann, Georg Phillipp 203
Temperley, Nicholas 1n, 172, 175, 177, 239n
Tenducci, Ferdinando 18, 97
Tessarini, Carlo 220n
Teynham, Lord 157
The Hague 124, 145, 147
Thompson, C&S 153, 224, 225, 228–9, 268, 269, 271, 273
Tibaldi, Giacomo 53
Tibaldi, Giuseppe 43
Tintoretto 158
Titian 158
Todi 142

INDEX

Tonelli, Caterina 47, 49
Tonioli, Antonio 147–8
Tonioli, Girolamo 65, 147–8
Tonioli, Vincenzo 148
Torelli, Francesco 61
Toti, Andrea 67
Totnes 221n
Tourte, François 284, 284n
Tradati, Paola 49
Traetta, Tommaso
  Buovo d'Antona 48
  Le serve rivali 56, 60, 69
  L'Olimpiade 42
Travaglia Rodeginda 39
Travers, John 261, 270, 270n, 280
Trebeschi, Giuseppe 65
Tricklir, Jean-Balthasar 135n
Trombetta, Joseph 30
Tudway, Thomas 9
Turchi, Teresa 63
Turchi, Vittoria 65
Twining, Thomas 294
Turin 40, 42, 48, 50, 52, 60, 62, 143, 148
Tyburn 84
Tyrawley, Lord 79

Ucedo, Giuseppe 41, 43
Uffenbach, John Friedrich Armond von 138
Ugolini, Pellegrino 43
Uttini, Francesco 133, 156

Valentine, John 96
Valentini, Giuseppe 156
Val(l)etti, Antonio 39, 41
Valsecchi, Marianna 31
Vanhal, Johann Baptist 249
Vanneschi, Francesco 142
Vaughan Williams, Ralph 177n
Venice,22, 23, 23n, 24, 25, 26, 27n, 36, 38, 46, 48, 54, 60, 62, 64, 66, 68, 69, 70, 139, 142, 148, 216n, 217, 222n
Vento, Matteo 31
Vercelli 42
Vernon, Joseph 84, 85, 95, 96, 97
Verona 27n, 40, 144
Versailles 282
Vestris, Gäeton 224n
Vico, Diana 139
Vienna 25, 52, 54, 68, 140, 141, 247, 248n
Vietinghof (Jun.) 246

Viganoni, Giuseppe 93, 94
Viganti, Giuseppe 43
Vincent, Thomas 21, 31, 32
Vinci, Leonardo 71, 217, 230
Virgil 160
Visconti, Gasparo 126, 126n, 148
Visconti, Luisa 45
Vitalba, Rosa 61
Vitturi, Bartolomeo 37
Vivaldi, Antonio 2, 229, 230

Wade, John F. 106n
Wagenseil, Georg Christoph 223, 224n
Wallfisch, Elizabeth 11n, 12n
Walond, William (Sen.) 214, 224n
Walond, William (Jun.) 274
Walpole, Sir Edward 155
Walpole, Horace 10, 22, 22n
Walsal (hymn tune) 176
Walsall 188
Walsh and Hare 127, 156, 220, 220n, 222
Walsh, John 133, 134, 150, 151, 152, 153, 157, 168n, 201–2, 228, 229, 262, 263, 271–2, 273, 277
Waltz (bass) 194, 201, 211
Wamsley 96
Warburton, Ernest 72n
Ward, William 155
Watkin, D. 127n
Watts, Robert 173n
Weaver, Sam 150
Webb 96
Webbe, Samuel (Sen.) 78, 79, 80, 80n, 92, 93, 99, 100, 106n, 109–12, 109n 113, 114, 115, 116, 118
Webbe, Samuel (Jun.) 78, 80, 80n, 93, 112, 114
Weber, William 7, 9, 23, 24, 256
Weichsell, Mrs 99
Welcker, John 147, 153, 154, 155, 156, 133n, 219
Weldon, John 4, 176, 268n
Wendeborn, Friedrich 282
Wesley, Charles (Sen.) 8, 112n, 243, 249
Wesley, Charles (Jun.) 243, 249
Wesley, John 171, 238n, 243, 251
Wesley, Samuel 11, 78, 80, 80n, 86, 93, 112–14, 112n, 115–16, 115n, 116n, 243, 249
White, Chapell 283n, 284, 296
Whitworth, Sir Charles 88, 98

Wiesentheid 252
Wilberforce, William 244, 244n
Williams, Thomas **88**
Winchester 269n
Wisentheid 134
Witvogel, Gerhardo Federico 150, 272
Wölfflin, Heinrich 2
Wood 79, 85, 92, 97
Woodcock, Robert 229, 230
Worgan, John 170
Wright, Daniel 271, 272, 273, 277
Wright, Mrs 212n
Wurzburg 141
Wynne, John 153

Yale University (Beinecke Library)
  234n, 235, 241, 241n
Young, Cecilia (Miss) 55, 61, 201,
  211
Young, Polly 31

Zaccarini, Teresa 51
Zambertini, Giacomo 61

Zamperini, Anna 21, 22, 22n, 24, 31,
  33, 55, 57, 60–7
Zamperini, Antonio 33, 47, 55, 57, 61,
  63, 65, 67
Zamperini, Cecilia 65
Zamperini, Elisabetta 61
Zamperini, Giandomenico 61
Zamperini, Giovanni 31, 61
Zamperini, Maria 61
Zanoni, Angelo 128, 139
Zappa, Francesco 133, 135, 147, 147n
Zaslaw, Neal 1n
Zeno, Apostolo 37
Zingoni, Giovanni Battista 27, 31
Zinzendorf, Count Nikolaus Ludwig
  von 235, 235n, 238n
Zittau 235
Zoffany 94
Zöllner, Eva 6
Zon, Bennett 106n
Zonca, Giovanni Battista 22n, 30, 45
Zuccari, Carlo 225